The Steinsaltz Mishne Torah

SEFER HAMADDA

YESODEI HATORAH • DEOT • TALMUD TORAH

Steinsaltz Center

KOREN

משנה תורה לרמב"ם שטיינזלץ

THE STEINSALTZ MISHNE TORAH

ספר המדע

SEFER HAMADDA

YESODEI HATORAH • DEOT • TALMUD TORAH

COMMENTARY BY

Rabbi Adin Even-Israel
Steinsaltz

STEINSALTZ CENTER

KOREN PUBLISHERS JERUSALEM

The Steinsaltz Mishne Torah
Volume 1B: *Sefer HaMadda*, Yesodei HaTorah • Deot • Talmud Torah

Paperback edition, ISBN 978-965-583-164-1

First Hebrew/English Edition, 2026

Koren Publishers Jerusalem Ltd.
PO Box 4044, Jerusalem 9104001, ISRAEL
PO Box 8531, New Milford, CT 06776, USA
www.korenpub.com

Steinsaltz Center
Steinsaltz Center is the parent organization
of institutions established by Rabbi Adin Even-Israel Steinsaltz
PO Box 45187, Jerusalem 91450 ISRAEL
Telephone: +972 2 646 0900, Fax +972 2 624 9454
www.steinsaltz-center.org

First printing, 2026

Printed in ROT

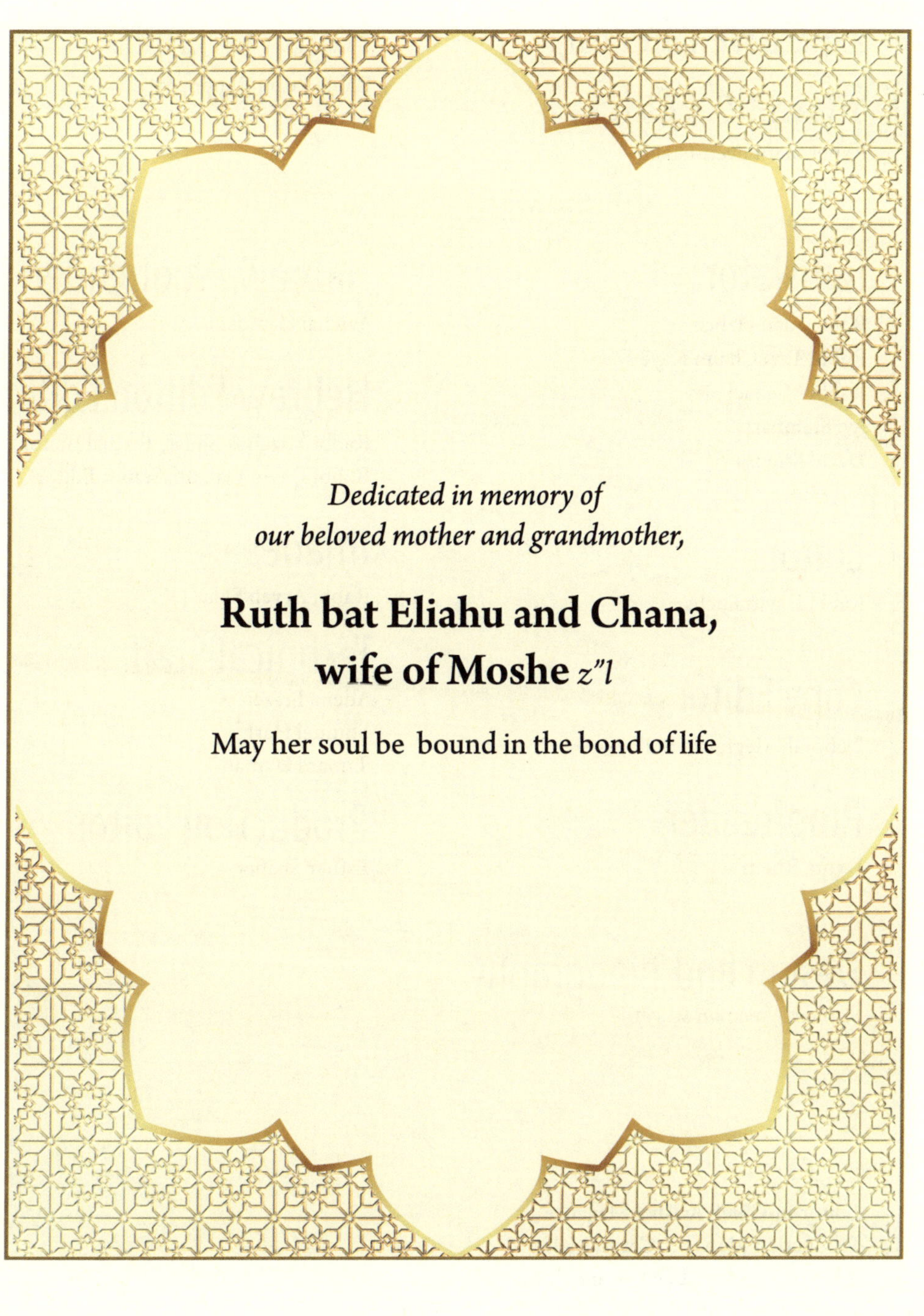

Dedicated in memory of
our beloved mother and grandmother,

Ruth bat Eliahu and Chana,
wife of Moshe *z"l*

May her soul be bound in the bond of life

Executive Director, Steinsaltz Center
Rabbi Meni Even-Israel

Editor-in-Chief
Rabbi Jason Rappoport

Translators
Rabbi Alan Haber
Rabbi Tzvi Chaim Kaye
Rabbi Michael Siev
Avi Steinhart
David Strauss

Editor
Rabbi David Fuchs

Copy Editor
Deborah Meghnagi Bailey

Proofreader
Dvora Rhein

Hebrew Proofreader
Avichai Gamdani

Hebrew Edition Editors
Rabbi Yitzchak Shilat, Textual Editor
Rabbi David Fialkoff, Senior Editor

Images
Rabbi Aryeh Sklar

Technical Staff
Adena Frazer
Shmuel Hart
Tamar Hayman

Production Editor
Esther Shafier

Design and Typography
Raphaël Freeman MISTD

Editor-in-Chief, Avishai Magence
Production Manager, Caryn Meltz
Typesetting, Rina Ben Gal and Tomi Mager
Cover Design, Eliyahu Misgav and Shmooel Lasry

Contents

"מְשֹׁךְ חַסְדְּךָ לְיֹדְעֶיךָ וְצִדְקָתְךָ לְיִשְׁרֵי לֵב" (תהלים לו, יא)

"Extend Your kindness* to those who know You,
and Your righteousness to the upright of heart" (Psalms 36:11)

סֵפֶר רִאשׁוֹן וְהוּא

סֵפֶר הַמַּדָּע

The first book is *Sefer HaMadda*

INSIGHTS OF THE LUBAVITCHER REBBE

*Extend Your kindness – מְשֹׁךְ חַסְדְּךָ: Since the *Mishne Torah* is designed as a kind of alternative to the Babylonian Talmud, there are certain similarities between the two works: 1) They both start with the letter *mem* and end with a final *mem*; b) In both, the beginning of the book and its end are linked, in terms of their content; the theme of peace in the case of the Talmud, and the knowledge of God in the *Mishne Torah* (*Torat Menaḥem, Hitvaaduyot, Parashat [Ki] Tavo* 5744; *Motzai Zot Ḥanuka* 5746).

Introduction to *Sefer HaMadda*

Sefer HaMadda includes both halakhot that are technical down to their finest details (such as the laws pertaining to idolatry), as well as far more abstract halakhot, whose philosophical content predominates over their practical laws. Most of the halakhot in *Sefer HaMadda* cannot be found, at least not in this form, in other works of halakha, both those that preceded the Rambam and also those that were written afterward.

In other words, this is a group of very basic topics, comprising the majority of *Sefer HaMadda*, which do not involve much in the way of practical halakha. This is one of the unique features of the *Mishne Torah* – not only does it present laws that have not been in effect since the destruction of the Temple, but it also engages with halakhot that do not offer concrete and immediately applicable rules of conduct.

It is possible that in *Sefer HaMadda* the Rambam brings together all the topics that in his opinion come under the rubric of the first of the Ten Commandments, which he himself defines as "to know that there is a God." Perhaps this is why he calls it *Sefer HaMadda*, "the Book of Knowledge," because while the other nine commandments involve practical instructions that subsequently devolve into the minutiae of halakhic cases, the first commandment presents an overall conception of the relationship between God and man.

In *Sefer HaMadda*, the Rambam analyses the specifics of this first commandment, with each of the *Hilkhot* sections of this book focusing on a particular aspect of this fundamental relationship between mankind and the Lord.

Accordingly, although each of the *Hilkhot* sections in *Sefer HaMadda* relates to different mitzvot, they all broadly deal with how a Jew must stand before God, in terms of his ways of thinking, moral behavior, Torah study, and mode of repentance. These halakhot thus address the Jew in the entirety of his being, in a manner that reflects King David's final instructions to his son Solomon:

"Know the God of your father and serve Him with a whole heart" (I Chronicles 28:9)

For this reason, all the *Hilkhot* sections in *Sefer HaMadda* share another common feature: They all include an introduction, as well as abstract philosophical ideas woven into their laws. Typically, the Rambam does not provide in the *Mishne Torah* any prefaces that stray beyond the basic halakhic realm. While there are introductory paragraphs to all books of the *Mishne Torah,* these serve to present general rules and guidelines for understanding the details of the ensuing laws. In *Sefer HaMadda,* by contrast, the introductions and reflective passages can be found not only in those *Hilkhot* that are more abstract in their nature (such as *Hilkhot Yesodei HaTorah*), but also in cases where the philosophical discussions complement their halakhot (*Hilkhot Teshuva*). Even in very detailed *Hilkhot,* as *Hilkhot Avoda Zara,* the Rambam starts with a background explanation of how there came to be idolatry in the world. In sum, the collection of *Hilkhot* in *Sefer HaMadda* are unique in that their philosophical analyses, "knowledge" itself, are important components of the laws. They are not merely decorative addendums but keys for comprehending all the halakhic particulars themselves. Accordingly, the Rambam formed a book from this collection of special *halakhot,* a large proportion of which are indeed unique to the Rambam. From this perspective, the book can be viewed as an introduction to the entire *Mishne Torah.*

הִלְכוֹת

יְסוֹדֵי הַתּוֹרָה

The Halakhot (Laws) of the Foundations of the Torah

יֵשׁ בִּכְלָלָן עֶשֶׂר מִצְוֹת, שֵׁשׁ מִצְוֹת עֲשֵׂה וְאַרְבַּע מִצְוֹת לֹא תַעֲשֶׂה, וְזֶה הוּא פְּרָטָן:

א) לֵידַע שֶׁיֵּשׁ שָׁם אֱלוֹהַּ. ב) שֶׁלֹּא יַעֲלֶה בְּמַחֲשָׁבָה שֶׁיֵּשׁ שָׁם אֱלוֹהַּ זוּלָתִי יי. ג) לְיַחֲדוֹ.
ד) לְאַהֲבוֹ. ה) לְיִרְאָה מִמֶּנּוּ. ו) לְקַדֵּשׁ שְׁמוֹ. ז) שֶׁלֹּא לְחַלֵּל אֶת שְׁמוֹ. ח) שֶׁלֹּא לְאַבֵּד דְּבָרִים שֶׁנִּקְרָא שְׁמוֹ עֲלֵיהֶן.
ט) לִשְׁמֹעַ מִן הַנָּבִיא הַמְדַבֵּר בִּשְׁמוֹ. י) שֶׁלֹּא לְנַסּוֹתוֹ.

וּבֵאוּר כָּל הַמִּצְוֹת הָאֵלּוּ בִּפְרָקִים אֵלּוּ.

These halakhot include ten mitzvot:
six positive mitzvot and four negative mitzvot.
Their enumeration follows:

1) To know that there is a God 2) Not to contemplate that there is another god apart from Him
3) To acknowledge His unity 4) To love Him 5) To fear Him 6) To sanctify His name
7) Not to desecrate His name 8) Not to eradicate items that have His name upon them
9) To listen to the prophet who speaks in His name 10) Not to test Him

All these mitzvot will be explained in the following chapters.

Hilkhot Yesodei HaTorah: Parallels to the mitzvot

The mitzva	*Sefer HaMitzvot*	The mitzva in *Hilkhot Yesodei HaTorah*
To know that there is a God	Positive mitzva 1	1:6
Not to contemplate that there is another god apart from Him	Negative mitzva 1	1:6
To acknowledge His unity	Positive mitzva 2	1:7
To love Him	Positive mitzva 3	2:1
To fear Him	Positive mitzva 4	2:1
To sanctify His name	Positive mitzva 9	5:1
Not to desecrate His name	Negative mitzva 63	5:1
Not to eradicate items that have His name upon them	Negative mitzva 65	6:1, 7
To listen to the prophet who speaks in His name	Positive mitzva 172	7:7
Not to test Him	Negative mitzva 64	10:5

Introduction to *Hilkhot Yesodei HaTorah*

These halakhot, like many others in *Sefer HaMadda*, include both abstract, general teachings, as well as practical rulings of halakha that are related to the same topics.

The basic subject matter of *Hilkhot Yesodei HaTorah* is the foundations of the faith of the Torah: the beliefs and recognized facts that form the fundamental basis for the existence of the Torah. All the halakhot of the Torah are in essence grounded in elemental principles. Since these principles are not brought together and presented in an orderly fashion in the Torah or in any other book, the Rambam felt that they must first be arranged systematically before the other mitzvot could be discussed.

From the perspective of the fundamental principles of the Torah, two major topics are clarified here that constitute the foundational basis of the entire Torah. The first section of these Halakhot delineates belief in God, both in general terms, and through more precise definitions that have religious and philosophical significance. This section also includes two halakhic chapters that address the practical ramifications of the proper attitude toward God: the laws of the sanctification of God's name, and the prohibition against eradicating holy writings. The second section deals with the basis of faith in relation to the Torah: the belief that the Torah is from Heaven, which is without doubt the basis for the requirement to observe the mitzvot. Here, too, the issues are presented in both the general and the particular, and they cover all the laws that pertain to the prophets: the distinction between a true and false prophecy, the practical implications of belief in a prophet, and how one is obligated to relate to an established prophet. The main significance of these topics is not in the particular details of their halakhot, but rather their importance as fundamental principles, since it is impossible for the Torah to be adhered to without faith in the Giver of the Torah, and without the belief that the Torah is from Heaven.

There is one more section in *Hilkhot Yesodei HaTorah*, and that is a description provided by the Rambam, in accordance with the best knowledge available at his time, of the overall structure of the universe. He considers this both an aspect of faith and an important stock of knowledge, for through it one can gain a comprehensive picture not only of the reality above nature, but also of the great panorama of nature itself.

In sum, all these themes provide the theoretical foundation for everything that will be discussed throughout the whole of the *Mishne Torah*. In other words, it presents the fundamentals that every person has to know and believe before they can proceed to the rest of the Torah, with all its myriad details.

Contents

Chapters 1–4: The Existence and Knowledge of God

Chapters 5–6: The Sanctification of God's Name

Chapter 6: The Prohibition against Eradicating God's Name and Sacred Items

Halakhot 1–6: Erasing the names of God
Halakha 7: Destroying Temple stones and consecrated wood
Halakha 8: Eradicating holy writings
Halakha 9: The status of the various appellations of God in the Bible

Chapters 7–10: Prophecy

Chapter 7: Prophecy

Halakhot 1–5: Those worthy of prophecy, and the prophetic experience
Halakha 6: The difference between the prophecy of Moses and that of the other prophets
Halakha 7: The purpose of prophecy, and believing in prophets

Chapter 8: The Prophecy of Moses

Halakhot 1–3: The belief in the prophecy of Moses

Chapter 9: A Prophet Is Subject to the Words of the Torah

Halakha 1: A prophet does not have the authority to innovate new mitzvot of the Torah
Halakha 2: The obligation to obey a prophet
Halakhot 3–5: The prophecy to violate a command of the Torah provisionally

Chapter 10: The Credibility of a Prophet

Halakhot 1–2: The credibility of a prophet as established by signs
Halakhot 3–4: The credibility of prophets in contrast to enchanters
Halakha 5: The status of a prophet as established by the testimony of another prophet; the prohibition against doubting a prophet

פֶּרֶק רִאשׁוֹן

CHAPTER 1

The Existence and Unity of God

Halakhot 1–6: The existence of God
Halakhot 7–12: The unity of God, and that He does not have a bodily form

Halakha 1

יְסוֹד הַיְסוֹדוֹת וְעַמּוּד הַחָכְמוֹת לֵידַע שֶׁיֵּשׁ שָׁם מָצוּי רִאשׁוֹן, וְהוּא מַמְצִיא כָּל הַנִּמְצָא, וְכָל הַנִּמְצָאִים מִן שָׁמַיִם וָאָרֶץ וּמַה בֵּינֵיהֶם לֹא נִמְצְאוּ אֶלָּא מֵאֲמִתַּת הִמָּצְאוֹ.

The foundation of foundations and the pillar of wisdoms[a] **is to know*** **that a Primary Being**[b] **exists**** **who brought all existence into being. All the beings in heaven and earth, and what is between them, came into existence only through** the essential **true existence of His being.**

FROM THE LUBAVITCHER REBBE

***To know – לֵידַע:** In his introduction to *Sefer HaMadda*, the Rambam quotes the verse: "Extend Your kindness to those who know You, and Your charity to the upright of heart" (Psalms 36:11). This verse describes the great reward that awaits those who fulfill the obligations presented at both the start and end of this *Sefer*. *Sefer HaMadda* begins with the knowledge of God, "those who know You," and the verse teaches that those who attain this receive a kindness from God that extends to them directly from Him. The *Sefer* ends with *Hilkhot Teshuva*, whose purpose is to straighten crooked hearts. Thus, "the upright of heart" merit "Your charity," which is a "tithe" or "fifth" of God's own property.

These two endeavors are mutually reinforcing. One's knowledge of God helps him repent, which is essentially the act of drawing near to God, a movement that is advanced through one's increased intellectual understanding of the Divine. The same applies in the opposite direction: In order to become close to God, one must first be a God-fearing person, which requires active repentance (*Torat Menaḥem*, *Hitvaaduyot*, *Parashat Emor* 5744).

****To know that a Primary Being exists – לֵידַע שֶׁיֵּשׁ שָׁם מָצוּי רִאשׁוֹן:** The Rambam maintains that the mitzva of "I am the Lord your God" (Exodus 20:2) is comprised not only of the basic belief in the existence of God, but also of all the details that he clarifies in the first Halakhot of the chapter. His source is likely the *Zohar* (2, 25a), the wording of which even parallels, to a certain extent, the language of the Rambam in Halakha 1, with its emphasis on the obligation to know. Accordingly, understanding and internalizing the Rambam's lengthy descriptions in his first few chapters is an actual fulfillment of a mitzva (*Torat Menaḥem*, *Hitvaaduyot*, 11 *Nisan*, *Aḥaron shel Pesaḥ*, *Parashat Emor* 5744; *Parashat Va'era* 5745; *Likkutei Siḥot* 26, p. 114).

NOTES

a. The Rambam is implying here that one cannot even begin to think about or contemplate anything, neither about oneself, nor about the world, without first assuming the existence of God, which precedes everything. When he refers to "the pillar of wisdoms" he means that, regardless of the field of wisdom in question, one who investigates always proceeds from one cause to the next, until ultimately arriving at the Holy One Blessed Be He. If anyone fails to reach this conclusion, it is merely due to intellectual laziness, for whoever understands the matter properly knows that we all begin with "the foundation of foundations and the pillar of wisdoms" (from a lecture in honor of the completion of the daily Rambam cycle, *Agudat Ḥemed*, 2015).

b. God (see Halakha 5), whose existence precedes the existence of all other beings. This precedence is both temporal and causal, as will be explained.

Halakha 2

וְאִם יַעֲלֶה עַל הַדַּעַת שֶׁהוּא אֵינוֹ מָצוּי – אֵין דָּבָר אַחֵר יָכוֹל לְהִמָּצְאוֹת.

If it were possible to **imagine that He does not exist,* nothing else could possibly exist.** Even if one could entertain the thought that the Primary Being does not exist, it would be impossible to think about any other form of existence.

Halakha 3

וְאִם יַעֲלֶה עַל הַדַּעַת שֶׁאֵין כָּל הַנִּמְצָאִים מִלְּבַדּוֹ מְצוּיִים – הוּא לְבַדּוֹ יִהְיֶה מָצוּי וְלֹא יִבָּטֵל הוּא לְבִטּוּלָם,

By contrast, **if one were to imagine that no beings apart from Him exist, He alone would exist, and He would not be nullified by their nullification.** The non-existence of all other entities would have no effect at all on the existence of the Primary Being.

שֶׁכָּל הַנִּמְצָאִים צְרִיכִין לוֹ, וְהוּא בָּרוּךְ הוּא אֵינוֹ צָרִיךְ לָהֶם וְלֹא לְאֶחָד מֵהֶם.

For all beings require Him, but He, blessed be He, does not require them, nor even any single **one of them.**

לְפִיכָךְ אֵין אֲמִתָּתוֹ כַּאֲמִתַּת אֶחָד מֵהֶם.

Therefore, the truth of His existence[a] **is not like the truth of** the existence of **any of them.** They all depend on Him and have no independent existence, whereas He alone is the absolute truth.

Halakha 4

הוּא שֶׁנָּבִיא אוֹמֵר: "וַיי אֱלֹהִים אֱמֶת" (ירמיהו י, י) – הוּא לְבַדּוֹ הָאֱמֶת, וְאֵין לְאַחֵר אֱמֶת כַּאֲמִתּוֹ.

This is the meaning of that **which the prophet states: "But the Lord God is truth"** (Jeremiah 10:10). **He alone is the truth, and no other** being **has a truth like His truth.**

וְהוּא שֶׁהַתּוֹרָה אוֹמֶרֶת: "אֵין עוֹד מִלְּבַדּוֹ" (דברים ד, לה), כְּלוֹמַר: אֵין שָׁם מָצוּי אֱמֶת מִלְּבַדּוֹ כְּמוֹתוֹ.

This is the meaning of that **which the Torah says: "There is no other besides Him"** (Deuteronomy 4:35). **In other words, there is no existing true being like Him, apart from Him.**[b]

NOTES

a. This knowledge cannot be merely a matter of thoughts, of words that someone might say. Anyone can speak, but what is required is understanding, for us to live by the ideas. This is also the meaning of "to know," that is, to know in exactly the same way that I know that my hand is my hand. I do not need proof, evidence, or interpretations: I simply know it to be true. Likewise, with regard to God, the first thing is to know, with an immediate, direct, all-encompassing knowledge.

What does one need to know? "That a Primary Being exists, who brought all existence into being." Here, the Rambam is not talking about the Holy One Blessed be He as the Creator of the world. He is not addressing all the many complicated topics that he analyzes elsewhere, such as the eternal nature of the Creator, and the like. Rather, he is referring to God as the Primary Being, in the sense that He "brought all existence into being." Thus, the truth of God's existence is the background, the foundation, the basis of everything in the world. All living beings are nothing but etchings, so to speak, of God's image. One must know this at every moment, including during times of trouble and, indeed, at all times: We must all know and believe that God is the foundation of our lives, and we must therefore cleave to and hold fast to Him (from a lecture in honor of the completion of the daily Rambam cycle, *Agudat Ḥemed*, 2015).

b. That is, the verse is not negating the existence of other beings, but instead it is saying that none of them have the value of absolute truth (in the sense of a continuous existence), for their existence can come to an end; they are not eternal like the Creator.

FROM THE LUBAVITCHER REBBE

***If it were possible to imagine that He does not exist – וְאִם יַעֲלֶה עַל הַדַּעַת שֶׁהוּא אֵינוֹ מָצוּי:** According to the Rambam, the mitzva of "I am the Lord your God" (Exodus 20:2) involves knowing these details of this fundamental idea that the existence of all created beings stems from the existence of the Creator. Nevertheless, the verse continues with "who took you out of the land of Egypt," since the aim is for us to understand both that there is a Divine Being who is above creation, and at the same time, that a connection is maintained between that which is above creation and creation itself (as can be learned from the miraculous exodus from Egypt and the ensuing giving of the Torah). The Rambam alludes to this idea in the first two Halakhot: God is connected to creation, for it is He "who brought all existence into being" (Halakha 1), but He is also above creation, as indicated in Halakha 2, with its emphasis on the existence of God irrespective of any creation. The initials of the Hebrew words of the Rambam's opening comments to the book: "The foundation of foundations and the pillar of wisdoms" form an acronym of the ineffable name of God, the Tetragrammaton, alluding to God Himself, who is beyond any definition and boundary, and thus links what exists above and below (*Torat Menaḥem*, *Hitvaaduyot*, *Parashat Yitro* 5750).

Halakha 5

הַמָּצוּי הַזֶּה הוּא אֱלוֹהַּ הָעוֹלָם, אֲדוֹן כָּל הָאָרֶץ, וְהוּא הַמַּנְהִיג הַגַּלְגַּל בְּכֹחַ שֶׁאֵין לוֹ קֵץ וְתַכְלִית, בְּכֹחַ שֶׁאֵין לוֹ הֶפְסֵק.

This being is the Lord of the world and the Master of the whole Earth. He controls the sphere with infinite and endless power, with a power that does not cease. This was the accepted definition (in the terminology of the scientific concepts of the time) of the Primary Force that activates everything.[a]

שֶׁהַגַּלְגַּל סוֹבֵב תָּמִיד, וְאִי אֶפְשָׁר שֶׁיִּסֹּב בְּלֹא מְסַבֵּב, וְהוּא בָּרוּךְ הוּא הוּא הַמְסַבֵּב אוֹתוֹ בְּלֹא יָד וְלֹא גוּף.

For the sphere is constantly revolving, and it is impossible for it to revolve without something causing it to revolve. And it is He, blessed be He, who causes it to revolve, without the use of **a hand** or any other **bodily matter.**

Halakha 6

וִידִיעַת דָּבָר זֶה - מִצְוַת עֲשֵׂה, שֶׁנֶּאֱמַר: "אָנֹכִי יי אֱלֹהֶיךָ" (שמות כ, ב; דברים ה, ו).

The knowledge of this concept, the fact that there is a Primary Being, and the relationship between the truth of His existence and the truth of the existence of all other beings, **is a positive mitzva,* as it is stated: "I am the Lord your God"**[b] (Exodus 20:2; Deuteronomy 5:6).

וְכָל הַמַּעֲלֶה עַל דַּעְתּוֹ שֶׁיֵּשׁ שָׁם אֱלוֹהַּ אַחֵר חוּץ מִזֶּה - עָבַר בְּלֹא תַעֲשֶׂה, שֶׁנֶּאֱמַר: "לֹא יִהְיֶה לְךָ אֱלֹהִים אֲחֵרִים עַל פָּנָי" (שם), וְכָפַר בָּעִקָּר,

Anyone who contemplates that another god exists apart from Him **has violated a prohibition, as it is stated: "You shall have no other gods before Me"** (Exodus 20:3; Deuteronomy 5:7), **and he has denied the** fundamental **principle** of the faith,

שֶׁזֶּה הוּא הָעִקָּר הַגָּדוֹל שֶׁהַכֹּל תָּלוּי בּוֹ.

for this is the great principle upon which the whole religion **depends.** The belief in the uniqueness of God forms the basis for all the mitzvot of the Torah.

Halakha 7

אֱלוֹהַּ זֶה - אֶחָד הוּא, אֵינוֹ לֹא שְׁנַיִם וְלֹא יָתֵר עַל שְׁנַיִם, אֶלָּא אֶחָד שֶׁאֵין כְּיִחוּדוֹ אֶחָד מִן הָאֲחָדִים הַנִּמְצָאִים בָּעוֹלָם:

This God is one. He is not two, or more than two, but one, in such a manner **that His unity is unlike** any **one of the unities that are found in the world.** The definition of God as "one" is not the same as the "one" used in any other context.

לֹא אֶחָד כְּמִין שֶׁהוּא כּוֹלֵל אֲחָדִים הַרְבֵּה, וְלֹא אֶחָד כְּגוּף שֶׁהוּא נֶחְלָק לְמַחְלָקוֹת וְלִקְצָווֹת, אֶלָּא יִחוּד שֶׁאֵין יִחוּד אַחֵר כְּמוֹתוֹ בָּעוֹלָם.

He is **not one like the type** of entity **that includes many** other **unities,** a whole comprised of smaller parts, **nor one like the body, that divides into** its constituent **portions and extremities,** its limbs. **Rather,** His **unity** is of such a kind **that there exists no unity like His in the world.**

NOTES

a. See chap. 3.

b. This verse, which is telling us that the Lord who is addressing Israel is God, is not merely providing information; it is commanding us to know and believe this truth.

BACKGROUND

For the sphere is constantly revolving – שֶׁהַגַּלְגַּל סוֹבֵב תָּמִיד:

An armillary sphere used to calculate movements of the heavenly bodies

FROM THE LUBAVITCHER REBBE

*The knowledge of this concept is a positive mitzva – וִידִיעַת דָּבָר זֶה מִצְוַת עֲשֵׂה: The Rambam considers knowledge of God to be a positive mitzva (see also *Sefer HaMitzvot*, positive mitzva 1). There were other early authorities, such as the Baal Halakhot Gedolot, who argued that this cannot be counted as a mitzva, because there is no significance to the concept of a commandment without presupposing belief in the One who commands, and if one already believes in the One who commands, what need is there for such a mitzva? Rather, belief is the basis of all the mitzvot, but is not a mitzva itself (see Ramban's commentary to *Sefer HaMitzvot*, positive mitzva 1). The Rambam's view, however, is that this mitzva is not that of the basic belief in the existence of God. Rather, presupposing that basic level of belief, the mitzva is to know that God is the source of everything that exists, and all the other details the Rambam includes in this chapter. That is why he waits until the sixth Halakha to state that this is a mitzva, rather than beginning the chapter with this statement (*Likkutei Siḥot* 26, p. 133).

אִלּוּ הָיוּ הָאֱלוֹהוֹת הַרְבֵּה – הָיוּ גּוּפִין וּגְוִיּוֹת, מִפְּנֵי שֶׁאֵין הַנִּמְנִין הַשָּׁוִין בִּמְצִיאָתָן נִפְרָדִין זֶה מִזֶּה אֶלָּא בַּמְּאֹרָעִים שֶׁיֶּאֶרְעוּ הַגּוּפוֹת וְהַגְּוִיּוֹת.

If there were many gods, they would have **bodies and corporeal forms, because entities that are equal** with respect to **their existence are separated from each other only through the circumstances involving bodies and corporeal forms.**[a]

וְאִלּוּ הָיָה הַיּוֹצֵר גּוּף וּגְוִיָּה – הָיָה לוֹ קֵץ וְתַכְלִית, שֶׁאִי אֶפְשָׁר לִהְיוֹת גּוּף שֶׁאֵין לוֹ קֵץ.

If the Maker had **a body and corporeal form, He would have a limit and an end,**[b] **because it is impossible for there to be a body that is not limited.**

וְכָל שֶׁיֵּשׁ לוֹ קֵץ וְתַכְלִית – יֵשׁ לְכֹחוֹ קֵץ וָסוֹף.

And for **any** being **that has a limit and an end, its power** also **has a limit and an end.** Since God's power is unlimited, it follows that He himself is unlimited, which negates the possibility of multiple deities.

וֵאלֹהֵינוּ בָּרוּךְ שְׁמוֹ, הוֹאִיל וְכֹחוֹ אֵין לוֹ קֵץ וְאֵינוֹ פָּסֵק, שֶׁהֲרֵי הַגַּלְגַּל סוֹבֵב תָּמִיד – אֵין כֹּחוֹ כֹּחַ גּוּף.

But with regard to **our God, blessed be His name, since His power has no limit and does not cease – for the sphere is continuously revolving – His power is not a physical power.**

וְהוֹאִיל וְאֵינוֹ גּוּף – לֹא יֶאֶרְעוּ מְאֹרְעוֹת הַגּוּפוֹת כְּדֵי שֶׁיְּהֵא נֶחְלָק וְנִפְרָד מֵאַחֵר. לְפִיכָךְ אִי אֶפְשָׁר שֶׁיִּהְיֶה אֶלָּא אֶחָד.

And since He is not a body, the circumstances involving bodies, which would divide and separate Him **from** any **other** body, **do not affect Him. Therefore, it is impossible for Him to be** anything **other than one.**

וִידִיעַת דָּבָר זֶה – מִצְוַת עֲשֵׂה, שֶׁנֶּאֱמַר: "יי אֱלֹהֵינוּ יי אֶחָד" (דברים ו,ד).

The knowledge of this concept, God's unity, is **a positive mitzva, as it is stated: "Hear, Israel: The Lord is our God, the Lord is one"** (Deuteronomy 6:4).

Halakha 8

הֲרֵי מְפֹרָשׁ בַּתּוֹרָה וּבַנָּבִיא שֶׁאֵין הַקָּדוֹשׁ בָּרוּךְ הוּא גּוּף וּגְוִיָּה, שֶׁנֶּאֱמַר: "כִּי יי הוּא הָאֱלֹהִים בַּשָּׁמַיִם מִמַּעַל וְעַל הָאָרֶץ מִתָּחַת" (דברים ד,לט), וְהַגּוּף לֹא יִהְיֶה בִּשְׁנֵי מְקוֹמוֹת.

Now, it is explicitly stated **in the Torah and in the Prophets that the Holy One blessed be He** does **not** have **a body or corporeal form, as it is stated: "That the Lord, He is the God in the heavens above and upon the earth below"** (Deuteronomy 4:39), **and a body cannot be in two places** at the same time.

וְנֶאֱמַר: "כִּי לֹא רְאִיתֶם כָּל תְּמוּנָה" (שם ד, טו), וְנֶאֱמַר: "וְאֶל מִי תְדַמְּיוּנִי וְאֶשְׁוֶה" (ישעיהו מ, כה), וְאִלּוּ הָיָה גּוּף – הָיָה דּוֹמֶה לִשְׁאָר גּוּפִים.

And it is stated: "As you did not see any image on the day that the Lord your God spoke to you at Horev" (Deuteronomy 4:15), **and it is stated: "To whom would you liken Me that I would be equal?"** (Isaiah 40:25), since God does not have a physical form. **Were He** to have a **body,** with the dimensions of a body, He **would resemble other bodies,** and could thus be likened to them.

NOTES

a. The proof of the unity of God follows from the fact that He does not have a body, for the necessary result of referring to multiple deities is that they are limited bodies, since the difference between entities of the same essence is expressed only through their different bodies and the particular circumstances associated with them.

b. When we speak of God as infinite, we are referring not only to the farthest boundaries of outer space, but also to His relationship with our familiar, supposedly more mundane reality. For these share the same characteristic; they are included in the all-encompassing nature of the Infinite. People have a tendency to feel that God, like a great ruler who has no time to deal with trivial matters, is too lofty to be involved in our concerns, even though this idea is contradicted by many verses in the Torah. They think that if God is dealing with stars and galaxies, He can't possibly care about the minor deeds of humans. However, the concept of infinity encompasses even the smallest things. A human ruler, even the most powerful one, cannot deal with every small matter, because he is limited, and therefore he has to focus only on pressing issues. However, for the Infinite, the distinction between vast and tiny disappears. Thus, the verse states: "Exalted above all nations is the Lord; above the heavens is His glory" (Psalms 113:4), meaning that, for the nations, God's exalted state is why He remains "above the heavens." We, by contrast, declare that He "sits on high" (Psalms 113:5), i.e., He is above the heavens as well, and that He nevertheless "looks down to see what is in heaven and earth" (Psalms 113:6); both of them, together (from the article "On the Foundations of Faith," published in the periodical *Shefa Rav*, 17).

Halakha 9

אִם כֵּן, מַה הוּא זֶה שֶׁנֶּאֱמַר בַּתּוֹרָה: "וְתַחַת רַגְלָיו" (שמות כד, י), "כְּתֻבִים בְּאֶצְבַּע אֱלֹהִים" (שם לא, יח; דברים ט, י), "יַד ה'" (שמות ט, ג; במדבר יא, כג ועוד), וְ"עֵינֵי ה'" (דברים יא, יב), וְ"אָזְנֵי ה'" (במדבר יא, א; יא, יח), וְכַיּוֹצֵא בַּדְּבָרִים הַלָּלוּ?

If this is **so,** that God has no body, **what is** the meaning of that **which is stated in the Torah,** with regard to the revelation at Sinai: **"Under His feet** was like a configuration of sapphire brick, and like the very heavens in purity" (Exodus 24:10); "the two Tablets of Testimony, tablets of stone, **written with the finger of God"** (Exodus 31:18; Deuteronomy 9:10); **"the hand of the Lord"** (e.g., Exodus 9:3, Numbers 11:23); **"the eyes of the Lord"** (Deuteronomy 11:12); **"the ears of the Lord"** (Numbers 11:1, 18), **and similar expressions?**

הַכֹּל לְפִי דַּעְתָּן שֶׁל בְּנֵי אָדָם הוּא שֶׁאֵינָן מַכִּירִין אֶלָּא הַגּוּפוֹת, וְדִבְּרָה תּוֹרָה כִּלְשׁוֹן בְּנֵי אָדָם, וְהַכֹּל כִּנּוּיִים הֵם, כְּמוֹ שֶׁנֶּאֱמַר: "אִם שַׁנּוֹתִי בְּרַק חַרְבִּי" (דברים לב, מא).

This is all in accordance with people's way of **thought,**[a] and their manner of grasping concepts, **for they are familiar only with bodies, and the Torah spoke in the language of men. They are all parables** and metaphors, **in the manner that it is stated: "Surely I will hone My flashing sword"**[b] (Deuteronomy 32:41).

וְכִי חֶרֶב יֵשׁ לוֹ וּבַחֶרֶב הוּא הוֹרֵג? אֶלָּא מָשָׁל, וְהַכֹּל מָשָׁל.

Now, does God **have a sword, and does He kill with a sword? Rather, this is a metaphor, and** likewise **all** such expressions are **metaphors** of God's actions and revelation.

רְאָיָה לְדָבָר זֶה, שֶׁנָּבִיא אֶחָד אוֹמֵר שֶׁרָאָה הַקָּדוֹשׁ בָּרוּךְ הוּא "לְבוּשֵׁהּ כִּתְלַג חִוָּר" (דניאל ז, ט), וְאַחֵר רָאָהוּ "חֲמוּץ בְּגָדִים מִבָּצְרָה" (ישעיהו סג, א),

A proof of this claim, that all corporeal descriptions of God are only metaphorical, is **that one prophet says that he saw the Holy One blessed be He** and **"His garment was like white snow"** (Daniel 7:9), **while another saw Him** coming **"red-clothed from Botzra"** (Isaiah 63:1).

וּמֹשֶׁה רַבֵּנוּ עַצְמוֹ רָאָהוּ עַל הַיָּם כְּגִבּוֹר עוֹשֵׂה מִלְחָמָה, וּבְסִינַי כִּשְׁלִיחַ צִבּוּר עָטוּף,

Moses, our teacher, himself saw Him at the splitting of the Red **Sea as a mighty** warrior, **waging war,**[c] **and** yet **at** Mount **Sinai,** Moses had a vision of God **as a prayer leader of a congregation, wrapped** in a tallit.[d]

לוֹמַר שֶׁאֵין לוֹ דְּמוּת וְצוּרָה, אֶלָּא הַכֹּל בְּמַרְאֵה הַנְּבוּאָה וּבְמַחֲזֶה.

This **tells us that He has no image or form,** since He reveals Himself in many ways, all of which are metaphors. **Rather,** it was **all** experienced **through prophetic vision and representation.**

וַאֲמִתַּת הַדָּבָר – אֵין דַּעְתּוֹ שֶׁל אָדָם יְכוֹלָה לְהַשִּׂיגוֹ וּלְחָקְרוֹ, וְזֶה הוּא שֶׁאָמַר הַכָּתוּב: "הַחֵקֶר אֱלוֹהַּ תִּמְצָא אִם עַד תַּכְלִית שַׁדַּי תִּמְצָא" (איוב יא, ז).

But the truth of this concept cannot be grasped or analyzed by human thought, and this is the meaning of **the verse: "Can you discover the understanding of God? Can you discover the purpose of the Almighty?"** (Job 11:7).

NOTES

a. Since infinity goes beyond our existence, it is very difficult to relate to it emotionally. The more we think about it, the further it seems to drift away from us. Accordingly, the Rambam rules that it is permitted, and to a certain extent even appropriate, to relate to God as the prophets speak about Him, in a poetic, rather than philosophically accurate manner. The Biblical phrases discussed here, as well as expressions such as "our Father" and "the King, girded in strength," which we use in prayer, cannot be understood in a literal manner, but they enable us to move from the cold realm of abstract thought to the realm of experience. Thus, when the average person goes to sleep, he lies down comfortably on his bed not by thinking that he is in the presence of the Infinite, but rather, that he is a subject of the King, or his Father. All of our prophets and Sages affirm that anthropomorphic expressions are a genuine element of our relationship with God. These are all poetic ways of speaking, and poetry lives through images that, while not factual descriptions of reality, as such, are true, in the emotional sense (from the article "On the Foundations of Faith," published in the periodical Shefa Rav, 17).

b. God says this at the end of the song of *Haazinu*.

c. As it is stated at the end of the Song at the Red Sea: "The Lord is a warrior" (Exodus 15:3).

d. When Moses ascended Mount Sinai alone, after the sin of the Golden Calf, God revealed to him the secret of His thirteen attributes of mercy. The Sages teach that He wrapped Himself in a tallit, a prayer shawl, like a prayer leader, and demonstrated to Moses how the prayer should be performed (see *Rosh HaShana* 17b).

Halakha 10

מַה הוּא זֶה שֶׁבִּקֵּשׁ מֹשֶׁה רַבֵּנוּ לְהַשִּׂיג כְּשֶׁאָמַר: "הַרְאֵנִי נָא אֶת כְּבֹדֶךָ" (שמות לג, יח)?

In that case, however, **what is that which Moses, our teacher, sought to comprehend, when he said: "Please show me Your glory"?** (Exodus 33:18). If God has no form, what did Moses ask to be shown?

בִּקֵּשׁ לֵידַע אֲמִתַּת הִמָּצְאוֹ שֶׁל הַקָּדוֹשׁ בָּרוּךְ הוּא עַד שֶׁיִּהְיֶה יָדוּעַ בְּלִבּוֹ כְּמוֹ יְדִיעַת אֶחָד מִן הָאֲנָשִׁים שֶׁרָאָה פָּנָיו וְנֶחְקְקָה צוּרָתוֹ בְּקִרְבּוֹ, שֶׁנִּמְצָא אוֹתוֹ הָאִישׁ נִפְרָד בְּדַעְתּוֹ מִשְּׁאָר הָאֲנָשִׁים.

He sought to know the truth of the existence of the Holy One blessed be He, until it would be known in his heart like the knowledge of a person whose face he has seen, and whose image has been engraved on his mind, such **that** the identity of **that person is distinguished in his mind from** that of **other men.**[a]

כָּךְ בִּקֵּשׁ מֹשֶׁה רַבֵּנוּ לִהְיוֹת מְצִיאַת הַקָּדוֹשׁ בָּרוּךְ הוּא נִפְרֶדֶת בְּלִבּוֹ מִשְּׁאָר מְצִיאַת הַנִּמְצָאִים, עַד שֶׁיֵּדַע אֲמִתַּת הִמָּצְאוֹ כְּמָה שֶׁהִיא. וֶהֱשִׁיבוֹ בָּרוּךְ הוּא שֶׁאֵין כֹּחַ בְּדַעַת הָאָדָם הַחַי, שֶׁהוּא מְחֻבָּר מִגּוּף וְנֶפֶשׁ, לְהַשִּׂיג אֲמִתַּת דָּבָר זֶה עַל בֻּרְיוֹ.

Thus, Moses, our teacher, sought for the existence of the Holy One blessed be He to be distinguished in his heart from the existence of all other beings, to the extent that he would know the truth of His existence as it is. However, God, **blessed be He, replied to him that it is not within the power of a living person, who is an amalgamation of body and soul,**[b] **to fully attain the truth of this matter.**[c]

וְהוֹדִיעוֹ בָּרוּךְ הוּא מַה שֶּׁלֹּא יָדַע אָדָם לְפָנָיו וְלֹא יֵדַע לְאַחֲרָיו, עַד שֶׁהִשִּׂיג מֵאֲמִתַּת הִמָּצְאוֹ דָּבָר שֶׁנִּפְרַד הַקָּדוֹשׁ בָּרוּךְ הוּא בְּדַעְתּוֹ מִשְּׁאָר הַנִּמְצָאִים, כְּמוֹ שֶׁיִּפָּרֵד אֶחָד מִן הָאֲנָשִׁים שֶׁרָאָה אֲחוֹרָיו וְהִשִּׂיג כָּל גּוּפוֹ וּמַלְבּוּשׁוֹ בְּדַעְתּוֹ מִשְּׁאָר הָאֲנָשִׁים. וְעַל דָּבָר זֶה רָמַז הַכָּתוּב וְאָמַר: "וְרָאִיתָ אֶת אֲחֹרָי וּפָנַי לֹא יֵרָאוּ" (שמות לג, כג).

Even so, God, **blessed be He, revealed to** Moses **that which no other man had known before him, and none would know after him, until he grasped in his mind, with regard to the truth of His existence,** the **fact that the Holy One blessed be He is distinguished from** all **other beings, just as** a certain **man is distinguished from** all **other men in one's mind when he has seen his back and comprehended** the shape **of his whole body and his clothing.**[d] **The verse** alludes **to this idea** when **it states: "And you will see My back, but My face will not be seen"** (Exodus 33:23).

NOTES

a. In other words, Moses' request is also presented in metaphorical terms. He wished to know the reality of God with the same clarity that the shape and image of another person are clear in the mind of someone who has seen him and has recognized the unique characteristics that differentiate him from others.

b. The Rambam's statement here is based on the verse: "as man shall not see Me and live" (Exodus 33:20). This verse can also be rendered: "as no man [*adam*] and living being [*ḥai*] may see Me and live." The Rambam interprets the term *adam* as referring to man's physical being and *ḥai* as referring to man's spiritual side. Man, comprised of a combination of the physical and spiritual, cannot perceive God with absolute clarity (Rabbi Shlomo Eiger).

c. God replied to Moses that anything that a person will ever grasp in his mind is limited by the fact that humans can fully understand only corporeal, physical things. Therefore, it is impossible for him to comprehend the whole truth of God's nature and existence.

d. Although God did not reveal to Moses a positive recognition of His existence (which is in any case unattainable for humans), Moses nevertheless attained a negative recognition of this truth, which is the essential difference between God's existence and the existence of anything else. Thus, he achieved a very high level of understanding, but only in a negative manner.

GLOSSES OF THE RAAVAD

"מַהוּ שֶׁבִּקֵּשׁ מֹשֶׁה רַבֵּנוּ כְּשֶׁאָמַר הַרְאֵנִי נָא אֶת כְּבֹדֶךָ בִּקֵּשׁ לֵידַע אֲמִתַּת הִמָּצְאוֹ שֶׁל הַקָּדוֹשׁ בָּרוּךְ הוּא עַד שֶׁיְּהֵא יָדוּעַ בַּלֵּב כְּמוֹ יְדִיעַת אֶחָד מִן הָאֲנָשִׁים שֶׁרָאָה."

"What is it that Moses, our teacher, sought when he said 'please show me Your glory'? He sought to know the truth of the existence of the Holy One blessed be He, until it would be known in the heart like the knowledge of a person whom he has seen."

אָמַר אַבְרָהָם: אֵין דַּעְתִּי מְיֻשֶּׁבֶת עָלַי דְּבָרָיו, וַהֲלֹא רָאָה עַל הַר סִינַי וּבְאַרְבָּעִים יוֹם שֶׁל לוּחוֹת הָרִאשׁוֹנוֹת מַה שֶּׁלֹּא רָאָה נָבִיא וְחוֹזֶה עַד שֶׁקִּנְּאוּ בּוֹ מַלְאֲכֵי הַשָּׁרֵת וּבִקְּשׁוּ לְדָחֲפוֹ, עַד שֶׁאָחַז בְּכִסֵּא הַכָּבוֹד (בבלי שבת פח, ב).

Avraham says: My mind is unsettled by the Rambam's **comments. For** Moses had already **seen on Mount Sinai,** and during **the forty days of** the giving **of the first Tablets, that which no prophet or seer had seen** before him, to such an extent **that the ministering angels were jealous of him and sought to push him away, until he grasped hold of** God's **Throne of Glory** (*Shabbat* 88b).

וְעוֹד אִלּוּ הָיְתָה זֹאת הַבַּקָּשָׁה, מַה צֹּרֶךְ בַּתְּשׁוּבָה לוֹמַר: "וְחַנֹּתִי אֶת אֲשֶׁר אָחֹן וְרִחַמְתִּי אֶת אֲשֶׁר אֲרַחֵם" (שמות לג, יט).

Furthermore, if this was Moses' **request, what is the relevance of the answer** that God **says: "And I will favor whom I will favor, and I will have mercy on whom I will have mercy"?** (Exodus 33:19).

אֲבָל לְפִי שֶׁאָמַר לוֹ הַבּוֹרֵא: "לֹא אֶעֱלֶה בְּקִרְבְּךָ...פֶּן אֲכֶלְךָ בַּדָּרֶךְ" (שם לג, ב), וּבִקֵּשׁ מֹשֶׁה שֶׁיָּשׁוּב וְהוּא אוֹמֵר 'הוֹדִיעֵנִי נָא אֶת כְּבוֹדֶךָ', וְאָמַר לוֹ 'יֵלְכוּ פָּנַי וַהֲנִיחוֹתִי לָךְ',

Rather, the request is **in accordance with** the development of the entire discussion between God and Moses presented in that chapter. **The Creator said to him: "I will not go up in your midst... lest I destroy you on the way"** (Exodus 33:2), **and Moses,** asking God **to return** to the people, **said to Him: "Inform me, please, of Your ways"** (Exodus 33:13), to which God **responded: "My Presence will go, and I will give you rest"** (Exodus 33:14).

וְאָמַר מֹשֶׁה "אִם אֵין פָּנֶיךָ הֹלְכִים", כְּלוֹמַר אַל תֹּאמַר כְּשֶׁנִּכָּנֵס בָּאָרֶץ תֵּלֵךְ עִמָּנוּ כִּי מִכָּאן לֹא נִסַּע עַד שֶׁתָּשׁוּב עִמָּנוּ, וְאָמַר לוֹ הַבּוֹרֵא "גַּם אֲשֶׁר דִּבַּרְתָּ אֶעֱשֶׂה".

Moses then said: "If Your Presence does not go, do not bring us up from here" (Exodus 33:15). **In other words, do not say that You will go with us** only **when we enter the Land, for we will not travel from here unless You return with us.** To this, **the Creator replied:** "This matter **that you have spoken, I will do as well"** (Exodus 33:17).

"וַיֹּאמַר הַרְאֵנִי נָא אֶת כְּבֹדֶךָ" כְּלוֹמַר אֲנִי רוֹצֶה לִרְאוֹת. "וַיֹּאמֶר אֲנִי אַעֲבִיר כָּל טוּבִי עַל פָּנֶיךָ וְקָרָאתִי בְשֵׁם" וְגוֹ'

Then Moses **said: "Please show me Your glory"** (Exodus 33:18), **that is, I wish to see** it happen. **"He said: I will pass all My goodness before you, and I will call with the name** of the Lord before you; and I will favor whom I will favor, and I will have mercy on whom I will have mercy" (Exodus 33:19).

וְאוֹדִיעֲךָ בְּעָבְרִי וְהָעָם אֲשֶׁר הִכְעִיסוּנִי יִהְיֶה מִי שֶׁאָחֹן עָלָיו וְלֹא כָּל כֻּלָּם. וּפָנִים וְאָחוֹר סוֹד גָּדוֹל וְאֵין רָאוּי לְגַלּוֹתוֹ לְכָל אָדָם. וְאוּלַי בַּעַל הַדְּבָרִים הַזֶּה לֹא יְדָעָהוּ.

This means that God said: **I will inform you of My passing** before you, **and the people who angered Me will be those "I will favor," but not all of them.** As for the mention of God's **"face" and "back"** (Exodus 33:20, 23), this **is a great secret that should not be revealed to all people, and perhaps this author did not know it.**

NOTES

a. See *Ḥagiga* 15a.

b. That is, no reverse side, which represents division.

c. See the Rambam's *Commentary on the Mishna*, *Hadkama LePerek Ḥelek*.

d. See Halakha 9.

e. See e.g., *Berakhot* 31b.

Halakha 11

וְכֵיוָן שֶׁנִּתְבָּרֵר שֶׁאֵינוֹ גּוּף וּגְוִיָּה, יִתְבָּאֵר שֶׁלֹּא יֶאֶרְעוֹ וְלֹא אֶחָד מִמְּאֹרְעוֹת הַגּוּף,

Since it has been established that God does **not** have **a body or corporeal form, it is** also **clear that none of the circumstances of the body are applicable to Him.** The characteristic qualities of physical entities cannot be ascribed to God:

לֹא חִבּוּר וְלֹא פֵּרוּד, וְלֹא מָקוֹם וְלֹא מִדָּה, וְלֹא עֲלִיָּה וְלֹא יְרִידָה, וְלֹא יָמִין וְלֹא שְׂמֹאל, וְלֹא פָּנִים וְלֹא אָחוֹר, וְלֹא יְשִׁיבָה וְלֹא עֲמִידָה.

Not the **connection** to another body, **or a division** into smaller parts, **nor** does He occupy any **place, or** have **measurements, or ascend or descend,** which are movements in space, **nor** does He go to the **right, left, front, or back, or stand or sit,** all of which refer only to bodies.

וְאֵינוֹ מָצוּי בִּזְמַן עַד שֶׁיִּהְיֶה לוֹ רֵאשִׁית וְאַחֲרִית וּמִנְיַן שָׁנִים. וְאֵינוֹ מִשְׁתַּנֶּה, שֶׁאֵין לוֹ דָּבָר שֶׁיִּגְרֹם לוֹ שִׁנּוּי.

He is not found in time, that is, the dimension of time does not apply to Him, **that He would possess a beginning, an end, or an age** in **years. He does not change, for there is nothing that can cause Him to change.**

וְאֵין לוֹ לֹא מָוֶת וְלֹא חַיִּים כְּחַיֵּי הַגּוּף הַחַי, וְלֹא סִכְלוּת וְלֹא חָכְמָה כְּחָכְמַת הָאִישׁ הֶחָכָם, לֹא שֵׁנָה וְלֹא הֲקָצָה, וְלֹא כַּעַס וְלֹא שְׂחוֹק, וְלֹא שִׂמְחָה וְלֹא עַצְבוּת, לֹא שְׁתִיקָה וְלֹא דִּבּוּר כְּדִבּוּר אָדָם. כָּךְ אָמְרוּ חֲכָמִים: אֵין לְמַעְלָה לֹא יְשִׁיבָה וְלֹא עֲמִידָה, לֹא עֹרֶף וְלֹא עִפּוּי.

God **has no death, or life, as** these apply to **the life of the living body, nor** does He have **foolishness, or wisdom like the wisdom of a wise man, or sleep or waking, or anger or laughter, or joy or sadness, or silence, or speech like human speech. The Sages said the following:**[a] "In the world **above there is no sitting; no standing; no back;**[b] **and no connection** to another body."[c]

Halakha 12

וְהוֹאִיל וְהַדָּבָר כֵּן הוּא, כָּל הַדְּבָרִים הַלָּלוּ וְכַיּוֹצֵא בָּהֶן שֶׁנֶּאֶמְרוּ בַּתּוֹרָה וּבְדִבְרֵי נְבִיאִים – הַכֹּל מָשָׁל וּמְלִיצָה הֵם, כְּמוֹ שֶׁנֶּאֱמַר: "יוֹשֵׁב בַּשָּׁמַיִם יִשְׂחָק" (תהלים ב, ד), "כִּעֲסוּנִי בְּהַבְלֵיהֶם" (דברים לב, כא), "כַּאֲשֶׁר שָׂשׂ יי" (שם כח, סג), וְכַיּוֹצֵא בָּהֶן,

Since this is the case, all these descriptions and the like, which attribute such qualities to God, and **which are stated in the Torah and the words of** the **prophets, are all metaphors and allegories,**[d] **as,** for example, **when it states: "He whose seat is in heaven will laugh"** (Psalms 2:4); **"they angered Me with their futilities"** (Deuteronomy 32:21); **"as the Lord rejoiced"** (Deuteronomy 28:63), **and other such** expressions.

עַל הַכֹּל אָמְרוּ חֲכָמִים: דִּבְּרָה תּוֹרָה כִּלְשׁוֹן בְּנֵי אָדָם. וְכֵן הוּא אוֹמֵר: "הַאֹתִי הֵם מַכְעִסִים" (ירמיהו ז, יט).

With regard to all these, **the Sages said: "The Torah spoke in the language of men,"**[e] **and** the verse **likewise states,** attesting that such characteristics do not apply to God: **"Is it Me that they anger?"** (Jeremiah 7:19). Do the sins of the children of Israel actually make God angry? Certainly not.

הֲרֵי הוּא אוֹמֵר: "אֲנִי יי לֹא שָׁנִיתִי" (מלאכי ג, ו), וְאִלּוּ הָיָה פְּעָמִים כּוֹעֵס וּפְעָמִים שָׂמֵחַ – הָיָה מִשְׁתַּנֶּה. וְכָל הַדְּבָרִים הָאֵלּוּ אֵינָם מְצוּיִים אֶלָּא לַגּוּפִים הָאֲפֵלִים הַשְּׁפָלִים, שֹׁכְנֵי בָּתֵּי חֹמֶר אֲשֶׁר בֶּעָפָר יְסוֹדָם. אֲבָל הוּא בָּרוּךְ הוּא יִתְעַלֶּה וְיִתְרוֹמֵם עַל כָּל זֶה.

It thus states: "For I, the Lord, did not change" (Malachi 3:6). The entire concept of change is inapplicable to God. **Now, were He sometimes angry and at** other **times joyful,** He **would change.** Thus, all human traits, such as anger and joy, do not apply to God. **All these qualities are found only in the dark, lowly bodies who dwell in houses of clay, whose founding is in dust.**[a] **But He, blessed be He, is exalted and elevated above all this.**

BACKGROUND

Opening of *Sefer Madda*, illustrated manuscript, thirteenth century

NOTES

a. This is a quote from Job 4:19 which refers to mortals, whose spirits reside within corporeal bodies, fashioned from the dust (see Genesis 2:7).

פֶּרֶק שֵׁנִי

CHAPTER 2

God's Knowledge and Providence

Halakhot 1–2:	The mitzvot to love and fear God
Halakha 3:	The types of created beings in the world
Halakhot 4–8:	The angels and their ranks
Halakhot 9–10:	God's knowledge
Halakhot 11–12:	Studying the Design of the Divine Chariot

Halakha 1

הָאֵל הַנִּכְבָּד וְהַנּוֹרָא הַזֶּה – מִצְוָה לְאָהֲבוֹ וּלְיִרְאָה מִמֶּנּוּ, שֶׁנֶּאֱמַר: "וְאָהַבְתָּ אֵת יי אֱלֹהֶיךָ" (דברים ו, ה; יא, א), וְנֶאֱמַר: "אֶת יי אֱלֹהֶיךָ תִּירָא" (שם ו, יג; י, כ).

This glorious and awesome God, it is **a mitzva to love Him and fear Him,*** **as it is stated: "You shall love the Lord your God"** (Deuteronomy 6:5, 11:1), **and it is stated: "You shall fear the Lord your God"** (Deuteronomy 6:13, 10:20).

FROM THE LUBAVITCHER REBBE

*It is a mitzva to love Him and fear Him – מִצְוָה לְאָהֲבוֹ וּלְיִרְאָה מִמֶּנּוּ: The Rambam presents the mitzvot of loving and fearing God together, which is unusual for him, since he typically lays out each mitzva and its sources separately. This is especially surprising in light of the fact that these two mitzvot involve very different, indeed, opposite emotional states: the closeness of love, in contrast to fear and keeping one's distance. The reason is that according to the Rambam, the love and fear of God are actually similar to one another, and they stem from the same source: By reflecting on God's "wonderful, great deeds and creations" one truly yearns "to know the Great Name," but since it is not possible for a created being to fully attain this, this thirst and passion continue to develop in him until they blossom into love. At the very same time, when he realizes how small and distant he is from God, "he will immediately recoil backward and be scared and afraid, knowing that he is a small, lowly, dark, and material creature" (Halakha 2), and that is the essence of the fear of God (*Torat Menaḥem, Hitvaaduyot, Parashat Mishpatim* 5747; *Likkutei Siḥot* 34, p. 32).

Halakha 2

וְהֵיאַךְ הִיא הַדֶּרֶךְ לְאַהֲבָתוֹ וְיִרְאָתוֹ? בְּשָׁעָה שֶׁיִּתְבּוֹנֵן הָאָדָם בְּמַעֲשָׂיו וּבְרוּאָיו הַנִּפְלָאִים הַגְּדוֹלִים וְיִרְאֶה מֵהֶם חָכְמָתוֹ שֶׁאֵין לָהּ עֵרֶךְ וְלֹא קֵץ – מִיָּד הוּא אוֹהֵב וּמְשַׁבֵּחַ וּמְפָאֵר וּמִתְאַוֶּה תַּאֲוָה גְּדוֹלָה לֵידַע הַשֵּׁם הַגָּדוֹל, כְּמוֹ שֶׁאָמַר דָּוִד: "צָמְאָה נַפְשִׁי לֵאלֹהִים לְאֵל חָי" (תהלים מב, ג).

What is the path one should follow in order **to love and fear** God? **When a person contemplates His wonderful, great deeds and creations and thereby realizes His incomparable, infinite wisdom, he will immediately love, praise, and glorify** Him, **and yearn with a great yearning to know the Great Name** of God, **as David said: "My soul thirsts for God, the living God Almighty"** (Psalms 42:3).

וּכְשֶׁמְּחַשֵּׁב בַּדְּבָרִים הָאֵלּוּ עַצְמָן, מִיָּד הוּא נִרְתָּע לַאֲחוֹרָיו וְיִירָא וְיִפְחַד, וְיוֹדֵעַ שֶׁהוּא בְּרִיָּה קְטַנָּה שְׁפָלָה אֲפֵלָה, עוֹמֵד בְּדַעַת קַלָּה מְעוּטָה לִפְנֵי תְּמִים דֵּעוֹת, כְּמוֹ שֶׁאָמַר דָּוִד: "כִּי אֶרְאֶה שָׁמֶיךָ וגו' מָה אֱנוֹשׁ כִּי תִזְכְּרֶנּוּ" וגו' (תהלים ח, ד–ה).

At the same time, **as he reflects on these** very **same matters, he will immediately recoil backward and be scared and afraid, knowing that he is a small, lowly, dark** and earthbound **creature, standing with** his **flimsy, slight knowledge before He who is complete in knowledge,**[a] **as David said: "When I see Your heavens,** the work of Your fingers, the moon and the stars You have made: **What is a mortal that You remember him?"** (Psalms 8:4–5). When David gazed at God's creations, he was led to contemplate the insignificance and relative worthlessness of mortals.

וּלְפִי הַדְּבָרִים הָאֵלּוּ אֲנִי מְבָאֵר כְּלָלִים גְּדוֹלִים מִמַּעֲשֵׂה רִבּוֹן הָעוֹלָמִים, כְּדֵי שֶׁיִּהְיוּ פֶּתַח לַמֵּבִין לֶאֱהֹב אֶת הַשֵּׁם, כְּמוֹ שֶׁאָמְרוּ חֲכָמִים בְּעִנְיַן אַהֲבָה: שֶׁמִּתּוֹךְ כָּךְ אַתָּה מַכִּיר אֶת מִי שֶׁאָמַר וְהָיָה הָעוֹלָם.

Based on these ideas, that reflecting on the works of God leads one to love and fear Him,[b] **I will explain important principles**[1] **concerning the deeds of the Master of the universe, so that there should be an opening for** a person of **understanding to love God, as the Sages said, regarding love, that you will thereby recognize the One who spoke and the world came into being.**[c]

Halakha 3

כָּל מַה שֶּׁבָּרָא הַקָּדוֹשׁ בָּרוּךְ הוּא בְּעוֹלָמוֹ נֶחֱלָק לִשְׁלֹשָׁה חֲלָקִים: מֵהֶם בְּרוּאִים שֶׁהֵם מְחֻבָּרִין מִגֹּלֶם וְצוּרָה, וְהֵם נֶהֱוִים וְנִפְסָדִים תָּמִיד, כְּמוֹ גּוּפוֹת הָאָדָם וְהַבְּהֵמָה וְהַצְּמָחִים וְהַמַּתָּכוֹת; וּמֵהֶם בְּרוּאִים שֶׁהֵם מְחֻבָּרִים מִגֹּלֶם וְצוּרָה, אֲבָל אֵינָם מִשְׁתַּנִּים מִגּוּף לְגוּף וּמִצּוּרָה לְצוּרָה כְּמוֹ הָרִאשׁוֹנִים,

Everything that the Holy One blessed be He created within His world can be divided into three categories. Some are created beings that are an amalgamation of matter and form.[d] **These are constantly coming into existence and ceasing to exist, such as the bodies of humans and animals, plants, and metals. Others are created beings that are** also **an amalgamation of matter and form, but they do not change from one body to another and from one form to the next, like** those in **the first** category.

HALAKHIC DISCUSSION

1. **Based on these ideas I will explain important principles – וּלְפִי הַדְּבָרִים הָאֵלּוּ אֲנִי מְבָאֵר כְּלָלִים גְּדוֹלִים:** In chapters 3 and 4, the Rambam will provide a scientific account of the structure of the universe, which he calls "the act of Creation" (4:10). For various opinions among the authorities regarding this depiction, see the appendix: "The Scientific Description of the World in *Hilkhot Yesodei HaTorah*."

NOTES

a. See Job 37:16.

b. See also 4:12.

c. The Sages said, on the passage: "You shall love the Lord your God.... These matters that I command you today shall be upon your heart" (Deuteronomy 6:5–6), that the way to attain the love of God is by placing "these matters" upon your heart, so "that you will thereby recognize the One who spoke and the world came into being, and cleave to His ways" (*Sifrei* on Deuteronomy 33). In a similar manner, understanding the works of creation can lead to the love of God.

d. "Matter" is the substance itself, which has no qualities, while "form" is all the qualities of the substance, such as its weight, color, structure, and so on. According to this worldview, "form" is a separate existence to "matter," even though they generally come together.

אֶלָּא צוּרָתָם קְבוּעָה בְּגָלְמָם לְעוֹלָם וְאֵינָם מִשְׁתַּנִּים כְּמוֹ אֵלּוּ, וְהֵם הַגַּלְגַּלִּים וְהַכּוֹכָבִים שֶׁבָּהֶן, וְאֵין גָּלְמָם כִּשְׁאָר גְּלָמִים וְלֹא צוּרָתָם כִּשְׁאָר צוּרוֹת. וּמֵהֶם בְּרוּאִים צוּרָה בְּלֹא גֹּלֶם כְּלָל, וְהֵם הַמַּלְאָכִים, שֶׁהַמַּלְאָכִים אֵינָן גּוּף וּגְוִיָּה, אֶלָּא צוּרוֹת נִפְרָדוֹת זוֹ מִזּוֹ.

Rather, their form is permanently fixed in their matter, and they do not change like those first entities.[a] **These are the spheres, and the stars** that revolve **in them. Their matter is not like other matter, and their form is not like other forms.**[b] Finally, **other created beings** have **a form without matter at all. These are the angels, for the angels** do **not** have **a body or corporeal form, but** are nevertheless **separate forms from each other.** They are spiritual beings, abstracted from any material substance, yet they are different forms from one another.[c]

Halakha 4

וּמַה הוּא זֶה שֶׁהַנְּבִיאִים אוֹמְרִים שֶׁרָאוּ הַמַּלְאָךְ אֵשׁ וּבַעַל כְּנָפַיִם?

What is the meaning **when the prophets say that they saw an angel of fire, or** an angel **with wings?** If the angels have no substance or body, why are they depicted as made of fire or as winged creatures?

הַכֹּל בְּמַרְאֵה הַנְּבוּאָה וְדֶרֶךְ חִידָה, לוֹמַר שֶׁאֵינוֹ גּוּף, וְאֵינוֹ כָּבֵד כַּגּוּפוֹת הַכְּבֵדִים,

All of these descriptions are elements **of prophetic visions and** are stated **in the manner of a parable,**[d] as a way of **saying that** the angel does **not** have **a body and has no weight like weighted bodies.** Thus, the parable is that angels have no bodies, like fire, and they also lack the qualities of a body, such as physical weight, as alluded to by their wings.

כְּמוֹ שֶׁנֶּאֱמַר: "כִּי יי אֱלֹהֶיךָ אֵשׁ אֹכְלָה הוּא" (דברים ד,כד), וְאֵינוֹ אֵשׁ, אֶלָּא מָשָׁל, וּכְמוֹ שֶׁנֶּאֱמַר: "עֹשֶׂה מַלְאָכָיו רוּחוֹת" (תהלים קד,ד).

This is **as it is stated: "For the Lord your God is a consuming fire"** (Deuteronomy 4:24), **and yet He is not fire. Rather,** this depiction of God is certainly **a metaphor,**[e] **and the same** can be said regarding **that which is stated: "He makes His angels winds"** (Psalms 104:4).

Halakha 5

וּבַמֶּה יִפָּרְדוּ הַצּוּרוֹת זוֹ מִזּוֹ, וַהֲרֵי אֵינָן גּוּפִין? לְפִי שֶׁאֵינָן שָׁוִין בִּמְצִיאָתָן,

What, then, **separates the forms** of the angels **from each other, seeing that they** do **not** have **bodies?**[f] They differ from one another **because they are unequal in** terms of **their existence,** that is, with respect to their qualities, the essence of their particular forms.

אֶלָּא כָּל אֶחָד מֵהֶם לְמַטָּה מִמַּעֲלָתוֹ שֶׁל חֲבֵרוֹ, וְהוּא מָצוּי מִכֹּחוֹ, זֶה לְמַעְלָה מִזֶּה,

Rather, each one of them is above or **below the level of the other, and exists through its effect, one above the other.** The relationship between the angels is one of cause and effect; the higher angel is the cause of the lower one.

NOTES

a. Even though they also have both a material basis ("matter") and qualities ("form"), their essence does not change, but remains the same forever.

b. According to this view, the stars are comprised of a special substance (the "fifth element"), which is dissimilar to the substance of our world. Their form also has qualities that do not exist in other entities.

c. See Halakha 5.

d. See 7:3.

e. See 1:9.

f. See 1:5.

וְהַכֹּל נִמְצָאִים מִכֹּחוֹ שֶׁל הַקָּדוֹשׁ בָּרוּךְ הוּא וְטוּבוֹ. וְזֶה הוּא שֶׁרָמַז שְׁלֹמֹה בְּחָכְמָתוֹ וְאָמַר: "כִּי גָבֹהַּ מֵעַל גָּבֹהַּ שֹׁמֵר" (קהלת ה, ז).

And they **all exist through the effect of the Holy One blessed be He, and His goodness. This is what Solomon is alluding to in his wisdom** when **he says: "For higher than high is watching**, and high ones are over them" (Ecclesiastes 5:7). In other words, the angels are not identical to one another, but rather they are on different levels.

Halakha 6

זֶה שֶׁאָמַרְנוּ לְמַטָּה מִמַּעֲלָתוֹ - אֵינָהּ מַעֲלַת מָקוֹם, כְּמוֹ אָדָם שֶׁיּוֹשֵׁב לְמַעְלָה מֵחֲבֵרוֹ,

When we said that each form of an angel is "**below the level of** the other,"[a] this **does not** refer to **height** as the term is used in reference to **space.** There is no difference between the angels in terms of physical location, with one situated above the other, **like a person who is sitting on a higher** level **than another.**

אֶלָּא כְּמוֹ שֶׁאוֹמְרִין בִּשְׁנֵי חֲכָמִים שֶׁאֶחָד גָּדוֹל מֵחֲבֵרוֹ בְּחָכְמָה, שֶׁהוּא לְמַעְלָה מִמַּעֲלָתוֹ שֶׁל זֶה, וּכְמוֹ שֶׁאוֹמְרִין בָּעִלָּה, שֶׁהִיא לְמַעְלָה מִן הֶעָלוּל.

Rather, it is **similar** to **when one says about two Sages, one of whom is greater in wisdom than the other, that he is** "on **a higher level than this** other Sage." It is also **similar** to the way **one says about a cause, that it is "higher than"** its **effect.**

Halakha 7

שִׁנּוּי שְׁמוֹת הַמַּלְאָכִים - עַל שֵׁם מַעֲלוֹתָם הוּא, וּלְפִיכָךְ נִקְרָאִים: חַיּוֹת הַקֹּדֶשׁ, וְהֵם לְמַעְלָה מִן הַכֹּל, וְאוֹפַנִּים, וְאֶרְאֶלִּים, וְחַשְׁמַלִּים, וּשְׂרָפִים, וּמַלְאָכִים, וֵאלֹהִים, וּבְנֵי אֱלֹהִים, וּכְרוּבִים, וְאִישִׁים.

The differences in the names of the angels accord with their respective **levels. They are therefore called the holy *ḥayyot*** (**and these** angels **are higher than all** the rest); ***ofanim***; ***erelim***; ***ḥashmalim***; **seraphim**; ***melakhim***; ***elohim***; **sons of *elohim***; ***keruvim***; **and *ishim***, which are the lowest level of angels.

כָּל אֵלּוּ עֲשָׂרָה הַשֵּׁמוֹת שֶׁנִּקְרְאוּ בָּהֶם הַמַּלְאָכִים - עַל שֵׁם עֶשֶׂר הַמַּעֲלוֹת שֶׁלָּהֶם הֵם. וּמַעֲלָה שֶׁאֵין לְמַעְלָה מִמֶּנָּה אֶלָּא מַעֲלַת הָאֵל בָּרוּךְ שְׁמוֹ, הִיא מַעֲלַת הַצּוּרוֹת שֶׁנִּקְרֵאת חַיּוֹת. לְפִיכָךְ נֶאֱמַר בַּנְּבוּאָה שֶׁהֵם תַּחַת הַכִּסֵּא.

All these ten names by which the angels are called are in accordance with their ten levels. The level above which there is no higher level other than that of God, blessed be He, is the level of the form called *ḥayyot*. Therefore, it is stated in a prophecy that they are below God's **throne** of glory.[b]

וּמַעֲלָה עֲשִׂירִית הִיא מַעֲלַת הַצּוּרָה שֶׁנִּקְרֵאת אִישִׁים, וְהֵם הַמַּלְאָכִים שֶׁמְּדַבְּרִים עִם הַנְּבִיאִים וְנִרְאִים לָהֶם בְּמַרְאֵה הַנְּבוּאָה. לְפִיכָךְ נִקְרְאוּ אִישִׁים, שֶׁמַּעֲלָתָם קְרוֹבָה מִמַּעֲלַת דַּעַת הָאָדָם.

The tenth level is the level of the form called *ishim*. These are the angels who communicate with the prophets, and are shown to them in prophetic visions. This is why they are called *ishim*, "men," **because their level is close to the level of human knowledge.** Their spiritual level and understanding are only slightly higher than that of people, and prophets actually attain the level of the *ishim*.[c]

NOTES

a. In the previous Halakha.

b. See Ezekiel 1:26.

c. See 7:1.

BACKGROUND

Keruvim – cherubs

Halakha 8

וְכָל הַצּוּרוֹת הָאֵלּוּ חַיִּים וּמַכִּירִים אֶת הַבּוֹרֵא וְיוֹדְעִין אוֹתוֹ דֵּעָה גְּדוֹלָה עַד לִמְאֹד, כָּל צוּרָה וְצוּרָה לְפִי מַעֲלָתָהּ, לֹא כְּפִי גָּדְלוֹ.

All these forms are living beings **who recognize the Creator and know Him** with **an immense knowledge, each of the forms in accordance with its level,** albeit **not in accordance with** God's **greatness,** which is infinite and unattainable.

אֲפִלּוּ מַעֲלָה הָרִאשׁוֹנָה אֵינָהּ יְכוֹלָה לְהַשִּׂיג אֲמִתַּת הַבּוֹרֵא כְּמָה שֶׁהִיא, אֶלָּא דַּעְתָּהּ קְצָרָה לְהַשִּׂיג.

Not even an angel of **the highest level,** the holy *ḥayyot,* **is able to conceive of the truth of the Creator as He is; rather, its mind is too limited to grasp** Him.

אֲבָל מַשֶּׂגֶת וְיוֹדַעַת יָתֵר מִמַּה שֶּׁמַּשֶּׂגֶת וְיוֹדַעַת צוּרָה שֶׁלְּמַטָּה מִמֶּנָּה. וְכֵן כָּל מַעֲלָה וּמַעֲלָה, עַד מַעֲלָה עֲשִׂירִית,

However, such an angel **does grasp and know more than the form below it grasps and knows. The same** applies to **each and every level,** down **to the tenth level.**

גַּם הִיא יוֹדַעַת הַבּוֹרֵא דֵּעָה שֶׁאֵין כֹּחַ בְּנֵי הָאָדָם הַמְחֻבָּרִין מִגֹּלֶם וְצוּרָה יָכוֹל לְהַשִּׂיג וְלֵידַע כְּמוֹתָהּ. וְהַכֹּל אֵינָם יוֹדְעִין אֶת הַבּוֹרֵא כְּמוֹ שֶׁהוּא יוֹדֵעַ עַצְמוֹ.

Angels of the tenth level, the *ishim,* **also know the Creator** with **a knowledge the like of which humans, who are** a limited **amalgamation of matter and form, cannot grasp and know.** Yet **none** of the angels **can know the Creator as He** alone **knows Himself.**

Halakha 9

כָּל הַנִּמְצָאִים חוּץ מִן הַבּוֹרֵא, מִצּוּרָה הָרִאשׁוֹנָה עַד יַתּוּשׁ קָטָן שֶׁיִּהְיֶה בְּטַבּוּר הָאָרֶץ – הַכֹּל מִכֹּחַ אֲמִתּוֹ נִמְצְאוּ.

All beings apart from the Creator, from the first form, the holy *ḥayyot,* **until** the **small gnat that can be** found **in the depths of the earth, all came into being through the power of His truth.**[a]

וּלְפִי שֶׁהוּא יוֹדֵעַ עַצְמוֹ וּמַכִּיר גָּדְלוֹ וְתִפְאַרְתּוֹ וַאֲמִתּוֹ – הוּא יוֹדֵעַ הַכֹּל, וְאֵין דָּבָר נֶעְלָם מִמֶּנּוּ.

Since He knows Himself, and recognizes His greatness, splendor, and truth, He knows everything, and nothing is hidden from Him. All beings are dependent upon and stem from "the truth of His existence," and thus, in a sense, He incorporates them all. Accordingly, through God's knowledge of Himself, He knows everything that exists in the world.

Halakha 10

הַקָּדוֹשׁ בָּרוּךְ הוּא מַכִּיר אֲמִתּוֹ וְיוֹדֵעַ אוֹתָהּ כְּמוֹת שֶׁהִיא. וְאֵינוֹ יוֹדֵעַ בְּדֵעָה שֶׁהִיא חוּץ מִמֶּנּוּ, כְּמוֹ שֶׁאָנוּ יוֹדְעִין, שֶׁאֵין אָנוּ וְדַעְתֵּנוּ אֶחָד.

The Holy One blessed be He recognizes His truth and knows it as it is. He does not know with a knowledge that is external to Him, in the manner that we know something, **for we and our knowledge are not one.** The separate category of "knowledge" does not apply to God in the way that we are one thing, and our knowledge another.

NOTES

a. As explained in 1:1–3.

אֲבָל הַבּוֹרֵא, הוּא וְדַעְתּוֹ וְחַיָּיו אֶחָד מִכָּל צַד וּמִכָּל פִּנָּה. שֶׁאִלְמָלֵי הָיָה חַי בְּחַיִּים וְיוֹדֵעַ בְּדֵעָה – הָיוּ שָׁם אֱלוֹהוֹת הַרְבֵּה: הוּא, וְחַיָּיו, וְדַעְתּוֹ.

Rather, for **the Creator, may He be blessed, He, His knowledge, and His life are one, in all aspects and perspectives. For if He lived** by partaking of **life, or knew** by partaking in **knowledge, there would be many gods: He, His life, and His knowledge.** If God's life and knowledge were separate from Him, they themselves would have to be on the level of deities, and thus there would be many gods.

וְאֵין הַדָּבָר כֵּן, אֶלָּא אֶחָד מִכָּל צַד וּמִכָּל פִּנָּה וּבְכָל דֶּרֶךְ יִחוּד.

But that is not so; rather, He is **one, in all aspects and perspectives, and in every manner of unity.** As explained, God's unity is absolute, and differs in kind from all other types of unity.

נִמְצֵאתָ אוֹמֵר: הוּא הַיּוֹדֵעַ, וְהוּא הַיָּדוּעַ, וְהוּא הַדֵּעָה עַצְמָהּ – הַכֹּל אֶחָד. וְדָבָר זֶה אֵין כֹּחַ בַּפֶּה לְאָמְרוֹ, וְלֹא בָּאֹזֶן לְשָׁמְעוֹ, וְלֹא בְּלֵב הָאָדָם לְהַכִּירוֹ עַל בֻּרְיוֹ.

It is thus the case that **He is the Knower, He is the Known,**[a] **and He is the Knowledge itself.**[b] **All is one. This idea is beyond the power of** our **mouths to express or** our **ears to hear, or within** the capacity of **the heart of man to conceptualize fully.**

וּלְפִיכָךְ אוֹמְרִין: "חֵי פַרְעֹה" (בראשית מב, טו-טז) וְ"חֵי נַפְשְׁךָ" (שמואל א א, כו ועוד), וְאֵין אוֹמְרִין: 'חֵי יי׳' אֶלָּא "חַי יי׳" (שופטים ח, יט ועוד), שֶׁאֵין הַבּוֹרֵא וְחַיָּיו שְׁנַיִם כְּמוֹ חַיֵּי הַגּוּפוֹת הַחַיִּים אוֹ כְּחַיֵּי הַמַּלְאָכִים.

Therefore, one can say: "By Pharaoh's life" (Genesis 42:15–16), **and "by your soul's life"** (e.g., I Samuel 1:26), **whereas one does not say "by the Lord's life"** but **rather "as the Lord lives"** (e.g., Judges 8:19), **for the Creator and His life are not two, like the lives of living bodies or like the lives of the angels.** One cannot refer to "God's life," since it is absolutely united with His essence; rather, one says "as the Lord lives," which is similar to describing Him as "the living God."

לְפִיכָךְ אֵינוֹ מַכִּיר הַבְּרוּאִים וְיוֹדְעָם מֵחֲמַת הַבְּרוּאִים, כְּמוֹת שֶׁאָנוּ יוֹדְעִים אוֹתָם, אֶלָּא מֵחֲמַת עַצְמוֹ יְדָעָם. לְפִיכָךְ, מִפְּנֵי שֶׁהוּא יוֹדֵעַ עַצְמוֹ – יָדַע הַכֹּל, שֶׁהַכֹּל נִסְמָךְ בַּהֲוָיָתוֹ לוֹ.

Accordingly, He does not recognize and know the created beings by virtue of observing **the created beings, as we know them, but rather He knows them by virtue of Himself. Consequently, since He knows Himself, He knows everything, for the existence of everything else depends upon Him.**

Halakha 11

דְּבָרִים אֵלּוּ שֶׁאָמַרְנוּ בְּעִנְיָן זֶה בִּשְׁנֵי פְּרָקִים אֵלּוּ – כְּמוֹ טִפָּה מִן הַיָּם הֵן מִמַּה שֶּׁצָּרִיךְ לְבָאֵר בְּעִנְיָן זֶה.

The ideas that we have stated on this topic in these two chapters, regarding the existence of God, His knowledge, the relationship between Him and the rest of existence, as well as the angels and their intellectual levels compared to human intellect, **are like a drop from the sea, of what it is necessary to explain this on this topic.**

NOTES

a. Since God knows things through His knowledge of Himself.

b. Which is not a separate essence, as was just explained.

NOTES

a. See 4:11.

b. See 4:13.

וּבֵאוּר כָּל הָעִקָּרִים שֶׁבִּשְׁנֵי פְּרָקִים אֵלּוּ, הוּא הַנִּקְרָא מַעֲשֵׂה מֶרְכָּבָה.

The explanation of all the fundamental **principles in these two chapters is called** the "Design of the Divine **Chariot** [*maaseh merkava*]."

Halakha 12

צִוּוּ חֲכָמִים הָרִאשׁוֹנִים שֶׁלֹּא לִדְרֹשׁ בִּדְבָרִים אֵלּוּ אֶלָּא לְאִישׁ אֶחָד בִּלְבַד,

The early Sages commanded that one should not expound on these ideas except to a single individual at a time, and not to a group, in case one of them fails to understand him properly without the teacher realizing it.[a]

וְהוּא שֶׁיִּהְיֶה חָכָם וּמֵבִין מִדַּעְתּוֹ,

He must be a wise person, **who can understand of his own accord,** and therefore he does not require a full explanation to arrive at the truth; mere hints are sufficient.

וְאַחַר כָּךְ מוֹסְרִין לוֹ רָאשֵׁי הַפְּרָקִים וּמוֹדִיעִין אוֹתוֹ שֶׁמֶץ מִן הַדָּבָר, וְהוּא מֵבִין מִדַּעְתּוֹ וְיוֹדֵעַ סוֹף הַדָּבָר וְעָמְקוֹ.

After that has been established to be the case, **he is taught the basic concepts, and** then **he is informed of a little of the** more complex **ideas, and he** will then **understand** more **of his own accord** until **he knows the full idea and its depth.**

וּדְבָרִים אֵלּוּ – דְּבָרִים עֲמֻקִּים הֵם עַד לִמְאֹד, וְאֵין כָּל דַּעַת וָדַעַת רְאוּיָה לְסָבְלָן, וַעֲלֵיהֶן אָמַר שְׁלֹמֹה בְּחָכְמָתוֹ דֶּרֶךְ מָשָׁל: "כְּבָשִׂים לִלְבוּשֶׁךָ" (משלי כז, כו).

These concepts are extremely profound ideas, and not every person's **intellect is suited to comprehend them. With regard to them, Solomon said, by way of metaphor: "The lambs** [*kevasim*] **will be for your garments"** (Proverbs 27:26).

כָּךְ אָמְרוּ חֲכָמִים בְּפֵרוּשׁ מָשָׁל זֶה: דְּבָרִים שֶׁהֵן כִּבְשׁוֹנוֹ שֶׁל עוֹלָם יִהְיוּ לִלְבוּשְׁךָ, כְּלוֹמַר לְךָ לְבַדְּךָ, וְאַל תִּדְרֹשׁ אוֹתָן בָּרַבִּים.

The Sages said the following, in explanation of this metaphor: "Things that constitute the concealed matters [*kivshono*] **of the world should be for your garments." That is,** they should be **for you alone,** like your garments that you do not share with others; **do not expound them in public.**

וַעֲלֵיהֶם אָמַר: "יִהְיוּ לְךָ לְבַדֶּךָ וְאֵין לְזָרִים אִתָּךְ" (שם ה, יז), וַעֲלֵיהֶן אָמַר: "דְּבַשׁ וְחָלָב תַּחַת לְשׁוֹנֵךְ" (שיר השירים ד, יא) – כָּךְ פֵּרְשׁוּ חֲכָמִים הָרִאשׁוֹנִים: דְּבָרִים שֶׁהֵן כִּדְבַשׁ וְחָלָב יִהְיוּ תַּחַת לְשׁוֹנֶךָ.

Another verse **states, regarding them: "They will be your own, and there will be nothing for strangers with you"** (Proverbs 5:17), **and** it is further **stated about them: "Honey and milk are under your tongue"** (Song of Songs 4:11), which **the early Sages explained as follows** (*Hagiga* 13a): **Ideas that are** as sweet **as honey and milk should be** kept **under your tongue,** and you should enjoy them by yourself.[b]

פֶּרֶק שְׁלִישִׁי

CHAPTER 3

The Spheres and the Elements

Halakhot 1–9: The celestial spheres
Halakhot 10–11: The four material elements

Halakha 1

וְהַגַּלְגַּלִּים הֵם הַנִּקְרָאִים שָׁמַיִם, וְרָקִיעַ, וּזְבוּל, וַעֲרָבוֹת, וְהֵם תִּשְׁעָה גַּלְגַּלִּים: גַּלְגַּל הַקָּרוֹב מִמֶּנּוּ הוּא גַּלְגַּל הַיָּרֵחַ, וְהַשֵּׁנִי שֶׁלְּמַעְלָה מִמֶּנּוּ גַּלְגַּל שֶׁבּוֹ הַכּוֹכָב שֶׁנִּקְרָא כּוֹכָב, וְגַלְגַּל שְׁלִישִׁי שֶׁלְּמַעְלָה מִמֶּנּוּ שֶׁבּוֹ נֹגַהּ,

The spheres[a] **are called heaven** [*shamayim*], **firmament** [*rakia*], **abode** [*zevul*], **and the skies** [*aravot*]; **and they are nine spheres.*** **The closest sphere to** the earth **is the sphere of the moon. The second sphere, which is higher than it, is the sphere that contains the planet called Mercury. The third sphere, which is higher than** that, **contains Venus.**

וְגַלְגַּל רְבִיעִי שֶׁבּוֹ חַמָּה, וְגַלְגַּל חֲמִישִׁי שֶׁבּוֹ מַאְדִּים, וְגַלְגַּל שִׁשִּׁי שֶׁבּוֹ כּוֹכַב צֶדֶק, וְגַלְגַּל שְׁבִיעִי שֶׁבּוֹ שַׁבְּתַאי, וְגַלְגַּל שְׁמִינִי שֶׁבּוֹ שְׁאָר כָּל הַכּוֹכָבִים שֶׁנִּרְאִים בָּרָקִיעַ, וְגַלְגַּל תְּשִׁיעִי הוּא גַּלְגַּל הַחוֹזֵר בְּכָל יוֹם מִן מִזְרָח לְמַעֲרָב.

The fourth sphere contains the sun; the fifth sphere contains Mars; the sixth sphere contains the planet Jupiter; the seventh sphere contains Saturn; the eighth sphere contains all the rest of the stars that can be seen in the firmament; while the ninth sphere is the sphere that revolves each day from east to west.

NOTES

a. According to the Rambam's approach, the spheres are actual conscious beings that resemble physical wheels, like the outer cover of a ball (see Halakha 9). The heavenly bodies revolve within and by force of the spheres.

FROM THE LUBAVITCHER REBBE

*Nine spheres – תִּשְׁעָה גַּלְגַּלִּים: In this chapter, the Rambam begins to clarify the "Act of Creation," after having explained the "Design of the Divine Chariot" in the previous two chapters. It is noteworthy that the Rambam refers in general terms to "nine spheres" (Halakha 1), and those entities which He created "beneath the firmament" (Halakha 10), which makes a total of ten. Ten is "the perfect number," and thus the Rambam alludes to the perfection of the "Act of Creation" (*Torat Menaḥem*, *Hitvaaduyot*, *Parashat Beshalaḥ*, *Parashat Mishpatim* 5757).

BACKGROUND

The spheres – וְהַגַּלְגַּלִּים:

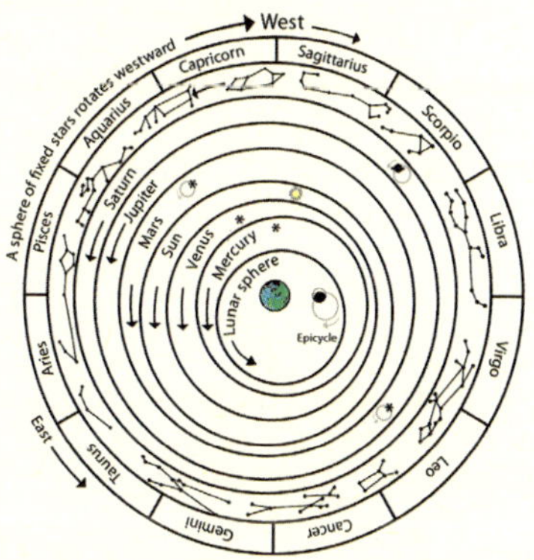

During the Rambam's time, the accepted astronomical theory was the one taught by Ptolemy (the geocentric theory), the main principle of which was that the earth is fixed in its place, the seven planets are likewise fixed in seven distinct "spheres," while the rest of the stars are fixed in an eighth wheel. These spheres revolve around the Earth at a constant speed from west to east. Around them there is a ninth wheel (the sphere of the constellations, or the Zodiac), which rotates the earth in the opposite direction – from east to west – in slightly less than a day, rotating with it all the spheres in this direction (see 3:1–6; *Hilkhot Kiddush HaHodesh* 11:7–13) [N.B. The proportions in the image have been adjusted in order to emphasize the differences; in practice the deviation of the center is far smaller than appears here].

וְהוּא הַמַּקִּיף אֶת הַכֹּל וּמְסַבֵּב אֶת הַכֹּל. וְזֶה שֶׁתֵּרָאֶה כָּל הַכּוֹכָבִים כְּאִלּוּ הֵן כֻּלָּן בְּגַלְגַּל אֶחָד, וְאַף עַל פִּי שֶׁיֵּשׁ בָּהֶם זֶה לְמַעְלָה מִזֶּה – מִפְּנֵי שֶׁהַגַּלְגַּלִּים טְהוֹרִים וְזַכִּים כִּזְכוּכִית וְכַסַּפִּיר, וּלְפִיכָךְ רוֹאִין כּוֹכָבִים שֶׁבְּגַלְגַּל הַשְּׁמִינִי מִתַּחַת גַּלְגַּל הָרִאשׁוֹן.

This ninth sphere **surrounds everything and encompasses everything.**[a] **The fact that all the stars appear to be in one sphere, even though some of them are higher than others, is because the spheres are pure and** entirely **transparent, like glass or sapphire. Therefore, the stars in the eighth sphere appear** to be **beneath** those of **the first sphere.**

Halakha 2

כָּל גַּלְגַּל וְגַלְגַּל מִשְּׁמוֹנַת הַגַּלְגַּלִּים שֶׁבָּהֶם הַכּוֹכָבִים נֶחֱלָק לְגַלְגַּלִּים הַרְבֵּה זֶה לְמַעְלָה מִזֶּה, כְּמוֹ גִּלְדֵי בְּצָלִים, מֵהֶם גַּלְגַּלִּים סוֹבְבִים מִמַּעֲרָב לְמִזְרָח, וּמֵהֶם סוֹבְבִים מִמִּזְרָח לְמַעֲרָב, כְּמוֹ הַגַּלְגַּל הַחוֹזֵר הַתְּשִׁיעִי. וְכֻלָּם אֵין בֵּינֵיהֶן מָקוֹם פָּנוּי.

Each and every one of the eight spheres that contain the stars themselves **divide into many spheres,**[b] **one above the other, like the layers of an onion. Some of them revolve from west to east, while others revolve from east to west, such as the revolving ninth sphere. There is no empty space between any of them;** rather, the spheres are positioned right up against one another.

Halakha 3

כָּל הַגַּלְגַּלִּים אֵינָם לֹא קַלִּים וְלֹא כְּבֵדִים, וְאֵין לָהֶם לֹא עֵין אָדֹם וְלֹא שָׁחֹר וְלֹא שְׁאָר עֵינוֹת. וְזֶה שֶׁאָנוּ רוֹאִין אוֹתָן כְּעֵין הַתְּכֵלֶת – לְמַרְאִית הָעַיִן בִּלְבַד הוּא, לְפִי גֹּבַהּ הָאֲוִיר. וְכֵן אֵין לָהֶם לֹא טַעַם וְלֹא רֵיחַ, לְפִי שֶׁאֵין אֵלּוּ הַמְּאֹרָעִים מְצוּיִים אֶלָּא בַּגּוּפוֹת שֶׁלְּמַטָּה מֵהֶם.

None of the spheres are light or heavy. They are neither a reddish hue, or black, or any other color. The fact that we see them as blue, the color of the sky, **is only** our **perception, due to the height of the skies.** Our eyes absorb the blue color from the light of the sun, but it is not the actual color of the spheres. **Likewise, they have neither taste nor smell, because these phenomena occur only in bodies that are lower than them.**

Halakha 4

כָּל הַגַּלְגַּלִּים הָאֵלּוּ הַמַּקִּיפִין אֶת הָעוֹלָם כֻּלּוֹ הֵן עֲגֻלִּין כַּדּוּר, וְהָאָרֶץ תְּלוּיָה בָּאֶמְצַע.

All of these spheres that encompass the entire world are spherical like a ball, while the Earth is suspended in the middle, all the spheres rotate around it.[c]

וְיֵשׁ לְמִקְצָת מִן הַכּוֹכָבִים גַּלְגַּלִּים קְטַנִּים שֶׁהֵן קְבוּעִין בָּהֶן, וְאֵין אוֹתָם הַגַּלְגַּלִּים מַקִּיפִין אֶת הָאָרֶץ, אֶלָּא גַּלְגַּל קָטָן שֶׁאֵינוֹ מַקִּיף קָבוּעַ בַּגַּלְגַּל הַגָּדוֹל הַמַּקִּיף.

Some of the planets have small spheres in which they are fixed. Those spheres do not encompass the Earth; rather, a small sphere which does not encompass the Earth **is fixed within a large sphere which does encompass** the Earth, and therefore their movement varies.

NOTES

a. In other words, the farthest sphere does not contain any particular star or celestial body, but it rotates constantly and continuously (from east to west and back again). The constant rotation of this sphere causes the rotation of the other spheres, which are adjacent to it.

b. There being many spheres helps to explain the movements of the planets, for they do not appear to go in a single direction, and the direction of their movement also varies.

c. See *Hilkhot Kiddush HaḤodesh* 11:13–14.

Halakha 5

מִסְפַּר כָּל הַגַּלְגַּלִּים הַמַּקִּיפִים אֶת כָּל הָעוֹלָם – שְׁמוֹנָה עָשָׂר, וּמִסְפַּר כָּל הַגַּלְגַּלִּים הַקְּטַנִּים שֶׁאֵינָן מַקִּיפִין – שְׁמוֹנָה.

The total number of spheres that encompass the entire Earth is **eighteen, while the number of all the small spheres that do not encompass** the Earth is **eight.**

וּמִמַּהֲלַךְ הַכּוֹכָבִים וִידִיעַת שִׁעוּר סְבִיבָתָן בְּכָל יוֹם וּבְכָל שָׁעָה, וּמִנְּטִיָּתָן לְרוּחַ צָפוֹן וְרוּחַ דָּרוֹם, וּמִגָּבְהָן מֵעַל הָאָרֶץ וּקְרִיבָתָן, יִוָּדַע מִסְפַּר כָּל אֵלּוּ הַגַּלְגַּלִּים וְצוּרַת הֲלִיכָתָן וְדֶרֶךְ הַקָּפָתָן,

From the movement of the planets and the knowledge of the extent of their revolutions each day and every hour, and from their positions, northward or southward, and from their distance above the Earth or their proximity to it, **the number of all these spheres, the form of their movement, and the path of their revolution can be ascertained.**

וְזוֹ הִיא חָכְמַת חֶשְׁבּוֹן תְּקוּפוֹת וּמַזָּלוֹת. וּסְפָרִים רַבִּים חִבְּרוּ בָּהּ חַכְמֵי יָוָן.

This is the science of calculating the astronomical seasons and constellations.[a] **Many books have been written on this** science **by the scholars of Greece,** and they form the basis for the descriptions presented here.[b]

Halakha 6

גַּלְגַּל הַתְּשִׁיעִי שֶׁהוּא מַקִּיף אֶת הַכֹּל, חִלְּקוּהוּ הַחֲכָמִים הַקַּדְמוֹנִים לִשְׁנֵים עָשָׂר חֵלֶק, כָּל חֵלֶק וָחֵלֶק הֶעֱלוּ לוֹ שֵׁם עַל שֵׁם צוּרָה שֶׁתֵּרָאֶה בּוֹ מִן הַכּוֹכָבִים שֶׁלְּמַטָּה מִמֶּנּוּ שֶׁהֵם מְכֻוָּנִים תַּחְתָּיו, וְהֵם הַמַּזָּלוֹת שֶׁשְּׁמוֹתָם: טָלֶה, שׁוֹר, תְּאוֹמִים, סַרְטָן, אַרְיֵה, בְּתוּלָה, מֹאזְנַיִם, עַקְרָב, קַשָּׁת, גְּדִי, דְּלִי, דָּגִים.

The ninth sphere, which encompasses all the others, **was divided by the early Sages into twelve parts. They gave each and every one of these sections a name, in accordance with the shape that appeared to be formed by the stars below it that correspond to it.**[c] **These** names **are the constellations,**[d] **which are called Aries, Taurus, Gemini, Cancer, Leo, Virgo, Libra, Scorpio, Sagittarius, Capricorn, Aquarius,** and **Pisces.**

Halakha 7

גַּלְגַּל הַתְּשִׁיעִי עַצְמוֹ – אֵין בּוֹ לֹא חֲלֻקָּה וְלֹא צוּרָה מִכָּל הַצּוּרוֹת הָאֵלּוּ וְלֹא כּוֹכָב, אֶלָּא בְּחִבּוּר הַכּוֹכָבִים שֶׁבַּגַּלְגַּל הַשְּׁמִינִי הוּא שֶׁיֵּרָאֶה בְּכוֹכָבִים גְּדוֹלִים שֶׁבּוֹ תַּבְנִית הַצּוּרוֹת הָאֵלּוּ אוֹ קָרוֹב מֵהֶן.

The ninth sphere itself has no division, or any of these shapes or a star, since it merely rotates the lower spheres. **Instead, the shape of these forms,** or something **resembling them, are seen through the combination of the stars in the eighth sphere, of the larger stars in** that sphere. The grouping of the large stars in the eighth sphere forms shapes that serve as the basis of the names of the constellations by which the parts of the ninth sphere are called.

NOTES

a. See *Hilkhot Kiddush HaḤodesh* 11:2.

b. See *Hilkhot Kiddush HaḤodesh* 17:24.

c. The fixed stars in the eighth sphere are arranged in groups based on the apparent shapes that they form, such as a ram (*aries* in Latin) or a bull (*taurus* in Latin), and so on. The twelve parts of the ninth sphere were named in accordance with these shapes.

d. Each of the constellations corresponds to the location of the sun in one of the months of the solar year (see *Hilkhot Kiddush HaḤodesh* 9:3).

BACKGROUND

These are the constellations – וְהֵם הַמַּזָּלוֹת:

Mosaic pavement of a sixth-century synagogue at Beth Alpha, Jezreel Valley, northern Israel, discovered in 1928 featuring the signs of the Zodiac

וְאֵלּוּ הַשְּׁתֵּים עֶשְׂרֵה צוּרוֹת לֹא הָיוּ מְכֻוָּנוֹת כְּנֶגֶד אוֹתָן הַחֲלָקִים אֶלָּא בִּזְמַן הַמַּבּוּל, שֶׁבּוֹ הֶעֱלוּ לָהֶן שֵׁמוֹת אֵלּוּ.

These twelve shapes corresponded to those parts only at the time of the flood, when they were given these names. Those twelve groups of stars were positioned at the time of the flood directly opposite the corresponding parts of the ninth sphere.[a]

אֲבָל בַּזְּמַן הַזֶּה כְּבָר סָבְבוּ מְעַט, לְפִי שֶׁכָּל הַכּוֹכָבִים שֶׁבְּגַלְגַּל שְׁמִינִי כֻּלָּם סוֹבְבִים כְּמוֹ הַשֶּׁמֶשׁ וְהַיָּרֵחַ, אֶלָּא שֶׁהֵן סוֹבְבִין בִּכְבֵדוּת. וְחֵלֶק שֶׁתְּהַלֵּךְ הַשֶּׁמֶשׁ כְּנֶגְדּוֹ בְּיוֹם אֶחָד – יֵלֵךְ כְּנֶגְדּוֹ כָּל כּוֹכָב מֵהֶם בְּקָרוֹב מִשִּׁבְעִים שָׁנָה.

However, in the present they have already revolved slightly from west to east,[b] **because all the stars in the eighth sphere revolve, like the sun and the moon, only** those stars **move more ponderously. The distance that the sun moves in its orbit on one day would take any of these stars approximately seventy years to move in its orbit.**

Halakha 8

כָּל הַכּוֹכָבִים הַנִּרְאִים – יֵשׁ מֵהֶן כּוֹכָבִים קְטַנִּים שֶׁהָאָרֶץ גְּדוֹלָה מֵאֶחָד מֵהֶן, וְיֵשׁ מֵהֶן כּוֹכָבִים שֶׁכָּל אֶחָד מֵהֶן גָּדוֹל מִן הָאָרֶץ כַּמָּה פְּעָמִים.

With regard to **all the visible stars, some are small ones,** such **that the Earth is larger than** each **one of them, while others are large stars, each one of which is several times larger than the Earth.**

וְהָאָרֶץ גְּדוֹלָה מִן הַיָּרֵחַ כְּמוֹ אַרְבָּעִים פְּעָמִים, וְהַשֶּׁמֶשׁ גְּדוֹלָה מִן הָאָרֶץ כְּמוֹ מֵאָה וְשִׁבְעִים פְּעָמִים.

The Earth is roughly forty times larger than the moon, in volume, not diameter, **and the sun approximately 170 times larger than the Earth.** This claim is based on the ancient assessment of the ratio between the Earth and the sun.

נִמְצָא הַיָּרֵחַ אֶחָד מִשֵּׁשֶׁת אֲלָפִים וּשְׁמוֹנֶה מֵאוֹת מִן הַשֶּׁמֶשׁ בְּקֵרוּב. וְאֵין בְּכָל הַכּוֹכָבִים כּוֹכָב גָּדוֹל מִן הַשֶּׁמֶשׁ, וְלֹא קָטָן מִכּוֹכָב שֶׁבְּגַלְגַּל שֵׁנִי.

Thus, the moon is about one 6,800th of the size **of the sun. None of the** other **stars is as large as the sun, nor** are any of them **smaller than Mercury, which is in the second sphere.**

Halakha 9

כָּל הַכּוֹכָבִים וְהַגַּלְגַּלִּים כֻּלָּם בַּעֲלֵי נֶפֶשׁ וְדֵעָה וְהַשְׂכֵּל הֵם, וְהֵם חַיִּים וְעוֹמְדִים וּמַכִּירִים אֶת מִי שֶׁאָמַר וְהָיָה הָעוֹלָם,

All of the stars and the spheres are not mere matter; rather, they **possess a soul, knowledge, and intellect. They are alive and stand in recognition of the One who spoke and the world came into being.**

NOTES

a. For example, the group of Aries was then exactly above the part of the firmament belonging to the month of April.

b. See *Hilkhot Kiddush HaḤodesh* 12:2.

כָּל אֶחָד וְאֶחָד לְפִי גָּדְלוֹ וּלְפִי מַעֲלָתוֹ, מְשַׁבְּחִים וּמְפָאֲרִים לְיוֹצְרָם כְּמוֹ הַמַּלְאָכִים. וּכְשֵׁם שֶׁמַּכִּירִים אֶת הַקָּדוֹשׁ בָּרוּךְ הוּא, כָּךְ מַכִּירִים אֶת עַצְמָן וּמַכִּירִין אֶת הַמַּלְאָכִים שֶׁלְּמַעְלָה מֵהֶן.

Every single one of them, in accordance with its size and level, praises and glorifies their Maker, like the angels. Just as they are aware of the Holy One blessed be He, they are also self-aware, and aware of the angels that are above them.

וְדַעַת הַכּוֹכָבִים וְהַגַּלְגַּלִּים מְעוּטָה מִדַּעַת הַמַּלְאָכִים וּגְדוֹלָה מִדַּעַת בְּנֵי הָאָדָם.

The knowledge of the stars and the spheres is less than the knowledge of the angels, but greater than the knowledge of humans.

Halakha 10

בָּרָא הָאֵל לְמַטָּה מִגַּלְגַּל הַיָּרֵחַ גֹּלֶם אֶחָד שֶׁאֵינוֹ כְּגֹלֶם הַגַּלְגַּלִּים,

God created, beneath the sphere of the moon, in the space between the sphere of the moon and the Earth, **one** type of **matter that is unlike the matter of the spheres.** This matter forms the basis for the various materials of our world.

וּבָרָא אַרְבַּע צוּרוֹת לְגֹלֶם זֶה, וְאֵינָם כְּצוּרַת הַגַּלְגַּלִּים, וְנִקְבְּעָה כָּל צוּרָה וְצוּרָה בְּמִקְצָת גֹּלֶם זֶה.

He created four forms for this matter, the qualities of the "four elements" that comprise our world, **which differ from the forms of the spheres.** The qualities of the four elements are dissimilar to that of the matter of the spheres, which is a kind of "fifth element." **Each of these forms was fixed in a portion of this matter.**

צוּרָה רִאשׁוֹנָה, צוּרַת הָאֵשׁ, נִתְחַבְּרָה בְּמִקְצָת גֹּלֶם זֶה וְנִהְיָה מִשְּׁנֵיהֶם גּוּף הָאֵשׁ. וְצוּרָה שְׁנִיָּה, צוּרַת הָרוּחַ, נִתְחַבְּרָה בְּמִקְצָתוֹ וְנִהְיָה מִשְּׁנֵיהֶם גּוּף הָרוּחַ.

The first form, the form of fire, became connected to a portion of this matter, and from the pair of them, the body of fire came into being. The second form, the form of air, likewise **became connected to a portion of this matter, and from the pair of them, the body of air came into being.**

וְצוּרָה שְׁלִישִׁית, צוּרַת הַמַּיִם, נִתְחַבְּרָה בְּמִקְצָתוֹ וְנִהְיָה מִשְּׁנֵיהֶם גּוּף הַמַּיִם. וְצוּרָה רְבִיעִית, צוּרַת הָאָרֶץ, נִתְחַבְּרָה בְּמִקְצָתוֹ וְנִהְיָה מִשְּׁנֵיהֶם גּוּף הָאָרֶץ.

Again, **the third form, the form of water, became connected to a portion of this matter, and from the pair of them, the body of water came into being.** Finally, **the fourth form, the form of earth,** also **became connected to a portion of this matter, and from the pair of them, the body of earth came into being.**

נִמְצָא לְמַטָּה מִן הָרָקִיעַ אַרְבָּעָה גּוּפִין מְחֻלָּקִין זֶה לְמַעְלָה מִזֶּה, וְכָל אֶחָד וְאֶחָד מַקִּיף אֶת שֶׁלְּמַטָּה מִמֶּנּוּ מִכָּל רוּחוֹתָיו כְּמוֹ גַּלְגַּל:

Thus, beneath the firmament there are four different bodies of matter, one higher than the other, each one encompassing the one below it from all directions, like a sphere.

הַגּוּף הָרִאשׁוֹן, הַסָּמוּךְ לְגַלְגַּל הַיָּרֵחַ, הוּא גּוּף הָאֵשׁ, לְמַטָּה מִמֶּנּוּ גּוּף הָרוּחַ, לְמַטָּה מִמֶּנּוּ גּוּף הַמַּיִם, לְמַטָּה מִמֶּנּוּ גּוּף הָאָרֶץ. וְאֵין בֵּינֵיהֶם מָקוֹם פָּנוּי בְּלֹא גּוּף כְּלָל.

The first of these bodies, which is adjacent to the sphere of the moon, is the body of fire. Beneath it is the body of air, beneath it the body of water, and lastly, **beneath it** is **the body of earth. There is no empty space without any body between them at all.**

Halakha 11

אַרְבָּעָה גּוּפוֹת הָאֵלּוּ אֵינָם בַּעֲלֵי נֶפֶשׁ, וְאֵינָם יוֹדְעִין וְלֹא מַכִּירִין, אֶלָּא כְּגוּפִים מֵתִים. וְיֵשׁ לְכָל אֶחָד וְאֶחָד מֵהֶם מִנְהָג שֶׁאֵינוֹ יוֹדְעוֹ וְלֹא מַשִּׂיגוֹ וְאֵינוֹ יָכוֹל לְשַׁנּוֹתוֹ.

In contrast to the spheres and the stars, **these four bodies do not possess souls, nor do they know** anything **or recognize** God. **Rather,** they are **like dead bodies. Each and every one of them has its nature, which it does not know or grasp, and which it cannot change.**

וְזֶה שֶׁאָמַר דָּוִד: "הַלְלוּ אֶת יי מִן הָאָרֶץ תַּנִּינִים וְכָל תְּהֹמוֹת, אֵשׁ וּבָרָד שֶׁלֶג וְקִיטוֹר" (תהלים קמח, ח) – עִנְיַן הַדְּבָרִים: הַלְלוּהוּ בְּנֵי אָדָם מִגְּבוּרוֹתָיו שֶׁתִּרְאוּ בָּאֵשׁ וּבָרָד וּבִשְׁאָר בְּרוּאִים שֶׁתִּרְאוּ לְמַטָּה מִן הָרָקִיעַ, שֶׁגְּבוּרָתָם תָּמִיד נִכֶּרֶת לַקָּטָן וְלַגָּדוֹל.

Regarding **that which David said: "Praise the Lord from the earth, sea creatures and all depths, fire and hail, snow and vapor"** (Psalms 148:7–8), when he appears to be calling on these forces of nature to praise God, that is not the case, for they are not conscious beings. Rather, **the meaning is as follows:** You **people, praise Him for His mighty works that you see in the fire and hail,** and in the **other creations that you can see beneath the firmament, because their might is always apparent to great and small** alike.

פֶּרֶק רְבִיעִי

CHAPTER 4

The Creatures of the World and the Human Soul

Halakhot 1–6: The qualities of the material elements and the bodies that are comprised of them

Halakhot 7–9: The human soul and its capacity for understanding

Halakhot 10–13: The "Act of Creation," the "Design of the Divine Chariot," and their study

Halakha 1

אַרְבָּעָה גּוּפִים הָאֵלּוּ, שֶׁהֵן אֵשׁ וְרוּחַ וּמַיִם וְאֶרֶץ – הֵם יְסוֹדוֹת כָּל הַנִּבְרָאִים לְמַטָּה מִן הָרָקִיעַ.

These four bodies, which are fire, air, water, and earth, are the fundamental **elements of** the substance of **all created beings beneath the firmament.**

וְכָל שֶׁיִּהְיֶה מֵאָדָם וּמִבְּהֵמָה וְעוֹף וְרֶמֶשׂ וְדָג וְצֶמַח וּמַתֶּכֶת וַאֲבָנִים טוֹבוֹת וּמַרְגָּלִיּוֹת וּשְׁאָר אַבְנֵי בִּנְיָן וְהָרִים וְגוּשֵׁי עָפָר – הַכֹּל גָּלְמוֹ מְחֻבָּר מֵאַרְבַּע יְסוֹדוֹת הָאֵלּוּ.

Everything, whether it is human, animal, fowl, crawling creature, fish, plant, metal, precious stone, pearl, other building stones, mountains, and even **lumps of earth, the matter** that comprises **all** of them **is a combination of these four elements.**

נִמְצְאוּ כָּל הַגּוּפִים שֶׁלְּמַטָּה מִן הָרָקִיעַ חוּץ מֵאַרְבָּעָה יְסוֹדוֹת הָאֵלּוּ, מְחֻבָּרִים מִגֹּלֶם וְצוּרָה, וְגֹלֶם שֶׁלָּהֶם מְחֻבָּר מֵאַרְבָּעָה יְסוֹדוֹת אֵלּוּ, אֲבָל כָּל אֶחָד מֵאַרְבָּעָה יְסוֹדוֹת אֵינוֹ מְחֻבָּר אֶלָּא מִגֹּלֶם וְצוּרָה בִּלְבַד.

Thus, all the bodies that are beneath the firmament, apart from these four elements themselves, **are a combination of matter and form,**[a] **and their matter is a combination of these four elements. However, each** separate **one of these four elements is a combination of** pure matter **and form alone,** not matter that is a combination of the four elements.

BACKGROUND

These four elements – מֵאַרְבַּע יְסוֹדוֹת הָאֵלּוּ:

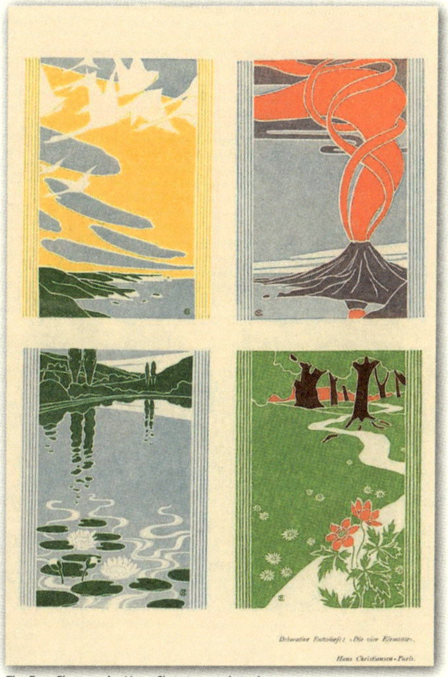

The Four Elements by Hans Christiansen (1898)

NOTES

a. As explained in 2:3.

Halakha 2

דֶּרֶךְ הָאֵשׁ וְהָרוּחַ לִהְיוֹת מַהֲלָכָם מִמַּטָּה, מִטַּבּוּר הָאָרֶץ, לְמַעְלָה, כְּלַפֵּי הָרָקִיעַ.

It is **the manner of fire and wind for their movement to be from below, from the center of the Earth, upward toward the firmament.** They naturally rise from the center of the planet upward.

וְדֶרֶךְ הַמַּיִם וְהָאָרֶץ לִהְיוֹת מַהֲלָכָם מִתַּחַת הָרָקִיעַ לְמַטָּה, לָאֶמְצַע, שֶׁאֶמְצַע הָרָקִיעַ הוּא הַמַּטָּה שֶׁאֵין לְמַטָּה מִמֶּנּוּ.

The manner of water and earth is for their movement to be from beneath the firmament downward, to the middle of the firmament, which is the center of the Earth, **for the middle of the firmament is the lowest spot of all.** Since the firmament is shaped like a ball, its center is the lowest spot in relation to its circumference.

וְאֵין הִלּוּכָם בְּדַעְתָּם וְלֹא בְּחֶפְצָם, אֶלָּא מִנְהָג שֶׁנִּקְבַּע בָּהֶם וְטֶבַע שֶׁנִּטְבַּע בָּהֶם.

They do not move consciously or willfully; rather, it is due to the **pattern established within them and** the **nature imprinted in them.**

טֶבַע הָאֵשׁ חַם יָבֵשׁ, וְהוּא קַל מִכֻּלָּם. וְהָרוּחַ חַם לַח, וְהַמַּיִם קָרִים לַחִים, וְהָאָרֶץ יְבֵשָׁה קָרָה, וְהִיא כְּבֵדָה מִכֻּלָּם.

The nature of fire is that it is **warm** and **dry, and it is the lightest of all** the elements. **Wind is warm** and **moist, and water is cold** and **moist, while earth,** which **is dry** and **cold, is the heaviest of all** the elements.

וְהַמַּיִם קַל מִמֶּנָּה, לְפִיכָךְ נִמְצָא לְמַעְלָה עַל הָאָרֶץ. וְהָרוּחַ קַל מִן הַמַּיִם, לְפִיכָךְ הוּא מְרַחֵף עַל פְּנֵי הַמַּיִם. וְהָאֵשׁ קַל מִן הָרוּחַ.

Water is lighter than earth, and **therefore it is found above earth. Wind is lighter than water,** and **therefore it hovers over the surface of the water.** Finally, **fire is lighter than wind.**

וּמִפְּנֵי שֶׁהֵם יְסוֹדוֹת לְכָל גּוּפִים שֶׁתַּחַת הָרָקִיעַ, יִמָּצֵא כָּל גּוּף וָגוּף מֵאָדָם וּבְהֵמָה וְחַיָּה וְעוֹף וְדָג וְצֶמַח וּמַתֶּכֶת וְאֶבֶן – גָּלְמוֹ מְחֻבָּר מֵאֵשׁ וְרוּחַ וּמַיִם וְעָפָר.

Since these are the basic **elements for all** the **bodies beneath the firmament, the result is** that **the matter of every single body – human, animal, beast, fowl, fish, plant, metal, or stone –** is some **combination of fire, wind, water, and earth.**

וְאַרְבַּעְתָּם יִתְעָרְבוּ בְּיַחַד, וְיִשְׁתַּנֶּה כָּל אֶחָד מֵהֶן בְּעֵת הָעֵרוּב, עַד שֶׁיִּמָּצֵא הַמְחֻבָּר מֵאַרְבַּעְתָּן אֵינוֹ דּוֹמֶה לְאֶחָד מֵהֶן כְּשֶׁהוּא לְבַדּוֹ.

The four of them intermingle, and each one of them changes during the process of their **combination, such that the combination of the four of them does not resemble any one of them by itself.** Each body comprised of the four elements contains different ratios of these elements.

וְאֵין בַּמְעֹרָב מֵהֶן אֲפִלּוּ חֵלֶק אֶחָד שֶׁהוּא אֵשׁ בִּפְנֵי עַצְמָהּ אוֹ מַיִם בִּפְנֵי עַצְמָן אוֹ אֶרֶץ בִּפְנֵי עַצְמָהּ אוֹ רוּחַ בִּפְנֵי עַצְמָהּ, אֶלָּא הַכֹּל נִשְׁתַּנּוּ וְנַעֲשׂוּ גּוּף אַחֵר.

In any combination of them, there is not even one portion of fire by itself, wind by itself, water by itself, or earth by itself. Rather, they have all changed and become a different body. The basic matter of each of the four elements is found only in their respective places, whereas everything on Earth is an amalgamation of them.

וְכָל גּוּף וָגוּף הַמְחֻבָּר מֵאַרְבַּעְתָּן, יִמָּצֵא בּוֹ קֹר וְחֹם לַח וְיָבֵשׁ כְּאֶחָד.

Each and every body that is a combination of these four elements **will have cold and warmth, moistness and dryness, together.** Each body contains all of the elements, only in different ratios.

אֲבָל יֵשׁ מֵהֶם גּוּפִים שֶׁיִּהְיֶה בָּהֶם חֲזָקָה מִיסוֹד הָאֵשׁ, כְּמוֹ בַּעֲלֵי נֶפֶשׁ חַיָּה, לְפִיכָךְ יֵרָאֶה בָּהֶם הַחֹם יָתֵר,

However, there are some bodies that have a more powerful aggregation **of the element of fire, such as creatures with living souls. Accordingly, warmth is more evident in them.** They produce heat to a greater extent than other created beings.

וְיֵשׁ מֵהֶם גּוּפִים שֶׁיִּהְיֶה בָּהֶם חֲזָקָה מִיסוֹד הָאָרֶץ, כְּמוֹ הָאֲבָנִים, לְפִיכָךְ יֵרָאֶה בָּהֶם הַיֹּבֶשׁ הַרְבֵּה.

Other bodies have a more powerful aggregation **of the element of earth, such as stones,** and **accordingly dryness is evident in them to** a far **greater** extent.

וְעַל הַדֶּרֶךְ הַזֶּה יִמָּצֵא גּוּף חַם יָתֵר מִגּוּף אַחֵר חַם, וְגוּף יָבֵשׁ יָתֵר מִגּוּף אַחֵר יָבֵשׁ.

In this manner, one body can be found to be **warmer than another warm body, and** likewise **one body drier than another dry body.**

וְכֵן יִמָּצֵא גּוּפִים יֵרָאֶה בָּהֶם הַקֹּר בִּלְבַד, וְגוּפִים יֵרָאֶה בָּהֶם הַלַּח בִּלְבַד, וְגוּפִים יֵרָאֶה בָּהֶן הַקֹּר וְהַיֹּבֶשׁ כְּאֶחָד בְּשָׁוֶה, אוֹ הַקֹּר וְהַלַּח כְּאֶחָד בְּשָׁוֶה, אוֹ הַחֹם וְהַיֹּבֶשׁ כְּאֶחָד בְּשָׁוֶה, אוֹ הַחֹם וְהַלַּח כְּאֶחָד בְּשָׁוֶה –

Similarly, there are bodies in which cold alone is evident, and other **bodies in which moistness alone is evident, while** in yet other **bodies, cold and dryness are equally evident, or cold and moistness equally** evident, **or warmth and dryness equally** evident, **or warmth and moistness equally** evident.

לְפִי רֹב הַיְסוֹד שֶׁהָיָה בְּעִקַּר הַתַּעֲרֹבֶת, יֵרָאוּ מַעֲשֵׂה אוֹתוֹ הַיְסוֹד וְטִבְעוֹ בַּגּוּף הַמְעֹרָב.

The effect of an element and its nature in the body accords with how predominant the element is in the basic combination formed by **the mixture.**

Halakha 3

וְכָל הַמְחֻבָּר מֵאַרְבָּעָה יְסוֹדוֹת אֵלּוּ, לָהֶם הוּא נִפְרָד בַּסּוֹף:

Everything that is a combination of these four elements will eventually break down into them, in accordance with the nature of every complex entity.

יֵשׁ שֶׁהוּא נִפְרָד לְאַחַר יָמִים אֲחָדִים, וְיֵשׁ שֶׁהוּא נִפְרָד לְאַחַר שָׁנִים רַבִּים. וְכָל שֶׁנִּתְחַבֵּר מֵהֶם – אִי אֶפְשָׁר שֶׁלֹּא יִפָּרֵד לָהֶם,

Some will break down after a few days, while others will break down only **after many years. But it is impossible for anything that is a combination of them not to break down into them.**

אֲפִלּוּ הַזָּהָב וְהָאֹדֶם אִי אֶפְשָׁר שֶׁלֹּא יִפָּסֵד וְיַחֲזֹר לִיסוֹדוֹתָיו, וְיַחֲזֹר מִקְצָתוֹ לָאֵשׁ וּמִקְצָתוֹ לַמַּיִם וּמִקְצָתוֹ לָרוּחַ וּמִקְצָתוֹ לָאָרֶץ.

It is **even impossible for gold and ruby,** a particular hard precious stone, **not to decay and return to their elements,** despite the fact that they appear to be resistant to the effects of other materials: **Part of them returns to be** fire, **part to be** water, **part to be air, and part to be earth.**

Halakha 4

הוֹאִיל וְכָל הַנִּפְרָד – לְאֵלּוּ יִפָּרֵד, לָמָּה נֶאֱמַר לָאָדָם: "וְאֶל עָפָר תָּשׁוּב" (בראשית ג, יט)?

Since every entity **that breaks down will break down into** all four of **these** elements, **why was Adam told: "You will return to the dust"** (Genesis 3:19), when he will actually break down into all four elements?

לְפִי שֶׁרֹב בִּנְיָנוֹ מִן הֶעָפָר. וְלֹא כָּל הַנִּפְסָד כְּשֶׁיִּפָּסֵד, מִיָּד יַחֲזוֹר לְאַרְבַּע הַיְסוֹדוֹת,

This is **because the majority of his structure is from dust. Not every** entity **that breaks down will immediately return, when it breaks down, into the four** primary **elements.**

אֶלָּא יִפָּסֵד וְיַחֲזוֹר לְדָבָר אַחֵר, וְדָבָר אַחֵר לְדָבָר אַחֵר, וְסוֹף הַדְּבָרִים יַחֲזוֹר לַיְסוֹדוֹת, וְנִמְצְאוּ כָּל הַדְּבָרִים חוֹזְרִין חֲלִילָה.

Rather, it can decay and change into something else, and that **something else can,** in turn, change **into** yet **something else, until it ultimately returns to the elements. Thus, all entities follow a cyclical** movement of being, changing, and adopting different characteristics after they have broken down.

Halakha 5

אַרְבָּעָה יְסוֹדוֹת הָאֵלּוּ מִשְׁתַּנִּים זֶה לָזֶה תָּמִיד בְּכָל יוֹם וּבְכָל שָׁעָה, מִקְצָתָן, לֹא כָּל גּוּפָן. כֵּיצַד?

These four elements are constantly changing into one another, each day and every hour, but only **part of them, not their entire body. How so?**

מִקְצָת הָאָרֶץ הַקְּרוֹבָה מִן הַמַּיִם מִשְׁתַּנֵּית וּמִתְפּוֹרֶרֶת וְנַעֲשֵׂית מַיִם. וְכֵן מִקְצָת הַמַּיִם הַסְּמוּכִין לָרוּחַ מִשְׁתַּנִּים וּמִתְמַסְמְסִין וְהוֹוִין רוּחַ. וְכֵן הָרוּחַ, מִקְצָתוֹ הַסָּמוּךְ לָאֵשׁ מִשְׁתַּנֶּה וּמִתְחוֹלֵל וְנַעֲשֶׂה אֵשׁ.

Part of the earth that is close to the water changes, crumbles, and becomes water. Likewise, part of the water that is close to the air changes, dissolves, and becomes air. And similarly in the case of **air, that part of it which is close to the fire changes, comes apart, and becomes fire.**

וְכֵן הָאֵשׁ, מִקְצָתָהּ הַסָּמוּךְ לָרוּחַ מִשְׁתַּנֶּה וּמִתְכַּנֵּס וְנַעֲשֶׂה רוּחַ. וְכֵן הָרוּחַ, מִקְצָתוֹ הַסָּמוּךְ לַמַּיִם מִשְׁתַּנֶּה וּמִתְכַּנֵּס וְנַעֲשֶׂה מַיִם. וְכֵן הַמַּיִם, מִקְצָתָן הַסָּמוּךְ לָאָרֶץ מִשְׁתַּנֶּה וּמִתְכַּנֵּס וְנַעֲשֶׂה אֶרֶץ.

Likewise with regard to **fire, part of the fire that is close to the wind changes, contracts, and becomes air. The same** applies to **that part of the air that is close to the water:** It **changes, contracts, and becomes water, and likewise the water that is close to the earth changes, contracts, and becomes earth.**

וְשִׁנּוּי זֶה – מְעַט מְעַט, וּלְפִי אֹרֶךְ הַיָּמִים. וְאֵין כָּל הַיְסוֹד מִשְׁתַּנֶּה עַד שֶׁיֵּעָשֶׂה כָּל הַמַּיִם רוּחַ אוֹ כָּל הָרוּחַ אֵשׁ, שֶׁאִי אֶפְשָׁר שֶׁיִּבָּטֵל אֶחָד מִן הַיְסוֹדוֹת הָאַרְבָּעָה,

This change unfolds **little by little over the course of time. The entire element does not change, such that all the water becomes air, or all the air fire, since it is impossible for** any **one of the four elements to be nullified.**

אֶלָּא מִקְצָת יִשְׁתַּנֶּה מֵאֵשׁ לְרוּחַ וּמִקְצָת מֵרוּחַ לְאֵשׁ. וְכֵן בֵּין כָּל אֶחָד וַחֲבֵרוֹ יִמָּצֵא הַשִּׁנּוּי בֵּין אַרְבַּעְתָּם, וְחוֹזְרוֹת חֲלִילָה.

Rather, part of the fire will change into air, and part of the air into fire. Similarly, a change will be found to occur **between each one of these four** elements **and the next, in a recurrent cycle.**

Halakha 6

וְשִׁנּוּי זֶה יִהְיֶה בִּסְבִיבַת הַגַּלְגַּל, וּמִסְּבִיבָתוֹ יִתְחַבְּרוּ אַרְבַּעְתָּם, וְיִהְיֶה מֵהֶם שְׁאָר גָּלְמֵי בְּנֵי אָדָם וְנֶפֶשׁ חַיָּה וְצֶמַח וְאֶבֶן וּמַתֶּכֶת.

This change is caused by the revolution of the sphere. The four elements **combine** by virtue **of its revolution, and from them are** formed **the rest of the matter of humans, living creatures, plants, stones, and metals.**

וְהָאֵל נוֹתֵן לְכָל גֹּלֶם וְגֹלֶם צוּרָה הָרְאוּיָה לוֹ עַל יְדֵי מַלְאָךְ הָעֲשִׂירִי, שֶׁהִיא הַצּוּרָה שֶׁנִּקְרֵאת אִישִׁים.

The Lord gives each and every matter the form that is appropriate for it through the agency of **an angel from the tenth** level. **These are the forms called *ishim*.**[a]

Halakha 7

לְעוֹלָם אֵין אַתָּה רוֹאֶה גֹּלֶם בְּלֹא צוּרָה אוֹ צוּרָה בְּלֹא גֹּלֶם, אֶלָּא לֵב הָאָדָם הוּא שֶׁמְּחַלֵּק הַגּוּף הַנִּמְצָא בְּדַעְתּוֹ, וְיוֹדֵעַ שֶׁהוּא מְחֻבָּר מִגֹּלֶם וְצוּרָה,

You will never see matter without form, or form without matter. One cannot observe pure matter or pure form. **Rather, it is man's perception that divides the body which exists in his mind,** thereby **knowing that it is a combination of matter and form.** In other words, we discern the difference between matter and form through our abstract analysis of entities.

וְיוֹדֵעַ שֶׁיֵּשׁ שָׁם גּוּפִים שֶׁגָּלְמָם מְחֻבָּר מֵאַרְבַּע יְסוֹדוֹת, וְגוּפִים שֶׁגָּלְמָם פָּשׁוּט וְאֵינוֹ מְחֻבָּר מִגֹּלֶם אַחֵר.

A person also **knows that there are bodies whose matter is a combination of the four elements, and** other **bodies,** the spheres and stars,[b] **whose matter is simple, and is not comprised of any** other **matter.**

וְהַצּוּרוֹת שֶׁאֵין לָהֶם גֹּלֶם אֵינָן נִרְאִין לָעַיִן, אֶלָּא בְּעֵין הַלֵּב הֵם יְדוּעִים, כְּמוֹ שֶׁיָּדַעְנוּ אֲדוֹן הַכֹּל בְּלֹא רְאִיַּת עַיִן.

The forms that have no matter, the angels,[c] **are invisible, and are known only through "the eye of the heart,"** human understanding, **just as we know** the existence of **the Master of everything without seeing** God with our **eyes.**

Halakha 8

נֶפֶשׁ כָּל בָּשָׂר הִיא צוּרָתוֹ שֶׁנָּתַן לוֹ הָאֵל, וְהַדַּעַת הַיְתֵרָה הַמְּצוּיָה בְּנַפְשׁוֹ שֶׁל אָדָם הִיא צוּרַת הָאָדָם הַשָּׁלֵם בְּדַעְתּוֹ,

The soul of all flesh, that is, the fundamental form of man, rather than his physical structure, **is the form that it was granted by God. The additional knowledge found in the human soul is** itself **the "form" of the man who is perfect in his knowledge.** This is the perfect human form.

NOTES

a. See 2:7.

b. See 2:3.

c. See 2:3.

וְעַל צוּרָה זוֹ נֶאֱמַר בַּתּוֹרָה: "נַעֲשֶׂה אָדָם בְּצַלְמֵנוּ כִּדְמוּתֵנוּ" (בראשית א, כו),

With regard to this form, it is stated in the Torah, in its description of God's decision to create man on the sixth day of creation: **"Let us make man in our image, in our likeness"** (Genesis 1:26).

כְּלוֹמַר שֶׁתִּהְיֶה לוֹ צוּרָה הַיּוֹדַעַת וּמַשֶּׂגֶת הַדֵּעוֹת שֶׁאֵין לָהֶם גֹּלֶם, עַד שֶׁיִּדְמֶה לָהֶן.

In other words, he should have a form that can know and grasp the existence of **entities that are not bodies,**[a] **until he can resemble them.** People have the ability to resemble the angels in terms of their knowledge.[b]

וְאֵינוֹ אוֹמֵר עַל צוּרָה זוֹ הַנִּכֶּרֶת לָעֵינַיִם, שֶׁהִיא הַפֶּה וְהַחֹטֶם וְהַלְּסָתוֹת וּשְׁאָר רֹשֶׁם הַגּוּף, שֶׁזּוֹ – תֹּאַר שְׁמָהּ.

This "image" [*tzelem*] mentioned in the verse **is not referring to this** physical **form, that is perceived by the eye, which** includes **the mouth, nose, cheeks, and the rest of the structure of the body, for that is called countenance** [*to'ar*]. The "image of God" is neither the corporeal body itself, nor the force of its physical life.

וְאֵינָהּ הַנֶּפֶשׁ הַמְּצוּיָה לְכָל נֶפֶשׁ חַיָּה, שֶׁבָּהּ אוֹכֵל וְשׁוֹתֶה וּמוֹלִיד וּמַרְגִּישׁ וּמְהַרְהֵר, אֶלָּא הַדֵּעָה, שֶׁהִיא צוּרַת הַנֶּפֶשׁ, וּבְצוּרַת הַנֶּפֶשׁ הַכָּתוּב מְדַבֵּר.

It is also **not the soul that is present in all living creatures, through which it eats, drinks, reproduces, senses, and thinks. Rather,** the "image of God" **is** man's unique **intellectual capacity, which is the form of the soul,**[c] **and the verse is speaking of** this **form of the soul.**

וּפְעָמִים רַבּוֹת תִּקָּרֵא זֹאת הַצּוּרָה נֶפֶשׁ וְרוּחַ, לְפִיכָךְ צָרִיךְ לְהִזָּהֵר בַּשֵּׁמוֹת שֶׁלֹּא תִּטְעֶה, וְכָל שֵׁם וָשֵׁם יִלָּמֵד מֵעִנְיָנוֹ.

This form is often called *nefesh* [soul] **or *ruaḥ*** [spirit]. **Therefore, one must be careful with regard to these names, not to err** between the different meanings of "soul." The precise denotation **of each and every name can be understood from its context.**

Halakha 9

אֵין צוּרַת הַנֶּפֶשׁ הַזֹּאת מְחֻבֶּרֶת מִן הַיְסוֹדוֹת כְּדֵי שֶׁתִּפָּרֵד לָהֶם, וְאֵינָהּ מִכֹּחַ הַנְּשָׁמָה עַד שֶׁתִּהְיֶה צְרִיכָה לַנְּשָׁמָה כְּמוֹ שֶׁהַנְּשָׁמָה צְרִיכָה לַגּוּף, אֶלָּא מֵאֵת יי מִן הַשָּׁמַיִם הִיא.

The form of this soul is not a combination of the elements, such that it will break down into them, nor does it come from the force of the *neshama*, which is the animating force of the body, **in which case it would require the *neshama*,** just as the ***neshama*** **requires the body. Rather, it is from God, from heaven.**

לְפִיכָךְ כְּשֶׁיִּפָּרֵד הַגֹּלֶם שֶׁהוּא מְחֻבָּר מִן הַיְסוֹדוֹת, וְתֹאבַד הַנְּשָׁמָה, מִפְּנֵי שֶׁאֵינָהּ מְצוּיָה אֶלָּא עִם הַגּוּף וּצְרִיכָה לַגּוּף בְּכָל מַעֲשֶׂיהָ – לֹא תִּכָּרֵת הַצּוּרָה הַזֹּאת, לְפִי שֶׁאֵינָהּ צְרִיכָה לַנְּשָׁמָה בְּמַעֲשֶׂיהָ,

Therefore, when the matter of the body, **which is a combination of the elements, breaks down** at death **and the *neshama* perishes – for** the *neshama* **exists only** when it is **together with the body and requires the body for all of its activity – this form will not perish, for it does not require the *neshama* for its activity.** The *nefesh* soul does not expire after one's death.[d]

NOTES

a. See 2:3.

b. See 7:1.

c. See also *Hilkhot Teshuva* 8:3.

d. See *Hilkhot Teshuva* 8:3.

אֶלָּא יוֹדַעַת וּמַשֶּׂגֶת הַדֵּעוֹת הַפְּרוּדוֹת מִן הַגְּלָמִים, וְיוֹדַעַת בּוֹרֵא הַכֹּל, וְעוֹמֶדֶת לְעוֹלָם וּלְעוֹלְמֵי עוֹלָמִים. הוּא שֶׁאָמַר שְׁלֹמֹה בְּחָכְמָתוֹ: "וְיָשֹׁב הֶעָפָר עַל הָאָרֶץ כְּשֶׁהָיָה וְהָרוּחַ תָּשׁוּב אֶל הָאֱלֹהִים אֲשֶׁר נְתָנָהּ" (קהלת יב,ז).

Rather, it knows and comprehends the entities that are separated from matter; it knows the Creator of everything, and it lasts forever and ever. This is the meaning of that **which Solomon said in his wisdom: "And the dust returns to the earth as it was, and the spirit** [*ruaḥ*] **returns to God who provided it"** (Ecclesiastes 12:7).

Halakha 10

כָּל הַדְּבָרִים הָאֵלּוּ שֶׁדִּבַּרְנוּ בְּעִנְיָן זֶה – כְּמַר מִדְּלִי הֵם, וּדְבָרִים עֲמֻקִּים הֵם, אֲבָל אֵינָם כְּעֹמֶק עִנְיַן פֶּרֶק רִאשׁוֹן וְשֵׁנִי. וּבֵאוּר כָּל אֵלּוּ הַדְּבָרִים שֶׁבְּפֶרֶק שְׁלִישִׁי וּרְבִיעִי הוּא הַנִּקְרָא מַעֲשֵׂה בְּרֵאשִׁית.

All of these ideas that we have explained on this topic are like a drop from a bucket,[a] **and they are profound matters. Nevertheless, they are not as deep as the subject matter of the first and second chapters. The explanation of all these concepts** presented **in the third and fourth chapters is called** the **"Act of Creation** [*maaseh bereshit*]."

וְכָךְ צִוּוּ חֲכָמִים הָרִאשׁוֹנִים, שֶׁאֵין דּוֹרְשִׁין גַּם בִּדְבָרִים הָאֵלּוּ בָּרַבִּים, אֶלָּא לְאָדָם אֶחָד בִּלְבַד מוֹדִיעִים דְּבָרִים אֵלּוּ וּמְלַמְּדִין אוֹתוֹ.

Accordingly, the early Sages commanded that these matters should not be expounded in public either,[b] in case they are inadequately understood. **Rather, one informs a single individual alone about these ideas, teaching him** in private.

Halakha 11

וּמַה בֵּין עִנְיַן מַעֲשֵׂה מֶרְכָּבָה לְעִנְיַן מַעֲשֵׂה בְּרֵאשִׁית?

Since they are both proscribed in public, **what is the difference between** teaching **the topic of** the **Design of** the Divine **Chariot and** teaching **the topic of** the **Act of Creation?**

שֶׁעִנְיַן מַעֲשֵׂה מֶרְכָּבָה – אֲפִלּוּ לְאֶחָד אֵין דּוֹרְשִׁין בּוֹ, אֶלָּא אִם כֵּן הָיָה חָכָם וּמֵבִין מִדַּעְתּוֹ, נוֹתְנִין לוֹ רָאשֵׁי הַפְּרָקִים.

The difference is **that one does not expound the topic** of the **Design of** the Divine **Chariot even to a single individual, unless he is a wise** person **who can understand of his own accord,** in which case **he is given the basic concepts.**

וְעִנְיַן מַעֲשֵׂה בְּרֵאשִׁית – מְלַמְּדִין אוֹתוֹ לְיָחִיד אַף עַל פִּי שֶׁאֵינוֹ מֵבִין אוֹתוֹ מִדַּעְתּוֹ, וּמוֹדִיעִין אוֹתוֹ כָּל שֶׁיָּכוֹל לֵידַע מִדְּבָרִים אֵלּוּ.

By contrast, **one may teach the topic of** the **Act of Creation to an individual even if he cannot understand it of his own accord, and one may inform him about everything that he can know of these ideas.** Even if everything has to be explained to him, and the basic concepts are not enough, it is permitted to teach him.

וְלָמָּה אֵין מְלַמְּדִין אוֹתוֹ לָרַבִּים? לְפִי שֶׁאֵין כָּל אָדָם יֵשׁ לוֹ דַּעַת רְחָבָה לְהַשִּׂיג פֵּרוּשׁ וּבֵאוּר כָּל הַדְּבָרִים עַל בֻּרְיָן.

Why, then, **may** the Act of Creation **not be taught in public? Because not every person has** sufficiently **broad knowledge to fully grasp the meaning and explanation of all these ideas,** even after receiving instruction.

NOTES

a. The expression is from Isaiah 40:15.

b. That is, public teaching about the Design of the Divine Chariot is also prohibited, in 2:12.

Halakha 12

בִּזְמַן שֶׁאָדָם מִתְבּוֹנֵן בִּדְבָרִים הָאֵלּוּ וּמַכִּיר כָּל הַבְּרוּאִים, מִמַּלְאָךְ וְגַלְגַּל וְאָדָם וְכַיּוֹצֵא בּוֹ, וְיִרְאֶה חָכְמָתוֹ שֶׁל הַקָּדוֹשׁ בָּרוּךְ הוּא בְּכָל הַיְצוּרִים וְכָל הַבְּרוּאִים – מוֹסִיף אַהֲבָה לַמָּקוֹם,

When a person reflects on these ideas, and recognizes all the created beings, from angels and **spheres,** down to **humans, and the like, and he observes the wisdom of the Holy One blessed be He** as manifested **in all creatures and in all created beings, his love for the Omnipresent will increase** as he wonders at the wisdom displayed in their creation.[a]

וְתִצְמְאָה נַפְשׁוֹ וְיִכְמַהּ בְּשָׂרוֹ לֶאֱהֹב הַמָּקוֹם בָּרוּךְ הוּא, וְיִירָא וְיִפְחַד מִשִּׁפְלוּתוֹ וְדַלּוּתוֹ וְקַלּוּתוֹ כְּשֶׁיַּעֲרֹךְ עַצְמוֹ לְאֶחָד מֵהַגּוּפוֹת הַקְּדוֹשִׁים הַגְּדוֹלִים,

His soul will thirst and his flesh yearn to love the Omnipresent, blessed be He. He will also **be scared and afraid due to his lowly and miserable insubstantial** state **when he compares himself to one of the holy and mighty bodies,** such as the spheres and the stars;

וְכָל שֶׁכֵּן לְאֶחָד מֵהַצּוּרוֹת הַטְּהוֹרוֹת הַנִּפְרָדוֹת מִן הַגְּלָמִים שֶׁלֹּא נִתְחַבְּרוּ בְּגֹלֶם כְּלָל, וְיִמְצָא עַצְמוֹ שֶׁהוּא כִּכְלִי מָלֵא בּוּשָׁה וּכְלִמָּה, רֵיק וְחָסֵר.

all the more so, when comparing himself **to one of the pure forms which are separated from matter and are not comprised of matter at all. He will realize that he is a vessel filled with shame and disgrace, empty and deficient.**

Halakha 13

וְעִנְיְנֵי אַרְבָּעָה פְּרָקִים אֵלּוּ שֶׁבְּחָמֵשׁ מִצְוֹת הָאֵלּוּ – הֵם שֶׁחֲכָמִים הָרִאשׁוֹנִים קוֹרְאִין אוֹתָן פַּרְדֵּס, כְּמוֹ שֶׁאָמְרוּ: אַרְבָּעָה נִכְנְסוּ לַפַּרְדֵּס. וְאַף עַל פִּי שֶׁגְּדוֹלֵי יִשְׂרָאֵל הָיוּ, וַחֲכָמִים גְּדוֹלִים הָיוּ, לֹא כֻּלָּם הָיָה בָּהֶן כֹּחַ לֵידַע וּלְהַשִּׂיג כָּל הַדְּבָרִים עַל בֻּרְיָן.

The topics of these four chapters, concerning these five mitzvot,[b] **are what the early Sages called** ***pardes*****,**[1] "orchard," **as they stated: "Four entered the** ***pardes*****"** (*Ḥagiga* 14b). **Even though they were great** leaders of **Israel and they were** all **great Sages, not all of them had the capability to fully know and grasp all of these ideas,** and thus some of them were harmed by the experience, as the Gemara there relates.

וַאֲנִי אוֹמֵר שֶׁאֵין רָאוּי לְהִטַּיֵּל בַּפַּרְדֵּס אֶלָּא מִי שֶׁנִּתְמַלֵּא כְּרֵסוֹ לֶחֶם וּבָשָׂר. וְלֶחֶם וּבָשָׂר זֶה הוּא לֵידַע בֵּאוּר הָאָסוּר וְהַמֻּתָּר וְכַיּוֹצֵא בָּהֶן מִשְּׁאָר הַמִּצְוֹת.

I maintain that it is improper for a person **to "stroll in the** ***pardes*****,"** that is, to contemplate these ideas, **unless he has** already **filled his belly with** the basic foods of **bread and meat. This "bread and meat" means knowing the explanation of what is permitted and what is prohibited**[2] **and the like, with regard to** all the **rest of the mitzvot.**

וְאַף עַל פִּי שֶׁדְּבָרִים אֵלּוּ דָּבָר קָטָן קְרָאוּ אוֹתָם חֲכָמִים, שֶׁהֲרֵי אָמְרוּ חֲכָמִים: דָּבָר גָּדוֹל – מַעֲשֵׂה מֶרְכָּבָה, וְדָבָר קָטָן – הֲוָיָה דְּאַבַּיֵּי וְרָבָא, אַף עַל פִּי כֵן רְאוּיִין הֵן לְהַקְדִּימָן, שֶׁהֵן מְיַשְּׁבִין דַּעְתּוֹ שֶׁל אָדָם תְּחִלָּה.

Even though the Sages called these topics "a small matter" – for the Sages said: "A great matter" is the **Design of** the Divine **Chariot, and a "small matter"** is, for example, halakhot that result from **the discussions of Abaye and Rava**[c] (*Bava Batra* 134a) **– nevertheless, it is fitting for them to receive precedence, because they settle a person's mind first.**

HALAKHIC DISCUSSION

1. **Are what the early Sages called** ***pardes*** **– הֵם שֶׁחֲכָמִים הָרִאשׁוֹנִים קוֹרְאִין אוֹתָן פַּרְדֵּס:** According to the Shakh, the *pardes* refers to books of philosophy, astronomy, and the wisdom of the Kabbala. There have been discussions over the generations regarding how much time one should devote to the study of these subjects.

2. **Knowing the explanation of what is permitted and what is prohibited – לֵידַע בֵּאוּר הָאָסוּר וְהַמֻּתָּר:** *Shulḥan Arukh, Yoreh De'a* 246:4. With regard to the Kabbala, the Shakh states that a person should not delve into such matters until he has "filled his belly" with the study of Mishna and Talmud. He also cites an opinion that one should not study Kabbala until the age of forty, since it requires holiness, purity, proper motivation, and cleanliness of thought (see *Hilkhot Talmud Torah* 1:12, 3:13). The Arizal maintains that conditions have changed over time in this regard, and that it is permitted and even a mitzva to reveal the wisdom of the Kabbala (his opinion is cited and clarified in the *Tanya, Iggeret HaKodesh* 26; see also *Shaarei Halakha UMinhag, Yoreh De'a* 3:71–74).

With regard to the general rule that "only one who has filled his belly with meat and wine should stroll in the *pardes*," Rabbi Abraham Isaac Kook explains that this is addressed specifically to a person who only wishes to fulfill his basic Torah obligations. However, if someone feels in his heart a particular desire to study the esoteric teachings of the Torah and become educated in the knowledge of God and His truth, he is obligated to do so. Indeed, his inclination toward these areas of study shows that he has a special talent for them and that he was created for this purpose (*Orot HaTorah* 9:12; see there for an in-depth analysis of this topic).

NOTES

a. See also 2:2; *Hilkhot Teshuva* 10:6.

b. The first five mitzvot listed at the start of these Halakhot: to know that there is a God; not to contemplate that there is another god apart from Him; to acknowledge His unity; to love Him; and to fear Him.

c. These are examples of common talmudic debates.

וְעוֹד, שֶׁהֵן הַטּוֹבָה הַגְּדוֹלָה שֶׁהִשְׁפִּיעַ הַקָּדוֹשׁ בָּרוּךְ הוּא לְיִשּׁוּב הָעוֹלָם הַזֶּה כְּדֵי לִנְחֹל חַיֵּי הָעוֹלָם הַבָּא, וְאֶפְשָׁר שֶׁיֵּדָעֵם הַכֹּל, גָּדוֹל וְקָטָן, אִישׁ וְאִשָּׁה, בַּעַל לֵב רָחָב וּבַעַל לֵב קָצָר.

Furthermore, they are the great good that the Holy One blessed be He has bestowed for the settlement of this world, in order that one will **inherit the life of the World to Come.** For one merits the World to Come by studying Torah and observing the mitzvot.[a] **Everyone can know** those halakhot, whether one is **great or small, man or woman,** whether **one has a broad mind,** which is capable of deep, reflective thought, **or** whether **one has a limited mind,** and is not so gifted intellectually.[b]

NOTES

a. See *Hilkhot Teshuva* 9:2.

b. See *Hilkhot Talmud Torah* 1:12.

פֶּרֶק חֲמִישִׁי

CHAPTER 5

The Sanctification and Desecration of God's Name

Halakha 1

כָּל בֵּית יִשְׂרָאֵל מְצֻוִּין עַל קִדּוּשׁ הַשֵּׁם הַגָּדוֹל הַזֶּה, שֶׁנֶּאֱמַר: "וְנִקְדַּשְׁתִּי בְּתוֹךְ בְּנֵי יִשְׂרָאֵל" (ויקרא כב, לב), וּמֻזְהָרִין שֶׁלֹּא לְחַלְּלוֹ, שֶׁנֶּאֱמַר: "וְלֹא תְחַלְּלוּ אֶת שֵׁם קָדְשִׁי" (שם).

The entire house of Israel are commanded regarding the sanctification of this great name of God, **as it is stated: "And I shall be sanctified among the children of Israel"** (Leviticus 22:32), **and they are warned not to desecrate** God's name, **as it is stated** in the same verse: **"And you shall not desecrate My holy name."**

כֵּיצַד? בְּשָׁעָה שֶׁיַּעֲמֹד גּוֹי וְיֶאֱנֹס אֶת יִשְׂרָאֵל לַעֲבֹר עַל אַחַת מִכָּל מִצְוֹת הָאֲמוּרוֹת בַּתּוֹרָה אוֹ יַהַרְגֶנּוּ – יַעֲבֹר וְלֹא יֵהָרֵג, שֶׁנֶּאֱמַר בַּמִּצְוֹת: "אֲשֶׁר יַעֲשֶׂה אֹתָם הָאָדָם וָחַי בָּהֶם" (שם יח, ה) – וְלֹא שֶׁיָּמוּת בָּהֶם. וְאִם מֵת וְלֹא עָבַר – הֲרֵי זֶה מִתְחַיֵּב בְּנַפְשׁוֹ.

How so? When a gentile arises and forces a Jew[1] **to violate one of the mitzvot stated in** the **Torah or he will kill him,** the Jew **should transgress**[2] that prohibition **and not be killed,**[3] **as it is stated with regard to the mitzvot:** "You shall keep My statutes... **which a man shall do and live by them"** (Leviticus 18:5) – **and not that he should die by them. If he died rather than transgress, he is held liable for his own life.** He is deserving of punishment for causing his own death.

HALAKHIC DISCUSSION

1. How so? When a gentile arises and forces a Jew – כֵּיצַד בְּשָׁעָה שֶׁיַּעֲמֹד גּוֹי וְיֶאֱנֹס אֶת יִשְׂרָאֵל: *Shulhan Arukh, Yoreh De'a* 157:1.

2. Should transgress – יַעֲבֹר: If he can save himself by giving up all of his money, he is obligated to do so rather than commit a transgression (Rema). The later authorities discuss the case of one who is threatened with harm to one of his limbs, whether or not this is considered a life-threatening situation, and the consensus is that one may be lenient (*Shakh*; see also *Pithei Teshuva* 157:15). They further state that one is not obligated to spend all that he possesses in order to fulfill a positive mitzva, but only up to one-fifth of his wealth (*Shakh*).

3. Should transgress that prohibition and not be killed – יַעֲבֹר וְאַל יֵהָרֵג: One should violate the prohibition even if it is uncertain that he will thereby spare himself (*Pithei Teshuva*).

Halakha 2

בַּמֶּה דְּבָרִים אֲמוּרִים? בִּשְׁאָר מִצְוֹת חוּץ מֵעֲבוֹדָה זָרָה וְגִלּוּי עֲרָיוֹת וּשְׁפִיכוּת דָּמִים. אֲבָל שָׁלֹשׁ עֲבֵרוֹת אֵלּוּ, אִם יֹאמַר לוֹ: 'עֲבֹר עַל אַחַת מֵהֶן אוֹ תֵּהָרֵג' – יֵהָרֵג וְאַל יַעֲבֹר.

In what case is this statement said? In the case of other mitzvot,[1] **excepting idol worship,**[2] **forbidden sexual relations,**[3] **and bloodshed.**[4] **However,** with regard to **these three sins, if one is told: "Transgress one of these or be killed,"**[5] **he must be killed and not transgress.**

בַּמֶּה דְּבָרִים אֲמוּרִים? בִּזְמַן שֶׁהַגּוֹי מִתְכַּוֵּן לַהֲנָאַת עַצְמוֹ, כְּגוֹן שֶׁאֲנָסוֹ לִבְנוֹת לוֹ בֵּיתוֹ בְּשַׁבָּת אוֹ לְבַשֵּׁל לוֹ תַּבְשִׁילוֹ, אוֹ אָנַס אִשָּׁה לְבָעֳלָהּ, וְכַיּוֹצֵא בָּזֶה.

In what case **is this statement said,** that for one of the other mitzvot the Jew must transgress and not be killed? **When the gentile's intention is his own pleasure, for example, he** seeks to **compel** the Jew **to build his house for him or cook his dish for him on Shabbat, or if he** wants to **force** a Jewish **woman to have relations with him, and the like.**

אֲבָל אִם נִתְכַּוֵּן לְהַעֲבִירוֹ עַל הַמִּצְוֹת בִּלְבַד: אִם הָיָה בֵּינוֹ לְבֵין עַצְמוֹ וְאֵין שָׁם עֲשָׂרָה מִיִּשְׂרָאֵל – יַעֲבֹר וְאַל יֵהָרֵג; וְאִם אֲנָסוֹ לְהַעֲבִירוֹ בַּעֲשָׂרָה מִיִּשְׂרָאֵל – יֵהָרֵג וְאַל יַעֲבֹר, וַאֲפִלּוּ לֹא נִתְכַּוֵּן לְהַעֲבִירוֹ אֶלָּא עַל מִצְוָה מִשְּׁאָר מִצְוֹת בִּלְבַד.

However, if his intention is solely to have the Jew **violate the mitzvot,** the following distinction applies: If the Jew **is alone, and there are not ten** other **Jews there, he should transgress and not be killed.**[6] **But if he** wishes to **compel him to transgress in** the presence of **ten Jews,**[7] **he must be killed and not transgress,**[8] **even if** the gentile **intended for him to violate only one of the other mitzvot,**[9] and it did not involve idol worship, forbidden sexual relations, or bloodshed.

HALAKHIC DISCUSSION

1. **In the case of other mitzvot – בִּשְׁאָר מִצְוֹת:** *Shulḥan Arukh, Yoreh De'a* 157:1.

2. **Idol worship – עֲבוֹדָה זָרָה:** It is prohibited to declare that one is an idol worshipper in order to avoid being killed, but it is permitted to change one's dress so as to not be recognized as a Jew, and one may even wear a garment consisting of the prohibited diverse kinds of wool and linen [*shaatnez*] for this purpose. One may also issue an ambiguous statement that can be taken to mean that one worships idols (*Shulḥan Arukh* and Rema on *Yoreh De'a* 157:2), but one may not do so for financial reasons, such as to avoid paying a tax, although a Torah scholar is permitted to do so (*Shakh*; see *Pitḥei Teshuva*). One who has been condemned to death may escape into an idolatrous house of worship (*Shulḥan Arukh* 157:3), but some maintain that it is prohibited to do this during a period of religious persecution (Rema).

3. **Forbidden sexual relations – גִּלּוּי עֲרָיוֹת:** A Jewish woman who is forced to have intercourse with a gentile is not considered to have engaged in forbidden sexual relations for the purposes of this law (Rema; the Taz and Shakh add that this is the case only if she is unmarried; see the *Gra*), but a Jew having intercourse with a gentile woman is considered forbidden sexual relations (*Taz*).

4. **Idol worship, forbidden sexual relations, and bloodshed – מֵעֲבוֹדָה זָרָה וְגִלּוּי עֲרָיוֹת וּשְׁפִיכוּת דָּמִים:** With regard to these three mitzvot, a person must allow himself to be killed rather than violate any relevant negative mitzva, even if it is not the main prohibition; for example, if he is forced to embrace and kiss a relative who is forbidden to him (Rema; see Halakha 9).

HALAKHIC DISCUSSION

5. **Transgress one of these or be killed – עֲבֹר עַל אַחַת מֵהֶן אוֹ תֵּהָרֵג:** If one is compelled to violate one of these prohibitions without performing an action, i.e., even in a situation where one is completely passive, such as a woman forced to have relations with a man, or if they wish to throw someone on a baby and thereby kill it, he does not have to give up his life to prevent this (Rema).

6. **He should transgress and not be killed – יַעֲבֹר וְאַל יֵהָרֵג:** If the gentile insists that the Torah of Moses is untrue, or some similar claim, and this is why he wishes to force the Jew to transgress, even if he does not intend for him to convert and it is all done in private, the Jew must let himself be killed rather than transgress, since this is equivalent to idol worship (*Pitḥei Teshuva*, citing Radbaz).

7. **In the presence of ten Jews – בַּעֲשָׂרָה מִיִּשְׂרָאֵל:** The same applies even if the ten Jews cannot see him but they are aware of the incident (*Shakh*).

8. **But if he wishes to compel him to transgress in the presence of ten Jews, he must be killed and not transgress – וְאִם אֲנָסוֹ לְהַעֲבִירוֹ בַּעֲשָׂרָה מִיִּשְׂרָאֵל יֵהָרֵג וְאַל יַעֲבֹר:** Some maintain that one has the right to give up his life even if the gentile's intention is not for him to violate his faith (see *Shakh*; Halakha 4).

9. **Only one of the other mitzvot – מִצְוָה מִשְּׁאָר מִצְוֹת בִּלְבַד:** Some contend that even if the act is prohibited only as a custom, one should still be killed rather than transgress (see *Beit Yosef* and *Shakh*). This law applies specifically to negative mitzvot, but one need not let himself be killed over a positive mitzva. If the circumstances require it and he wishes to give up his life, he may do so even for a positive mitzva (Rema).

Halakha 3

וְכָל הַדְּבָרִים הָאֵלּוּ – שֶׁלֹּא בִּשְׁעַת הַשְּׁמָד. אֲבָל בִּשְׁעַת הַשְּׁמָד, וְהוּא כְּשֶׁיַּעֲמֹד מֶלֶךְ רָשָׁע כִּנְבוּכַדְנֶאצַּר וַחֲבֵרָיו וְיִגְזֹר שְׁמָד עַל יִשְׂרָאֵל לְבַטֵּל דָּתָם אוֹ מִצְוָה מִן הַמִּצְווֹת – יֵהָרֵג וְאַל יַעֲבֹר אֲפִלּוּ עַל אַחַת מִשְּׁאָר מִצְווֹת, בֵּין נֶאֱנַס בְּתוֹךְ עֲשָׂרָה בֵּין נֶאֱנַס בֵּינוֹ לְבֵין גּוֹיִם.

All of these distinctions apply **when it is not a time of** religious **persecution. However, in a time of persecution,**[1] **which is,** for example, **when a king as wicked as Nebuchadnezzar and his ilk arises and issues** a decree of **persecution against the Jews,**[2] **to nullify their religion or one of the mitzvot, one should be killed and not transgress even one of the other mitzvot, whether he** is being **forced** to do so **among ten** Jews or **whether** he is being **forced** to act only **among gentiles.**

Halakha 4

כָּל מִי שֶׁנֶּאֱמַר בּוֹ יַעֲבֹר וְאַל יֵהָרֵג, וְנֶהֱרַג וְלֹא עָבַר – הֲרֵי זֶה מִתְחַיֵּב בְּנַפְשׁוֹ. וְכָל מִי שֶׁנֶּאֱמַר בּוֹ יֵהָרֵג וְאַל יַעֲבֹר, וְנֶהֱרַג וְלֹא עָבַר – הֲרֵי זֶה קִדֵּשׁ אֶת הַשֵּׁם.

With regard to **anyone about whom it is stated** that the halakha is that **he should transgress and not be killed,** and yet **he was killed and did not transgress, he is held liable for his own life.**[3] **And** in the case of **anyone regarding whom it is stated** that **he should be killed and not transgress, and he was** indeed **killed and did not transgress, he has sanctified** God's **name.**[4]

וְאִם הָיָה בַּעֲשָׂרָה מִיִּשְׂרָאֵל – הֲרֵי זֶה קִדֵּשׁ אֶת הַשֵּׁם בָּרַבִּים, כְּדָנִיֵּאל חֲנַנְיָה מִישָׁאֵל וַעֲזַרְיָה, וּכְרַבִּי עֲקִיבָה וַחֲבֵרָיו, וְאֵלּוּ הֵם הֲרוּגֵי מַלְכוּת שֶׁאֵין מַעֲלָה עַל מַעֲלָתָם, וַעֲלֵיהֶם נֶאֱמַר: "כִּי עָלֶיךָ הֹרַגְנוּ כָל הַיּוֹם נֶחְשַׁבְנוּ כְּצֹאן טִבְחָה" (תהלים מד, כג), וַעֲלֵיהֶם נֶאֱמַר: "אִסְפוּ לִי חֲסִידָי כֹּרְתֵי בְרִיתִי עֲלֵי זָבַח" (שם נ, ה).

If he was in the presence of **ten Jews, he has sanctified** God's **name in public, like Daniel,**[a] **Hananya, Mishael, and Azarya,**[b] **and like Rabbi Akiva and his colleagues.**[c] **These are the ones executed by the** wicked **government, above whom there is no** person at **a higher level. With regard to them,** the verse **states: "For we are killed all day long for You; we are accounted as sheep for slaughter"** (Psalms 44:23), **and** another verse states **regarding them: "Gather My devoted ones, those who establish a covenant with Me by sacrifice"**[d] (Psalms 50:5).

וְכָל מִי שֶׁנֶּאֱמַר בּוֹ יֵהָרֵג וְאַל יַעֲבֹר, וְעָבַר וְלֹא נֶהֱרַג – הֲרֵי זֶה מְחַלֵּל אֶת הַשֵּׁם. וְאִם הָיָה בַּעֲשָׂרָה מִיִּשְׂרָאֵל – הֲרֵי חִלֵּל אֶת הַשֵּׁם בָּרַבִּים, וּבִטֵּל מִצְוַת עֲשֵׂה שֶׁהִיא קִדּוּשׁ הַשֵּׁם, וְעָבַר עַל מִצְוַת לֹא תַעֲשֶׂה שֶׁהִיא חִלּוּל הַשֵּׁם.

And in the case of **anyone regarding whom it is stated** that **he should be killed and not transgress,**[5] **and yet he transgressed and was not killed, he has desecrated** God's **name. If he was in** the presence of **ten Jews, he has desecrated** God's **name in public, negated** the fulfillment of **a positive mitzva, which is the sanctification of** God's **name, and violated a negative mitzva, which is the desecration of** God's **name.**

HALAKHIC DISCUSSION

1. **In a time of persecution – בִּשְׁעַת הַשְּׁמָד:** *Shulhan Arukh, Yoreh De'a* 157:1.

2. **And issues a decree of persecution against the Jews – וְיִגְזֹר שְׁמָד עַל יִשְׂרָאֵל:** If the decree of persecution applies to other nations as well, it is not necessary to let oneself be killed (Rema).

3. **And he was killed and did not transgress, he is held liable for his own life – וְנֶהֱרַג וְלֹא עָבַר הֲרֵי זֶה מִתְחַיֵּב בְּנַפְשׁוֹ:** *Shulhan Arukh, Yoreh De'a* 157:1. The *Shulhan Arukh* adds that in a case where the gentile seeks to force the Jew to transgress one of the mitzvot in order to violate his faith, one has permission to be stringent and allow himself to be killed, even if it is not in the presence of ten Jews. The later authorities dispute the ruling of halakha in such a situation (*Shakh*; see the appendix: "Martyrdom").

4. **He has sanctified God's name – הֲרֵי זֶה קִדֵּשׁ אֶת הַשֵּׁם:** The Shelah states that one recites the following blessing for the sanctification of God's name: "Who sanctified us with His mitzvot and commanded us to sanctity His name in public" (*Pithei Teshuva*).

5. **And anyone about whom it is stated that he should be killed and not transgress – וְכָל מִי שֶׁנֶּאֱמַר בּוֹ יֵהָרֵג וְאַל יַעֲבֹר:** The early authorities dispute whether a person who is concerned that he will be unable to withstand the test and allow himself to be killed is permitted to kill himself in order to avoid such a state of affairs (*Beit Yosef*; see the appendix: "Martyrdom").

NOTES

a. Who prayed to God against the decree of King Darius, and was therefore thrown into the lions' den (Daniel, chap. 6).

b. Who were thrown into a fiery furnace for refusing to bow down to the image set up by Nebuchadnezzar (Daniel, chap. 3).

c. Who gave up their lives for the Torah (*Sanhedrin* 110b).

d. This verse is expounded as referring to the righteous in each generation who sacrifice their lives for the sake of the covenant established with God.

וְאַף עַל פִּי כֵן, מִפְּנֵי שֶׁעָבַר בְּאֹנֶס, אֵין מַלְקִין אוֹתוֹ, וְאֵין צָרִיךְ לוֹמַר שֶׁאֵין מְמִיתִין אוֹתוֹ בֵּית דִּין, אֲפִלּוּ הָרַג בְּאֹנֶס, שֶׁאֵין מַלְקִין וּמְמִיתִין אֶלָּא לָעוֹבֵר בִּרְצוֹנוֹ בְּעֵדִים וְהַתְרָאָה, שֶׁנֶּאֱמַר בַּנּוֹתֵן מִזַּרְעוֹ לַמֹּלֶךְ: "וְנָתַתִּי אֲנִי אֶת פָּנַי בָּאִישׁ הַהוּא" (ויקרא כ, ה, ושם: וְשַׂמְתִּי אֲנִי אֶת פָּנַי), וּמִפִּי הַשְּׁמוּעָה לָמְדוּ: "הַהוּא" – לֹא אָנוּס וְלֹא שׁוֹגֵג וְלֹא מֻטְעֶה.

Nevertheless, since he transgressed under duress, he is not flogged, and needless to say he is not executed by **the court, even if he killed** someone **under duress. For** the courts **flog and execute only one who transgresses willingly,** in the presence of **witnesses, and** after **a warning** had been given, **as is stated with regard to one who gives** one **of his offspring to Molech,** a form of idolatry:[a] **"I will direct My attention to that man"** (Leviticus 20:5), **and** the Sages **learned, on the basis of the** Oral **tradition, that** the phrase **"that** man**"** teaches that this applies only to one who worshipped Molech intentionally, **but not one** who is **compelled** to transgress, **nor** one who does so **unwittingly, nor** one who **was mistaken.**[b]

וּמָה אִם עֲבוֹדָה זָרָה שֶׁהִיא חֲמוּרָה מִן הַכֹּל, הָעוֹבֵד אוֹתָהּ בְּאֹנֶס אֵינוֹ חַיָּב כָּרֵת, וְאֵין צָרִיךְ לוֹמַר מִיתַת בֵּית דִּין, קַל וָחֹמֶר לִשְׁאָר מִצְוֹת הָאֲמוּרוֹת בַּתּוֹרָה. וּבָעֲרָיוֹת הוּא אוֹמֵר: "וְלַנַּעֲרָה לֹא תַעֲשֶׂה דָבָר" (דברים כב, כו, ושם: וְלַנַּעֲרָ).

Now, if in the case of Molech, a form of **idol worship, which is more severe than all** other sins,[c] **one who worships it under duress is** nevertheless **not liable to** ***karet***,[d] **and needless to say** he is not liable to the **court-imposed death penalty,** ***a fortiori*** the same applies **to the other mitzvot stated in the Torah.** Likewise, **in** the case of **forbidden sexual relations,** the Torah **states: "But to the young woman you shall do nothing"** (Deuteronomy 22:26). This verse, which is referring to a betrothed young woman who was raped, also proves that one who sins under duress is not punished.[e]

Halakha 5

נָשִׁים שֶׁאָמְרוּ לָהֶם גּוֹיִם: 'תְּנוּ לָנוּ אַחַת מִכֶּם וּנְטַמֵּא אוֹתָהּ, וְאִם לָאו נְטַמֵּא אֶת כֻּלְּכֶם' – יְטַמְּאוּ כֻּלָּם וְאַל יִמְסְרוּ לָהֶם נֶפֶשׁ אַחַת מִיִּשְׂרָאֵל. וְכֵן אִם אָמְרוּ לָהֶם גּוֹיִם: 'תְּנוּ לָנוּ אֶחָד מִכֶּם וְנַהַרְגֶנּוּ, וְאִם לָאו נַהֲרֹג כֻּלְּכֶם' – יֵהָרְגוּ כֻּלָּם וְאַל יִמְסְרוּ לָהֶם נֶפֶשׁ אַחַת מִיִּשְׂרָאֵל.

In the case of **women who were told by gentiles:**[1] **"Give us one of you and we will defile her, and if** you do **not** do so **we will defile all of you," they should all be defiled and not hand over to them a single Jewish soul. Similarly, if gentiles told** a group of Jews: **"Give us one of you and we will kill him,**[2] **and if** you do **not** do so **we will kill all of you," they should all be killed and not hand over to them a single Jewish soul.**

HALAKHIC DISCUSSION

1. Women who were told by gentiles – נָשִׁים שֶׁאָמְרוּ לָהֶם גּוֹיִם: *Shulḥan Arukh, Yoreh De'a* 157:1.

2. Give us one of you and we will kill him – תְּנוּ לָנוּ אֶחָד מִכֶּם וְנַהַרְגֶנּוּ: They should not hand him over even if the gentiles merely wish to torture or rob him (*Taz*).

NOTES

a. See *Hilkhot Avoda Zara* 6:3.

b. See *Kiddushin* 43a.

c. See *Hilkhot Avoda Zara* 2:4.

d. Excision from the World to Come. One who worships idols is liable only if he did so willingly (see *Hilkhot Avoda Zara* 3:1).

e. See also *Hilkhot Sanhedrin* 20:2. Some editions of the Rambam include a section of text here, which the Rambam would probably have agreed with, even if he did not write it (*Yad Peshuta*): "If, however, one could save himself and flee from under the power of a wicked king and [yet] he does not do [so], he is like a dog returning to its vomit [see Proverbs 26:11]. He is called an intentional idol worshipper, and he will be banished from the World to Come and will descend to the lowest level of Gehenna."

וְאִם יִחֲדוּהוּ לָהֶם וְאָמְרוּ: 'תְּנוּ לָנוּ פְּלוֹנִי אוֹ נַהֲרֹג אֶת כֻּלְּכֶם': אִם הָיָה מְחֻיָּב מִיתָה כְּשֶׁבַע בֶּן בִּכְרִי – יִתְּנוּ אוֹתוֹ לָהֶם, וְאֵין מוֹרִין לָהֶם כֵּן לְכַתְּחִלָּה; וְאִם אֵינוֹ חַיָּב – יֵהָרְגוּ כֻּלָּם וְאַל יִמְסְרוּ לָהֶם נֶפֶשׁ אַחַת מִיִּשְׂרָאֵל.

But if the gentiles **singled out** a specific person **for themselves**[1] **and said: "Give us so-and-so or we will kill all of you,"** the following distinction applies: **If** that individual **is liable to** receive the **death** penalty,[2] **like Sheva, son of Bikhri,**[a3] **they may give him** over **to them, but they are not instructed** to do **so** ***ab initio***, for it is still better not to hand him over. **If he is not liable** to receive the death penalty, **they should all be killed and not hand over to them a single Jewish soul.**[4]

Halakha 6

כְּעִנְיַן שֶׁאָמְרוּ בַּאֲנָסִין, כָּךְ אָמְרוּ בְּחֳלָאִים. כֵּיצַד? מִי שֶׁחָלָה וְנָטָה לָמוּת, וְאָמְרוּ הָרוֹפְאִים שֶׁרְפוּאָתוֹ בְּדָבָר פְּלוֹנִי מֵאִסּוּרִין שֶׁבַּתּוֹרָה – עוֹשִׂין לוֹ.

Just as the Sages **stated** these principles **with regard to** one who is forced to act **under duress** by gentiles, that he may sin rather than die, **they said the same with regard to sicknesses.**[5] **How so? One who became ill and tended toward death, and the doctors said that his cure is a certain procedure**[6] that involves violating one **of the prohibitions in the Torah,** it is nevertheless **done for him.**[7]

וּמִתְרַפְּאִין בְּכָל אִסּוּרִין שֶׁבַּתּוֹרָה בִּמְקוֹם סַכָּנָה, חוּץ מֵעֲבוֹדָה זָרָה וְגִלּוּי עֲרָיוֹת וּשְׁפִיכוּת דָּמִים, שֶׁאֲפִלּוּ בִּמְקוֹם סַכָּנָה אֵין מִתְרַפְּאִין בָּהֶם. וְאִם עָבַר וְנִתְרַפֵּא – עוֹנְשִׁין אוֹתוֹ בֵּית דִּין עֹנֶשׁ הָרָאוּי לוֹ.

One may be healed through all of the prohibitions in the Torah in a situation of a danger,[8] **except for idol worship,**[9] **forbidden sexual relations, and bloodshed, for one may not be healed through** one of those three sins **even in a dangerous situation. If one transgressed** one of these three sins **and was healed** through one of them, **the court punishes him with his appropriate punishment.**

HALAKHIC DISCUSSION

1. But if the gentiles singled out a specific person for themselves – וְאִם יִחֲדוּהוּ לָהֶם: If that person has committed crimes against the government, for example, if he has forged money and the like, it is permitted to hand him over even if the gentiles have not singled him out, because he has endangered the whole community through his actions (*Baer Heitev*).

2. If that individual is liable to receive the death penalty – אִם הָיָה מְחֻיָּב מִיתָה: The Rema cites a dissenting opinion, according to which they should hand him over even if he is not liable to receive the death penalty. The later authorities rule in accordance with the Rambam (*Taz*).

3. Liable to death, like Sheva, son of Bikhri – מְחֻיָּב מִיתָה כְּשֶׁבַע בֶּן בִּכְרִי: This applies even if he is not liable to death according to Torah law, but only according to the laws of the gentile government (*Taz*).

4. They should all be killed and not hand over to them a single Jewish soul – יֵהָרְגוּ כֻּלָּם וְאַל יִמְסְרוּ לָהֶם נֶפֶשׁ אַחַת מִיִּשְׂרָאֵל: If the gentiles demand a specific number of people, but they do not care who they are, it is permitted to try to prevent a particular person from being taken even though this means that someone else will definitely be chosen instead. It is also permitted to perform a lottery for this purpose (*Pitḥei Teshuva*). During times of persecution, the ruling authorities indeed had to face such difficult questions (see, for example, Responsa *Memaamakim* 5:1, composed during the Holocaust). The authorities have stated that "it is hard to issue rulings in this regard, and the Sages said about such a matter that, just as it is a mitzva for a person to say that which will be heeded, so is it a mitzva for a person not to say that which will not be heeded (*Yevamot* 65b), and (Amos 5:13) 'the prudent at that time shall be silent'" (*Noda BiYehuda Tinyana*, *Yoreh De'a* 74).

5. They said the same with regard to sicknesses – כָּךְ אָמְרוּ בְּחֳלָאִים: *Shulḥan Arukh*, *Yoreh De'a* 155:2–3.

6. And the doctors said that his cure is a certain procedure – וְאָמְרוּ הָרוֹפְאִים שֶׁרְפוּאָתוֹ בְּדָבָר פְּלוֹנִי: This is permitted only if he is an expert doctor, or if the cure is well established (Rema).

7. It is done for him – עוֹשִׂין לוֹ: Even if the invalid does not want to be cured through this prohibition, his wishes are disregarded and he is forced to comply with the doctors' instructions (*Pitḥei Teshuva*).

NOTES

a. Who was liable to receive the death penalty for rebelling against King David (II Samuel, chap. 20).

HALAKHIC DISCUSSION

8. One may be healed through all of the prohibitions in the Torah in a dangerous situation – וּמִתְרַפְּאִין בְּכָל אִסּוּרִין שֶׁבַּתּוֹרָה בִּמְקוֹם סַכָּנָה: If the treatment can be administered in a permitted manner, it must be performed in that way, even if they will have to wait a while, provided that the invalid's life is not thereby endangered (Rema).

9. Except for idol worship – חוּץ מֵעֲבוֹדָה זָרָה: Accordingly, if a Jew is treated by a gentile, and the gentile instructs him to take an herb that is worshipped, the Jew is prohibited to follow that treatment. If the gentile did not mention the specific idolatry, but simply said that he should take a particular herb, then even if all the herbs of that type are worshipped, it is permitted for the Jew to take it, although some prohibit this (*Shulḥan Arukh*, *Yoreh De'a* 155:2).

Halakha 7

וּמִנַּיִן שֶׁאֲפִלּוּ בִּמְקוֹם סַכָּנַת נְפָשׁוֹת אֵין עוֹבְרִין עַל אַחַת מִשָּׁלֹשׁ עֲבֵרוֹת אֵלּוּ? שֶׁנֶּאֱמַר: "וְאָהַבְתָּ אֵת יי אֱלֹהֶיךָ בְּכָל לְבָבְךָ וּבְכָל נַפְשְׁךָ וּבְכָל מְאֹדֶךָ" (דברים ו,ה) – אֲפִלּוּ הוּא נוֹטֵל אֶת נַפְשְׁךָ.

From where is it derived that even in a life-threatening situation one may not violate any **one of these three prohibitions? As it is stated: "You shall love the Lord your God with all your heart, and with all your soul, and with all your might"** (Deuteronomy 6:5), which implies that one may not worship idols, but must remain faithful to God **even if He takes your soul.** This accounts for one of the three cardinal sins, idol worship.

וַהֲרִיגַת נֶפֶשׁ מִיִּשְׂרָאֵל לְרַפּוֹת נֶפֶשׁ אַחֶרֶת אוֹ לְהַצִּיל אָדָם מִיַּד אַנָּס – דָּבָר שֶׁהַדַּעַת נוֹטָה לוֹ הוּא, שֶׁאֵין מְאַבְּדִין נֶפֶשׁ מִפְּנֵי נֶפֶשׁ.

With regard to **killing a Jew to heal another person, or to save a person from a violent individual, it stands to reason that** one person's **life should not be sacrificed for** that of **another.**

וַעֲרָיוֹת הֻקְּשׁוּ לִנְפָשׁוֹת, שֶׁנֶּאֱמַר: "כִּי כַּאֲשֶׁר יָקוּם אִישׁ עַל רֵעֵהוּ וּרְצָחוֹ נֶפֶשׁ כֵּן הַדָּבָר הַזֶּה" (שם כב,כו).

And finally, having **forbidden sexual relations is juxtaposed** in the Torah **to** killing **people, as it is stated** in the verse cited above, involving a raped betrothed woman: "But to the young woman you shall do nothing; the young woman has no sin worthy of death, **as just like a man rises against his neighbor and murders him, so is this matter"** (Deuteronomy 22:26).

Halakha 8

בַּמֶּה דְּבָרִים אֲמוּרִים שֶׁאֵין מִתְרַפְּאִין בִּשְׁאָר אִסּוּרִין אֶלָּא בִּמְקוֹם סַכָּנָה? בִּזְמַן שֶׁהֵן דֶּרֶךְ הֲנָאָתָן, כְּמוֹ שֶׁמַּאֲכִילִין אֶת הַחוֹלֶה שְׁקָצִים וּרְמָשִׂים אוֹ חָמֵץ בְּפֶסַח, אוֹ שֶׁמַּאֲכִילִין אוֹתוֹ בְּיוֹם הַכִּפּוּרִים.

In what case **is this statement said,**[1] **that one may be healed through** the violation of **other prohibitions only in a situation of danger? When** they are used **in the typical manner that they are enjoyed. For example, when an invalid is fed repugnant creatures and creeping animals, or leavened bread on Passover, or if one is fed on Yom Kippur.**[a]

אֲבָל שֶׁלֹּא דֶּרֶךְ הֲנָאָתָן, כְּגוֹן שֶׁעוֹשִׂין לוֹ רְטִיָּה אוֹ מְלוּגְמָה מֵחָמֵץ אוֹ מֵעָרְלָה, אוֹ שֶׁמַּשְׁקִין אוֹתוֹ דְּבָרִים שֶׁיֵּשׁ בָּהֶן מַר מְעֹרָב עִם אִסּוּרֵי מַאֲכָל, שֶׁהֲרֵי אֵין בָּהֶן הֲנָיָה לַחֵךְ – הֲרֵי זֶה מֻתָּר, וַאֲפִלּוּ שֶׁלֹּא בִּמְקוֹם סַכָּנָה,

However, if the prohibited substances are used **not in the typical manner of their enjoyment, for example, if one makes** a smeared **bandage or a poultice**[b] **from leaven** on Passover, **or from** ***orla*****,**[c] **or when one is given something to drink that contains bitter** foods **mixed with forbidden foods**[d] – **since** one's **palate derives no enjoyment** from the taste – **it is permitted**[2] **even if it is not a situation of danger.**

חוּץ מִכִּלְאֵי הַכֶּרֶם וּבָשָׂר בְּחָלָב, שֶׁהֵן אֲסוּרִין אֲפִלּוּ שֶׁלֹּא דֶּרֶךְ הֲנָאָתָן, לְפִיכָךְ אֵין מִתְרַפְּאִין בָּהֶן אֲפִלּוּ שֶׁלֹּא דֶּרֶךְ הֲנָאָה, אֶלָּא בִּמְקוֹם סַכָּנָה.

This is the case for all forbidden foods **except for diverse kinds in a vineyard and** a mixture of **milk and meat, for they are prohibited even** when used **not in the typical manner of their enjoyment.**[e] **Consequently, one may not be healed with them even not in a manner of** their **enjoyment, unless it is a situation of danger.**

HALAKHIC DISCUSSION

1. In what case is this statement said – בַּמֶּה דְּבָרִים אֲמוּרִים: *Shulhan Arukh, Yoreh De'a* 155:3.

2. However, if the prohibited substances are used not in the typical manner of their enjoyment… it is permitted – אֲבָל שֶׁלֹּא דֶּרֶךְ הֲנָאָתָן...הֲרֵי זֶה מֻתָּר: If the issue is a rabbinic prohibition, one may be healed even by using the substances in the typical manner of their enjoyment, provided that he does not eat or drink a forbidden food (Rema). The later authorities state that an invalid whose life is not in danger may not swallow something that is prohibited to eat by Torah law, since that is considered its typical manner of enjoyment. If the forbidden food has dried up completely until it is like the bark of a tree, with no moisture at all, one may be lenient and eat it, since this is regarded as not its typical manner of enjoyment (*Pithei Teshuva*; with regard to swallowing pills, see the appendix on *Sefer Kedusha, Laws of Forbidden Foods*: "The Kosher Status of Medicines").

NOTES

a. See also *Hilkhot Shevitat Asor* 2:8.

b. When chewed food is placed on the skin as a cure.

c. Fruit of a tree during the first three years after its planting, which it is prohibited to eat.

d. See also *Hilkhot Maakhalot Asurot* 14:11.

e. This is because the prohibition in these two cases is not written in terms of eating them, but rather expressed in a different manner (see *Hilkhot Maakhalot Asurot* 14:10).

Halakha 9

מִי שֶׁנָּתַן עֵינָיו בְּאִשָּׁה, וְחָלָה וְנָטָה לָמוּת, וְאָמְרוּ רוֹפְאִים: 'אֵין לוֹ רְפוּאָה עַד שֶׁתִּבָּעֵל לוֹ', אֲפִלּוּ הָיְתָה פְּנוּיָה, וַאֲפִלּוּ לְדַבֵּר עִמּוֹ מֵאֲחוֹרֵי גָּדֵר – אֵין מוֹרִין לוֹ בְּכָךְ,

In the case of **one who has set his eyes upon** a certain **woman to** the extent that **he has become sick and tends toward death, and the doctors say** that **"he has no remedy other than her having relations with him," even if she is unmarried,** and thus no Torah prohibition is involved, **and even** if he just wants her **to speak with him** in private **behind a fence, he may not be instructed** to do **so.**

וְיָמוּת וְלֹא יוֹרוּ לוֹ לְדַבֵּר עִמּוֹ מֵאֲחוֹרֵי הַגָּדֵר, שֶׁלֹּא יְהוּ בְּנוֹת יִשְׂרָאֵל הֶפְקֵר, וְיָבֹאוּ בִּדְבָרִים אֵלּוּ לִפְרֹץ בַּעֲרָיוֹת.

Instead, **he should die rather than be instructed** that **she may speak with him behind a fence.** The purpose of this stringent halakha is to ensure **that Jewish women will not be treated with disregard, and come, through these events, to breach** the boundaries **of forbidden sexual relations.**

Halakha 10

כׇּל הָעוֹבֵר מִדַּעְתּוֹ בְּלֹא אֹנֶס עַל אַחַת מִכׇּל מִצְוֹת הָאֲמוּרוֹת בַּתּוֹרָה, בְּשָׁאט בְּנֶפֶשׁ לְהַכְעִיס – הֲרֵי זֶה מְחַלֵּל אֶת הַשֵּׁם.

Anyone who knowingly, when not under duress, transgresses one of the mitzvot that are stated in the Torah, impudently, to express insolence toward God, he **desecrates** God's **name.**

וּלְפִיכָךְ נֶאֱמַר בִּשְׁבוּעַת שֶׁקֶר: "וְחִלַּלְתָּ אֶת שֵׁם אֱלֹהֶיךָ אֲנִי יי" (ויקרא יט,יב).

It is therefore stated with regard to taking **a false oath: "As you will profane the name of your God: I am the Lord"** (Leviticus 19:12). This teaches that even though taking a false oath is not one of the cardinal sins, its violation still constitutes the desecration of God's name,[a] and the same applies to any sin performed as a way of expressing insolence toward God.

וְאִם עָבַר בַּעֲשָׂרָה מִיִּשְׂרָאֵל – הֲרֵי זֶה חִלֵּל אֶת הַשֵּׁם בָּרַבִּים. וְכֵן כׇּל הַפּוֹרֵשׁ מֵעֲבֵרָה אוֹ עָשָׂה מִצְוָה לֹא מִפְּנֵי דָּבָר בָּעוֹלָם, לֹא פַּחַד וְלֹא יִרְאָה וְלֹא לְבַקֵּשׁ כָּבוֹד, אֶלָּא מִפְּנֵי הַבּוֹרֵא בָּרוּךְ הוּא, כִּמְנִיעַת יוֹסֵף הַצַּדִּיק עַצְמוֹ מֵאֵשֶׁת רַבּוֹ – הֲרֵי זֶה מְקַדֵּשׁ אֶת הַשֵּׁם.

If he transgressed in the presence of **ten Jews, he has desecrated** God's **name in public.** In a **similar** vein, **anyone who withdraws from a transgression or performs a mitzva not for any ulterior motive, not out of fright or fear, and not to seek honor, but** solely **because of the Creator blessed be He,** just **like Joseph the Righteous withheld himself from his master's wife,**[b] **he** thereby **sanctifies** God's **name.**

NOTES

a. See also *Hilkhot Shevuot* 12:1.

b. Joseph refused to listen to the exhortations of Potifar's wife to lie with her, declaring: "How can I do this great evil, and sin to God?" (Genesis 39:9).

Halakha 11

וְיֵשׁ דְּבָרִים אֲחֵרִים שֶׁהֵם בִּכְלַל חִלּוּל הַשֵּׁם, וְהוּא שֶׁיַּעֲשֶׂה אָדָם גָּדוֹל בַּתּוֹרָה וּמְפֻרְסָם בַּחֲסִידוּת דְּבָרִים שֶׁהַבְּרִיּוֹת מְרַנְּנוֹת אַחֲרָיו בִּשְׁבִילָן, וְאַף עַל פִּי שֶׁאֵינָם עֲבֵרוֹת – הֲרֵי זֶה חִלֵּל אֶת הַשֵּׁם.

There are other things that are also included in the category **of the desecration of** God's **name. This is when a person who is a great Torah scholar and renowned for** his **piety performs deeds on account of which people speak disparagingly of him, even though they are not transgressions. This** person **has desecrated** God's **name.**

כְּגוֹן שֶׁלּוֹקֵחַ וְאֵינוֹ נוֹתֵן דְּמֵי הַלֶּקַח לְאַלְתַּר, וְהוּא יֵשׁ לוֹ, וְנִמְצְאוּ הַמּוֹכְרִין תּוֹבְעִין וְהוּא מַקִּיפָן,

This applies, **for example, if** such an individual **purchases** an item **and does not give the money of the purchase immediately,**[a] provided that **he has** the funds available. **Thus, the sellers** in this case **demand** payment **and** yet **he buys at credit.**

אוֹ שֶׁיַּרְבֶּה בִּשְׂחוֹק אוֹ בַּאֲכִילָה וּשְׁתִיָּה אֵצֶל עַמֵּי הָאָרֶץ וּבֵינֵיהֶן, אוֹ שֶׁאֵין דִּבּוּרוֹ בְּנַחַת עִם הַבְּרִיּוֹת וְאֵינוֹ מְקַבְּלָן בְּסֵבֶר פָּנִים יָפוֹת, אֶלָּא בַּעַל קְטָטָה וְכַעַס, וְכַיּוֹצֵא בִּדְבָרִים הָאֵלּוּ. הַכֹּל לְפִי גָּדְלוֹ שֶׁל חָכָם, צָרִיךְ שֶׁיְּדַקְדֵּק עַל עַצְמוֹ וְיַעֲשֶׂה לִפְנִים מִשּׁוּרַת הַדִּין.

Or if he laughs immoderately, or engages **in eating and drinking with and among boorish** people,[b] **or if he does not speak gently to** all **people and does not receive them with a pleasant countenance, but is a quarrelsome, angry person, and similar conduct. Everything** depends **on the stature of the** Torah **scholar.** A great scholar **must be** especially **particular with himself and act beyond the letter of the law.**

וְכֵן אִם דִּקְדֵּק הֶחָכָם עַל עַצְמוֹ, וְהָיָה דִּבּוּרוֹ בְּנַחַת עִם הַבְּרִיּוֹת וְדַעְתּוֹ מְעֹרֶבֶת עִמָּהֶם, וּמְקַבְּלָן בְּסֵבֶר פָּנִים יָפוֹת, וְנֶעֱלָב מֵהֶן וְאֵינוֹ עוֹלְבָן, מְכַבֵּד לָהֶם וַאֲפִלּוּ לַמְקִלִּין לוֹ, וְנוֹשֵׂא וְנוֹתֵן בֶּאֱמוּנָה, וְלֹא יַרְבֶּה בַּאֲרִיחוּת עַמֵּי הָאָרֶץ וִישִׁיבָתָן, וְלֹא יֵרָאֶה תָּמִיד אֶלָּא עוֹסֵק בַּתּוֹרָה, עָטוּף בְּצִיצִית, מֻכְתָּר בִּתְפִלִּין, וְעוֹשֶׂה בְּכָל מַעֲשָׂיו לִפְנִים מִשּׁוּרַת הַדִּין, וְהוּא שֶׁלֹּא יִתְרַחֵק הַרְבֵּה וְלֹא יִשְׁתּוֹמֵם, עַד שֶׁיִּמָּצְאוּ הַכֹּל מְקַלְּסִין אוֹתוֹ וְאוֹהֲבִין אוֹתוֹ וּמִתְאַוִּין לְמַעֲשָׂיו – הֲרֵי זֶה קִדֵּשׁ אֶת הַשֵּׁם, וְעָלָיו הַכָּתוּב אוֹמֵר: "וַיֹּאמֶר לִי עַבְדִּי אָתָּה יִשְׂרָאֵל אֲשֶׁר בְּךָ אֶתְפָּאָר" (ישעיהו מט,ג).

In a **similar** vein, **if the** Torah **scholar is particular with himself; speaks gently to** all **people;**[c] **is engaged with the concerns of others; receives them with a pleasant countenance;** allows himself **to be insulted by them and does not insult them** in return;[d] **honors them,** including **even those who disrespect him; conducts his business faithfully,** fairly and with integrity; **is not a frequent guest of boorish** people **or** attends **their gatherings; and is invariably seen only engaging in Torah, wrapped in ritual fringes, crowned with phylacteries,**[e] **and performing all his actions beyond the letter of the law – provided he does not** act in such an extreme fashion that he **separates himself too much** from others **and is not** thereby left **isolated**[f] – and he conducts himself in this manner **to** the extent **that all are found to praise him, love him, and yearn** to imitate **his deeds, he has sanctified** God's **name. With regard to** such an individual, **the verse states: "He said to me: You are My servant, Israel, in whom I glory"** (Isaiah 49:3).

NOTES

a. See also *Hilkhot Deot* 5:13.

b. See also *Hilkhot Deot* 2:7, 5:2.

c. See also *Hilkhot Deot* 5:7.

d. See *Hilkhot Talmud Torah* 7:13.

e. See *Hilkhot Tefillin UMezuza VeSefer Torah* 4:25.

f. See *Hilkhot Deot* 3:1.

פֶּרֶק שִׁשִּׁי

CHAPTER 6

The Prohibition Against Eradicating God's Name and Sacred Items

Halakhot 1–6:	Erasing the names of God
Halakha 7:	Destroying Temple stones and consecrated wood
Halakha 8:	Eradicating holy writings
Halakha 9:	The status of the various appellations of God in the Bible

Halakha 1

כָּל הַמְאַבֵּד שֵׁם מִן הַשֵּׁמוֹת הַקְּדוֹשִׁים הַטְּהוֹרִים שֶׁנִּקְרָא בָּהֶן הַקָּדוֹשׁ בָּרוּךְ הוּא – לוֹקֶה מִן הַתּוֹרָה, שֶׁהֲרֵי הוּא אוֹמֵר בַּעֲבוֹדָה זָרָה: "וְאִבַּדְתֶּם אֶת שְׁמָם מִן הַמָּקוֹם הַהוּא, לֹא תַעֲשׂוּן כֵּן לַיי אֱלֹהֵיכֶם" (דברים יב, ג–ד).

Whoever destroys one of the holy, pure names by which the Holy One blessed be He is called is flogged by Torah law, for it is stated with regard **to idol worship: "And you shall eradicate their name.... You shall not do so to the Lord your God"** (Deuteronomy 12:3–4).

Halakha 2

וְשִׁבְעָה שֵׁמוֹת הֵן: הַשֵּׁם שֶׁנִּכְתָּב יוֹ"ד הֵ"א וָא"ו הֵ"א, וְהוּא הַשֵּׁם הַמְפֹרָשׁ, אוֹ הַנִּכְתָּב אַלֶ"ף דַּא"ל נוּ"ן יוֹ"ד; וְאֵל, וֶאֱלוֹהַּ, וֵאלֹהִים, וְאֶהְיֶה, וְשַׁדַּי, וּצְבָאוֹת. כָּל הַמּוֹחֵק אֲפִלּוּ אוֹת אַחַת מִשִּׁבְעָה שֵׁמוֹת אֵלּוּ – לוֹקֶה.

There are seven names[1] for God: **The name that is written** with the letters ***yod-heh-vav-heh*****, which is the ineffable name** of God, the Tetragrammaton, **or which is** the name **written** with the letters ***alef-dalet-nun-yod*****,**[2] the "name of Lordship," which is the manner in which one pronounces the Tetragrammaton;[a] and the names ***El*****;** ***Elo'a*****;** ***Elohim*****;** ***Eheyeh*****;** ***Shaddai*****;** **and** ***Tzevaot*****. Anyone who erases**[3] **even one letter from** any of **these seven names is flogged.**[4]

NOTES

a. *Hilkhot Tefilla UVirkat Kohanim* 14:10; see *Hilkhot Avoda Zara* 2:7.

HALAKHIC DISCUSSION

1. There are seven names – וְשִׁבְעָה שֵׁמוֹת הֵן: *Shulḥan Arukh, Yoreh De'a* 276:9.

2. That is written *alef-dalet-nun-yod* – הַנִּכְתָּב אַלֶ"ף דַּא"ל נוּ"ן יוֹ"ד: If one wrote the name with a line between each letter, some say that this is no different than writing the actual name itself (*Avnei Nezer, Yoreh De'a* 665), while others are more lenient (see *Shevet HaLevi* 3:170; *Peninei Halakha, Likkutim* 1, 5:8).

3. Anyone who erases – כָּל הַמּוֹחֵק: With regard to deleting names of God written on a computer screen, the later authorities note that there are several reasons for leniency here: First, this is not considered actual writing; second, such writing is meant to be deleted, or at least removed; third, the erasure is performed in an indirect manner (Responsa *Teshuvot VeHanhagot* 3:326; Responsa *Ateret Paz* 1, vol. 2, *Yoreh De'a* 13:4).

4. Anyone who erases even one letter... is flogged – כָּל הַמּוֹחֵק אֲפִלּוּ אוֹת אַחַת...לוֹקֶה: It is permitted to dismantle a name that is comprised of letters designed to be taken apart (such as the letters of a printing press), although some are stringent in this case (*Pitḥei Teshuva* 276:17). With regard to erasing God's name from a Torah scroll that requires emendation, see *Shulḥan Arukh, Yoreh De'a* 276:11–12.

Halakha 3

כָּל הַנִּטְפָּל לַשֵּׁם מִלְּפָנָיו – מֻתָּר לְמָחֳקוֹ. כְּגוֹן לָמֶ״ד מִ׳לַייָ׳, וּבֵי״ת מִ׳בֵּאלֹהִים׳, וְכַיּוֹצֵא בָּהֶן – אֵינָן כִּקְדֻשַּׁת הַשֵּׁם. וְכָל הַנִּטְפָּל לַשֵּׁם מֵאֲחוֹרָיו, כְּגוֹן כָּא״ף שֶׁל ׳אֱלֹהֶיךָ׳, וְכָא״ף מֵי״ם שֶׁל ׳אֱלֹהֵיכֶם׳, וְכַיּוֹצֵא בָּהֶן – אֵינָן נִמְחָקִין, וַהֲרֵי הֵן כִּשְׁאָר אוֹתִיּוֹת שֶׁל שֵׁם, מִפְּנֵי שֶׁהַשֵּׁם מְקַדְּשָׁן.

With regard to **any** letter **used as a prefix to** God's **name,**[1] **it is permitted to erase it. For example,** the letter ***lamed* of *l'Adonai*,** or the letter ***bet* of *b'Elohim*, and the like. They do not** possess the same degree **of holiness as the name** itself. However, **any** letter **used as a suffix to** God's **name, such as** the letter ***khaf* of *elohekha*,** or the letters ***khaf* and *mem* of *eloheikhem*, and the like, may not be erased, and they are like the other letters of** God's **name.** This is **because the name sanctifies them.**

וְאַף עַל פִּי שֶׁנִּתְקַדְּשׁוּ וְאָסוּר לְמָחֳקָן – הַמּוֹחֵק אֵלּוּ הָאוֹתִיּוֹת הַנִּטְפָּלוֹת אֵינוֹ לוֹקֶה, אֲבָל מַכִּין אוֹתוֹ מַכַּת מַרְדּוּת.

But although they were sanctified, and it is prohibited to erase them, one who erases these letters that are connected as suffixes to the name of God **is not flogged. However,** the court **strikes him with lashes for rebelliousness,** which one receives for intentionally violating rabbinic decrees.

Halakha 4

כָּתַב אָלֶ״ף לָמֶ״ד מֵ׳אֱלֹהִים׳, יוֹ״ד הֵ״א מֵ׳יי׳ – אֵינוֹ נִמְחָק. וְאֵין צָרִיךְ לוֹמַר ׳יָהּ׳, שֶׁהוּא שֵׁם בִּפְנֵי עַצְמוֹ, מִפְּנֵי שֶׁזֶּה הַשֵּׁם מִקְצָת שֵׁם הַמְפֹרָשׁ הוּא.

If **one wrote** the letters ***alef*** and ***lamed* from** the name ***Elohim***[2] or the letters ***yod* and *heh* from** the name written with the letters ***yod-heh-vav-heh*,** those letters **may not be erased. Needless to say,** this applies if he intended to write the name ***Yah*** with the letters *yod* and *heh*, **because this name is part of the ineffable name,** and is therefore considered a name in its own right.

אֲבָל הַכּוֹתֵב שִׁי״ן דָּלֶ״ת מִ׳שַּׁדַּי׳, צָדִ״י בֵּי״ת מִ׳צְּבָאוֹת׳ – הֲרֵי זֶה נִמְחָק.

However, if one writes the letters ***shin*** and ***dalet* from the name *Shaddai*,** or the letters ***tzadi*** and ***beit* from the name *Tzevaot*,** those letters **may be erased.**

GLOSSES OF THE RAAVAD

״כָּתַב אֵל מֵאֱלֹהִים וְיָהּ מִיהו־ה אֵינוֹ נִמְחָק.״ אָמַר אַבְרָהָם: זֶה אֵינוֹ כְּלוּם שֶׁלֹּא אָמְרוּ אֶלָּא אֵל מֵאֱלֹהִים וְיָהּ מִיהו־ה, אֲבָל שַׁד מִשַּׁדַּי וְצַב מִצְּבָאוֹת הֲרֵי אֵלּוּ נִמְחָקִין.

"One wrote *El* from *Elohim* or *Ya* from *yod-heh-vav-heh*, those letters may not be erased." Avraham says: This is worthless, for the Sages only said that ***El* from *Elohim* and *Ya* from** the name written with the letters ***yod-heh-vav-heh*** may not be erased, **but *Shad* from *Shaddai* and *Tzav* from *Tzevaot* may be erased.**[a]

NOTES

a. Evidently the Raavad had a different version of the text of the Rambam than the one before us today.

HALAKHIC DISCUSSION

1. Any letter used as a prefix to God's name – כָּל הַנִּטְפָּל לַשֵּׁם מִלְּפָנָיו: *Shulḥan Arukh, Yoreh De'a* 276:9.

2. One wrote *alef* and *lamed* from *Elohim* – כָּתַב אָלֶ״ף לָמֶ״ד מֵאֱלֹהִים: *Shulḥan Arukh, Yoreh De'a* 276:10. As for the form of the name of God that appears in prayer books, with two letters *yod* next to each other and another one above them, one may erase it if there is a great need to do so (Rema, *Yoreh De'a* 276:10), and the same applies if it was written simply as two letters *yod* (*Pitḥei Teshuva*; *Arukh HaShulḥan*). Some authorities permit these names to be erased even if there is no need (*Sefer Ḥasidim* 935; see *Yeḥaveh Daat* 4:50). With regard to shorthand ways of writing the name of God, such as a letter *heh* with a stroke above it, or the acronym *beit-ayin-zayin-heh* in Hebrew (which stands for *be'ezrat Hashem*, with the help of God) and the like, some maintain that it is permitted to erase them, but one should not treat them in a degrading manner (*Arukh HaShulḥan*; *Tzitz Eliezer* 22:51), whereas others contend that they should not be erased unless there is a good reason (*Pitḥei Teshuva*; see *Iggerot Moshe, Yoreh De'a* 2:138).

Most authorities agree that it is permitted to erase shorthand names that do not include any of the letters of God, such as a *dalet* with a stroke above it. For this reason it is customary to write the letters *beit-samekh-dalet* (an acronym for *besiyata diShmaya*, "with the help of Heaven") rather than *beit-heh* (*Barukh Hashem*, "blessed be the Lord") at the start of letters of correspondence (*Iggerot Moshe, Yoreh De'a* 2:138; *Betzel HaḤokhma* 4:105; see *Yeḥaveh Daat* 3:78, where it is stated that there is no problem with writing *beit-heh* at the start of a letter of correspondence). As for names of God in other languages, such as the English word "God" itself, they have the status of appellations of God and therefore it is permitted to erase them (Rabbi Akiva Eiger on *Yoreh De'a* 276:9; see *Hilkhot Sanhedrin* 26:3), although some rule stringently that they should not be erased if they are written out in Hebrew letters (see *Pitḥei Teshuva* on 276:11).

NOTES

a. See *Hilkhot Keriat Shema* 3:4.

b. *Hilkhot Mikvaot* 1:12.

BACKGROUND

He wraps a reed – כּוֹרֵךְ עָלָיו גֶּמִי:

Reeds

Halakha 5

שְׁאָר הַכִּנּוּיִין שֶׁמְּשַׁבְּחִין בָּהֶן הַקָּדוֹשׁ בָּרוּךְ הוּא, כְּגוֹן חַנּוּן וְרַחוּם, הַגָּדוֹל הַגִּבּוֹר וְהַנּוֹרָא, הַנֶּאֱמָן, קַנָּא וְחָזָק, וְכַיּוֹצֵא בָּהֶן – הֲרֵי הֵן כִּשְׁאָר דִּבְרֵי הַקֹּדֶשׁ, וּמֻתָּר לְמָחֳקָן.

The **other appellations with which the Holy One blessed be He is praised, such as Gracious and Compassionate, the Great, the Mighty, the Awesome, the Faithful, Zealous, and Powerful, and the like, are similar to other sacred texts, and it is permitted to erase them.**[1]

Halakha 6

כְּלִי שֶׁהָיָה שֵׁם כָּתוּב עָלָיו – קוֹצֵץ אֶת מְקוֹם הַשֵּׁם וְגוֹנְזוֹ. אֲפִלּוּ הָיָה הַשֵּׁם חָקוּק בִּכְלִי מַתָּכוֹת אוֹ בִּכְלִי זְכוּכִית, וְהִתִּיךְ הַכְּלִי – הֲרֵי זֶה לוֹקֶה, אֶלָּא חוֹתֵךְ אֶת מְקוֹמוֹ וְגוֹנְזוֹ. וְכֵן אִם הָיָה שֵׁם כָּתוּב עַל בְּשָׂרוֹ – הֲרֵי זֶה לֹא יִרְחַץ וְלֹא יָסוּךְ וְלֹא יַעֲמֹד בִּמְקוֹם הַטִּנֹּפֶת.

With regard to **a utensil that has a name** of God **written on it,**[2] **one cuts off the area of the name and inters it. Even if the name was engraved on a metal or glass utensil, and one melted the utensil, he is flogged. Instead, one cuts off its area and inters it. Similarly, if a name** of God **was written on one's flesh, he may not bathe** in case the name is erased by the water, **or smear** oil on his flesh, **or stand in a place of filth,** where there is excrement and the like, due to the sanctity of the name.[a]

נִזְדַּמְּנָה לוֹ טְבִילָה שֶׁל מִצְוָה – כּוֹרֵךְ עָלָיו גֶּמִי וְטוֹבֵל. וְאִם לֹא מָצָא גֶּמִי – מְסַבֵּב אַחֲרָיו. וְלֹא יְהַדֵּק, כְּדֵי שֶׁלֹּא יָחֹץ,

If an immersion by means of which one fulfills a **mitzva happened** to present itself **to him,**[3] **he wraps a reed over** God's name **and** then **immerses. If he cannot find a reed, he should** continue to **search** until he finds one. **He should not** wrap the reed so **tightly** around his skin **that it will form a barrier** between his skin and the water. A barrier between one's skin and the water invalidates a ritual immersion.[b]

שֶׁלֹּא אָמְרוּ לִכְרֹךְ עָלָיו אֶלָּא מִפְּנֵי שֶׁאָסוּר לַעֲמֹד בִּפְנֵי הַשֵּׁם עָרֹם.

For the Sages **said** that he should **wrap** a reed **around it only because it is prohibited to stand in the presence of** God's **name** when one is **naked.** Consequently, it is enough to wrap the reed around the name; he does not have to place it tightly upon it.

HALAKHIC DISCUSSION

1. Similar to other sacred texts, and it is permitted to erase them – הֲרֵי הֵן כִּשְׁאָר דִּבְרֵי הַקֹּדֶשׁ וּמֻתָּר לְמָחֳקָן: Even so, one should not erase them for no reason (Responsa *Ein Yitzḥak* 5:4; see Halakha 8).

2. A utensil that has a name of God written on it – כְּלִי שֶׁהָיָה שֵׁם כָּתוּב עָלָיו: *Shulḥan Arukh, Yoreh De'a* 276:13. One should not write a name of God on anything other than a book, *ab initio*, lest it comes to be treated in a disrespectful manner. Accordingly, one should take care not to write God's name in a letter of correspondence (Rema).

3. If an immersion by means of which he fulfills a mitzva happened to present itself to him – נִזְדַּמְּנָה לוֹ טְבִילָה שֶׁל מִצְוָה: Although the name on his skin will be erased during the immersion, it is permitted because it will be erased through an indirect action. It is prohibited to cause this kind of erasure to occur by taking any other, active, measure, such as by placing water right next to one's skin so that it will fall on the name and rub it out (*Arukh HaShulḥan, Yoreh De'a* 276:36).

Halakha 7

הַסּוֹתֵר אֲפִלּוּ אֶבֶן אַחַת דֶּרֶךְ הַשְׁחָתָה מִן הַמִּזְבֵּחַ אוֹ מִן הַהֵיכָל אוֹ מִשְּׁאָר הָעֲזָרָה – לוֹקֶה, שֶׁנֶּאֱמַר בַּעֲבוֹדָה זָרָה: "כִּי אֶת מִזְבְּחֹתָם תִּתֹּצוּן" (שמות לד, יג), וְכָתוּב: "לֹא תַעֲשׂוּן כֵּן לַיי" (דברים יב, ד).

One who dismantles even one stone[a] **in a destructive manner from the altar, or from the Sanctuary, or from** the **rest of the** Temple **courtyard, is flogged, as it is stated** with regard **to idol worship: "Rather, you shall smash their altars"** (Exodus 34:13), **and it is written:** "You shall smash their altars... **You shall not do so to the Lord your God"** (Deuteronomy 12:3–4).

וְכֵן הַשּׂוֹרֵף עֲצֵי הַקֹּדֶשׁ דֶּרֶךְ הַשְׁחָתָה – לוֹקֶה, שֶׁנֶּאֱמַר: "וַאֲשֵׁרֵיהֶם תִּשְׂרְפוּן... לֹא תַעֲשׂוּן" (שם יב, ג–ד).

Likewise, one who burns consecrated wood[b] **in a destructive manner is flogged, as it is stated: "And their sacred trees you shall burn in fire... You shall not do so to the Lord your God"** (Deuteronomy 12:3–4).

Halakha 8

כִּתְבֵי הַקֹּדֶשׁ כֻּלָּן וּפֵרוּשֵׁיהֶן וּבֵאוּרֵיהֶן – אָסוּר לִשְׂרֹף אוֹתָן אוֹ לְאַבְּדָן בַּיָּד. וְהַמְאַבֵּד בַּיָּד – לוֹקֶה מַכַּת מַרְדּוּת. בַּמֶּה דְּבָרִים אֲמוּרִים? בְּכִתְבֵי הַקֹּדֶשׁ שֶׁכְּתָבוּ אוֹתָן יִשְׂרָאֵל בִּקְדֻשָּׁה.

With regard to **all sacred writings,** including **their commentaries and their explanations,**[1] **it is prohibited to burn them or eradicate them through direct action.** In the case of **one who did eradicate** them **through direct action,** the court **strikes him with lashes for rebelliousness. In what** case **is this statement said? In** the case of **sacred writings that were written by a Jew with** the intent that they would be **sacred.**[2]

אֲבָל מִין יִשְׂרְאֵלִי שֶׁכָּתַב סֵפֶר תּוֹרָה – שׂוֹרְפִין אוֹתוֹ עִם הָאַזְכָּרוֹת שֶׁבּוֹ, מִפְּנֵי שֶׁאֵינוֹ מַאֲמִין בִּקְדֻשַּׁת הַשֵּׁם, וְלֹא כְּתָבוֹ אֶלָּא וְהוּא מַעֲלֶה בְּדַעְתּוֹ שֶׁזֶּה כִּשְׁאָר הַדְּבָרִים, וְהוֹאִיל וְדַעְתּוֹ כֵּן – לֹא נִתְקַדֵּשׁ הַשֵּׁם, וּמִצְוָה לְשָׂרְפוֹ כְּדֵי שֶׁלֹּא לְהַנִּיחַ שֵׁם לַמִּינִים וְלֹא לְמַעֲשֵׂיהֶם. אֲבָל גּוֹי שֶׁכָּתַב אֶת הַשֵּׁם – גּוֹנְזִין אוֹתוֹ. וְכֵן כִּתְבֵי הַקֹּדֶשׁ שֶׁבָּלוּ אוֹ שֶׁכְּתָבָן גּוֹי – יִגָּנְזוּ.

However, if **a Jewish heretic,** one who denies the existence or unity of God,[c] **wrote a Torah scroll, one burns it together with the names of God it contains.**[d] This is **because he does not believe in the sanctity of** God's **name**[3] **and wrote it only with the thought that it is like other texts. Since that is his intent,** any **name** of God he writes **is not sanctified, and it is a mitzva to burn it**[4] **so that no remembrance will be left of the heretics or their deeds.** If, **however,** it was **a gentile who wrote the name, it is interred. Likewise, sacred writings that became tattered,**[e] **or which were written by a gentile, should be interred.**

HALAKHIC DISCUSSION

1. **All sacred writings, including their commentaries and their explanations** – כִּתְבֵי הַקֹּדֶשׁ כֻּלָּן וּפֵרוּשֵׁיהֶן וּבֵאוּרֵיהֶן: These texts have sanctity not only when they are handwritten, but also when they are printed (*Taz* on *Shulḥan Arukh*, *Yoreh De'a* 271:8; with regard to the manner of their internment, see the appendix: "Interring Printed Sacred Texts").

2. **That were written by a Jew with the intent that they would be sacred** – שֶׁכְּתָבוּ אוֹתָן יִשְׂרָאֵל בִּקְדֻשָּׁה: The name of God must be written with the intention for it to be sacred (*Hilkhot Tefillin UMezuza VeSefer Torah* 1:15). A holy name that was written without such intent may be erased for the purpose of emending a Torah scroll (*Shakh* on *Shulḥan Arukh*, *Yoreh De'a* 276:9). If, for example, one meant to write the name Yehuda, which consists of the letters *yod-heh-vav-dalet-heh*, and he accidentally omitted the letter *dalet* (leaving *yod-heh-vav-heh*, the Tetragrammaton), this name has no sanctity and one may erase it (*Beit Yosef*).

3. **One burns it together with the names of God it contains, because he does not believe in the sanctity of God's name** – שׂוֹרְפִין אוֹתוֹ עִם הָאַזְכָּרוֹת שֶׁבּוֹ מִפְּנֵי שֶׁאֵינוֹ מַאֲמִין בִּקְדֻשַּׁת הַשֵּׁם: *Shulḥan Arukh*, *Yoreh De'a* 281:1, *Oraḥ Ḥayyim* 334:21. According to the Rambam, a *min*, translated here as a "heretic," is one who denies the existence or unity of God, whereas according to Rashi and other early authorities, *min* means someone who is dedicated to idol worship (see *Hilkhot Teshuva* 3:7, and the "Halakhic Discussion" there). In their opinion, a Torah scroll written by a *min* is burned because it was certainly written for idolatrous purposes, and the *Shulḥan Arukh* rules likewise (see *Beit Yosef* on *Oraḥ Ḥayyim* 39:4 and *Beur Halakha* there; *Beit Yosef* and *Shulḥan Arukh*, *Oraḥ Ḥayyim* 334:21; *Shulḥan Arukh*, *Yoreh De'a* 281:1, and *Shakh* there).

4. **And it is a mitzva to burn it** – וּמִצְוָה לְשָׂרְפוֹ: The later authorities dispute the law with regard to books written by missionaries that contain holy names of God. Some maintain that it is a mitzva to burn them (*Iggerot Moshe*, *Yoreh De'a* 1:172), whereas others disagree, arguing that those who print these texts do not have idol worship in mind (*Tzitz Eliezer* 15, 32:3; see *Shevet HaLevi* 2:143).

NOTES

a. See also *Hilkhot Beit HaBeḥira* 1:17.

b. Wood that has been consecrated for the maintenance of the Temple (Responsa of the Rambam, 160).

c. As explained in *Hilkhot Teshuva* 3:7.

d. See also *Hilkhot Tefillin UMezuza VeSefer Torah* 1:13.

e. See also *Hilkhot Tefillin UMezuza VeSefer Torah* 10:3.

Halakha 9

כָּל הַשֵּׁמוֹת הָאֲמוּרוֹת בְּאַבְרָהָם – קֹדֶשׁ. אַף זֶה שֶׁנֶּאֱמַר: ״אֲדֹנָי אִם נָא מָצָאתִי חֵן בְּעֵינֶיךָ״ (בראשית יח, ג) – הֲרֵי הוּא קֹדֶשׁ.

All the names of God **that are stated in** the section involving **Abraham** and the angels are **sacred.** The name *Adonai*, which appears repeatedly in the description of the angels' visit to Abraham (Genesis chap. 18), refers to God. **Even this** name **that is stated** in the following verse: **"He said: My Lord** [*Adonai*], **if indeed I have found favor in Your eyes"** (Genesis 18:3), **is sacred.**

כָּל הַשֵּׁמוֹת הָאֲמוּרוֹת בְּלוֹט – חֹל, חוּץ מִזֶּה: ״אַל נָא אֲדֹנָי, הִנֵּה נָא מָצָא עַבְדְּךָ חֵן״ (שם יט, יח–יט).

By contrast, **all the names** of God **that are stated in** the section involving **Lot** and the angels are **non-sacred**[1] **except for this** one: **"Please, no, my Lord. Please, behold, Your servant has found favor"** (Genesis 19:18–19). The same name, *adonai*, when it is used in Genesis chap. 19, refers to the angels, and it means "my lord," with only that one exception.

כָּל הַשֵּׁמוֹת הָאֲמוּרוֹת בְּגִבְעַת בִּנְיָמִין – קֹדֶשׁ.

All the names of God **that are stated in** the section involving **Giva of Benjamin** are **sacred.** The children of Israel asked God whether they should wage war against the tribe of Benjamin (Judges chap. 20). Although it would seem that the answer they were given failed to materialize, those names nevertheless refer to God.

כָּל הַשֵּׁמוֹת הָאֲמוּרוֹת בְּמִיכָה – חֹל. כָּל הַשֵּׁמוֹת הָאֲמוּרוֹת בְּנָבוֹת – קֹדֶשׁ.

All the names of God **that are stated in** the section involving the idol of **Mikha** (Judges chap. 17–18) are **non-sacred.** Those names refer to idolatry, not God. **All the names** of God **that are stated in** the section involving **Navot** are **sacred.** When Ahav falsely accused Navot of blasphemy: "You blessed God and the king" (1 Kings 21:10, 21:13), the wicked king was not referring to his own form of idol worship.

כָּל שְׁלֹמֹה הָאָמוּר בְּשִׁיר הַשִּׁירִים – קֹדֶשׁ, וַהֲרֵי הוּא כִּשְׁאָר הַכִּנּוּיִין, חוּץ מִזֶּה: ״הָאֶלֶף לְךָ שְׁלֹמֹה״ (שיר השירים ח, יב). כָּל מַלְכַיָּא הָאָמוּר בְּדָנִיֵּאל – חֹל, חוּץ מִזֶּה: ״אַנְתְּ מַלְכָּא מֶלֶךְ מַלְכַיָּא״ (דניאל ב, לז), וַהֲרֵי הוּא כִּשְׁאָר הַכִּנּוּיִין.

Every mention of **"Solomon"** [*Shlomo*] **in Song of Songs is sacred,**[2] since they allude to God, one of whose names is *Shalom*, Peace, **and it is like the other appellations** of God,[a] **except for this** one: **"The thousand is for you, Solomon"** (8:12). **Every** mention of **"king" in** the book of **Daniel** is **non-sacred,** because they all refer to King Nebuchadnezzar, **except for this** one: **"You, King, King of kings"** (Daniel 2:37), **and it is like the other appellations** of God.

HALAKHIC DISCUSSION

1. All the names that are stated in the section involving Lot are non-sacred – כָּל הַשֵּׁמוֹת הָאֲמוּרוֹת בְּלוֹט חֹל: The same applies to any of the other seven names of God: If they were written as non-sacred names, it is permitted to erase them (*Shakh* on *Yoreh De'a* 276:12).

2. Every Solomon in Song of Songs is sacred – כָּל שְׁלֹמֹה הָאָמוּר בְּשִׁיר הַשִּׁירִים קֹדֶשׁ: The Rema accordingly states (*Yoreh De'a* 276:13) that for this reason some are careful not to write out the word *shalom* ["peace"] in full, since it is a name of God, although the later authorities maintain that one need not be concerned about this (*Shakh*; *Gra*). Some suggest that it is a problem only if one is writing *shalom* in the context of sending greetings to another, but if one is writing about, say, the state of peace in the world, or a letter to a person named Shalom, there is no need for concern (*Pitḥei Teshuva*; *Arukh HaShulḥan*). Similarly, if one writes the word in such a manner that it is clear that he does not intend to bless his correspondent with the name of God, for example if he writes "*shalom* to you" or "*shalom* and blessings," this too is a reason for leniency (*Iggerot Moshe*, *Oraḥ Ḥayyim* 4, 40:3, although the conclusion there is that it is preferable to be stringent even in such a case).

NOTES

a. And may not, therefore, be eradicated (see Halakha 8).

פֶּרֶק שְׁבִיעִי
CHAPTER 7
Prophecy

Halakhot 1–5:	Those worthy of prophecy, and the form of the prophetic experience
Halakha 6:	The difference between the prophecy of Moses and that of the other prophets
Halakha 7:	The purpose of prophecy, and believing in prophets

Halakha 1

מִיסוֹדֵי הַדָּת לֵידַע שֶׁהָאֵל מְנַבֵּא אֶת בְּנֵי הָאָדָם. וְאֵין הַנְּבוּאָה חָלָה אֶלָּא עַל חָכָם גָּדוֹל בְּחָכְמָה, גִּבּוֹר בְּמִדּוֹתָיו, וְלֹא יְהֵא יִצְרוֹ מִתְגַּבֵּר עָלָיו בְּדָבָר בָּעוֹלָם, אֶלָּא הוּא מִתְגַּבֵּר בְּדַעְתּוֹ עַל יִצְרוֹ תָּמִיד, בַּעַל דֵּעָה רְחָבָה נְכוֹנָה עַד מְאֹד.

One of the foundations of the faith is **to know that God grants prophecy*** **to people. Prophecy is bestowed only upon a very wise sage** who is **mighty in his character, whose** evil **inclination never overcomes him with respect to** any **issue in the world. Rather, he always overcomes his inclination through** the power of **his mind. He** also **possesses** a **very broad, meticulous intellect.**

אָדָם שֶׁהוּא מְמֻלָּא בְּכָל הַמִּדּוֹת הָאֵלּוּ, שָׁלֵם בְּגוּפוֹ, כְּשֶׁיִּכָּנֵס לַפַּרְדֵּס וְיִמָּשֵׁךְ בְּאוֹתָן הָעִנְיָנוֹת הַגְּדוֹלִים הָרְחוֹקִים, וְתִהְיֶה לוֹ דַּעַת נְכוֹנָה לְהָבִין וּלְהַשִּׂיג, וְהוּא מִתְקַדֵּשׁ וְהוֹלֵךְ, וּפוֹרֵשׁ מִדַּרְכֵי כְּלַל הָעָם הַהוֹלְכִים בְּמַחְשַׁכֵּי הַזְּמַן, וְהוֹלֵךְ וּמְזָרֵז עַצְמוֹ וּמְלַמֵּד נַפְשׁוֹ שֶׁלֹּא תִּהְיֶה לוֹ מַחֲשָׁבָה כְּלָל בְּאֶחָד מִדְּבָרִים בְּטֵלִים וְלֹא מֵהַבְלֵי הַזְּמַן וְתַחְבּוּלוֹתָיו,

A person who is full of all these attributes, and **is physically sound, when he enters the** ***pardes***[a] **and is drawn into these great concepts,** which are **far removed** from the minds of most people, **and he has** a sufficiently **meticulous intellect to understand and grasp** them, **and he becomes increasingly holy, and he separates himself from the paths of the masses of the people who follows the darkness of time,**[b] will approach the level of prophecy. **He** must **continue rousing himself and teaching his soul not to have any thought at all about** even **one of** all the **worthless ideas or the vanities and** transitory **ruses**[c] **of the times.**

FROM THE LUBAVITCHER REBBE

*One of the foundations of the faith is to know that God grants prophecy – מִיסוֹדֵי הַדָּת לֵידַע שֶׁהָאֵל מְנַבֵּא: The Rambam discuss the topic of prophecy at great length, for four whole chapters. Although prophecy has been taken from us since the passing of the last prophets, the Rambam nevertheless maintains that "prophecy will return to Israel" and that it is a sign of the approaching Messiah (*Iggeret Teiman*). Accordingly, the knowledge of this topic is important for all generations, since even in our times, prophecy and the Divine Spirit have a certain influence (*Torat Menaḥem*, *Hitvaaduyot*, *Parashat Shofetim* 5751).

NOTES

a. A term for the fundamental, secret teachings of the Torah; the "Act of Creation" and the "Design of the Divine Chariot" (see 4:13).

b. They are led by the momentary enticements of the age, and are thus like the blind, walking in darkness.

c. They are called "ruses" because it is as though the vanities are tricking a person into distraction by their worthless calls for attention.

אֶלָּא דַעְתּוֹ תָּמִיד פְּנוּיָה לְמַעְלָה, קְשׁוּרָה תַּחַת הַכִּסֵּא לְהָבִין בְּאוֹתָן הַצּוּרוֹת הַקְּדוֹשׁוֹת הַטְּהוֹרוֹת, וּמִסְתַּכֵּל בְּחָכְמָתוֹ שֶׁל הַקָּדוֹשׁ בָּרוּךְ הוּא כֻּלָּהּ מִצּוּרָה רִאשׁוֹנָה עַד טַבּוּר הָאָרֶץ, וְיוֹדֵעַ מֵהֶם גָּדְלוֹ – מִיָּד רוּחַ הַקֹּדֶשׁ שׁוֹרָה עָלָיו.

Instead, his mind should **be constantly directed upward, bound under the** divine **Throne,** persistently cleaving to God's Throne and reflecting on the forms of the angels and their levels,[a] in an effort **to comprehend those holy, pure forms, and** he should be **gazing at the wisdom of the Holy One blessed be He in its entirety,**[b] **from** the **primary** spiritual **form,** the holy *ḥayyot*, down **to the center of the earth,** the most corporeal of places, **comprehending His greatness through them.** Once he attains this level, **the Divine Spirit will immediately rest upon him.**

וּבְעֵת שֶׁתָּנוּחַ עָלָיו הָרוּחַ, תִּתְעָרֵב נַפְשׁוֹ בְּמַעֲלַת הַמַּלְאָכִים הַנִּקְרָאִים אִישִׁים, וְיֵהָפֵךְ לְאִישׁ אַחֵר, וְיָבִין בְּדַעְתּוֹ שֶׁאֵינוֹ כְּמוֹת שֶׁהָיָה, אֶלָּא שֶׁנִּתְעַלָּה עַל מַעֲלַת שְׁאָר בְּנֵי אָדָם הַחֲכָמִים, כְּמוֹ שֶׁנֶּאֱמַר בְּשָׁאוּל: "וְהִתְנַבִּיתָ עִמָּם וְנֶהְפַּכְתָּ לְאִישׁ אַחֵר" (שמואל א י, ו).

When the Divine **Spirit rests upon him, his soul will become intermingled with** the souls of the **level of the angels called** ***ishim.*** His degree of intellectual achievement will rise until it resembles the attainment of the lowest degree of the angels, those who speak with the prophets.[c] **He will be transformed into a different man, and will realize that he is not** the same person **as he** previously **was; rather, he has been elevated above the level of other wise men, as is stated with regard to Saul:** "The spirit of the Lord will rest upon you, **and you will prophesy with them, and you will be transformed into another man"** (I Samuel 10:6).

Halakha 2

הַנְּבִיאִים – מַעֲלוֹת מַעֲלוֹת הֵן. כְּמוֹ שֶׁיֵּשׁ בַּחָכְמָה חָכָם גָּדוֹל מֵחֲבֵרוֹ, כָּךְ בַּנְּבוּאָה נָבִיא גָּדוֹל מִנָּבִיא.

There are various levels among the prophets. Just as with regard to wisdom, one **sage is greater than another, so too in** the case of **prophecy,** one **prophet is greater than** another **prophet.**

וְכֻלָּן אֵין רוֹאִין מַרְאֵה הַנְּבוּאָה אֶלָּא בַּחֲלוֹם בְּחֶזְיוֹן הַלַּיְלָה, אוֹ בַּיּוֹם אַחַר שֶׁתִּפֹּל עֲלֵיהֶן תַּרְדֵּמָה, כְּמוֹ שֶׁנֶּאֱמַר: "בַּמַּרְאָה אֵלָיו אֶתְוַדָּע בַּחֲלוֹם אֲדַבֶּר בּוֹ" (במדבר יב, ו).

Nevertheless, **they all see the prophetic vision only in a dream, in a visionary** experience of **the night, or during the daytime after** a similar **slumber has fallen upon them,** a weakness of the senses and body, **as it is stated: "I will reveal Myself to him in a vision; in a dream I will speak to him"** (Numbers 12:6).

וְכֻלָּן כְּשֶׁמִּתְנַבְּאִין, אֵבְרֵיהֶן מִזְדַּעְזְעִין וְכֹחַ הַגּוּף כּוֹשֵׁל וְעֶשְׁתּוֹנוֹתֵיהֶם מִתְטָרְפוֹת, וְתִשָּׁאֵר הַדֵּעָה פְּנוּיָה לְהָבִין מַה שֶּׁתִּרְאֶה,

All of them, when they prophesy, their limbs tremble, their physical powers fail them, **their senses become confused, and** thus **their minds are free to understand what they see.**

NOTES

a. Which reach all the way up to God's Throne of Glory; see 2:7.

b. Since God's wisdom can be seen in His works and creations (2:2).

c. See 2:7.

כְּמוֹ שֶׁנֶּאֱמַר בְּאַבְרָהָם: "וְהִנֵּה אֵימָה חֲשֵׁכָה גְדֹלָה נֹפֶלֶת עָלָיו" (בראשית טו,יב), וּכְמוֹ שֶׁנֶּאֱמַר בְּדָנִיֵּאל: "וְהוֹדִי נֶהְפַּךְ עָלַי לְמַשְׁחִית וְלֹא עָצַרְתִּי כֹּחַ" (דניאל י,ח).

As it is stated with regard to Abraham, at the prophecy of the Covenant between the Parts: **"And, behold, a dread, a great darkness, fell upon him"** (Genesis 15:12), **and it is stated regarding Daniel,** when he experienced one of his visions: **"My glory[a] was transformed for me into destruction, and I retained no strength"** (Daniel 10:8).

Halakha 3

הַדְּבָרִים שֶׁמּוֹדִיעִין לַנָּבִיא בְּמַרְאֵה הַנְּבוּאָה – דֶּרֶךְ מָשָׁל מוֹדִיעִין לוֹ, וּמִיָּד יֵחָקֵק בְּלִבּוֹ פִּתְרוֹן הַמָּשָׁל בְּמַרְאֵה הַנְּבוּאָה, וְיֵדַע מַה הוּא. כְּמוֹ הַסֻּלָּם שֶׁרָאָה יַעֲקֹב אָבִינוּ וּמַלְאָכִים עוֹלִים וְיוֹרְדִים בּוֹ, וְהוּא הָיָה מָשָׁל לַמַּלְכֻיּוֹת וְשִׁעְבּוּדָן,

The message that a prophet is told in his **prophetic vision is told to him in the manner of a metaphor. Immediately,** however, **the interpretation of the metaphor of the prophetic vision is engraved upon his heart,** as soon as the prophet sees it, **and he knows what it is. For example, the ladder that our forefather Jacob saw** in his dream at Beit El (Genesis 28:10–22), **with the angels ascending and descending it, which was an allegory for the** gentile **kingdoms and their subjugation** of Jacob's descendants.

וּכְמוֹ הַחַיּוֹת שֶׁרָאָה יְחֶזְקֵאל, וְהַסִּיר הַנָּפוּחַ וּמַקֵּל שָׁקֵד שֶׁרָאָה יִרְמְיָה, וְהַמְּגִלָּה שֶׁרָאָה יְחֶזְקֵאל, וְהָאֵיפָה שֶׁרָאָה זְכַרְיָה.

Other **examples** include **the creatures that Ezekiel saw** in his vision of the Divine Chariot (Ezekiel chap. 1), which represented a revelation of God; **the boiling pot and the branch of an almond tree that Jeremiah saw** at the start of his prophetic career (Jeremiah 1:11–14), which were metaphors for the future destruction that would befall Judah; **the scroll that Ezekiel saw;[b] and the ephah that Zechariah saw.[c]**

וְכֵן שְׁאָר הַנְּבִיאִים, יֵשׁ שֶׁהֵן אוֹמְרִין הַמָּשָׁל וּפִתְרוֹנוֹ כְּמוֹ אֵלּוּ, וְיֵשׁ שֶׁהֵן אוֹמְרִין הַפִּתְרוֹן בִּלְבַד. וּפְעָמִים אוֹמְרִין הַמָּשָׁל בִּלְבַד בְּלֹא פִּתְרוֹן, כְּמִקְצָת דִּבְרֵי יְחֶזְקֵאל וּזְכַרְיָה. וְכֻלָּם בְּמָשָׁל וְדֶרֶךְ חִידָה הֵם מִתְנַבְּאִים.

This same applies to **the other prophets. Some relate the metaphor and its interpretation, as those did.[d] Others relate only the interpretation.** Most of the time, the prophet conveys only the meaning of the visions he experienced, without describing the actual images that he saw. **On occasion, they relate only the metaphor without** its **interpretation, as** is true of **a few of the statements of Ezekiel and Zechariah.** In any case, **they all prophesy through metaphors and by way of allegories,** not in a clear manner, unlike the prophecy of Moses our teacher.[e]

NOTES

a. His countenance.

b. God showed Ezekiel a large scroll that had writing on both sides, and then instructed him to eat it (Ezekiel 2:9–3:3). This is a general metaphor for his prophecy and the appropriate attitude toward it.

c. Zechariah saw an ephah (a large measuring vessel), with a woman inside it being taken to the land of Shinar (Zechariah 5:5–11).

d. That is, in those aforementioned cases where the verses record the specific metaphorical image the prophet saw.

e. See Halakha 6.

Halakha 4

כָּל הַנְּבִיאִים אֵין מִתְנַבְּאִין בְּכָל עֵת שֶׁיִּרְצוּ, אֶלָּא מְכַוְּנִין דַּעְתָּן וְיוֹשְׁבִין שְׂמֵחִים וְטוֹבֵי לֵב וּמִתְבּוֹדְדִין, שֶׁאֵין הַנְּבוּאָה שׁוֹרָה לֹא מִתּוֹךְ עַצְבוּת וְלֹא מִתּוֹךְ עַצְלוּת, אֶלָּא מִתּוֹךְ שִׂמְחָה.

None of the prophets can simply **prophesy at any time they wish** to. **Rather, they must concentrate their focus** on the intellectual ideas mentioned above, **and sit in a joyful, happy state, while secluding themselves. For prophecy does not rest** on a person **neither from** an atmosphere of **sadness, nor from** an atmosphere of **heaviness** of body and mind, **but from** an atmosphere imbued with **joy.**

לְפִיכָךְ בְּנֵי הַנְּבִיאִים לִפְנֵיהֶם "נֵבֶל וְתֹף וְחָלִיל וְכִנּוֹר", וְהֵם מְבַקְשִׁים הַנְּבוּאָה.

Accordingly, "the sons of the prophets," that is, the prophets' disciples who wish to prophesy,[a] as stated with regard to a group of prophets that Saul encountered, **had before them "a lyre, a drum, a flute, and a harp"** (I Samuel 10:5), **and they** were thereby **seeking prophecy.**

NOTES

a. See the next Halakha.

BACKGROUND

Harp

Drum

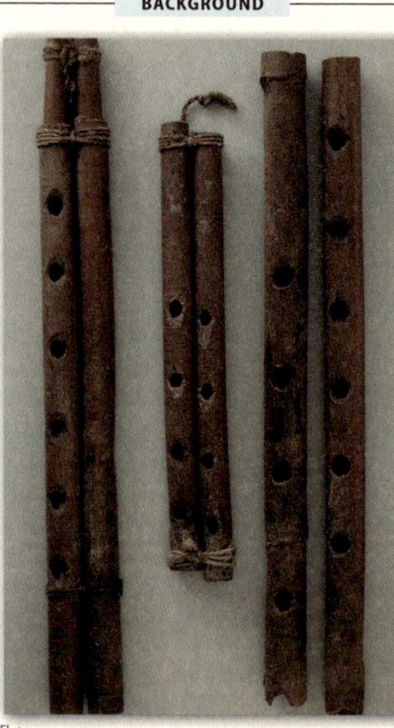
Flutes

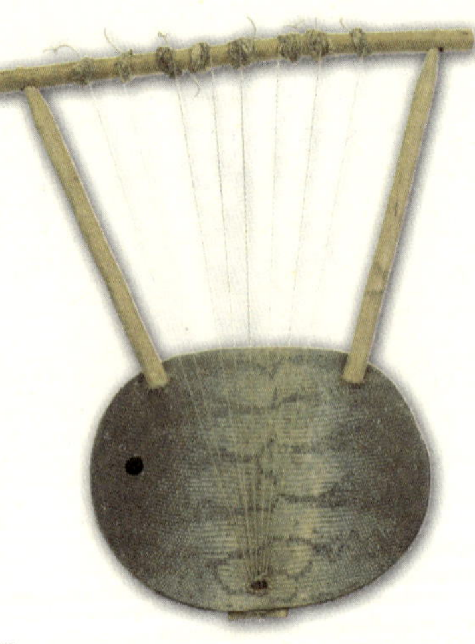
Lyre

A lyre, a drum, a flute, and a harp – נֵבֶל וְתֹף וְחָלִיל וְכִנּוֹר: Prophecy cannot rest upon a person when he is sad or languid, but only when he is happy. Therefore, the prophets' disciples would always have a harp, drum, flute, and lyre when they were seeking prophecy.

וְזֶה הוּא שֶׁנֶּאֱמַר: "וְהֵמָּה מִתְנַבְּאִים" (שמואל א י,ה), כְּלוֹמַר מְהַלְּכִין בְּדֶרֶךְ הַנְּבוּאָה עַד שֶׁיִּנָּבְאוּ, כְּמוֹ שֶׁאַתָּה אוֹמֵר: 'פְּלוֹנִי מִתְגַּדֵּל'.

This is the meaning of that **which is stated,** in the same verse: **"And they will be prophesying,"** **that is, following the path of prophecy until they would prophesy, as one says: "So-and-so** is doing so well that he **will** soon **be** achieving **greatness."**

Halakha 5

אֵלּוּ שֶׁהֵם מְבַקְּשִׁים לְהִתְנַבֵּא הֵם הַנִּקְרָאִים בְּנֵי הַנְּבִיאִים. וְאַף עַל פִּי שֶׁמְּכַוְּנִין דַּעְתָּן – אֶפְשָׁר שֶׁתִּשְׁרֶה עֲלֵיהֶן שְׁכִינָה, וְאֶפְשָׁר שֶׁלֹּא תִּשְׁרֶה.

Those who seek to prophesy are called "the sons, disciples, **of the prophets."** However, **even if they concentrate their focus** in the correct manner, **it is possible that the Divine Presence will rest upon them, and it is** also **possible that it will not rest** upon them.

Halakha 6

כָּל הַדְּבָרִים שֶׁאָמַרְנוּ הֵן דֶּרֶךְ הַנְּבוּאָה לְכָל הַנְּבִיאִים הָרִאשׁוֹנִים וְהָאַחֲרוֹנִים, חוּץ מִמֹּשֶׁה רַבֵּנוּ וְרַבָּן שֶׁל כָּל הַנְּבִיאִים.

Everything that we have said is an accurate description of **the path of prophecy for all the early and later prophets, except for Moses our teacher,** the **master of all prophets.**

וּמַה הֶפְרֵשׁ יֵשׁ בֵּין נְבוּאַת מֹשֶׁה לִשְׁאָר כָּל הַנְּבִיאִים? שֶׁכָּל הַנְּבִיאִים בַּחֲלוֹם אוֹ בְּמַרְאָה, וּמֹשֶׁה רַבֵּנוּ וְהוּא עֵר וְעוֹמֵד, שֶׁנֶּאֱמַר: "וּבְבֹא מֹשֶׁה אֶל אֹהֶל מוֹעֵד לְדַבֵּר אִתּוֹ וַיִּשְׁמַע אֶת הַקּוֹל" (במדבר ז, פט).

What is the difference between the prophecy of Moses and that of **all the other prophets?** The difference is **that all the** other **prophets** prophesy **in** a night **dream or through a vision** in the daytime, when their bodies are weak and their senses blurred,[a] **whereas Moses our teacher** would prophesy **while he was awake and standing** upright, **as it is stated: "When Moses went into the Tent of Meeting to speak with Him, he heard the voice"** (Numbers 7:89).

כָּל הַנְּבִיאִים עַל יְדֵי מַלְאָךְ, לְפִיכָךְ רוֹאִין מַה שֶּׁהֵן רוֹאִין בְּמָשָׁל וְחִידָה. מֹשֶׁה רַבֵּנוּ לֹא עַל יְדֵי מַלְאָךְ, שֶׁנֶּאֱמַר: "פֶּה אֶל פֶּה אֲדַבֶּר בּוֹ" (במדבר יב, ח), וְנֶאֱמַר: "וְדִבֶּר יי אֶל מֹשֶׁה פָּנִים אֶל פָּנִים" (שמות לג, יא), וְנֶאֱמַר: "וּתְמֻנַת יי יַבִּיט" (במדבר יב, ח),

Furthermore, **all the** other **prophets** prophesy only **through the medium of an angel,**[b] and **therefore they perceive whatever they see only by means of metaphors and allegories,** such that their interpretation of what they see is required. By contrast, **Moses our teacher** would prophesy **without the medium of an angel, as it is stated: "Mouth to mouth I will speak with him"** (Numbers 12:8), **and it is stated: "The Lord would speak to Moses face-to-face"** (Exodus 33:11), **and it is stated: "And the image of the Lord he will behold"** (Numbers 12:8).

NOTES

a. As stated in Halakha 2.

b. See *The Guide for the Perplexed* 1:37, 2:48.

כְּלוֹמַר שֶׁאֵין שָׁם מָשָׁל, אֶלָּא רוֹאֶה הַדָּבָר עַל בֻּרְיוֹ, בְּלֹא חִידָה בְּלֹא מָשָׁל. הוּא שֶׁהַתּוֹרָה מְעִידָה עָלָיו: "וּמַרְאֶה וְלֹא בְחִידֹת" (שם) – שֶׁאֵינוֹ מִתְנַבֵּא בְּחִידָה, אֶלָּא בְּמַרְאֶה, שֶׁרוֹאֶה הַדָּבָר עַל בֻּרְיוֹ.

In other words, there was no metaphor; rather, he would perceive the matter clearly, without an allegory. This is the meaning of that **which the Torah testifies regarding him: "And a vision that is not in riddles"** (Numbers 12:8), **that** is, **he does not prophesy through an allegory, but in "a vision,"** in **which he perceives the matter clearly.**

כָּל הַנְּבִיאִים יְרֵאִין וְנִבְהָלִין וּמִתְמוֹגְגִים, וּמֹשֶׁה רַבֵּנוּ אֵינוֹ כֵּן. הוּא שֶׁהַכָּתוּב אוֹמֵר: "כַּאֲשֶׁר יְדַבֵּר אִישׁ אֶל רֵעֵהוּ" (שמות לג,יא) – כְּמוֹ שֶׁאֵין אָדָם נִבְהָל לִשְׁמֹעַ דִּבְרֵי חֲבֵרוֹ, כָּךְ הָיָה כֹּחַ בְּדַעְתּוֹ שֶׁל מֹשֶׁה רַבֵּנוּ לְהָבִין דִּבְרֵי הַנְּבוּאָה וְהוּא עוֹמֵד עַל עָמְדוֹ שָׁלֵם.

Another difference is that **all the** other **prophets are scared, frightened, and petrified,**[a] **but not so Moses our teacher. This is** the meaning of that **which the verse states: "As a man speaks to his neighbor"** (Exodus 33:11). **Just as a person is not frightened by hearing the words of another** individual, **so too the mind of Moses had the power to understand the words of** his **prophecy while he was standing in a composed state.**

כָּל הַנְּבִיאִים אֵין מִתְנַבְּאִים בְּכָל עֵת שֶׁיִּרְצוּ. מֹשֶׁה רַבֵּנוּ אֵינוֹ כֵּן, אֶלָּא כָּל זְמַן שֶׁיַּחְפֹּץ רוּחַ הַקֹּדֶשׁ לוֹבַשְׁתּוֹ וּנְבוּאָה שׁוֹרָה עָלָיו, וְאֵינוֹ צָרִיךְ לְכַוֵּן דַּעְתּוֹ וּלְהִזְדַּמֵּן לָהּ, שֶׁהֲרֵי הוּא מְכֻוָּן וּמְזֻמָּן וְעוֹמֵד כְּמַלְאֲכֵי הַשָּׁרֵת. לְפִיכָךְ מִתְנַבֵּא בְּכָל עֵת, שֶׁנֶּאֱמַר: "עִמְדוּ וְאֶשְׁמְעָה מַה יְצַוֶּה יי לָכֶם" (במדבר ט,ח).

In addition, **all the** other **prophets cannot prophesy at any time they wish** to do so,[b] but **not so Moses our teacher. Rather, whenever he wished, the Divine Spirit would enfold him, and prophecy would rest upon him. He did not have to concentrate his focus and prepare himself for it, for** his mind **was** always **concentrated, prepared, and ready, like the ministering angels. Accordingly, he could prophesy at any time, as it is stated:** "Moses said to them: **Stand, and I will hear what the Lord will command you"** (Numbers 9:8).[c]

וּבָזֶה הִבְטִיחוֹ הָאֵל, שֶׁנֶּאֱמַר: "לֵךְ אֱמֹר לָהֶם שׁוּבוּ לָכֶם לְאָהֳלֵיכֶם, וְאַתָּה פֹּה עֲמֹד עִמָּדִי" (דברים ה,כו–כז). הָא לָמַדְתָּ שֶׁכָּל הַנְּבִיאִים כְּשֶׁהַנְּבוּאָה מִסְתַּלֶּקֶת, חוֹזְרִין לְאָהֳלָם, שֶׁהוּא צָרְכֵי הַגּוּף כֻּלָּן, כִּשְׁאָר הָעָם, לְפִיכָךְ אֵינָן פּוֹרְשִׁין מִנְּשׁוֹתֵיהֶן.

The Lord promised Moses **in this** regard, **as it is stated** after the giving of the Torah at Sinai, when all Israel saw the revelation of God and were thus like prophets themselves:[d] **"Go say to them: Return to your tents. But you, stand here with Me"** (Deuteronomy 5:27–28). **You learn** from **this** verse **that** in the case of **all the** other **prophets, when the prophecy departs** from them, **they return to their "tents,"** which refers to **all bodily requirements, like other people. Therefore, they do not separate from their wives.**

וּמֹשֶׁה רַבֵּנוּ לֹא חָזַר לְאָהֳלוֹ הָרִאשׁוֹן, לְפִיכָךְ פֵּרַשׁ מִן הָאִשָּׁה לְעוֹלָם, וּמִכָּל הַדּוֹמֶה לָהּ, וְנִקְשְׁרָה דַּעְתּוֹ בְּצוּר הָעוֹלָמִים, וְלֹא נִסְתַּלֵּק הַהוֹד מֵעָלָיו לְעוֹלָם, וְקָרַן עוֹר פָּנָיו, וְנִתְקַדֵּשׁ כַּמַּלְאָכִים.

But as implied by the verse, **Moses our teacher did not return to his former "tent." Consequently, he separated himself from** his **wife forever, and from everything of that** nature. Instead, **he bound his mind to the Everlasting Rock, and the glory never left him. The skin of his face radiated,**[e] **and he became holy like the angels.**

NOTES

a. As depicted in Halakha 2.

b. Rather, they have to prepare themselves beforehand (Halakha 4), and even then their efforts might not meet with success (Halakha 5).

c. Moses said this to the people who wanted to know what they should do after being unable to sacrifice the Paschal offering due to their state of ritual impurity.

d. See 8:1–2.

e. As a result of speaking with the Divine Presence (see Exodus 34:29).

Halakha 7

הַנָּבִיא – אֶפְשָׁר שֶׁתִּהְיֶה נְבוּאָתוֹ לְעַצְמוֹ בִּלְבַד, לְהַרְחִיב לִבּוֹ וּלְהוֹסִיף דַּעְתּוֹ עַד שֶׁיֵּדַע מַה שֶּׁלֹּא הָיָה יוֹדֵעַ מֵאוֹתָן הַדְּבָרִים הַגְּדוֹלִים;

With regard to **a prophet, it is possible that his prophecy will be for his own sake alone, to expand his mind and increase his knowledge until he knows something that he did not** previously **know about those lofty concepts.**

וְאֶפְשָׁר שֶׁיִּשְׁתַּלַּח לְעַם מֵעַמֵּי הָאָרֶץ אוֹ לְאַנְשֵׁי עִיר אוֹ מַמְלָכָה, לְכוֹנֵן אוֹתָם וּלְהוֹדִיעָם מַה יַּעֲשׂוּ אוֹ לִמְנֹעַ אוֹתָם מִמַּעֲשִׂים הָרָעִים שֶׁבִּידֵיהֶם.

It is also possible that he will be sent to one of the peoples of the world, or to the residents of a particular **city or kingdom, to teach them and inform them of what they should do, or to prevent them from** continuing with **the evil deeds that they maintain.**

וּכְשֶׁמְּשַׁלְּחִין אוֹתוֹ, נוֹתְנִין לוֹ אוֹת וּמוֹפֵת, כְּדֵי שֶׁיֵּדְעוּ הָעָם שֶׁהָאֵל שְׁלָחוֹ בֶּאֱמֶת.

When he is sent on such a mission, **he is given a sign or a wonder** to perform to confirm his status as a prophet, **so that the people will know that the Lord truly sent him.**

וְלֹא כָּל הָעוֹשֶׂה אוֹת וּמוֹפֵת מַאֲמִינִין אוֹתוֹ שֶׁהוּא נָבִיא, אֶלָּא אָדָם שֶׁהָיִינוּ יוֹדְעִין בּוֹ מִתְּחִלָּתוֹ שֶׁהוּא רָאוּי לִנְבוּאָה בְּחָכְמָתוֹ וּבְמַעֲשָׂיו שֶׁנִּתְעַלָּה בָּהֶן עַל כָּל בְּנֵי גִילוֹ,

Not everyone who performs signs or wonders should be **believed as a prophet. Rather, only a person who was known beforehand to be worthy of prophecy,** in terms of **his wisdom and his deeds, that in them he surpasses all the members of his generation.**

וְהָיָה מְהַלֵּךְ בְּדַרְכֵי הַנְּבוּאָה וּבִקְדֻשָּׁתָהּ וּפְרִישׁוּתָהּ, וְאַחַר כָּךְ בָּא וְעָשָׂה אוֹת וּמוֹפֵת וְאָמַר שֶׁהָאֵל שְׁלָחוֹ – מִצְוָה לִשְׁמֹעַ מִמֶּנּוּ, שֶׁנֶּאֱמַר: "אֵלָיו תִּשְׁמָעוּן" (דברים יח, טו).

If **he is following the paths of prophecy, with its** ways of **sanctity and separation** from worldly affairs, **and then performs a sign or wonder and states that the Lord sent him,** it is **a mitzva to listen to him, as it is stated** by Moses: "A prophet from your midst, from your brethren, like me, the Lord your God will establish for you; **him, you shall heed"** (Deuteronomy 18:15). That is, Moses instructed the people to heed such a person if he is worthy of prophecy "like me."

וְאֶפְשָׁר שֶׁיַּעֲשֶׂה אוֹת וּמוֹפֵת וְאֵינוֹ נָבִיא, וְזֶה הָאוֹת יֵשׁ לוֹ דְּבָרִים בְּגַוּוֹ,

It is possible that this person **will perform a sign or wonder and** yet **he is not a prophet, and that sign has** another **factor behind it,** such as magic or sleight of hand.

אַף עַל פִּי כֵן מִצְוָה לִשְׁמֹעַ לוֹ. הוֹאִיל וְאָדָם גָּדוֹל הוּא וְחָכָם וְרָאוּי לִנְבוּאָה – מַעֲמִידִין אוֹתוֹ עַל חֶזְקָתוֹ, שֶׁבְּכָךְ נִצְטַוִּינוּ.

Even so, it is **a mitzva to listen to him: Since he is a great person and a wise** individual, **worthy of prophecy, we accept him** as maintaining **his** established **status** as fit for prophecy, and thus his sign is presumed to be true, **for we have thus been commanded.**[a]

NOTES

a. See *Hilkhot Sanhedrin* 20:1, 24:1; *Hilkhot Edut* 3:4.

כְּמוֹ שֶׁנִּצְטַוִּינוּ לַחְתֹּךְ הַדִּין עַל פִּי שְׁנֵי עֵדִים כְּשֵׁרִים וְאַף עַל פִּי שֶׁאֶפְשָׁר שֶׁהֵעִידוּ בְּשֶׁקֶר, הוֹאִיל וּכְשֵׁרִים הֵם אֶצְלֵנוּ – מַעֲמִידִין אוֹתָן עַל כַּשְׁרוּתָן.

This is **like** the manner that **we are commanded to render judgment in accordance with the** testimony of **two witnesses. Even though they may testify falsely, since** as far as **we** know, **they are valid** witnesses, **we accept them** as maintaining **their** established status of **validity.**

וּבִדְבָרִים הָאֵלּוּ וְכַיּוֹצֵא בָּהֶן נֶאֱמַר: "הַנִּסְתָּרֹת לַיי אֱלֹהֵינוּ וְהַנִּגְלֹת לָנוּ וּלְבָנֵינוּ" וגו' (דברים כט, כח), וְנֶאֱמַר: "כִּי הָאָדָם יִרְאֶה לַעֵינַיִם וַיי יִרְאֶה לַלֵּבָב" (שמואל א טז,ז).

With regard to such cases and the like, it is stated: "The concealed are for the Lord our God, but the revealed are for us and for our children…" (Deuteronomy 29:28), **and it is stated: "For man sees into the eyes, but the Lord sees into the heart"** (I Samuel 16:7). Anything that is "concealed" from people and is in "the heart" is God's responsibility ("for the Lord our God") and is not the concern of man.

פֶּרֶק שְׁמִינִי

CHAPTER 8

The Prophecy of Moses

Halakhot 1–3: The belief in the prophecy of Moses

Halakha 1

מֹשֶׁה רַבֵּנוּ, לֹא הֶאֱמִינוּ בּוֹ יִשְׂרָאֵל מִפְּנֵי הָאוֹתוֹת שֶׁעָשָׂה, שֶׁהַמַּאֲמִין עַל פִּי הָאוֹתוֹת יֵשׁ בְּלִבּוֹ דֹּפִי, שֶׁאֶפְשָׁר שֶׁיֵּעָשֶׂה הָאוֹת בְּלָאט וְכִשּׁוּף.

With regard to the prophecy of **Moses our teacher, the Israelites did not believe in him on account of the signs that he performed. For one who believes based on signs** always **harbors doubts in his heart, for it is possible for a sign to be performed through** acts of **magic or sorcery.**

אֶלָּא כָּל הָאוֹתוֹת שֶׁעָשָׂה מֹשֶׁה בַּמִּדְבָּר – לְפִי הַצֹּרֶךְ עֲשָׂאָן, לֹא לְהָבִיא רְאָיָה עַל הַנְּבוּאָה: צָרַךְ לְהַשְׁקִיעַ אֶת הַמִּצְרִיִּים – קָרַע אֶת הַיָּם וְהִצְלִילָם בּוֹ;

Rather, all the signs that Moses performed in the wilderness were done to fulfill a specific **need, not as proof of his prophecy.** Thus, for example, **it was necessary to drown the Egyptians,** and therefore **he split the sea and drowned them in it.**

צָרַכְנוּ לְמָזוֹן – הוֹרִיד לָנוּ הַמָּן; צָמְאוּ – בָּקַע לָהֶם אֶת הָאֶבֶן; כָּפְרוּ בּוֹ עֲדַת קֹרַח – בָּלְעָה אוֹתָם הָאָרֶץ. וְכֵן שְׁאָר כָּל הָאוֹתוֹת.

The Israelites **required food, so he brought down the manna for** them. They **became thirsty,** and accordingly **he split the stone for them,** and water gushed out. **The assembly of Korah denied him,** and therefore **the earth swallowed them up. The same** applies **to all the other signs.**

וּבַמֶּה הֶאֱמִינוּ בּוֹ? בְּמַעֲמַד הַר סִינַי, שֶׁעֵינֵינוּ רָאוּ וְלֹא זָר, וְאָזְנֵינוּ שָׁמְעוּ וְלֹא אַחֵר, הָאֵשׁ וְהַקּוֹלוֹת וְהַלַּפִּידִים,

By virtue of **what** then, **did they believe in him?** They believed in him because **of the event at Mount Sinai. For our** own **eyes saw, and not** those of **a stranger,** and likewise **our** own **ears heard and not** those of **another, the fire, thunder, and lightning.**

וְהוּא נִגַּשׁ אֶל הָעֲרָפֶל, וְהַקּוֹל מְדַבֵּר אֵלָיו, וַאֲנוּ שׁוֹמְעִים: 'מֹשֶׁה מֹשֶׁה, לֵךְ אֱמֹר לָהֶם כָּךְ וְכָךְ'. וְכֵן הוּא אוֹמֵר: "פָּנִים בְּפָנִים דִּבֶּר יי עִמָּכֶם" (דברים ה,ד), וְנֶאֱמַר: "לֹא אֶת אֲבֹתֵינוּ כָּרַת יי אֶת הַבְּרִית הַזֹּאת" (שם ה, ג).

Moses "**approached to the fog**" (Exodus 20:18), **the voice** of God **spoke to him, while we heard: "Moses, Moses, go tell them such-and-such." It thus states: "Face-to-face the Lord spoke with you"** (Deuteronomy 5:4), **and it is stated: "Not with our forefathers did the Lord establish this covenant,** but with us, we, who are here, all of us alive today" (Deuteronomy 5:3).

וּמִנַּיִן שֶׁבְּמַעֲמַד הַר סִינַי לְבַדּוֹ הִיא הָרְאָיָה לִנְבוּאָתוֹ שֶׁהִיא אֱמֶת שֶׁאֵין בּוֹ דֹּפִי? שֶׁנֶּאֱמַר: "הִנֵּה אָנֹכִי בָּא אֵלֶיךָ בְּעַב הֶעָנָן בַּעֲבוּר יִשְׁמַע הָעָם בְּדַבְּרִי עִמָּךְ וְגַם בְּךָ יַאֲמִינוּ לְעוֹלָם" (שמות יט, ט) –

From where is it derived that the event at Mount Sinai alone is the proof of the truth of Moses' **prophecy that** leaves **no** room for **doubts? For it is stated** by God to Moses, before the giving of the Torah at Sinai: **"Behold, I am coming to you in a thickness of the cloud, so that the people will hear while I speak with you and they will believe also in you forever"** (Exodus 19:9).

מִכְּלָל שֶׁקֹּדֶם דָּבָר זֶה לֹא הֶאֱמִינוּ בּוֹ נֶאֱמָנוּת שֶׁהִיא עוֹמֶדֶת לְעוֹלָם, אֶלָּא נֶאֱמָנוּת שֶׁיֵּשׁ אַחֲרֶיהָ הִרְהוּר וּמַחֲשָׁבָה.

It can be learned **by inference** from this verse **that before this event** the people **did not believe in** Moses **with a faith that would last forever, but rather with a faith followed by** mistrustful **contemplations and thoughts** of doubt.

Halakha 2

נִמְצְאוּ אֵלּוּ שֶׁשֻּׁלַּח לָהֶם הֵם הָעֵדִים עַל נְבוּאָתוֹ שֶׁהִיא אֱמֶת, וְאֵינוֹ צָרִיךְ לַעֲשׂוֹת לָהֶם אוֹת, שֶׁהֵם וְהוּא אֶחָד בַּדָּבָר,

Thus, those to whom Moses **was sent,** all the Israelites, **are themselves the witnesses to the truth of his prophecy,** for they saw with their own eyes that God spoke to Moses. Accordingly, **it was not necessary** for him **to perform a sign for them. For he and they are one in this regard,** and there is no difference between them with respect to the truth of Moses' prophecy.

כִּשְׁנֵי עֵדִים שֶׁרָאוּ דָּבָר אֶחָד בְּיַחַד, שֶׁכָּל אֶחָד מֵהֶם עֵד לַחֲבֵרוֹ שֶׁהוּא אוֹמֵר אֱמֶת, וְאֵין אֶחָד מֵהֶם צָרִיךְ לְהָבִיא רְאָיָה לַחֲבֵרוֹ.

This is **like two witnesses who saw the same event together, each one of which** serves as **a witness to the other that he is telling the truth, and neither one of them has to bring a proof regarding the other.** When a witness observes something together with another, there is no need for him to provide evidence that the other witness is telling the truth, since he himself saw the same thing. Thus, his own testimony about the event also attests to his companion's trustworthiness.

כָּךְ מֹשֶׁה רַבֵּנוּ – כָּל יִשְׂרָאֵל עֵדִים לוֹ אַחַר מַעֲמַד הַר סִינַי, וְאֵינוֹ צָרִיךְ לַעֲשׂוֹת לָהֶם אוֹת.

The same applies to **Moses our teacher: All Israel were witnesses to his** prophecy **after the event at Mount Sinai, and it was unnecessary for him to perform** another **sign for them.**

וְזֶה הוּא שֶׁאָמַר לוֹ הַקָּדוֹשׁ בָּרוּךְ הוּא בִּתְחִלַּת נְבוּאָתוֹ, בְּעֵת שֶׁנָּתַן לוֹ הָאוֹתוֹת לַעֲשׂוֹתָן בְּמִצְרַיִם,

This is the meaning of that **which the Holy One blessed be He said to** Moses **at the start of his prophetic calling,** at the burning bush, **when** God commanded him to bring the Israelites out of Egypt, and **gave him the signs to perform in Egypt** in order to prove to the people that he was a prophet of God.[a]

וְאָמַר לוֹ: "וְשָׁמְעוּ לְקֹלֶךָ" (שמות ג, יח), יָדַע מֹשֶׁה רַבֵּנוּ שֶׁהַמַּאֲמִין עַל פִּי הָאוֹתוֹת יֵשׁ בְּלִבּוֹ דֹּפִי וּמְהַרְהֵר וּמְחַשֵּׁב,

In this regard, God **said to him: "They will heed your voice"** (Exodus 3:18). Now, **Moses our teacher knew that one who believes on the basis of signs harbors doubts in his heart, and** retains suspicious **contemplations and thoughts** of doubt.

וְהָיָה נִשְׁמָט מִלֵּילֵךְ, וְאָמַר: "וְהֵן לֹא יַאֲמִינוּ לִי" (שם ד,א). עַד שֶׁהוֹדִיעוֹ הַקָּדוֹשׁ בָּרוּךְ הוּא שֶׁאֵלּוּ הָאוֹתוֹת אֵינָן אֶלָּא עַד שֶׁיֵּצְאוּ מִמִּצְרַיִם,

Therefore, **he sought to evade having to go** on the mission, **saying: "But, behold, they will neither believe me,** nor will they heed my voice" (Exodus 4:1), **until the Holy One blessed be He informed him that these signs were** designed to establish trust only **until they left Egypt.**

וְאַחַר שֶׁיֵּצְאוּ וְיַעַמְדוּ עַל הָהָר הַזֶּה, יִסְתַּלֵּק הַהִרְהוּר שֶׁמְּהַרְהֲרִין אַחֲרֶיךָ, שֶׁאֲנִי נוֹתֵן לְךָ כָּאן אוֹת שֶׁיֵּדְעוּ שֶׁאֲנִי שְׁלַחְתִּיךָ בֶּאֱמֶת מִבַּתְּחִלָּה, וְלֹא יִשָּׁאֵר בְּלִבָּן הִרְהוּר.

But after they had left, and they would stand at the foot of **this mountain,** where God was speaking to him, "all doubtful **contemplations they have against you will be removed, for I am giving you a sign here,** so **that they will know that I truly sent you from the outset.** Thus, **no distrust will remain in their hearts."**

הוּא שֶׁהַכָּתוּב אוֹמֵר: "וְזֶה לְּךָ הָאוֹת כִּי אָנֹכִי שְׁלַחְתִּיךָ בְּהוֹצִיאֲךָ אֶת הָעָם מִמִּצְרַיִם תַּעַבְדוּן אֶת הָאֱלֹהִים עַל הָהָר הַזֶּה" (שם ג, יב).

This is the meaning of that **which the verse states: "And this is your sign that I sent you: When you take the people out of Egypt, you will serve God upon this mountain"** (Exodus 3:12). The true sign that God sent him would occur when they served God at Mount Sinai, at the giving of the Torah.

נִמְצֵאתָ אוֹמֵר, שֶׁכָּל נָבִיא שֶׁיַּעֲמֹד אַחַר מֹשֶׁה רַבֵּנוּ – אֵין אָנוּ מַאֲמִינִין בּוֹ מִפְּנֵי הָאוֹת לְבַדּוֹ, כְּדֵי שֶׁנֹּאמַר: אִם יַעֲשֶׂה אוֹת נִשְׁמַע לוֹ לְכָל מַה שֶּׁיֹּאמַר, אֶלָּא מִפְּנֵי הַמִּצְוָה שֶׁצִּוָּנוּ מֹשֶׁה בַּתּוֹרָה וְאָמַר: אִם נָתַן אוֹת – "אֵלָיו תִּשְׁמָעוּן" (דברים יח, טו).

It is thus the case that we do not believe in any prophet who arises after Moses our teacher on account of any **sign alone, that we would say: "If he performs a sign we will listen to everything he says." Rather,** we believe in him **because of the mitzva that Moses commanded us in the Torah,** when **he said: If he provides a sign, "him you shall heed"** (Deuteronomy 18:15), whether or not the sign is true.

כְּמוֹ שֶׁצִּוָּנוּ לַחְתֹּךְ הַדָּבָר עַל פִּי שְׁנֵי עֵדִים, וְאַף עַל פִּי שֶׁאֵין אָנוּ יוֹדְעִין אִם אֱמֶת הֵעִידוּ אִם שֶׁקֶר, כָּךְ מִצְוָה לִשְׁמֹעַ מִזֶּה הַנָּבִיא אִם הָאוֹת אֱמֶת אוֹ בְּכִשּׁוּף וָלָאט.

Just as we are commanded to render judgment in accordance with the testimony of **two witnesses even though we do not know if they testified truthfully or falsely, so too** it is **a mitzva to listen to this prophet,** despite the fact that we do not know **whether the sign is true or** performed **through magic or sorcery.**

NOTES

a. These signs were the transformation of his staff into a serpent, his hand becoming leprous, and a little water from the Nile turning into blood (see Exodus 4:1–9).

Halakha 3

לְפִיכָךְ, אִם עָמַד נָבִיא וְעָשָׂה אוֹתוֹת וּמוֹפְתִים גְּדוֹלִים, וּבִקֵּשׁ לְהַכְחִישׁ נְבוּאָתוֹ שֶׁל מֹשֶׁה רַבֵּנוּ – אֵין שׁוֹמְעִין לוֹ,

Consequently, if a prophet arises and performs great signs and wonders but he seeks to deny the prophecy of Moses our teacher, which is the Torah, in all its details and mitzvot, **we may not listen to him.**

וְאָנוּ יוֹדְעִין בְּיִחוּד שֶׁאוֹתָן הָאוֹתוֹת בְּלָאט וְכִשּׁוּף הֵן, לְפִי שֶׁנְּבוּאַת מֹשֶׁה רַבֵּנוּ אֵינָהּ עַל פִּי הָאוֹתוֹת כְּדֵי שֶׁנַּעֲרֹךְ אוֹתוֹת זֶה לְאוֹתוֹת זֶה,

We can know for certain that those signs were performed **through magic or sorcery. For the prophecy of Moses our teacher is not based on signs, that we could engage in a comparison between the signs performed by this** prophet **and the signs of that** prophet, and thereby determine which prophet is more reliable.

אֶלָּא בְּעֵינֵינוּ רְאִינוּהָ וּבְאָזְנֵינוּ שְׁמַעֲנוּהָ כְּמוֹ שֶׁשָּׁמַע הוּא.

Rather, we saw with our own **eyes and heard with our** own **ears, just as** Moses himself saw and **heard.**

הָא לְמָה הַדָּבָר דּוֹמֶה? לְעֵדִים שֶׁהֵעִידוּ לְאָדָם עַל דָּבָר שֶׁרָאָה בְּעֵינָיו שֶׁאֵינוֹ כְּמוֹ שֶׁרָאָה – שֶׁאֵינוֹ שׁוֹמֵעַ לָהֶן, אֶלָּא יוֹדֵעַ בְּוַדַּאי שֶׁהֵן עֵדֵי שֶׁקֶר.

To what is this matter comparable? To witnesses who testified to a person regarding something he had seen with his own **eyes, that it was not as he saw it. He would not listen to them; rather, he would know for certain that they are false witnesses.**

לְפִיכָךְ אָמְרָה תּוֹרָה שֶׁאִם בָּא הָאוֹת וְהַמּוֹפֵת, "לֹא תִשְׁמַע אֶל דִּבְרֵי הַנָּבִיא הַהוּא" (דברים יג,ד), שֶׁהֲרֵי זֶה בָּא אֵלֶיךָ בְּאוֹת וּמוֹפֵת לְהַכְחִישׁ מַה שֶּׁרָאִיתָ בְּעֵינֶיךָ.

Therefore, the Torah states that if such **a sign or wonder will come, "you shall not heed the words of that prophet"** (Deuteronomy 13:3–4). **For this** person **comes to you with a sign and wonder** in order **to deny what you saw with your** own **eyes.**

וְהוֹאִיל וְאֵין אָנוּ מַאֲמִינִין בְּמוֹפֵת אֶלָּא מִפְּנֵי הַמִּצְוָה שֶׁצִּוָּנוּ מֹשֶׁה, הֵיאַךְ נְקַבֵּל מֵאוֹת זֶה שֶׁבָּא לְהַכְחִישׁ נְבוּאָתוֹ שֶׁל מֹשֶׁה שֶׁרָאִינוּ וְשֶׁשָּׁמַעְנוּ?

Since we believe in a sign only because of the mitzva that Moses commanded us, how can we accept this sign that comes from a person who wishes **to deny the prophecy of Moses which we** ourselves **saw and heard?**

פֶּרֶק תְּשִׁיעִי

CHAPTER 9

A Prophet Is Subject to the Words of the Torah

Halakha 1:	A prophet does not have the authority to innovate new mitzvot of the Torah
Halakha 2:	The obligation to obey a prophet
Halakhot 3–5:	The prophecy to violate a command of the Torah provisionally

Halakha 1

דָּבָר בָּרוּר וּמְפֹרָשׁ בַּתּוֹרָה שֶׁהִיא מִצְוָה עוֹמֶדֶת לְעוֹלָם וּלְעוֹלְמֵי עוֹלָמִים, אֵין לָהּ לֹא שִׁנּוּי וְלֹא גֵּרָעוֹן וְלֹא תּוֹסֶפֶת,

It is a clear and explicit statement in the Torah that the Torah itself **is an eternal commandment**[a] **that stands forever and ever, without change, subtraction, or addition,**

שֶׁנֶּאֱמַר: "אֵת כָּל הַדָּבָר אֲשֶׁר אָנֹכִי מְצַוֶּה אֶתְכֶם אֹתוֹ תִשְׁמְרוּ לַעֲשׂוֹת לֹא תֹסֵף עָלָיו וְלֹא תִגְרַע מִמֶּנּוּ" (דברים יג, א), וְנֶאֱמַר: "וְהַנִּגְלֹת לָנוּ וּלְבָנֵינוּ עַד עוֹלָם לַעֲשׂוֹת אֶת כָּל דִּבְרֵי הַתּוֹרָה הַזֹּאת" (שם כט, כח) –

as it is stated: "All this matter that I command you, you shall take care to perform; you shall not add to it and you shall not subtract from it" (Deuteronomy 13:1), **and it is stated: "But the revealed are for us and for our children forever, to perform all the matters of this Torah"** (Deuteronomy 29:28).

הָא לָמַדְתָּ שֶׁכָּל דִּבְרֵי תּוֹרָה מְצֻוִּין אָנוּ לַעֲשׂוֹתָן עַד עוֹלָם. וְכֵן הוּא אוֹמֵר: "חֻקַּת עוֹלָם לְדֹרֹתֵיכֶם" (ויקרא ג, יז ועוד), וְנֶאֱמַר: "לֹא בַשָּׁמַיִם הִוא" (דברים ל, יב).

You learn from **this that we are commanded to fulfill all the words of the Torah forever. It likewise states: "It shall be an eternal statute for your generations"** (Leviticus 3:17 and elsewhere), **and it is stated: "It is not in the heavens"** (Deuteronomy 30:12). That is, the Torah and its mitzvot are no longer dependent upon a revelation from the heavens, such as through prophecy.

הָא לָמַדְתָּ שֶׁאֵין נָבִיא רַשַּׁאי לְחַדֵּשׁ דָּבָר מֵעַתָּה.

You learn from **this that a prophet is not permitted to initiate** or change **any matter** of halakha **from now** on.

NOTES

a. See *Hilkhot Teshuva* 3:8.

לְפִיכָךְ אִם יַעֲמֹד אִישׁ, בֵּין מִיִּשְׂרָאֵל בֵּין מִן הָאֻמּוֹת, וְיַעֲשֶׂה אוֹת וּמוֹפֵת וְיֹאמַר שֶׁיי שְׁלָחוֹ לְהוֹסִיף מִצְוָה אוֹ לִגְרֹעַ מִצְוָה, אוֹ לְפָרֵשׁ בְּמִצְוָה מִן הַמִּצְוֹת פֵּרוּשׁ שֶׁלֹּא שָׁמַעְנוּ מִמֹּשֶׁה, אוֹ שֶׁאָמַר שֶׁאוֹתָן הַמִּצְוֹת שֶׁנִּצְטַוּוּ בָּהֶן יִשְׂרָאֵל אֵינָן לְעוֹלָם וּלְדוֹרֵי דּוֹרוֹת אֶלָּא מִצְוֹת לְפִי זְמַן הָיוּ – הֲרֵי זֶה נְבִיא שֶׁקֶר, שֶׁהֲרֵי בָּא לְהַכְחִישׁ נְבוּאָתוֹ שֶׁל מֹשֶׁה,

Therefore, if a person will arise, whether from the Jewish people or from one of the gentile **nations, and perform a sign or wonder, saying that God sent him to add a mitzva, subtract a mitzva, explain one of the mitzvot in a manner that we did not hear as** a halakha transmitted to **Moses** from Sinai, **or if he says that those mitzvot that were commanded to the Jews are not forever and** for **all generations, but were given for** a limited **time, this is a false prophet, for he comes to deny the prophecy of Moses.**

וּמִיתָתוֹ בְּחֶנֶק, עַל שֶׁהֵזִיד לְדַבֵּר בְּשֵׁם יי אֲשֶׁר לֹא צִוָּהוּ, שֶׁהוּא בָּרוּךְ שְׁמוֹ צִוָּה לְמֹשֶׁה שֶׁהַמִּצְוָה הַזֹּאת "לָנוּ וּלְבָנֵינוּ עַד עוֹלָם" (דברים כט, כח), וְ"לֹא אִישׁ אֵל וִיכַזֵּב" (במדבר כג, יט).

His death is by strangulation, since he intentionally said in the name of God something **that** God **did not command him, because He, blessed be His name, commanded Moses that this commandment is "for us and for our children forever"** (Deuteronomy 29:28), **and "God is not a man that He will lie"** (Numbers 23:19). Unlike people, God would not issue false statements; rather, His word lasts forever.

Halakha 2

אִם כֵּן, לָמָּה נֶאֱמַר בַּתּוֹרָה: "נָבִיא אָקִים לָהֶם מִקֶּרֶב אֲחֵיהֶם כָּמוֹךָ וְנָתַתִּי דְבָרַי בְּפִיו וְדִבֶּר אֲלֵיהֶם אֵת כָּל אֲשֶׁר אֲצַוֶּנּוּ" (דברים יח, יח)?

If so, why is it stated in the Torah: "I will establish a prophet for them from among their brethren, like you, and I will place My words in his mouth, and he will speak to them everything that I will command him"? (Deuteronomy 18:18). What is the purpose of sending a prophet?

לֹא לַעֲשׂוֹת דָּת הוּא בָּא, אֶלָּא לְצַוּוֹת עַל דִּבְרֵי הַתּוֹרָה וּלְהַזְהִיר הָעָם שֶׁלֹּא יַעַבְרוּ עָלֶיהָ, כְּמוֹ שֶׁאָמַר הָאַחֲרוֹן שֶׁבָּהֶם: "זִכְרוּ תּוֹרַת מֹשֶׁה עַבְדִּי" (מלאכי ג, כב).

This prophet will **not come to establish** a new **faith, but to command** the Jews **regarding the statements of the Torah, and to warn the people not to violate it, as the last of** the prophets **said: "Remember the Torah of Moses My servant"** (Malachi 3:22).

וְכֵן אִם צִוָּנוּ בְּדִבְרֵי הָרְשׁוּת, כְּגוֹן: 'לְכוּ לְמָקוֹם פְּלוֹנִי' אוֹ 'אַל תֵּלְכוּ', 'עֲשׂוּ מִלְחָמָה הַיּוֹם' אוֹ 'אַל תַּעֲשׂוּ', 'בְּנוּ חוֹמָה זוֹ' אוֹ 'אַל תִּבְנוּהָ' – מִצְוָה לִשְׁמֹעַ לוֹ,

In a **similar** vein, **if** a prophet **commanded us** to do something **that** involved **a voluntary matter** which does not involve a positive or negative mitzva, **such as "go to that place," or "do not go** there," or **"wage war today," or "do not do** so," or **"build a wall," or "do not build it,"** it is **a mitzva to listen to him.**

וְהָעוֹבֵר עַל דְּבָרָיו חַיָּב מִיתָה בִּידֵי שָׁמַיִם, שֶׁנֶּאֱמַר: "וְהָיָה הָאִישׁ אֲשֶׁר לֹא יִשְׁמַע אֶל דְּבָרַי אֲשֶׁר יְדַבֵּר בִּשְׁמִי אָנֹכִי אֶדְרֹשׁ מֵעִמּוֹ" (דברים יח, יט).

One who violates his orders is liable to receive **death at the hand of Heaven, as it is stated: "It shall be, that the man who will not heed My words that he will speak in My name, I will demand it from him"** (Deuteronomy 18:19).

Halakha 3

וְכֵן נָבִיא שֶׁעָבַר עַל דִּבְרֵי עַצְמוֹ, וְהַכּוֹבֵשׁ נְבוּאָתוֹ – חַיָּב מִיתָה בִּידֵי שָׁמַיִם. וּבִשְׁלָשְׁתָּן נֶאֱמַר: "אָנֹכִי אֶדְרֹשׁ מֵעִמּוֹ" (דברים יח, יט).

Similarly, a prophet who violates his own prophetic **statement,** failing to act in accordance with the instruction he received from God, **or who suppresses his prophecy** and refuses to share it with the public, **is liable to death at the hand of Heaven. Regarding the three of them**[a] **it is stated: "I will demand it from him"** (Deuteronomy 18:19).

וְכֵן אִם יֹאמַר לָנוּ הַנָּבִיא, שֶׁנּוֹדַע לָנוּ שֶׁהוּא נָבִיא, לַעֲבֹר עַל אַחַת מִכָּל מִצְוֹת הָאֲמוּרוֹת בַּתּוֹרָה אוֹ עַל מִצְוֹת הַרְבֵּה, בֵּין קַלּוֹת בֵּין חֲמוּרוֹת, לְפִי שָׁעָה – מִצְוָה לִשְׁמֹעַ לוֹ.

Furthermore, if a prophet who is already established to us as a true **prophet**[b] **tells us to transgress one of the mitzvot that is stated in the Torah, or many mitzvot, whether the minor or major ones,** but only temporarily, as a **provisional** edict,[c] it is **a mitzva to listen to him.**

וְכָךְ לָמַדְנוּ מֵחֲכָמִים הָרִאשׁוֹנִים מִפִּי הַשְּׁמוּעָה: בַּכֹּל, אִם יֹאמַר לְךָ הַנָּבִיא עֲבֹר עַל דִּבְרֵי תּוֹרָה, כְּאֵלִיָּהוּ בְּהַר הַכַּרְמֶל – שְׁמַע לוֹ, חוּץ מֵעֲבוֹדָה זָרָה.

We thus learned from the early Sages on the basis of the Oral **tradition: With regard to all** cases, **if a prophet tells you to violate the words of the Torah, like Elijah on Mount Carmel, listen to him, except** if it involves **idol worship** (*Sanhedrin* 90a).

וְהוּא שֶׁיִּהְיֶה הַדָּבָר לְפִי שָׁעָה, כְּגוֹן אֵלִיָּהוּ בְּהַר הַכַּרְמֶל שֶׁהִקְרִיב עוֹלָה בַּחוּץ, וִירוּשָׁלַיִם נִבְחֲרָה, וְהַמַּקְרִיב בַּחוּץ חַיָּב כָּרֵת. וּמִפְּנֵי שֶׁהוּא נָבִיא, מִצְוָה לִשְׁמֹעַ לוֹ. וְגַם בָּזֶה נֶאֱמַר: "אֵלָיו תִּשְׁמָעוּן" (דברים יח, טו).

Now, this is the law only **if the** prophet's **order is** indeed **provisional. For example, Elijah sacrificed an offering outside** the Temple,[d] **on Mount Carmel, and** yet at that time **Jerusalem** had already been **chosen, and one who sacrifices outside** the Temple **is liable to** receive ***karet***,[e] excision from the World to Come. **But since he was a prophet,** it was **a mitzva to listen to him. With regard to such** cases **as well, it is stated: "Him you shall heed"** (Deuteronomy 18:15).

וְאִלּוּ שָׁאֲלוּ אֶת אֵלִיָּהוּ וְאָמְרוּ לוֹ: 'נֶעֱקֹר מַה שֶּׁכָּתוּב בַּתּוֹרָה: "פֶּן תַּעֲלֶה עֹלֹתֶיךָ בְּכָל מָקוֹם אֲשֶׁר תִּרְאֶה" (דברים יב, יג)?', הָיָה אוֹמֵר: 'לֹא, אֶלָּא הַמַּקְרִיב בַּחוּץ לְעוֹלָם חַיָּב כָּרֵת כְּמוֹ שֶׁצִּוָּה מֹשֶׁה. אֲבָל אֲנִי הַיּוֹם אַקְרִיב בַּחוּץ בִּדְבַר יי, כְּדֵי לְהַכְחִישׁ נְבִיאֵי הַבַּעַל'.

Had those present **asked Elijah** about this, **and said** the following **to him: "Can we** really **uproot that which is written in the Torah:** 'Beware, **lest you offer up your burnt offerings in any place that you see.** Rather, in the place that the Lord will choose… there you shall offer up your burnt offerings'" (Deuteronomy 12:13–14), **he would have said** in response: "**Not** so; **rather, one who sacrifices outside** the Temple is generally **liable to** receive ***karet***, and this law applies **forever, as Moses said. However, I will sacrifice today** alone **outside** the Temple, **by the word of God, in order to refute the prophets of Baal."**

וְעַל הַדֶּרֶךְ הַזֹּאת, אִם צִוּוּ כָּל הַנְּבִיאִים לַעֲבֹר לְפִי שָׁעָה – מִצְוָה לִשְׁמֹעַ לָהֶם. וְאִם אָמְרוּ שֶׁהַדָּבָר נֶעֱקַר לְעוֹלָם – מִיתָתָן בְּחֶנֶק, שֶׁהַתּוֹרָה אָמְרָה: "לָנוּ וּלְבָנֵינוּ עַד עוֹלָם" (דברים כט, כח).

In this manner, if any of the prophets command us to transgress a prohibition **provisionally, it is a mitzva to listen to them. But if they say that the matter has been uprooted forever, their death is by strangulation, for the Torah has stated** that its mitzvot are **"for us and for our children forever"** (Deuteronomy 29:28).

NOTES

a. That is, these two prophets and one who disobeys a prophet, as mentioned in the previous Halakha.

b. See 10:2.

c. Compare *Hilkhot Mamrim* 2:4.

d. When Elijah wished to prove that the prophets of the Baal were false prophets, he built an altar on Mount Carmel and sacrificed an offering upon it (see I Kings 18:30–40).

e. See *Hilkhot Beit HaBeḥira* 1:3; *Hilkhot Maaseh HaKorbanot*, chap. 18.

Halakha 4

וְכֵן אִם עָקַר דָּבָר מִדְּבָרִים שֶׁלָּמַדְנוּ מִפִּי הַשְּׁמוּעָה, אוֹ שֶׁאָמַר בְּדִין מִדִּינֵי תּוֹרָה שֶׁיי צִוָּה לוֹ שֶׁהַדִּין כָּךְ הוּא, וַהֲלָכָה כְּדִבְרֵי פְּלוֹנִי – הֲרֵי זֶה נְבִיא שֶׁקֶר וְיֵחָנֵק,

Likewise, a prophet who **uproots one of the things that we learned on the basis of the** Oral **tradition, or states with regard to one of the laws of the Torah,** which is subject to a dispute among the Sages, **that God commanded him that the law is such-and-such, and** that the **halakha is in accordance with** the Sage **So-and-So, he is a false prophet and should be strangled.**

אַף עַל פִּי שֶׁעָשָׂה אוֹת, שֶׁהֲרֵי בָּא לְהַכְחִישׁ תּוֹרָה שֶׁאָמְרָה: "לֹא בַשָּׁמַיִם הִיא" (שם ל,יב). אֲבָל לְפִי שָׁעָה – שׁוֹמְעִין לוֹ בַּכֹּל.

This applies **even if he performed a sign, for he is coming to deny the Torah, which states: "It is not in the heavens"** (Deuteronomy 30:12). But if he said that this is the case **provisionally, one listens to him in all** instances.

Halakha 5

בַּמֶּה דְּבָרִים אֲמוּרִים? בִּשְׁאָר מִצְוֹת. אֲבָל בַּעֲבוֹדָה זָרָה – אֵין שׁוֹמְעִין לוֹ, וַאֲפִלּוּ לְפִי שָׁעָה.

In what case **is this statement said? In** the case of the **other mitzvot. With regard to idol worship, however, one does not listen to him even provisionally.**

וַאֲפִלּוּ עָשָׂה אוֹתוֹת וּמוֹפְתִים גְּדוֹלִים וְאָמַר שֶׁיי צִוָּהוּ שֶׁתֵּעָבֵד עֲבוֹדָה זָרָה הַיּוֹם בִּלְבַד אוֹ בְּשָׁעָה זוֹ בִּלְבַד – הֲרֵי זֶה דִּבֵּר סָרָה עַל יי,

Even if he performs great signs and wonders and says that God commanded him that this object of **idol worship should be worshipped today alone, or only at this hour, he has "spoken fabrication about the Lord"** (Deuteronomy 13:6),

וְעַל זֶה צִוָּה הַכָּתוּב וְאָמַר: "וּבָא הָאוֹת וְהַמּוֹפֵת...לֹא תִשְׁמַע אֶל דִּבְרֵי הַנָּבִיא הַהוּא אוֹ אֶל חוֹלֵם הַחֲלוֹם...כִּי דִבֶּר סָרָה עַל יי אֱלֹהֵיכֶם" וגו' (דברים יג,ג–ו),

and concerning such an individual **the verse commanded and said: "And the sign or the wonder** that he spoke to you **comes to pass,** saying: Let us follow other gods that you did not know, and serve them; **you shall not heed the words of that prophet, or that dreamer of a dream . . . because he spoke fabrication about the Lord your God"** (Deuteronomy 13:3–6).

שֶׁהֲרֵי זֶה בָּא לְהַכְחִישׁ נְבוּאָתוֹ שֶׁל מֹשֶׁה, וּלְפִיכָךְ נֵדַע בְּוַדַּאי שֶׁהוּא נְבִיא שֶׁקֶר, וְכָל שֶׁעָשָׂה – בְּלָאט וְכִשּׁוּף עָשָׂה, וְיֵחָנֵק.

For this person **is coming to deny the prophecy of Moses, and therefore we know for certain that he is a false prophet, and everything he did was performed through sorcery and magic.** Consequently, **he should be strangled.** Moses himself stated that anyone who instructs us to worship idols, even if he backs up his claim with signs and wonders, is a false prophet who is enticing us away from God, and is liable to death.[a] Moses did not mention any reservation here about a temporary, provisional edit, and it has already been established that one who denies the prophecy of Moses is undoubtedly a false prophet.[b]

NOTES

a. See *Hilkhot Avoda Zara* 5:1.

b. See 8:3.

פֶּרֶק עֲשִׂירִי

CHAPTER 10

The Credibility of a Prophet

Halakhot 1–2:	The credibility of a prophet as established by signs
Halakhot 3–4:	The credibility of prophets in contrast to enchanters
Halakha 5:	The status of a prophet as established by the testimony of another prophet; the prohibition against doubting a prophet

Halakha 1

כָּל נָבִיא שֶׁיַּעֲמֹד לָנוּ וְיֹאמַר שֶׁיי שְׁלָחוֹ – אֵינוֹ צָרִיךְ לַעֲשׂוֹת אוֹת כְּאֶחָד מֵאוֹתוֹת מֹשֶׁה רַבֵּנוּ אוֹ כְּאוֹתוֹת אֵלִיָּהוּ וֶאֱלִישָׁע שֶׁיֵּשׁ בָּהֶן שִׁנּוּי מִנְהֲגוֹ שֶׁל עוֹלָם,

Any prophet who arises before **us and declares that God has sent him does not have to perform a sign like one of the signs performed by Moses our teacher, or like the signs of Elijah or Elisha, which involve a change** to **the natural order.**

אֶלָּא הָאוֹת שֶׁלּוֹ שֶׁיֹּאמַר דְּבָרִים הָעֲתִידִין לִהְיוֹת בָּעוֹלָם וְיֵאָמְנוּ דְּבָרָיו,

Rather, his sign is that he says things that will happen in the world in the future, and his statements are subsequently **verified,**

שֶׁנֶּאֱמַר: ״וְכִי תֹאמַר בִּלְבָבֶךָ אֵיכָה נֵדַע אֶת הַדָּבָר״ וכו׳ (דברים יח,כא).

as it is stated: "If you say in your heart: How shall we know the matter that the Lord did not speak? That which a prophet will speak in the name of the Lord, and the matter will not be and will not come to pass, that is the matter that the Lord did not speak" (Deuteronomy 18:21–22).

לְפִיכָךְ, כְּשֶׁיָּבֹא אָדָם הָרָאוּי לִנְבוּאָה בִּמְלַאֲכוּת יי, וְלֹא יָבֹא לְהוֹסִיף וְלֹא לִגְרֹעַ אֶלָּא לַעֲבֹד אֶת יי בְּמִצְוֹת הַתּוֹרָה, אֵין אוֹמְרִין לוֹ: ׳קְרַע לָנוּ הַיָּם׳ אוֹ ׳הַחֲיֵה מֵת׳ וְכַיּוֹצֵא בָּאֵלּוּ, ׳וְאַחַר כָּךְ נַאֲמִין בְּךָ׳,

Therefore, if a person who is worthy of prophecy[a] **comes on a mission from God, and he does not come to add or subtract** from the mitzvot, **but** rather he instructs us **to serve God through the mitzvot of the Torah, we do not tell him: "Split the sea for us," or "revive the dead" or something similar, "and then we will believe in you."**

NOTES

a. See 7:1.

NOTES

a. See *Hilkhot Avoda Zara* 11:6–9.

אֶלָּא אוֹמְרִין לוֹ: 'אִם נָבִיא אַתָּה – אֱמֹר לָנוּ דְּבָרִים הָעֲתִידִין לִהְיוֹת', וְהוּא אוֹמֵר, וְאָנוּ מְחַכִּים לוֹ לִרְאוֹת הֲיָבֹאוּ דְּבָרָיו.

Instead, we say to him: "If you are a prophet, tell us things that will happen in the future." He says what will happen, **and we wait to see if his statements come** to pass.

אִם לֹא יָבֹאוּ, וַאֲפִלּוּ נָפַל דָּבָר אֶחָד קָטָן – בְּיָדוּעַ שֶׁהוּא נְבִיא שֶׁקֶר. וְאִם בָּאוּ דְּבָרָיו כֻּלָּם – יִהְיֶה בְּעֵינֵינוּ נֶאֱמָן.

If his forecasts **do not come** to pass, **even if one small** detail **failed to materialize, he is clearly a false prophet. If all of his statements come** to pass, **we should deem him credible** for the time being, until he has been examined many times and fully established as a prophet, as stated in the next Halakha.

Halakha 2

וּבוֹדְקִין אוֹתוֹ פְּעָמִים הַרְבֵּה. אִם נִמְצְאוּ דְּבָרָיו נֶאֱמָנִין כֻּלָּם – הֲרֵי זֶה נְבִיא אֱמֶת, כְּמוֹ שֶׁנֶּאֱמַר בִּשְׁמוּאֵל: "וַיֵּדַע כָּל יִשְׂרָאֵל מִדָּן וְעַד בְּאֵר שָׁבַע כִּי נֶאֱמָן שְׁמוּאֵל לְנָבִיא לַיי" (שמואל א ג, כ).

We examine him in this manner **many times** over. **If all of his statements prove credible, he is a true prophet, as it is stated regarding Samuel: "All Israel from Dan to Beersheba knew that Samuel was faithful as a prophet of the Lord"** (I Samuel 3:20).

Halakha 3

וַהֲלֹא הַמְעוֹנְנִים וְהַקּוֹסְמִים אוֹמְרִין מַה עָתִיד לִהְיוֹת, וּמַה הֶפְרֵשׁ בֵּין הַנָּבִיא וּבֵינָם?

Now, since soothsayers and enchanters also **say what will happen in the future,** claiming that they have various ways of foretelling events,[a] **what,** then, **is the difference between a prophet and them?**

אֶלָּא שֶׁהַמְעוֹנְנִים וְהַקּוֹסְמִים וְכַיּוֹצֵא בָּהֶן – מִקְצָת דִּבְרֵיהֶן מִתְקַיְּמִין וּמִקְצָתָן אֵין מִתְקַיְּמִין, כָּעִנְיָן שֶׁנֶּאֱמַר: "יַעַמְדוּ נָא וְיוֹשִׁיעֻךָ הֹבְרֵי שָׁמַיִם הַחֹזִים בַּכּוֹכָבִים מוֹדִיעִם לֶחֳדָשִׁים מֵאֲשֶׁר יָבֹאוּ עָלָיִךְ" (ישעיהו מז, יג) – "מֵאֲשֶׁר" וְלֹא 'כָּל אֲשֶׁר'.

The difference is **that** in the case of **soothsayers, enchanters, and the like, some of their statements are fulfilled while others of them are not fulfilled, in the manner that it is stated: "Let now the astrologers, the stargazers, the monthly prognosticators stand and save you from that which will come upon you"** (Isaiah 47:13). The verse states **"from that," and not "all that."** The prophet is mocking those who rely on stargazers and the like, pointing out that they never know all of "that which will come upon you."

וְאֶפְשָׁר שֶׁלֹּא יִתְקַיֵּם מִדִּבְרֵיהֶם כְּלוּם אֶלָּא יִטְעוּ בַּכֹּל, כָּעִנְיָן שֶׁנֶּאֱמַר: "מֵפֵר אֹתוֹת בַּדִּים וְקֹסְמִים יְהוֹלֵל" (שם מד, כה).

It is also **possible that none of their statements will be fulfilled, but** rather **they will err in all** of them, **as it is stated** that it is God **"who negates the omens of deceivers and leads diviners astray"** (Isaiah 44:25) by confusing their minds.

אֲבָל הַנָּבִיא - כָּל דְּבָרָיו קַיָּמִין, שֶׁנֶּאֱמַר: ״כִּי לֹא יִפֹּל מִדְּבַר יי אַרְצָה״ (מלכים ב י, י), וְכֵן הוּא אוֹמֵר: ״הַנָּבִיא אֲשֶׁר אִתּוֹ חֲלוֹם יְסַפֵּר חֲלוֹם וַאֲשֶׁר דְּבָרִי אִתּוֹ יְדַבֵּר דְּבָרִי אֱמֶת מַה לַתֶּבֶן אֶת הַבָּר נְאֻם יי״ (ירמיהו כג, כח),

In the case of **a prophet, by contrast, all of his statements are fulfilled, as it is stated: "For nothing of the word of the Lord will fall to the ground"** (II Kings 10:10), **and the verse likewise states: "The prophet who has a dream will relate a dream, and he who has My word will speak My word of truth. What is the chaff to the grain? – The utterance of the Lord"** (Jeremiah 23:28).

כְּלוֹמַר שֶׁדִּבְרֵי הַקּוֹסְמִים וְהַחֲלוֹמוֹת כַּתֶּבֶן שֶׁנִּתְעָרֵב בּוֹ מְעַט בָּר, וּדְבַר יי כַּבָּר שֶׁאֵין בּוֹ תֶּבֶן כְּלָל.

In other words, the words of enchanters and dreamers are like chaff with a little grain mixed in them, mostly worthless, but with a bit of truth, **whereas the word of God is like grain without any chaff at all.**

וּבְדָבָר זֶה הִבְטִיחַ הַכָּתוּב וְאָמַר, שֶׁאוֹתָן הַדְּבָרִים שֶׁמּוֹדִיעִין הַמְעוֹנְנִין וְהַקּוֹסְמִים לָאֻמּוֹת וּמְכַזְּבִין, הַנָּבִיא יוֹדִיעַ לָכֶם דִּבְרֵי הָאֱמֶת

In this regard, the verse promised and said, concerning those things of which **soothsayers and enchanters inform the nations and** thereby **deceive** them, for their predictions do not come to pass, that **a prophet will inform you of the truth of the matter.**

וְאֵין אַתֶּם צְרִיכִין לִמְעוֹנֵן וְקוֹסֵם וְכַיּוֹצֵא בּוֹ, שֶׁנֶּאֱמַר: ״לֹא יִמָּצֵא בְךָ מַעֲבִיר בְּנוֹ וּבִתּוֹ בָּאֵשׁ וגו׳ כִּי הַגּוֹיִם הָאֵלֶּה וגו׳ נָבִיא מִקִּרְבְּךָ מֵאַחֶיךָ״ וגו׳ (דברים יח, י–טו).

Thus, **you do not need a soothsayer or an enchanter,** or anything **like that, as it is stated: "There shall not be found among you anyone who passes his son or his daughter through the fire,** a sorcerer, a soothsayer.... **For these nations** from whom you are taking possession heed soothsayers and sorcerers; but you, not so did the Lord your God give to you. **A prophet from your midst, from your brethren,** like me, the Lord your God will establish for you" (Deuteronomy 18:10–15).

הָא לָמַדְתָּ שֶׁאֵין הַנָּבִיא עוֹמֵד לָנוּ אֶלָּא לְהוֹדִיעֵנוּ דְּבָרִים הָעֲתִידִים לִהְיוֹת בָּעוֹלָם, מִשֹּׂבַע וְרָעָב, מִלְחָמָה וְשָׁלוֹם, וְכַיּוֹצֵא בָּהֶן. וַאֲפִלּוּ צָרְכֵי יָחִיד מוֹדִיעַ לוֹ, כְּשָׁאוּל שֶׁאָבְדָה לוֹ אֲבֵדָה וְהָלַךְ לַנָּבִיא לְהוֹדִיעוֹ מְקוֹמָהּ. כַּיּוֹצֵא בְּאֵלּוּ הַדְּבָרִים הוּא שֶׁיֹּאמַר הַנָּבִיא, לֹא שֶׁיַּעֲשֶׂה דָּת אַחֶרֶת אוֹ יוֹסִיף מִצְוָה אוֹ יִגְרַע.

You learn from **this that a prophet will arise for us only in order to inform us of future events that will occur in the world, for example** if there will be **plenty or famine, war or peace, and the like. He** might **even inform** a particular **individual of his needs, such as Saul, when he lost an object and went to the prophet** for him **to inform him of its place.**[a] **These are the kinds of things that a prophet will say; he will not establish a different faith,**[b] **or add or subtract a mitzva.**

BACKGROUND

Like chaff with a little grain mixed in... like grain without any chaff at all – כַּתֶּבֶן שֶׁנִּתְעָרֵב בּוֹ מְעַט בָּר...כַּבָּר שֶׁאֵין בּוֹ תֶּבֶן כְּלָל:

Chaff mixed with grain (left hand) and grain without chaff (right hand)

NOTES

a. When some donkeys belonging to Kish, Saul's father, became lost, Saul went to ask Samuel where they were (I Samuel 9:1–11).

b. As stated in 9:1–2.

Halakha 4

דִּבְרֵי הַפֻּרְעָנוּת שֶׁהַנָּבִיא אוֹמֵר, כְּגוֹן שֶׁיֹּאמַר: 'פְּלוֹנִי יָמוּת' אוֹ 'שָׁנָה פְּלוֹנִית שְׁנַת רָעָב' אוֹ 'מִלְחָמָה', וְכַיּוֹצֵא בִּדְבָרִים אֵלּוּ, אִם לֹא עָמְדוּ דְּבָרָיו – אֵין בָּזֶה הַכְחָשָׁה לִנְבוּאָתוֹ, וְאֵין אוֹמְרִין: הִנֵּה דִּבֵּר וְלֹא בָּא, שֶׁהַקָּדוֹשׁ בָּרוּךְ הוּא "אֶרֶךְ אַפַּיִם וְרַב חֶסֶד וְנִחָם עַל הָרָעָה" (יואל ב, יג; יונה ד, ב),

In a case where **a prophet issues a statement of retribution, for example if he says: "So-and-so will die," or "such-and-such a year will be a year of famine" or** "a year of **war," or a similar statement,** even **if his statements do not stand** the test of time, **this does not contradict** the truth **of his prophecy, and** here **we do not say: "Behold, he spoke and** his prediction **did not come** to pass." **For the Holy One Blessed be He is "slow to anger, and abounding in kindness, and reconsidering of harm"** (Joel 2:13; Jonah 4:2).

וְאֶפְשָׁר שֶׁעָשׂוּ תְּשׁוּבָה וְנִסְלַח לָהֶם כְּאַנְשֵׁי נִינְוֵה, אוֹ שֶׁתָּלָה לָהֶם כְּחִזְקִיָּה.

It is thus **possible that** the subjects of the retribution **repented and were forgiven, like the people of Nineveh,**[a] **or their** retribution **was held in abeyance,** as in the case of **Hizkiyahu.**[b]

אֲבָל אִם הִבְטִיחַ עַל טוֹבָה וְאָמַר שֶׁיִּהְיֶה כָּךְ וְכָךְ, וְלֹא בָּאָה הַטּוֹבָה שֶׁאָמַר – בְּיָדוּעַ שֶׁהוּא נְבִיא שֶׁקֶר, שֶׁכָּל דְּבַר טוֹבָה שֶׁיִּגְזֹר הָאֵל, אֲפִלּוּ עַל תְּנַאי – אֵינוֹ חוֹזֵר. הָא לָמַדְתָּ, שֶׁבְּדִבְרֵי הַטּוֹבָה בִּלְבַד יִבָּחֵן הַנָּבִיא.

If, however, a prophet **promised a good** event, **saying that such-and-such will occur, and the good of which he spoke did not come** about, **he is clearly a false prophet. For** regarding **any good that the Lord decrees, even if it is conditional, He does not renege** on it. **You learn** from **this that a prophet can be examined only through his statements** that predict **a good** outcome. If the good event that he predicted does not come to pass, the only explanation is that he is a false prophet.

הוּא שֶׁיִּרְמְיָהוּ אוֹמֵר בִּתְשׁוּבָתוֹ לַחֲנַנְיָה בֶּן עַזּוּר, כְּשֶׁהָיָה יִרְמְיָה מִתְנַבֵּא לְרָעָה וַחֲנַנְיָה לְטוֹבָה, אָמַר לוֹ: 'חֲנַנְיָה, אִם לֹא יַעַמְדוּ דְּבָרַי – אֵין בָּזֶה רְאָיָה שֶׁאֲנִי נְבִיא שֶׁקֶר, אֲבָל אִם לֹא יַעַמְדוּ דְּבָרֶיךָ – יִוָּדַע שֶׁאַתָּה נְבִיא שֶׁקֶר', שֶׁנֶּאֱמַר: "אַךְ שְׁמַע נָא אֶת הַדָּבָר הַזֶּה" וכו' (ירמיהו כח, ז, ושם: אַךְ שְׁמַע נָא הַדָּבָר הַזֶּה).

This is the meaning of that **which Jeremiah said in his response to Hananya, the son of Azur,** a false prophet of the time, **when Jeremiah was prophesying a bad** event **and Hananya a good** outcome.[c] Jeremiah **said to him: "Hananya, if my words do not stand, this is no proof that I am a false prophet,** since any prophecy of doom might fail to materialize if the people repent, **but if your words do not stand, you will be known** to be **a false prophet," as it is stated: "However, please hear this matter…"** (Jeremiah 28:7).

NOTES

a. Jonah prophesied doom upon the people of Nineveh, but the decree was nullified due to their repentance (Jonah, chap. 3).

b. When King Hizkiyahu was ill, the prophet Isaiah informed him that he would die, but in merit of his repentance he was granted an addition fifteen years of life (see Isaiah, chap. 38).

c. Jeremiah prophesied that the Temple and Jerusalem would be destroyed, whereas Hananya not only declared that the destruction would not occur, but he added that those who had already been exiled (the exile of Yekhonya) would return in two years (see Jeremiah, chap. 28).

Halakha 5

נָבִיא שֶׁהֵעִיד לוֹ נָבִיא אַחֵר שֶׁהוּא נָבִיא – הֲרֵי זֶה בְּחֶזְקַת נָבִיא, וְאֵין זֶה הַשֵּׁנִי צָרִיךְ חֲקִירָה, שֶׁהֲרֵי מֹשֶׁה רַבֵּנוּ הֵעִיד לִיהוֹשֻׁעַ, וְהֶאֱמִינוּ בוֹ כָּל יִשְׂרָאֵל קֹדֶם שֶׁיַּעֲשֶׂה אוֹת, וְכֵן לְדוֹרוֹת.

A prophet about whom another prophet testifies that he is a true **prophet has the presumptive status of a prophet. This second** prophet **does not require investigation. For Moses our teacher testified regarding Joshua, and all the Israelites believed in him before he performed a sign. The same** applies **for** all subsequent **generations.**

נָבִיא שֶׁנּוֹדְעָה נְבוּאָתוֹ וְהָאֱמְנוּ דְּבָרָיו פַּעַם אַחַר פַּעַם אוֹ שֶׁהֵעִיד לוֹ נָבִיא, וְהָיָה הוֹלֵךְ בְּדַרְכֵי הַנְּבוּאָה – אָסוּר לְחַשֵּׁב אַחֲרָיו וּלְהַרְהֵר בִּנְבוּאָתוֹ שֶׁמָּא אֵינָהּ אֱמֶת,

With regard to **a prophet whose prophecy has been established, and his statements have been verified time after time, or** if another **prophet testified** that he is a true prophet, **and he follows in the paths of prophecy,** acting in the proper manner that leads to prophecy,[a] **it is prohibited to think** suspiciously **about him or to harbor doubts concerning his prophecy that it might not be true.**

וְאָסוּר לְנַסּוֹתוֹ יָתֵר מִדַּאי, וְלֹא נִהְיֶה הוֹלְכִים וּמְנַסִּים לְעוֹלָם, שֶׁנֶּאֱמַר: "לֹא תְנַסּוּ אֶת יי אֱלֹהֵיכֶם כַּאֲשֶׁר נִסִּיתֶם בַּמַּסָּה" (דברים ו, טז), שֶׁאָמְרוּ: "הֲיֵשׁ יי בְּקִרְבֵּנוּ אִם אָיִן" (שמות יז, ז).

It is also **prohibited to test him too much,** by asking for yet another sign, for **we may not go on testing** prophets **forever, as it is stated: "You shall not test the Lord your God, as you tested Him in Masa"** (Deuteronomy 6:16), **when** the people complained to Moses over the lack of water[b] and **said: "Is the Lord among us, or not?"** (Exodus 17:7). This was an expression of doubt over Moses' prophetic leadership, as to whether he had indeed been sent by God.

אֶלָּא מֵאַחַר שֶׁנּוֹדַע שֶׁזֶּה נָבִיא – יַאֲמִינוּ וְיֵדְעוּ כִּי יי בְּקִרְבָּם, וְלֹא יְהַרְהֲרוּ וְלֹא יְחַשְּׁבוּ אַחֲרָיו, כְּעִנְיָן שֶׁנֶּאֱמַר: "וְיָדְעוּ כִּי נָבִיא הָיָה בְתוֹכָם" (יחזקאל ב, ה; לג, לג).

Rather, once it has been established that this individual **is a prophet, they must believe in him and know that God is in their midst. They must not harbor doubts or think** suspiciously **about him, in the manner that it is stated: "They will know that a prophet had been among them"** (Ezekiel 2:5, 33:33). God declared to Ezekiel that although the people would not believe him at first, they would ultimately realize that he had been speaking the truth.

בְּרִיךְ רַחֲמָנָא דְּסַיְּעַן

Blessed is the Merciful One, who has assisted us.

NOTES

a. See 7:7.

b. See Exodus 17:1–7.

הִלְכוֹת דֵּעוֹת

The Halakhot (Laws) of Character Traits

יֵשׁ בִּכְלָלָן אַחַת עֶשְׂרֵה מִצְוֹת, חָמֵשׁ מִצְוֹת עֲשֵׂה וְשֵׁשׁ מִצְוֹת לֹא תַעֲשֶׂה, וְזֶה הוּא פְּרָטָן:

א) לְהִדַּמּוֹת בִּדְרָכָיו. ב) לְהִדַּבֵּק בְּיוֹדְעָיו. ג) לֶאֱהֹב אֶת רֵעִים. ד) לֶאֱהֹב אֶת הַגֵּרִים. ה) שֶׁלֹּא לִשְׂנֹא אַחִים. ו) לְהוֹכִיחַ.
ז) שֶׁלֹּא לְהַלְבִּין פָּנִים. ח) שֶׁלֹּא לְעַנּוֹת אֲמֵלָלִים. ט) שֶׁלֹּא לַהֲלֹךְ רָכִיל. י) שֶׁלֹּא לִנְקֹם. יא) שֶׁלֹּא לִנְטֹר.

וּבֵאוּר כָּל הַמִּצְוֹת הָאֵלּוּ בִּפְרָקִים אֵלּוּ.

These halakhot include eleven mitzvot:
five positive mitzvot and six negative mitzvot.
Their enumeration follows:

1) To resemble God in His ways 2) To cleave to those who know Him
3) To love one's fellows 4) To love converts 5) Not to hate one's brothers 6) To reprove
7) Not to humiliate others 8) Not to oppress the downtrodden 9) Not to go about as a talebearer
10) Not to take vengeance 11) Not to bear a grudge

These eleven mitzvot will be explained in the following chapters.

Hilkhot Deot: Parallels to the mitzvot

The mitzva	*Sefer HaMitzvot*	The mitzva in *Hilkhot Deot*
To resemble God in His ways	Positive mitzva 8	1:5–6
To cleave to those who know Him	Positive mitzva 6	6:2
To love one's fellows	Positive mitzva 206	6:3
To love converts	Positive mitzva 207	6:4
Not to hate one's brothers	Negative mitzva 302	6:5
To reprove	Positive mitzva 208	6:6–7
Not to humiliate others	Negative mitzva 303	6:8
Not to oppress the downtrodden	Negative mitzva 256	6:10
Not to go about as a talebearer	Negative mitzva 301	7:1
Not to take vengeance	Negative mitzva 304	7:7
Not to bear a grudge	Negative mitzva 305	7:8

Introduction to *Hilkhot Deot*

No specific major tractate of the Talmud serves as the basis for *Hilkhot Deot*. However, there is something resembling these laws in the so-called "Minor Tractate" *Masekhet Derekh Eretz*, which deals with rules of etiquette. These come closest to the character traits discussed in these Halakhot.

While this section, *Hilkhot Deot*, contains several positive and negative mitzvot of the Torah concerning a person's conduct in his relations with others, it also analyzes general ethical principles, as well as rules that involve an ostensibly different area of life, the preservation of one's health. Each of these topics has its place in these chapters, and notwithstanding the essential differences between them, it can be said that the theme that connects these diverse issues is the Rambam's view that they are all part of the preservation of health, in the broader sense of the well-being of both body and soul. In his role as a physician, the Rambam was one of the first doctors to develop the concept of psychosomatic medicine, which argues that one's spiritual and material life interact in ways that can be both harmful and beneficial.

Hilkhot Deot offers broad moral guidelines for the overall path that a person should follow in life for the peace of both society and his own soul, as well as similar guidelines to follow for his physical health. These laws, essentially, direct us in how to live in order to be able to walk in the ways of God. The focus here, in both the physical and the spiritual sense, is on determining the balanced path, which ensures that one who follows it will be healthy in body and soul. The particular laws from the Torah that are included in these chapters, such as the mitzva to love one's fellows and the prohibitions against hating and taking vengeance, can be seen as part of this overall scheme through which a person attains a healthy, whole state of being as he follows the path of God. These halakhot, at their core, are not merely a collection of specific mitzvot, but a method for living a holy life that cannot be summed up in simple, unambiguous directives. They form an overall approach by which a person attains health and wholeness, for the sake of the service of God.

Contents

Chapters 1–5: Proper Conduct for Character Traits and Health

Chapters 6–7: Mitzvot Relating to Such Conduct

Chapter 6: The Mitzvot Involving the Love of One's Fellows

Halakhot 1–2:	Keeping away from the wicked and cleaving to the Sages
Halakhot 3–4:	Loving one's fellow and the convert
Halakhot 5–9:	The prohibition against hatred and the mitzva of reproof
Halakha 10:	Taking care not to harm orphans and widows

Chapter 7: Prohibitions Against Harming Others

Halakhot 1–6:	Gossip, slander, and defamation
Halakhot 7–8:	Taking revenge and bearing a grudge

פֶּרֶק רִאשׁוֹן

CHAPTER 1

The Proper Mode of Conduct

Halakhot 1–2:	The differences in people's characters
Halakhot 3–7:	The middle path

Halakha 1

דֵּעוֹת הַרְבֵּה יֵשׁ לְכָל אֶחָד וְאֶחָד מִבְּנֵי אָדָם, וְזוֹ מְשֻׁנָּה מִזּוֹ וּרְחוֹקָה מִמֶּנָּה בְּיוֹתֵר:

Every single person has many character traits, and **each of them** can therefore be **very different and far removed** in their specific character traits **from** other people.

יֵשׁ אָדָם שֶׁהוּא בַּעַל חֵמָה כּוֹעֵס תָּמִיד; וְיֵשׁ אָדָם שֶׁדַּעְתּוֹ מְיֻשֶּׁבֶת עָלָיו וְאֵינוֹ כּוֹעֵס כְּלָל, וְאִם כָּעַס, יִכְעֹס כַּעַס מְעַט בְּכַמָּה שָׁנִים.

There is one type of **person who is wrathful** and **constantly angry, while there is** another type of **person whose mind is settled and who never grows angry, and if he does become angry, he will** only **be a little angry,** and even then, only once **in several years.**

וְיֵשׁ אָדָם שֶׁהוּא גְּבַהּ לֵב בְּיוֹתֵר, וְיֵשׁ שֶׁהוּא שְׁפַל רוּחַ עַד מְאֹד. וְיֵשׁ שֶׁהוּא בַּעַל תַּאֲוָה, לֹא תִשְׂבַּע נַפְשׁוֹ מֵהֲלֹךְ בְּתַאֲוָתָהּ; וְיֵשׁ שֶׁהוּא טְהוֹר גּוּף בְּיוֹתֵר, לֹא יִתְאַוֶּה אֲפִלּוּ לִדְבָרִים מְעַטִּים שֶׁהַגּוּף צָרִיךְ לָהֶם.

There is a type of **person who is very proud, and** in contrast **there is one who is extremely self-effacing. There is** a type of **lustful** person **whose soul will never be satisfied from pursuing its desires, and there is** a contrasting kind of person **who is very pure** in his **body,**[a] **who does not desire even** the **little amount that the body requires.**

וְיֵשׁ בַּעַל נֶפֶשׁ רְחָבָה, שֶׁלֹּא תִשְׂבַּע נַפְשׁוֹ מִכָּל מָמוֹן הָעוֹלָם, כְּעִנְיָן שֶׁנֶּאֱמַר: "אֹהֵב כֶּסֶף לֹא יִשְׂבַּע כֶּסֶף" (קהלת ה, ט); וְיֵשׁ מְקַצֵּר, שֶׁדַּיּוֹ אֲפִלּוּ דָּבָר מְעַט שֶׁלֹּא יְסַפֵּק לוֹ, וְלֹא יִרְדֹּף לְהַשִּׂיג כָּל צָרְכּוֹ.

There is an avaricious type **whose soul will never be satisfied,** not even **with all the money in the world, in the manner that it is stated: "A lover of silver will never be satisfied with silver"** (Ecclesiastes 5:9), **and there is** a person **who limits** himself, and does not desire possessions at all, **for whom even a little is enough, which does not** even **satisfy** his needs, **and** yet **he will not pursue** more **to attain all his requirements.**

NOTES

a. He is free from the temptation of physical cravings.

וְיֵשׁ שֶׁהוּא מְסַגֵּף עַצְמוֹ בָּרָעָב, וְקוֹבֵץ עַל יָדוֹ, וְאֵינוֹ אוֹכֵל פְּרוּטָה מִשֶּׁלּוֹ אֶלָּא בְּצַעַר גָּדוֹל; וְיֵשׁ שֶׁהוּא מְאַבֵּד כָּל מָמוֹנוֹ בְּיָדוֹ לְדַעְתּוֹ. וְעַל דְּרָכִים אֵלּוּ שְׁאָר כָּל הַדֵּעוֹת,

There is a type of person **who torments himself with hunger, gathering** all he possesses **close to himself.**[a] **He spends a minimum sum of his own,** and that **only at** the cost of **great discomfort.** Meanwhile, **there is** another type of person **who knowingly wastes all the money in his possession. All** the **rest of the traits follow these same patterns.**

כְּגוֹן מְהוֹלֵל וְאוֹנֵן, וְכִילַי וְשׁוֹעַ, וְאַכְזָרִי וְרַחֲמָן, וְרַךְ לֵבָב וְאַמִּיץ לֵב, וְכָל כַּיּוֹצֵא בָּהֶן.

There is a spectrum, with different people having traits at each end of the extremes. **For example,** some are permanently **euphoric and** others are permanently **dour;** some are **stingy and** some are **generous;** some are **cruel and** some are **compassionate;** some are **fainthearted and** some are **brave, and** so on, with **all similar** traits.

Halakha 2

וְיֵשׁ בֵּין כָּל דֵּעָה וְדֵעָה הָרְחוֹקָה מִמֶּנָּה בַּקָּצֶה הָאַחֵר דֵּעוֹת בֵּינוֹנִיּוֹת, זוֹ רְחוֹקָה מִזּוֹ. וְכָל הַדֵּעוֹת – יֵשׁ מֵהֶן דֵּעוֹת שֶׁהֵן לָאָדָם מִתְּחִלַּת בְּרִיָּתוֹ לְפִי טֶבַע גּוּפוֹ, וְיֵשׁ מֵהֶן דֵּעוֹת שֶׁטִּבְעוֹ שֶׁל אָדָם זֶה מְכֻוָּן וְעָתִיד לְקַבֵּל אוֹתָם בִּמְהֵרָה יָתֵר מִשְּׁאָר הַדֵּעוֹת, וְיֵשׁ מֵהֶן שֶׁאֵינָן לָאָדָם מִתְּחִלַּת בְּרִיָּתוֹ, אֶלָּא לָמַד אוֹתָם מֵאֲחֵרִים, אוֹ שֶׁנִּפְנָה לָהֶן מֵעַצְמוֹ לְפִי מַחֲשָׁבָה שֶׁעָלְתָה בְּלִבּוֹ, אוֹ שֶׁשָּׁמַע שֶׁזּוֹ הַדֵּעָה טוֹבָה לוֹ וּבָהּ רָאוּי לֵילֵךְ, וְהִנְהִיג עַצְמוֹ בָּהּ עַד שֶׁנִּקְבְּעָה.

Between each character **trait and the trait that is farthest from it at the other extreme, there are intermediate traits, which are** also **far removed from one another.**[b]

וְכָל הַדֵּעוֹת – יֵשׁ מֵהֶן דֵּעוֹת שֶׁהֵן לָאָדָם מִתְּחִלַּת בְּרִיָּתוֹ לְפִי טֶבַע גּוּפוֹ,

With regard to **all the traits, there are certain traits that a person has from the start of his creation, in accordance with the nature of his body.**

וְיֵשׁ מֵהֶן דֵּעוֹת שֶׁטִּבְעוֹ שֶׁל אָדָם זֶה מְכֻוָּן וְעָתִיד לְקַבֵּל אוֹתָם בִּמְהֵרָה יָתֵר מִשְּׁאָר הַדֵּעוֹת,

There are also some traits for which a certain person's nature is best **suited, and which he can acquire over the course of time more easily than other traits.**

וְיֵשׁ מֵהֶן שֶׁאֵינָן לָאָדָם מִתְּחִלַּת בְּרִיָּתוֹ, אֶלָּא לָמַד אוֹתָם מֵאֲחֵרִים, אוֹ שֶׁנִּפְנָה לָהֶן מֵעַצְמוֹ לְפִי מַחֲשָׁבָה שֶׁעָלְתָה בְּלִבּוֹ, אוֹ שֶׁשָּׁמַע שֶׁזּוֹ הַדֵּעָה טוֹבָה לוֹ וּבָהּ רָאוּי לֵילֵךְ,

Yet **other traits he does not have from his conception, but he learned them from others, or turned to them of his own accord following a thought that arose in his mind, or because he heard that it was a proper trait for him which he should follow.**

NOTES

a. He is so miserly that he is willing to starve himself rather than spend any of his savings.

b. That is, there are many possible intermediate levels of character traits.

וְהִנְהִיג עַצְמוֹ בָּהּ עַד שֶׁנִּקְבְּעָה.

He therefore **conducted himself in accordance with** that trait **until it became established** in his character.[a]

Halakha 3

שְׁנֵי קְצָווֹת הָרְחוֹקוֹת זוֹ מִזּוֹ שֶׁבְּכָל דֵּעָה וְדֵעָה אֵינָן דֶּרֶךְ טוֹבָה, וְאֵין רָאוּי לוֹ לָאָדָם לָלֶכֶת בָּהֶן וְלֹא לְלַמְּדָן לְעַצְמוֹ.

The two extremes of each and every trait, which are far removed from one another, are not a good path. It is unworthy for a person to follow them, or train himself in them.

וְאִם מָצָא טִבְעוֹ נוֹטֶה לְאַחַת מֵהֶן אוֹ מוּכָן לְאַחַת מֵהֶן, אוֹ שֶׁכְּבָר לָמַד אַחַת מֵהֶן וְנָהַג בָּהּ – יַחֲזִיר עַצְמוֹ לַמּוּטָב וְיֵלֵךְ בְּדֶרֶךְ הַטּוֹבִים, וְהִיא הַדֶּרֶךְ הַיְשָׁרָה.

If he finds his nature tending toward one of them, or ready to follow **one of them, or if he has already learned one of the extremes and conducted himself accordingly, he should bring himself back to** the **good** way **and walk in the path of the good. This** middle road is called **the straight path.**[b]

Halakha 4

הַדֶּרֶךְ הַיְשָׁרָה הִיא מִדָּה בֵּינוֹנִית שֶׁבְּכָל דֵּעָה וְדֵעָה מִכָּל דֵּעוֹת שֶׁיֵּשׁ לָאָדָם, וְהִיא הַדֵּעָה שֶׁהִיא רְחוֹקָה מִשְּׁנֵי הַקְּצָווֹת רִחוּק שָׁוֶה, וְאֵינָהּ קְרוֹבָה לֹא לָזוֹ וְלֹא לָזוֹ. וּלְפִיכָךְ צִוּוּ חֲכָמִים הָרִאשׁוֹנִים שֶׁיְּהֵא אָדָם שָׁם דֵּעוֹתָיו תָּמִיד וּמְשַׁעֵר אוֹתָם וּמְכַוֵּן אוֹתָם בַּדֶּרֶךְ הָאֶמְצָעִית, כְּדֵי שֶׁיְּהֵא שָׁלֵם.

The straight path is the intermediate measure of each and every trait, of all the traits that a person possesses. It is the trait which is equidistant from the two extremes, without being closer to either of them. Therefore, the early Sages commanded a man to appraise his traits constantly, and to measure them and direct them along the middle path, so that he will be sound in his character traits.

כָּל אָדָם שֶׁדֵּעוֹתָיו כֻּלָּם דֵּעוֹת בֵּינוֹנִיּוֹת מְמֻצָּעוֹת – נִקְרָא חָכָם.

How so? One **should not be wrathful** and **easily angered, but** also **not like a dead** person, **who feels nothing.**[c] **Rather,** he should be **intermediate** in this regard: He should **grow angry only over a major issue that is worthy of one's anger, in order to prevent a similar occurrence** on **another occasion.**[d]

כֵּיצַד? לֹא יְהֵא בַּעַל חֵמָה נוֹחַ לִכְעֹס, וְלֹא כְּמֵת שֶׁאֵינוֹ מַרְגִּישׁ, אֶלָּא בֵּינוֹנִי: לֹא יִכְעֹס אֶלָּא עַל דָּבָר גָּדוֹל שֶׁרָאוּי לִכְעֹס עָלָיו, כְּדֵי שֶׁלֹּא יֵעָשֶׂה כַּיּוֹצֵא בּוֹ פַּעַם אַחֶרֶת.

Likewise, he should desire only those things that the body needs and without which it cannot exist, in the manner that it is stated: "The righteous eats to satisfy his soul"[e] (Proverbs 13:25).

וְכֵן לֹא יִתְאַוֶּה אֶלָּא לִדְבָרִים שֶׁהַגּוּף צָרִיךְ לָהֶם וְאִי אֶפְשָׁר לִחְיוֹת בְּזוּלָתָן, כָּעִנְיָן שֶׁנֶּאֱמַר: "צַדִּיק אֹכֵל לְשֹׂבַע נַפְשׁוֹ" (משלי יג, כה).

Similarly, one should toil in his business affairs only to attain that which he requires for his livelihood, rather than to grow wealthy, **in the manner that it is stated: "A little is good for the righteous"** (Psalms 37:16).

NOTES

a. If a person makes the active decision to behave regularly in a particular fashion, he can acquire a trait even though he has no innate affinity for it.

b. It is also known as the intermediate path, or the path of moderation.

c. By not reacting at all to anything that goes against his wishes.

d. That is, when the anger is justified and will serve a future benefit (see 2:3).

e. To fulfill the requirements of his body to support his soul.

וְכֵן לֹא יִהְיֶה עָמֵל בְּעִסְקוֹ אֶלָּא לְהַשִּׂיג דָּבָר שֶׁצָּרִיךְ לוֹ לְחַיֵּי שָׁעָה, כְּעִנְיָן שֶׁנֶּאֱמַר: "טוֹב מְעַט לַצַּדִּיק" (תהלים לז, טז). וְלֹא יְקַבֵּץ יָדוֹ בְּיוֹתֵר, וְלֹא יְפַזֵּר כָּל מָמוֹנוֹ, אֶלָּא נוֹתֵן צְדָקָה כְּפִי מִסַּת יָדוֹ, וּמַלְוֶה כָּרָאוּי לְמִי שֶׁצָּרִיךְ. וְלֹא יְהֵא מְהוֹלֵל וְשׂוֹחֵק, וְלֹא עָצֵב וְאוֹנֵן,

One should not be tightfisted, nor throw his money around, but **rather he should give charity in accordance with his means and lend as appropriate to whoever needs** money. **He should not be ecstatic and laugh** all the time, **nor sad and morose.**

אֶלָּא שָׂמֵחַ כָּל יָמָיו בְּנַחַת, בְּסֵבֶר פָּנִים יָפוֹת. וְכֵן שְׁאָר דֵּעוֹתָיו. וְדֶרֶךְ זוֹ הִיא דֶּרֶךְ הַחֲכָמִים.

Rather, he should be cheerful all his days, but **quietly** so, **with a friendly countenance. The same** applies **to his other** character **traits. This path is the path of the wise. Any person whose traits are all intermediate** and balanced **is called wise.**

Halakha 5

וּמִי שֶׁהוּא מְדַקְדֵּק עַל עַצְמוֹ בְּיוֹתֵר וְיִתְרַחֵק מִדֵּעָה בֵּינוֹנִית מְעַט לְצַד זֶה אוֹ לְצַד זֶה – נִקְרָא חָסִיד. כֵּיצַד? מִי שֶׁיִּתְרַחֵק מִגֹּבַהּ הַלֵּב עַד הַקָּצֶה הָאַחֲרוֹן וְיִהְיֶה שְׁפַל רוּחַ בְּיוֹתֵר – נִקְרָא חָסִיד,

One who is extremely particular with himself and moves slightly away from the intermediate trait, to one side or the other,[a] **is called pious. How so? One who moves** far **away from pride, to the other extreme, and is exceptionally self-effacing, is called pious.**

וְזוֹ הִיא מִדַּת חֲסִידוּת. וְאִם נִתְרַחֵק עַד הָאֶמְצַע בִּלְבַד, וְיִהְיֶה עָנָו – נִקְרָא חָכָם, וְזוֹ הִיא מִדַּת חָכְמָה. וְעַל דֶּרֶךְ זוֹ שְׁאָר כָּל הַדֵּעוֹת. וַחֲסִידִים הָרִאשׁוֹנִים הָיוּ מַטִּין דֵּעוֹת שֶׁלָּהֶם מִדֶּרֶךְ הָאֶמְצָעִית כְּנֶגֶד שְׁתֵּי הַקְּצָווֹת:

This is an attribute of piety. If he moves away from pride **only to the middle** point, **and is humble, he is called wise, and this is an attribute of wisdom. The same** applies **to all the other character traits. The early** generations of **pious** individuals **would incline their** character **traits from the middle path toward** one of **the two extremes.**[b]

יֵשׁ דֵּעָה שֶׁמַּטִּין אוֹתָהּ כְּנֶגֶד הַקָּצֶה הָאַחֲרוֹן, וְיֵשׁ דֵּעָה שֶׁמַּטִּין אוֹתָהּ כְּנֶגֶד הַקָּצֶה הָרִאשׁוֹן, וְזֶה הוּא לִפְנִים מִשּׁוּרַת הַדִּין.

For some traits they would incline toward the latter extreme, while for other traits they would incline toward the former extreme. This is conduct that goes **beyond the letter of the law.**

וּמְצֻוִּים אָנוּ לָלֶכֶת בִּדְרָכִים אֵלּוּ הַבֵּינוֹנִיִּים, וְהֵם הַדְּרָכִים הַטּוֹבִים וְהַיְשָׁרִים, שֶׁנֶּאֱמַר: "וְהָלַכְתָּ בִּדְרָכָיו" (דברים כח, ט).

We are commanded to walk in these intermediate paths, and they are the good and straight paths, as it is stated: "And you shall walk in His ways" (Deuteronomy 28:9).

Halakha 6

כָּךְ לָמְדוּ בְּפֵרוּשׁ מִצְוָה זוֹ: מַה הוּא נִקְרָא חַנּוּן – אַף אַתָּה הֱיֵה חַנּוּן, מַה הוּא נִקְרָא רַחוּם – אַף אַתָּה הֱיֵה רַחוּם, מַה הוּא נִקְרָא קָדוֹשׁ – אַף אַתָּה הֱיֵה קָדוֹשׁ.

The Sages **learned the following explanation of this mitzva: Just as** God **is called "compassionate," you too should be compassionate; just as He is called "merciful," you too should be merciful; just as He is called "Holy," you too should be holy.**

NOTES

a. That is, to the side which is better for his character.

b. They would apply this principle to every attribute, as a safeguard to proper conduct (see the Rambam's *Shemoneh Perakim*, chap. 4).

וְעַל דֶּרֶךְ זוֹ קָרְאוּ הַנְּבִיאִים לָאֵל בְּכָל אוֹתָן הַכִּנּוּיִים: אֶרֶךְ אַפַּיִם, וְרַב חֶסֶד, צַדִּיק, וְיָשָׁר, תָּמִים, גִּבּוֹר, וְחָזָק, וְכַיּוֹצֵא בָּהֶן, לְהוֹדִיעַ שֶׁאֵלּוּ דְּרָכִים טוֹבִים וִישָׁרִים הֵם, וְחַיָּב אָדָם לְהַנְהִיג עַצְמוֹ בָּהֶן וּלְהִדַּמּוֹת כְּפִי כֹּחוֹ.

In a similar manner, the prophets called God by all those appellations: "long-suffering," "abundant in kindness," "righteous," "just," "perfect," "mighty," "powerful," and the like. The prophets used these names for God in order **to inform** us **that these are** characteristic of **good and straight paths. A person is obligated to conduct himself in accordance with them and to resemble Him to the extent of his ability.**

Halakha 7

וְכֵיצַד יַרְגִּיל אָדָם עַצְמוֹ בְּדֵעוֹת אֵלּוּ עַד שֶׁיִּקָּבְעוּ בּוֹ? יַעֲשֶׂה וְיִשְׁנֶה וִישַׁלֵּשׁ בַּמַּעֲשִׂים שֶׁעוֹשֶׂה עַל פִּי הַדֵּעוֹת הָאֶמְצָעִיּוֹת, וְיַחֲזֹר בָּהֶן תָּמִיד, עַד שֶׁיִּהְיוּ מַעֲשֵׂיהֶן קַלִּים עָלָיו וְלֹא יִהְיֶה בָּהֶם טֹרַח, וְיִקָּבְעוּ הַדֵּעוֹת בְּנַפְשׁוֹ.

How should a person accustom himself to these traits until they are established in his character?[a] **He should perform** those **actions that he carries out in accordance with the middle traits once, twice, and three times, repeating them constantly, until these acts become easy for him and do not involve any effort.** Then **these traits will become established in his soul.**

וּלְפִי שֶׁהַשֵּׁמוֹת הָאֵלּוּ שֶׁנִּקְרָא בָּהֶן הַיּוֹצֵר הֵן הַדֶּרֶךְ הַבֵּינוֹנִית שֶׁאָנוּ חַיָּבִין לָלֶכֶת בָּהּ, נִקְרֵאת דֶּרֶךְ זוֹ דֶּרֶךְ יי.

Since these names by which our **Maker is called**[b] **constitute the intermediate path that we are obligated to follow, this path is called "the path of the Lord."**

וְהִיא שֶׁלִּמְּדָהּ אַבְרָהָם אָבִינוּ לְבָנָיו, שֶׁנֶּאֱמַר: "כִּי יְדַעְתִּיו לְמַעַן אֲשֶׁר יְצַוֶּה אֶת בָּנָיו וְאֶת בֵּיתוֹ אַחֲרָיו וְשָׁמְרוּ דֶּרֶךְ יי לַעֲשׂוֹת צְדָקָה וּמִשְׁפָּט" (בראשית יח, יט).

This approach **was taught by our forefather Abraham to his descendants, as it is stated: "For I know him, so that he shall command his children and his household after him, and they will observe the path of the Lord, to perform righteousness and justice"** (Genesis 18:19).

וְהַהוֹלֵךְ בְּדֶרֶךְ זוֹ מֵבִיא טוֹבָה וּבְרָכָה לְעַצְמוֹ, שֶׁנֶּאֱמַר: "לְמַעַן הָבִיא יי עַל אַבְרָהָם אֵת אֲשֶׁר דִּבֶּר עָלָיו" (שם).

One who follows this path brings goodness and blessing upon himself, as stated in the continuation of the same verse: **"So that the Lord will bring upon Abraham that which He spoke of him."**

NOTES

a. And become natural to him.

b. "Long-suffering," "abundant in kindness," and all the other appellations listed in Halakha 6.

פֶּרֶק שֵׁנִי

CHAPTER 2

The Way to Develop Various Character Traits

Halakhot 1–2:	Moral illnesses and their remedies
Halakha 3:	Those character traits regarding which one must adopt an extreme position
Halakhot 4–6:	The suitable manner of speech
Halakha 7:	The appropriate path for various character traits

Halakha 1

חוֹלֵי הַגּוּף טוֹעֲמִין הַמַּר מָתוֹק וְהַמָּתוֹק מַר. וְיֵשׁ מִן הַחוֹלִים מִי שֶׁמִּתְאַוֶּה וְתָאֵב לְמַאֲכָלוֹת שֶׁאֵינָן רְאוּיִין לַאֲכִילָה, כְּגוֹן הֶעָפָר וְהַפֶּחָם, וְשׂוֹנֵא הַמַּאֲכָלוֹת הַטּוֹבִים, כְּגוֹן הַפַּת וְהַבָּשָׂר – הַכֹּל לְפִי רֹב הַחֹלִי.

Those who are physically ill taste the bitter as sweet and the sweet as bitter.[a] **Among the sick are those who desire and crave inedible foods, such as earth and charcoal, while hating good foods, such as bread and meat. All depends on the severity of the sickness.**

כָּךְ בְּנֵי אָדָם שֶׁנַּפְשׁוֹתֵיהֶם חוֹלוֹת מְאַוִּים וְאוֹהֲבִים הַדֵּעוֹת הָרָעוֹת, וְשׂוֹנְאִים הַדֶּרֶךְ הַטּוֹבָה וּמִתְעַצְּלִים לָלֶכֶת בָּהּ, וְהִיא כְּבֵדָה עֲלֵיהֶן לִמְאֹד לְפִי חָלְיָם.

The same applies to **people whose souls are sick:**[b] **They crave and love bad traits, hate the good path, and are** too **lazy to follow it. They find it highly onerous,**[c] **in accordance with their malady.**

וְכֵן יְשַׁעְיָהוּ אוֹמֵר בַּאֲנָשִׁים הַלָּלוּ: "הוֹי הָאֹמְרִים לָרַע טוֹב וְלַטּוֹב רָע, שָׂמִים חֹשֶׁךְ לְאוֹר וְאוֹר לְחֹשֶׁךְ, שָׂמִים מַר לְמָתוֹק וּמָתוֹק לְמָר" (ישעיהו ה, כ).

Thus, the prophet **Isaiah states about such people: "Woe! Those who say of evil, good, and of good, evil; they render darkness into light and light into darkness; they render bitter into sweet and sweet into bitter"** (Isaiah 5:20).

וַעֲלֵיהֶם נֶאֱמַר: "הָעֹזְבִים אָרְחוֹת יֹשֶׁר לָלֶכֶת בְּדַרְכֵי חֹשֶׁךְ" (משלי ב, יג).

With regard to them, the verse **states: "Those who forsake the paths of uprightness to walk in the ways of darkness"** (Proverbs 2:13). They prefer an evil, dark path to a good and upright one.

NOTES

a. Certain diseases affect one's sense of taste, to such an extent that sometimes an invalid might desire to eat things that are not enjoyable for a healthy person, and which are even harmful.

b. Who have become accustomed to bad character traits.

c. Difficult to implement.

What is the remedy for those whose souls are sick? They should go to the wise, for the wise **are the healers of souls. They will heal** the **sickness** of **their** character **traits by teaching them** how to behave **until they have returned them to the good path.**

וּמַה הִיא תַּקָּנַת חוֹלֵי נְפָשׁוֹת? יֵלְכוּ אֵצֶל הַחֲכָמִים, שֶׁהֵם רוֹפְאֵי הַנְּפָשׁוֹת, וִירַפְּאוּ חָלְיָם בַּדֵּעוֹת שֶׁמְּלַמְּדִין אוֹתָם עַד שֶׁיַּחֲזִירוּם לַדֶּרֶךְ הַטּוֹבָה.

Regarding those who recognize their bad traits and yet **do not go to the wise to heal them, Solomon said: "Fools scorn wisdom and admonition"**[a] (Proverbs 1:7).

וְהַמַּכִּירִים בַּדֵּעוֹת הָרָעוֹת שֶׁלָּהֶם וְאֵינָם הוֹלְכִים אֵצֶל הַחֲכָמִים לְרַפֵּא אוֹתָם – עֲלֵיהֶם אָמַר שְׁלֹמֹה: "וּמוּסָר אֱוִילִים בָּזוּ" (משלי א, ז).

Halakha 2

How exactly **are they healed?** In the case of **one who is wrathful, he is told to accustom himself** to adopt such an attitude **that if he is beaten or cursed** he will **not react at all. He should follow this course** of behavior for **a long time, until the anger is uprooted from his heart.**[b]

וְכֵיצַד הִיא רְפוּאָתָם? מִי שֶׁהוּא בַּעַל חֵמָה – אוֹמְרִין לוֹ לְהַנְהִיג עַצְמוֹ שֶׁאִם הֻכָּה וְקֻלַּל לֹא יַרְגִּישׁ כְּלָל, וְיֵלֵךְ בְּדֶרֶךְ זוֹ זְמַן מְרֻבֶּה עַד שֶׁתֵּעָקֵר הַחֵמָה מִלִּבּוֹ.

If he is prideful, he should **accustom himself to severe degradation: He should sit below everyone** else, **dress in tattered rags that shame their wearer, and similar** practices, **until the arrogance is uprooted from him and he returns to the middle path, which is the good path. When he returns to the middle path, he should follow it all** the rest of **his days.**

וְאִם הָיָה גְּבַהּ לֵב – יַנְהִיג עַצְמוֹ בְּבִזָּיוֹן הַרְבֵּה, וְיֵשֵׁב לְמַטָּה מִן הַכֹּל, וְיִלְבַּשׁ בְּלוֹיֵי סְחָבוֹת הַמְבַזִּין אֶת לוֹבְשֵׁיהֶן, וְכַיּוֹצֵא בִּדְבָרִים אֵלּוּ, עַד שֶׁיֵּעָקֵר גֹּבַהּ הַלֵּב מִמֶּנּוּ וְיַחֲזֹר לַדֶּרֶךְ הָאֶמְצָעִית, שֶׁהִיא הַדֶּרֶךְ הַטּוֹבָה, וְלִכְשֶׁיַּחֲזֹר לַדֶּרֶךְ הָאֶמְצָעִית יֵלֵךְ בָּהּ כָּל יָמָיו.

One should follow this method with regard to all the rest of the traits: If he is far removed from the middle, **at one of the extremes, he should move himself** all the way to **the other extreme, and conduct himself accordingly for a long time until he returns to the proper path, which is the intermediate attribute for each and every trait.**

וְעַל קַו זֶה יַעֲשֶׂה בִּשְׁאָר כָּל הַדֵּעוֹת: אִם הָיָה רָחוֹק לַקָּצֶה הָאֶחָד – יַרְחִיק עַצְמוֹ לַקָּצֶה הַשֵּׁנִי, וְיִנְהַג בּוֹ זְמַן מְרֻבֶּה עַד שֶׁיַּחֲזֹר לַדֶּרֶךְ הַטּוֹבָה, וְהִיא מִדָּה בֵּינוֹנִית שֶׁבְּכָל דֵּעָה וְדֵעָה.

Halakha 3

However, **there are traits regarding which a person is prohibited to follow the intermediate** path.[c] **Instead,** he should **move** all the way **to the other extreme.** One example of this **is arrogance: It is not** considered following **the good path for a person to be merely humble. Rather, he must be self-effacing, and his spirit very lowly. It is thus stated about Moses our teacher** that he was **"very humble"** (Numbers 12:3), **and not just "humble."**

וְיֵשׁ דֵּעוֹת שֶׁאָסוּר לוֹ לָאָדָם לִנְהֹג בָּהֶן בְּבֵינוֹנִית, אֶלָּא יִתְרַחֵק עַד הַקָּצֶה הָאַחֵר, וְהוּא גֹּבַהּ הַלֵּב, שֶׁאֵין הַדֶּרֶךְ הַטּוֹבָה שֶׁיִּהְיֶה הָאָדָם עָנָו בִּלְבַד, אֶלָּא שֶׁיִּהְיֶה שְׁפַל רוּחַ וְתִהְיֶה רוּחוֹ נְמוּכָה לִמְאֹד. וּלְפִיכָךְ נֶאֱמַר בְּמֹשֶׁה רַבֵּנוּ: "עָנָו מְאֹד" (במדבר יב, ג), וְלֹא נֶאֱמַר 'עָנָו' בִּלְבַד.

NOTES

a. For they have no wish to improve their conduct.

b. Until he is no longer filled with rage whenever something happens that is not to his liking.

c. Since in these cases even the intermediate path is flawed.

וּלְפִיכָךְ צִוּוּ חֲכָמִים: מְאֹד מְאֹד הֱוֵי שְׁפַל רוּחַ. וְעוֹד אָמְרוּ, שֶׁכָּל הַמַּגְבִּיהַּ לִבּוֹ כָּפַר בָּעִקָּר, שֶׁנֶּאֱמַר: "וְרָם לְבָבֶךָ וְשָׁכַחְתָּ אֶת יי אֱלֹהֶיךָ" (דברים ח, יד). וְעוֹד אָמְרוּ: בְּשַׁמְתָּא דְּאִית בֵּיהּ גַּסּוּת הָרוּחַ, וַאֲפִלּוּ מִקְצָתָהּ.

Accordingly, the Sages instructed: "Have extreme humility of spirit" (*Avot* 4:4). **They further stated** that **anyone who is arrogant has denied the fundamental** tenet of the faith,[a] **as it is stated: "And your heart will grow haughty, and you will forget the Lord your God"** (Deuteronomy 8:14; see *Sota* 4b). **In addition, they said** that **one who has arrogance should be excommunicated, even if** he has **only a little of this** trait (see *Sota* 5a).

וְכֵן הַכַּעַס – דֵּעָה רָעָה הִיא עַד לִמְאֹד, וְרָאוּי לָאָדָם שֶׁיִּתְרַחֵק מִמֶּנָּה עַד הַקָּצֶה הָאַחֵר וִילַמֵּד עַצְמוֹ שֶׁלֹּא יִכְעֹס וַאֲפִלּוּ עַל דָּבָר שֶׁרָאוּי לִכְעֹס עָלָיו.

The same applies to **anger. It is an exceptionally bad trait, and** thus **it is fitting for a person to distance himself from it to the other extreme. He should train himself not to become angry** at all, **even over something that is deserving of anger.**[b]

וְכֵן אִם רָצָה לְהַטִּיל אֵימָה עַל בָּנָיו וּבְנֵי בֵיתוֹ אוֹ עַל הַצִּבּוּר אִם הָיָה פַּרְנָס, וְרָצָה לִכְעֹס עֲלֵיהֶם כְּדֵי שֶׁיַּחְזְרוּ לַמּוּטָב – יַרְאֶה עַצְמוֹ בִּפְנֵיהֶם שֶׁהוּא כּוֹעֵס כְּדֵי לְיַסְּרָם, וְתִהְיֶה דַּעְתּוֹ מְיֻשֶּׁבֶת בֵּינוֹ לְבֵין עַצְמוֹ, כְּאָדָם שֶׁהוּא מְדַמֶּה אִישׁ בִּשְׁעַת כַּעֲסוֹ, וְהוּא אֵינוֹ כּוֹעֵס.

Likewise, if he wishes to impose fear upon his children and the members of **his household,**[c] **or upon the community – if he is** a communal **leader – and wishes to be angry at them in order that they will return to the right** way, **he should act in their presence as** though he were **angry, in order to reprove them, while remaining inwardly calm.** Thus, he should be **like one who pretends to be a man in a rage, without** actually **being angry.**

אָמְרוּ חֲכָמִים הָרִאשׁוֹנִים: כָּל הַכּוֹעֵס כְּאִלּוּ עוֹבֵד עֲבוֹדָה זָרָה, וְאָמְרוּ שֶׁכָּל הַכּוֹעֵס, אִם חָכָם הוּא – חָכְמָתוֹ מִסְתַּלֶּקֶת מִמֶּנּוּ, וְאִם נָבִיא הוּא – נְבוּאָתוֹ מִסְתַּלֶּקֶת מִמֶּנּוּ. וּבַעֲלֵי כַעַס – אֵין חַיֵּיהֶם חַיִּים.

The early Sages said: Anyone who gets angry is like an idol worshipper (*Shabbat* 105b).[d] **They** further **said: Anyone who becomes angry, if he is a scholar, his wisdom departs from him; if he is a prophet, his prophecy departs from him** (*Pesaḥim* 66b). **The life of the wrathful is not a life** worthy of the name.[e]

לְפִיכָךְ צִוּוּ לְהִתְרַחֵק מִן הַכַּעַס עַד שֶׁיַּנְהִיג עַצְמוֹ שֶׁלֹּא יַרְגִּישׁ אֲפִלּוּ לִדְבָרִים הַמַּכְעִיסִין, וְזוֹ הִיא הַדֶּרֶךְ הַטּוֹבָה.

The Sages **therefore instructed** a person **to distance himself from anger until he has become accustomed not to react even to events that** naturally **provoke anger, and this is the good path.**

וְדֶרֶךְ הַצַּדִּיקִים: הֵן עֲלוּבִין וְאֵינָן עוֹלְבִין, שׁוֹמְעִין חֶרְפָּתָן וְאֵינָן מְשִׁיבִין, עוֹשִׂין מֵאַהֲבָה וּשְׂמֵחִים בְּיִסּוּרִים, עֲלֵיהֶם הַכָּתוּב אוֹמֵר: "וְאֹהֲבָיו כְּצֵאת הַשֶּׁמֶשׁ בִּגְבֻרָתוֹ" (שופטים ה, לא).

The path of the righteous is that **they are insulted and** yet **do not insult** others, **they hear their shame and do not respond, they act out of love and rejoice** in their own **suffering. With regard to them, the verse states: "And all those who love Him are like the sun coming out in its might"**[f] (Judges 5:31; *Shabbat* 88b and elsewhere).

NOTES

a. Since it is as though he worships himself.

b. The intermediate level of this trait was presented in 1:4.

c. So that they will fear him and conduct themselves appropriately.

d. This is derived from the verse: "There shall not be a strange god within you" (Psalms 81:10), as the Gemara states: "What is the strange god that is within a person's body… the evil inclination" (*Shabbat* 105b). When one grows angry, it is as though he has allowed foreign forces to take him over.

e. Since they fly into a rage whenever anything goes against their wishes.

f. Even though they are currently downtrodden, in the future they will shine like the light of the sun at its brightest.

Halakha 4

לְעוֹלָם יַרְבֶּה אָדָם בִּשְׁתִיקָה, וְלֹא יְדַבֵּר אֶלָּא אוֹ בִּדְבַר חָכְמָה אוֹ בִּדְבָרִים שֶׁצָּרִיךְ לָהֶן לְחַיֵּי גוּפוֹ. אָמְרוּ עַל רַב, תַּלְמִיד רַבֵּנוּ הַקָּדוֹשׁ, שֶׁלֹּא שָׂח שִׂיחָה בְּטֵלָה כָּל יָמָיו, וְזוֹ הִיא שִׂיחַת רֹב כָּל אָדָם.

A person should always accustom himself to silence, and to speak only words of wisdom[a] or on matters that he requires for his physical welfare. It is stated about Rav,[b] a student of our holy Rabbi, Rabbi Yehuda HaNasi, that he never engaged in idle speech all his days, and yet this is the main conversation of most people.

וַאֲפִלּוּ בְּצָרְכֵי הַגּוּף לֹא יַרְבֶּה אָדָם דְּבָרִים. וְעַל זֶה צִוּוּ חֲכָמִים וְאָמְרוּ: כָּל הַמַּרְבֶּה דְּבָרִים – מֵבִיא חֵטְא, וְאָמְרוּ: לֹא מָצָאתִי לַגּוּף טוֹב אֶלָּא שְׁתִיקָה.

One should not speak excessively even when talking about one's physical needs.[c] In this regard, the Sages commanded and said: "One who talks too much causes sin,"[d] and they further said: "I have found nothing better for the body than silence" (*Avot* 1:17).

וְכֵן בְּדִבְרֵי תּוֹרָה וּבְדִבְרֵי חָכְמָה, יִהְיוּ דִּבְרֵי הֶחָכָם מְעַטִּים וְעִנְיָנֵיהֶם מְרֻבִּים, וְהוּא שֶׁצִּוּוּ חֲכָמִים וְאָמְרוּ: לְעוֹלָם יִשְׁנֶה אָדָם לְתַלְמִידָיו דֶּרֶךְ קְצָרָה.

Likewise, even when one speaks about matters of Torah or matters of general wisdom, the words of the wise should be succinct, with much content. This is what the Sages commanded when they said: "A person should always teach his students in a concise manner" (*Pesaḥim* 3b).

אֲבָל אִם הָיוּ הַדְּבָרִים מְרֻבִּים וְהָעִנְיָן מוּעָט – הֲרֵי זוֹ סִכְלוּת, וְעַל זֶה נֶאֱמַר: "כִּי בָּא הַחֲלוֹם בְּרֹב עִנְיָן וְקוֹל כְּסִיל בְּרֹב דְּבָרִים" (קהלת ה, ב).

If, however, the words one uses are many, while the topic is short, this is foolishness, and with regard to this it is stated: "For a dream comes with a multitude of details,[e] and a fool's voice with a multitude of words" (Ecclesiastes 5:2).

Halakha 5

סְיָג לַחָכְמָה – שְׁתִיקָה. לְפִיכָךְ לֹא יְמַהֵר לְהָשִׁיב, וְלֹא יַרְבֶּה לְדַבֵּר,

"The fence protecting wisdom is silence"[f] (*Avot* 3:17). Accordingly, one should not rush to answer, nor speak excessively.

וִילַמֵּד לַתַּלְמִידִים בְּשׁוּבָה וָנַחַת, בְּלֹא צְעָקָה, בְּלֹא אֲרִיכוּת לָשׁוֹן. הוּא שֶׁשְּׁלֹמֹה אוֹמֵר: "דִּבְרֵי חֲכָמִים בְּנַחַת נִשְׁמָעִים" (קהלת ט, יז).

He should teach his students in a state of repose, calmly,[g] without shouting or engaging in lengthy speeches. This is the meaning of that which Solomon said: "The words of the wise are heard when spoken softly" (Ecclesiastes 9:17).

NOTES

a. Or words of Torah, as explained below.

b. The leading Sage of the first generation of amoraic scholars in Babylonia, and a disciple of the compiler of the Mishna, Rabbi Yehuda HaNasi.

c. Despite the fact that it is permitted to talk about such matters.

d. Since one will end up saying inappropriate things.

e. Worthless ideas are often expressed in great detail.

f. Remaining silent helps one preserve his wisdom.

g. These expressions are from Isaiah 30:15.

Halakha 6

אָסוּר לָאָדָם לְהַנְהִיג עַצְמוֹ בְּדִבְרֵי חֲלָקוֹת וּפִתּוּי, וְלֹא תִּהְיֶה אַחַת בַּפֶּה וְאַחַת בַּלֵּב, אֶלָּא תּוֹכוֹ כְּבָרוֹ, וְהָעִנְיָן שֶׁבַּלֵּב הוּא הַדָּבָר שֶׁבַּפֶּה.

It is prohibited for a person to conduct himself by using **words of flattery and falsehoods.**[1] **He should not say one** thing **with** his **mouth and** think **one** other thing **in** his **heart** (*Bava Metzia* 49a). **Rather, his inside should be like his outside:**[a] **The idea** he has **in his heart should be the** same as the **statement on his lips.**

וְאָסוּר לִגְנֹב דַּעַת הַבְּרִיּוֹת, אֲפִלּוּ דַּעַת הַגּוֹי. כֵּיצַד? לֹא יִמְכֹּר לַגּוֹי בְּשַׂר נְבֵלָה בִּכְלַל שְׁחוּטָה, וְלֹא מִנְעָל שֶׁל מֵתָה בִּמְקוֹם מִנְעָל שֶׁל שְׁחוּטָה.

It is prohibited to deceive people, even gentiles.[b] **How so? One may not sell meat of a carcass to a gentile as though it were ritually slaughtered meat,**[c] **nor a shoe made from** the hide of **an animal that died** of natural causes **instead of a shoe made from** the hide of **a slaughtered animal.**[d]

וְלֹא יְסָרֵב בַּחֲבֵרוֹ שֶׁיֹּאכַל אֶצְלוֹ וְהוּא יוֹדֵעַ שֶׁאֵינוֹ אוֹכֵל, וְיַרְבֶּה לוֹ בְּתִקְרֹבֶת וְהוּא יוֹדֵעַ שֶׁאֵינוֹ מְקַבֵּל, יִפְתַּח לוֹ חָבִיּוֹת שֶׁהוּא צָרִיךְ לִפְתֹּחַ אוֹתָן לְמָכְרָן כְּדֵי לְפַתּוֹתוֹ שֶׁבִּשְׁבִיל כְּבוֹדוֹ פָּתַח,

Similarly, **one should not importune another** person **to eat with him**[2] **when he knows that he will not eat** with him, **or** send another person **many gifts while knowing that** the other **will not accept** them. One may **not open barrels** supposedly **for** a specific person **when** in any case **he has to open them to sell them,** if he does so **in order to deceive him into thinking that he opened them in his honor.**[e]

וְכֵן כָּל כַּיּוֹצֵא בָּזֶה. אֲפִלּוּ מִלָּה אַחַת שֶׁל פִּתּוּי וְשֶׁל גְּנֵבַת הַדַּעַת אֲסוּרָה, אֶלָּא שְׂפַת אֱמֶת וְרוּחַ נָכוֹן וְלֵב טָהוֹר מִכָּל עָמָל וְהַוּוֹת.

This applies **in all similar cases. Even a single word of deception or falsehood is prohibited. Rather,** one should use **only truthful speech,** and have **a steadfast spirit, and a heart** that is **pure of all lies and evil.**

Halakha 7

לֹא יִהְיֶה אָדָם בַּעַל שְׂחוֹק וְהָתֵל, וְלֹא עָצֵב וְאוֹנֵן, אֶלָּא שָׂמֵחַ. כָּךְ אָמְרוּ חֲכָמִים: שְׂחוֹק וְקַלּוּת רֹאשׁ מַרְגִּילִין לְעֶרְוָה. וְצִוּוּ שֶׁלֹּא יְהֵא אָדָם פָּרוּץ בִּשְׂחוֹק, וְלֹא עָצֵב וּמִתְאַבֵּל, אֶלָּא מְקַבֵּל אֶת כָּל הָאָדָם בְּסֵבֶר פָּנִים יָפוֹת.

A person should not be full of jests and mockery, nor sad and morose, but happy. In this regard, **the Sages said: "Mocking and frivolity lead to immorality"**[f] (*Avot* 3:17). **They** also **instructed that a person should not laugh uncontrollably, nor be sad and mournful, but receive everyone with a friendly countenance.**

NOTES

a. His conduct should match his thoughts and feelings (e.g., *Yoma* 72b).

b. Just as one may not steal from a gentile or swindle him out of money (*Hilkhot Geneiva* 7:8; *Hilkhot Gezeila VaAveda* 11:3–5).

c. Because the gentile will think that he is receiving better quality and more expensive meat than the Jew actually gave him.

d. A shoe from the hide of a slaughtered animal was more valuable than one made from a carcass.

e. In all three of these examples, the person is misled into thinking that he was seeking to accord him respect.

f. They can lead one to sexual transgressions.

BACKGROUND

A shoe made from the hide of an animal that died of natural causes instead of a shoe made from the hide of a slaughtered animal – מִנְעָל שֶׁל מֵתָה בִּמְקוֹם מִנְעָל שֶׁל שְׁחוּטָה:

Shoe made from the hide of an animal

HALAKHIC DISCUSSION

1. It is prohibited for a person to conduct himself by using words of flattery and falsehoods – אָסוּר לָאָדָם לְהַנְהִיג עַצְמוֹ בְּדִבְרֵי חֲלָקוֹת וּפִתּוּי: *Shulhan Arukh, Hoshen Mishpat* 228:6, 8.

2. One should not importune another person to eat with him – וְלֹא יְסָרֵב בַּחֲבֵרוֹ שֶׁיֹּאכַל אֶצְלוֹ: It is permitted, however, to extend the invitation once or twice, even though he knows that the other person does not want to come, since this is considered respectful conduct (*Sefer Meirat Einayim*).

וְכֵן לֹא יִהְיֶה בַּעַל נֶפֶשׁ רְחָבָה נִבְהָל לַהוֹן, וְלֹא עָצֵל וּבָטֵל מִמְּלָאכָה, אֶלָּא בַּעַל עַיִן טוֹבָה, מְעַט עֵסֶק וְעוֹסֵק בַּתּוֹרָה, וְאוֹתוֹ הַמְּעַט שֶׁהוּא חֶלְקוֹ – יִשְׂמַח בּוֹ. וְלֹא יִהְיֶה לֹא בַּעַל קְטָטָה, וְלֹא בַּעַל קִנְאָה, וְלֹא בַּעַל תַּאֲוָה, וְלֹא רוֹדֵף אַחַר הַכָּבוֹד.

Similarly, one should not be avaricious, rushing after wealth,[a] **nor lazy and idle from** performing **labor. Rather, he should have a good eye, engaging minimally in** his **business** affairs, **and occupy himself with the Torah,**[b] **while rejoicing in that little which is his portion. He should not be quarrelsome, or an envious or lustful** person, **or one who pursues honor.**

כָּךְ אָמְרוּ חֲכָמִים: הַקִּנְאָה וְהַתַּאֲוָה וְהַכָּבוֹד מוֹצִיאִין אֶת הָאָדָם מִן הָעוֹלָם. כְּלָלוֹ שֶׁל דָּבָר: יֵלֵךְ בַּמִּדָּה הַבֵּינוֹנִית שֶׁבְּכָל דֵּעָה וְדֵעָה, עַד שֶׁיִּהְיוּ כָּל דֵּעוֹתָיו מְכֻוָּנוֹת בָּאֶמְצָעִית.

The Sages thus said: "Envy, lust, and the seeking of honor drive a person out of the world"[c] (*Avot* 4:28). **In sum, one should follow the intermediate attribute of each and every** character **trait until all his traits are aligned in the middle.**

וְהוּא שֶׁשְּׁלֹמֹה אוֹמֵר: "וְכָל דְּרָכֶיךָ יִכֹּנוּ" (משלי ד, כו).

This is the meaning of that which **Solomon said:** "Smooth the track of your feet, **and all your ways will be established"**[d] (Proverbs 4:26).

NOTES

a. The expression is from Proverbs 28:22.

b. See *Avot* 4:12. He should do only what is necessary to earn a living (see 1:4; *Hilkhot Talmud Torah* 3:7–9).

c. Since these attributes are harmful to the person himself.

d. When they are aligned along the middle path.

∻ פֶּרֶק שְׁלִישִׁי

CHAPTER 3

The Purpose of Following the Straight Path

Halakha 1:	The prohibition against adopting extreme measures of abstinence
Halakhot 2–3:	Directing all one's actions for the sake of Heaven

Halakha 1

שֶׁמָּא יֹאמַר אָדָם: הוֹאִיל וְהַתַּאֲוָה וְהַכָּבוֹד וְכַיּוֹצֵא בָּהֶן דֶּרֶךְ רָעָה הֵן וּמוֹצִיאִין אֶת הָאָדָם מִן הָעוֹלָם, אֶפְרֹשׁ מֵהֶן בְּיוֹתֵר וְאֶתְרַחֵק לַצַּד הָאַחֲרוֹן,

A person might say: "Since lust, honor, and the like, are a bad path that remove a person from the world,[a] I shall greatly abstain from them and distance myself to the other extreme."

עַד שֶׁלֹּא יֹאכַל בָּשָׂר, וְלֹא יִשְׁתֶּה יַיִן, וְלֹא יִשָּׂא אִשָּׁה, וְלֹא יֵשֵׁב בְּדִירָה נָאָה, וְלֹא יִלְבַּשׁ מַלְבּוּשׁ נָאֶה אֶלָּא הַשַּׂק וְהַצֶּמֶר הַקָּשֶׁה וְכַיּוֹצֵא בָּהֶן, כְּגוֹן כָּמְרֵי אֱדוֹם – גַּם זוֹ דֶּרֶךְ רָעָה הִיא, וְאָסוּר לֵילֵךְ בָּהּ.

He might adopt this attitude **to** such an extent **that he will not eat meat, drink wine, marry a woman, live in a fine home,** or **wear fine clothing,** but **rather** put on **sackcloth and coarse wool**[b] **and the like,** following the **example of Christian priests** and monks.[c] Yet **this is also a bad path and it is prohibited to follow it.**

NOTES

a. As stated in 2:7.

b. In order to derive no pleasure from the clothes he wears.

c. Who follow such ascetic practices.

BACKGROUND

Sackcloth – הַשַּׂק:

Sackcloth

Coarse wool – וְהַצֶּמֶר הַקָּשֶׁה:

Coarse wool tunic from Egypt, sixth century CE

הַמְהַלֵּךְ בְּדֶרֶךְ זוֹ נִקְרָא חוֹטֵא. הֲרֵי הוּא אוֹמֵר בְּנָזִיר: ״וְכִפֶּר עָלָיו מֵאֲשֶׁר חָטָא עַל הַנָּפֶשׁ״ (במדבר ו, יא). אָמְרוּ חֲכָמִים: וּמָה אִם נָזִיר שֶׁלֹּא פֵּרַשׁ אֶלָּא מִן הַיַּיִן צָרִיךְ כַּפָּרָה, הַמּוֹנֵעַ עַצְמוֹ מִכָּל דָּבָר עַל אַחַת כַּמָּה וְכַמָּה.

One who follows this path is called a sinner, and the verse **thus states with regard to a nazirite: "And make atonement for him, for he sinned by the soul"**[a] (Numbers 6:11). In this context, **the Sages said: "Just as this** person, **who abstained only from wine,**[b] nevertheless **requires atonement,**[c] **one who afflicts himself** by abstaining **from everything, all the more so** that he is a sinner" (*Nazir* 19a).

לְפִיכָךְ צִוּוּ חֲכָמִים שֶׁלֹּא יִמְנַע אָדָם עַצְמוֹ אֶלָּא מִדְּבָרִים שֶׁמְּנָעָה הַתּוֹרָה בִּלְבַד, וְלֹא יִהְיֶה אוֹסֵר עַצְמוֹ בִּנְדָרִים וּבִשְׁבוּעוֹת עַל דְּבָרִים הַמֻּתָּרִים. כָּךְ אָמְרוּ חֲכָמִים: לֹא דַּיֶּךָ מַה שֶּׁאָסְרָה תּוֹרָה, אֶלָּא שֶׁאַתָּה אוֹסֵר עָלֶיךָ דְּבָרִים אֲחֵרִים?!

Therefore, the Sages commanded that a person may abstain only from those things which the Torah withheld from him,[d] **and he should not prohibit himself permitted things by means of vows and oaths. The Sages thus stated: "Is it not enough for you what the Torah has prohibited, that you prohibit additional things upon yourself?!"** (Jerusalem Talmud, *Nedarim* 9:1).

וּבִכְלַל הַזֶּה, אֵלּוּ שֶׁמִּתְעַנִּין תָּמִיד – אֵינָן בְּדֶרֶךְ טוֹבָה. וְאָסְרוּ חֲכָמִים שֶׁיְּהֵא אָדָם מְסַגֵּף עַצְמוֹ בְּתַעֲנִית. וְעַל כָּל הַדְּבָרִים הָאֵלּוּ וְכַיּוֹצֵא בָּהֶן צִוָּה שְׁלֹמֹה וְאָמַר: ״אַל תְּהִי צַדִּיק הַרְבֵּה וְאַל תִּתְחַכַּם יוֹתֵר לָמָּה תִּשּׁוֹמֵם״ (קהלת ז, טז).

This directive that one may not prohibit things upon himself **includes those who fast constantly. They are not on a good path,** for **the Sages prohibited a person to mortify himself through fasting.**[1] **With regard to all of the above, and similar** deeds, **Solomon commanded and said: "Do not be overly righteous, and do not be exceedingly wise; why should you destroy yourself?"**[e] (Ecclesiastes 7:16).

Halakha 2

צָרִיךְ הָאָדָם שֶׁיְּכַוֵּן כָּל מַעֲשָׂיו כֻּלָּם כְּדֵי לֵידַע אֶת הַשֵּׁם בָּרוּךְ הוּא בִּלְבַד, וְיִהְיֶה שִׁבְתּוֹ וְקוּמוֹ וְדִבּוּרוֹ הַכֹּל לְעֻמַּת זֶה הַדָּבָר. כֵּיצַד? כְּשֶׁיִּשָּׂא וְיִתֵּן אוֹ יַעֲשֶׂה מְלָאכָה לִטֹּל שָׂכָר, לֹא יִהְיֶה בְּלִבּוֹ קִבּוּץ מָמוֹן בִּלְבַד,

A person should direct every single one of his actions[f2] **toward the sole purpose of knowing the Lord, blessed be He. His** habits of **rest, his rising, and his** manner of **speech should all be designed to this end. How so? When involved in business dealings, or working for a wage, he should not think only of amassing money.**

אֶלָּא יַעֲשֶׂה דְּבָרִים הָאֵלּוּ כְּדֵי שֶׁיִּמְצָא דְּבָרִים שֶׁהַגּוּף צָרִיךְ לָהֶן מֵאֲכִילָה וּשְׁתִיָּה וִישִׁיבַת בַּיִת וּנְשִׂיאַת אִשָּׁה.

Rather, he should do these things in order that he can use the money to **attain** those **things that the body requires: food; drink; a home residence; and marrying a woman.**

וְכֵן כְּשֶׁיֹּאכַל וְיִשְׁתֶּה וְיִבְעֹל, לֹא יָשִׂים עַל לִבּוֹ לַעֲשׂוֹת דְּבָרִים הַלָּלוּ כְּדֵי לֵהָנוֹת בִּלְבַד, עַד שֶׁנִּמְצָא שֶׁאֵינוֹ אוֹכֵל וְשׁוֹתֶה אֶלָּא הַמָּתוֹק לַחֵךְ וְיִבְעֹל כְּדֵי לֵהָנוֹת,

Likewise, when one eats, drinks, and has sexual intercourse, he should not have in mind to do these things solely for pleasure, with the result **that he will eat and drink only that which is sweet to the palate and have intercourse** merely **for pleasure.**

HALAKHIC DISCUSSION

1. **The Sages prohibited a person to mortify himself through fasting – וְאָסְרוּ חֲכָמִים שֶׁיְּהֵא אָדָם מְסַגֵּף עַצְמוֹ בְּתַעֲנִית**: *Shulḥan Arukh, Oraḥ Ḥayyim* 571:1. The *Shulḥan Arukh* states that if a person has the strength to fast he is called holy, but if not, for example if he is sick or weak, he is called a sinner. Torah scholars and schoolteachers are not permitted to fast, since this might affect their sacred tasks (see the "Halakhic Discussion" on *Hilkhot Talmud Torah* 2:3). The later authorities state that one who knows he has sinned is obligated to fast in atonement (*Taz*; *Magen Avraham*), and this includes Torah scholars, although schoolteachers should not be stringent in this regard (*Shaarei Teshuva*).

2. **A person should direct every single one of his actions – צָרִיךְ הָאָדָם שֶׁיְּכַוֵּן כָּל מַעֲשָׂיו כֻּלָּם**: *Shulḥan Arukh, Oraḥ Ḥayyim* 231:1.

NOTES

a. This is referring to one who took a vow of naziriteship and became ritually impure through contact with the dead while he was a nazirite.

b. A nazirite is prohibited from benefiting from all products of the vine (see *Hilkhot Nezirut* 1:1).

c. For depriving himself of a permitted pleasure.

d. As prescribed by the halakha.

e. Destructive consequences can result from such conduct.

f. When taking care of his physical needs.

אֶלָּא יָשִׂים עַל לִבּוֹ שֶׁיֹּאכַל וְיִשְׁתֶּה כְּדֵי לְהַבְרוֹת גּוּפוֹ וְאֵבָרָיו בִּלְבַד. לְפִיכָךְ לֹא יֹאכַל כָּל שֶׁהַחֵךְ מִתְאַוֶּה, כְּמוֹ הַכֶּלֶב וְהַחֲמוֹר, אֶלָּא יֹאכַל דְּבָרִים הַמּוֹעִילִים לוֹ, אִם מָרִים אִם מְתוּקִים.

Rather, he should have in mind to eat and drink only in order to be healthy in his body and limbs. Therefore, one should not eat all that the palate desires, like a dog or a donkey. Instead, he should eat things that are beneficial for him,[a] whether they are bitter or sweet.

וְלֹא יֹאכַל דְּבָרִים הָרָעִים לַגּוּף, אַף עַל פִּי שֶׁהֵן מְתוּקִים לַחֵךְ. כֵּיצַד? מִי שֶׁהָיָה בְּשָׂרוֹ חַם – לֹא יֹאכַל בָּשָׂר וְלֹא דְּבַשׁ וְלֹא יִשְׁתֶּה יַיִן, כְּעִנְיָן שֶׁאָמַר שְׁלֹמֹה דֶּרֶךְ מָשָׁל: "אָכֹל דְּבַשׁ הַרְבּוֹת לֹא טוֹב" וגו' (משלי כה, כז).

He should likewise **not eat things that are harmful to the body, even though they are sweet to the palate. How so? One who has a warm constitution[b] should not eat meat or honey, or drink wine, as Solomon stated by way of a parable: "Eating much honey is no good..."** (Proverbs 25:27).

וְשׁוֹתֶה מֵי הָעֻלְשִׁין אַף עַל פִּי שֶׁהוּא מַר, שֶׁנִּמְצָא שֶׁהוּא אוֹכֵל וְשׁוֹתֶה דֶּרֶךְ רְפוּאָה בִּלְבַד כְּדֵי שֶׁיִּבְרִיא וְיַעֲמֹד שָׁלֵם, הוֹאִיל וְאִי אֶפְשָׁר לָאָדָם לִחְיוֹת אֶלָּא בַּאֲכִילָה וּשְׁתִיָּה.

One should drink endive juice,[c] even though it is bitter, for he will thus be eating and drinking for medical reasons alone, in order to be healthy and stand whole in body, **since a person cannot survive without eating and drinking.**

וְכֵן כְּשֶׁיִּבְעֹל, לֹא יִבְעֹל אֶלָּא כְּדֵי לְהַבְרוֹת גּוּפוֹ וּכְדֵי לְקַיֵּם אֶת הַזֶּרַע.

Similarly, when one engages in intercourse he should do so only in order to keep his body healthy[d] and in order to have children.[1]

לְפִיכָךְ אֵינוֹ בּוֹעֵל כָּל זְמַן שֶׁיִּתְאַוֶּה, אֶלָּא כָּל עֵת שֶׁיֵּדַע שֶׁהוּא צָרִיךְ לְהוֹצִיא שִׁכְבַת זֶרַע, כְּמוֹ דֶּרֶךְ הָרְפוּאוֹת, אוֹ לְקַיֵּם אֶת הַזֶּרַע.

Accordingly, one should not engage in intercourse whenever he feels the urge, but at **any time when he knows that he requires a seminal emission, such as for medical reasons, or to have children.**

GLOSSES OF THE RAAVAD

וְכֵן כְּשֶׁיִּבְעֹל לֹא יִבְעֹל אֶלָּא כָּל עֵת שֶׁיֵּדַע שֶׁהוּא צָרִיךְ לְהוֹצִיא שִׁכְבַת זֶרַע כְּמוֹ דֶּרֶךְ הָרְפוּאוֹת אוֹ לְקַיֵּם הַזֶּרַע. אָמַר אַבְרָהָם: וְכֵן לְמִצְוַת עוֹנָה אִם הִיא מַקְפֶּדֶת.

"Accordingly, one should not engage in intercourse whenever he feels the urge, but at any time when he knows that he requires a seminal emission, such as for medical reasons, or to have children." Avraham says: And also in order **to** fulfill **the mitzva of conjugal rights, if** his wife **is particular** about this.

Halakha 3

הַמַּנְהִיג עַצְמוֹ עַל פִּי הָרְפוּאָה, אִם שָׂם עַל לִבּוֹ שֶׁיִּהְיֶה כָּל גּוּפוֹ וְאֵבָרָיו שְׁלֵמִים חֲזָקִים בִּלְבַד, וְשֶׁיִּהְיוּ לוֹ בָּנִים עוֹשִׂין מְלַאכְתּוֹ וַעֲמֵלִין לְצָרְכּוֹ – אֵין זוֹ דֶּרֶךְ טוֹבָה.

Even in the case of **one who conducts himself in accordance** with the dictates of **medical** advice, **if the only** thing **he has in mind is that his entire body and limbs will be whole and strong, and that he will have sons who will do his work and toil for his needs, this is not a good path.[e]**

HALAKHIC DISCUSSION

1. In order to keep his body healthy and in order to have children – לְהַבְרוֹת גּוּפוֹ וּכְדֵי לְקַיֵּם אֶת הַזֶּרַע: *Shulḥan Arukh*, *Even HaEzer* 25:2. Another legitimate reason is in order to fulfill the mitzva of conjugal rights (*Shulḥan Arukh*, in accordance with the gloss of the Raavad; see also *Hilkhot Ishut*, chap. 25).

NOTES

a. Which improve his health (for more details, see chap. 4).

b. And thus the doctors have said that certain foods are harmful for him.

c. Water in which the endive plant has been soaked, which was considered medically beneficial.

d. When it is necessary for reasons of health (for more details, see 4:19).

e. Since he is solely focused on his physical needs.

אֶלָּא יָשִׂים עַל לִבּוֹ שֶׁיִּהְיֶה גּוּפוֹ שָׁלֵם וְחָזָק כְּדֵי שֶׁתִּהְיֶה נַפְשׁוֹ יְשָׁרָה לָדַעַת אֶת יי, שֶׁאִי אֶפְשָׁר שֶׁיָּבִין וְיִסְתַּכֵּל בַּחָכְמוֹת וְהוּא חוֹלֶה אוֹ אֶחָד מֵאֵבָרָיו כּוֹאֵב. וְיָשִׂים עַל לִבּוֹ שֶׁיִּהְיֶה לוֹ בֵּן, אוּלַי יִהְיֶה חָכָם וְגָדוֹל בְּיִשְׂרָאֵל.

Instead, he should have in mind that his body will be whole and strong in order that his soul will be upright, to know God.[a] **For it is impossible to understand and reflect on wisdom when one is ill, or if one of his limbs hurts. One should** likewise **have in mind that** if **he will have a son, perhaps he will be a wise and great** scholar **in Israel.**

נִמְצָא הַמְהַלֵּךְ בְּדֶרֶךְ זוֹ כָּל יָמָיו כֻּלָּן – עוֹבֵד אֶת יי תָּמִיד, אֲפִלּוּ בְּשָׁעָה שֶׁנּוֹשֵׂא וְנוֹתֵן, וַאֲפִלּוּ בְּשָׁעָה שֶׁבּוֹעֵל, מִפְּנֵי שֶׁמַּחֲשַׁבְתּוֹ בַּכֹּל כְּדֵי שֶׁיִּמְצָא צְרָכָיו, עַד שֶׁיִּהְיֶה גּוּפוֹ שָׁלֵם לַעֲבֹד אֶת יי.

Thus, one who walks in this path all his days will be serving God constantly,[b] **even when he is involved** in his **business dealings, and even when engaged in intercourse, since his intent in all matters is to fulfill his needs such that his body will be whole,** in order **to serve God.**

וַאֲפִלּוּ בְּשָׁעָה שֶׁהוּא יָשֵׁן, אִם יָשֵׁן לָדַעַת כְּדֵי שֶׁתָּנוּחַ דַּעְתּוֹ עָלָיו וְיָנוּחַ גּוּפוֹ כְּדֵי שֶׁלֹּא יֶחֱלֶה וְלֹא יוּכַל לַעֲבֹד אֶת יי וְהוּא חוֹלֶה – נִמְצֵאת שֵׁנָה שֶׁלּוֹ עֲבוֹדָה לַמָּקוֹם בָּרוּךְ הוּא.

Even when one sleeps, if he goes to sleep with the intention that his mind will calm and his **body rest in order that he will not become sick, and** he **will be unable to serve God when he is sick, the result** is that **his sleep is a service to the Omnipresent, blessed be He.**

וְעַל עִנְיָן זֶה צִוּוּ חֲכָמִים וְאָמְרוּ: וְכָל מַעֲשֶׂיךָ יִהְיוּ לְשֵׁם שָׁמַיִם. וְהוּא שֶׁאָמַר שְׁלֹמֹה בְּחָכְמָתוֹ: "בְּכָל דְּרָכֶיךָ דָעֵהוּ וְהוּא יְיַשֵּׁר אֹרְחֹתֶיךָ" (משלי ג, ו).

In this regard, the Sages commanded and said: "All your deeds should be for the sake of Heaven"* (*Avot* 2:15)**, and this is what Solomon said in his wisdom: "In all your ways, know Him,**[c] **and He will smooth your paths"** (Proverbs 3:6).

FROM THE LUBAVITCHER REBBE

*All your deeds should be for the sake of Heaven – וְכָל מַעֲשֶׂיךָ יִהְיוּ לְשֵׁם שָׁמַיִם: Generally, the two maxims: "Let all your deeds be for the sake of Heaven" (*Avot* 2:17) and: "In all your ways, know Him" (Proverbs 3:6) are interpreted as expressing two different ideas. "For the sake of Heaven" implies that although the actions themselves are taken for one's body and the like, they should lead to a later fulfillment of the service of God (i.e., being healthy frees one to perform mitzvot). By contrast, "In all your ways, know Him" is typically understood as saying that the action itself constitutes the service of the Divine. The Rambam (at the end of Halakha 3) links the two concepts, for his wording indicates that even actions that are "for the sake of Heaven," themselves constitute the service of God. For example, staying healthy is a fulfillment of the command: "You shall greatly take care of your lives" (Deuteronomy 4:15), and working for one's livelihood helps build the world, as it is stated: "He formed it to be inhabited" (Isaiah 45:18) (*Torat Menaḥem*, *Hitvaaduyot*, *Parashat Bo* 5748).

NOTES

a. To reflect on the existence and unity of God, which is a positive mitzva (see *Hilkhot Yesodei HaTorah* 1:1–7).

b. Since all of his actions are geared toward the service of God.

c. That is, all your deeds should be for the sake of knowing God.

פֶּרֶק רְבִיעִי

CHAPTER 4

The Health of the Body

Halakhot 1–3:	Eating
Halakhot 4–5:	Sleeping
Halakhot 6–15:	Beneficial and harmful foods
Halakhot 16–17:	Bathing
Halakhot 18–19:	Bloodletting and sexual intercourse
Halakhot 20–23:	General health guidelines

Halakha 1

הוֹאִיל וֶהֱיוֹת הַגּוּף בָּרִיא וְשָׁלֵם מִדַּרְכֵי יי הוּא, שֶׁהֲרֵי אִי אֶפְשָׁר שֶׁיָּבִין אוֹ יֵדַע וְהוּא חוֹלֶה – צָרִיךְ אָדָם לְהַרְחִיק עַצְמוֹ מִדְּבָרִים הַמְאַבְּדִין אֶת הַגּוּף, וּלְהַנְהִיג עַצְמוֹ בִּדְבָרִים הַמַּבְרִים הַמַּחֲלִימִים,

Since it has been established that **having a healthy, whole body is** one **of the paths** by which one can follow **God**[a] – **for it impossible for one to understand or know** anything about the Divine **when he is sick – a person should keep himself far from those things that harm the body,**[1] **while accustoming himself to those things which lead to health and recovery.**

וְאֵלּוּ הֵן:

These are as follows:

לְעוֹלָם לֹא יֹאכַל אָדָם אֶלָּא כְּשֶׁהוּא רָעֵב וְלֹא יִשְׁתֶּה אֶלָּא כְּשֶׁהוּא צָמֵא, וְאַל יַשְׁהֶה נְקָבָיו אֲפִלּוּ רֶגַע אֶחָד, אֶלָּא כָּל זְמַן שֶׁצָּרִיךְ לְהַשְׁתִּין אוֹ לְהָסֵךְ אֶת רַגְלָיו יַעֲמֹד מִיָּד.

A person should eat only when he is hungry, and drink only when he is thirsty. One should not delay relieving himself even for a single **moment;**[b2] **rather, whenever he needs to urinate or relieve himself**[c] **he should arise** to do so **immediately.**

HALAKHIC DISCUSSION

1. **A person should keep himself far from those things that harm the body** – **צָרִיךְ אָדָם לְהַרְחִיק עַצְמוֹ מִדְּבָרִים הַמְאַבְּדִין אֶת הַגּוּף**: With regard to healthy practices and cures in modern times, see the appendix: "Medicine in the Talmud and in the Rambam."

2. **One should not delay relieving himself even for a single moment** – **וְאַל יַשְׁהֶה נְקָבָיו אֲפִלּוּ רֶגַע אֶחָד**: *Shulḥan Arukh, Oraḥ Ḥayyim* 3:17. It is permitted to delay defecating until one can find a suitably secluded spot for the purpose (*Mishna Berura*).

NOTES

a. See 3:3.

b. See also *Hilkhot Maakhalot Asurot* 17:31.

c. Defecate.

Halakha 2

לֹא יֹאכַל אָדָם עַד שֶׁתִּתְמַלֵּא כְּרֵסוֹ, אֶלָּא יִפְחֹת כְּמוֹ רְבִיעַ מִשָּׂבְעָתוֹ. וְלֹא יִשְׁתֶּה מַיִם בְּתוֹךְ הַמָּזוֹן, אֶלָּא מְעַט וּמָזוּג בְּיַיִן,

A person should not eat until his stomach is full. Rather, he should eat roughly a quarter less than he requires **to be full. One should not drink water during the meal, apart from a little, and** that small amount of water should be **mixed with wine.**

וּכְשֶׁיַּתְחִיל הַמָּזוֹן לְהִתְאַכֵּל בְּמֵעָיו, שׁוֹתֶה מַה שֶּׁהוּא צָרִיךְ לִשְׁתּוֹת. וְלֹא יַרְבֶּה לִשְׁתּוֹת מַיִם, אֲפִלּוּ כְּשֶׁיִּתְאַכֵּל הַמָּזוֹן. וְלֹא יֹאכַל עַד שֶׁיִּבְדֹּק עַצְמוֹ יָפֶה יָפֶה, שֶׁמָּא יְהֵא צָרִיךְ לִנְקָבָיו.

When the food starts to be digested in his intestines, he may drink what he requires to drink, but he should not drink too **much water, even when the food has been digested. One should not eat until he has examined himself thoroughly, lest he needs to relieve himself** first.

לֹא יֹאכַל אָדָם עַד שֶׁיְּהַלֵּךְ קֹדֶם אֲכִילָה עַד שֶׁיַּתְחִיל גּוּפוֹ לָחֹם, אוֹ יַעֲשֶׂה מְלָאכָה אוֹ יִתְיַגֵּעַ בְּיֶגַע אַחֵר.

A person should not eat until he has taken a walk before eating, so **that his body starts to warm up, or he should perform labor or exert himself with some other task.**[a]

כְּלָלוֹ שֶׁל דָּבָר: יְעַנֶּה גּוּפוֹ וְיִיגַע כָּל יוֹם בַּבֹּקֶר עַד שֶׁיַּתְחִיל גּוּפוֹ לָחֹם, וְיִשְׁקֹט מְעַט עַד שֶׁתִּתְיַשֵּׁב נַפְשׁוֹ, וְאוֹכֵל. וְאִם רָחַץ בְּחַמִּין אַחַר שֶׁיָּגַע – הֲרֵי זֶה טוֹב, וְאַחַר כָּךְ שׁוֹהֶה מְעַט וְאוֹכֵל.

The general principle is that one should strain his body and exert himself every day in the morning, until his body starts to warm up, and then **he should rest a little until his mind has settled, and** then he should **eat. If he bathes in hot water after** this **exertion, that is a good** practice. **He should then wait a short while and eat.**

Halakha 3

לְעוֹלָם כְּשֶׁיֹּאכַל אָדָם יֵשֵׁב בִּמְקוֹמוֹ אוֹ יַטֶּה עַל שְׂמֹאל, וְלֹא יְהַלֵּךְ וְלֹא יִרְכַּב וְלֹא יִיגַע וְלֹא יְזַעֲזֵעַ גּוּפוֹ וְלֹא יְטַיֵּל עַד שֶׁיִּתְאַכֵּל הַמָּזוֹן שֶׁבְּמֵעָיו. וְכָל הַמְטַיֵּל אַחַר אֲכִילָתוֹ אוֹ שֶׁיָּגַע – הֲרֵי זֶה מֵבִיא עַל עַצְמוֹ חֳלָאִים רָעִים וְקָשִׁים.

A person should always eat sitting in his place or reclining to the **left** side.[b] **One should not walk, ride, exert or subject his body to shocks, or take a stroll, until the food in his intestines has been digested. Anyone who takes a stroll or exerts** himself **after eating brings serious and severe illnesses upon himself.**

Halakha 4

הַיּוֹם וְהַלַּיְלָה – אַרְבַּע וְעֶשְׂרִים שָׁעוֹת. דַּי לוֹ לָאָדָם לִישֹׁן שְׁלִישָׁן, שֶׁהוּא שְׁמוֹנֶה שָׁעוֹת.

The daytime and nighttime together consist of **twenty-four hours. It is enough for a person to sleep a third of these** hours, **which** amounts to **eight hours.**[1]

וְיִהְיוּ בְּסוֹף הַלַּיְלָה, כְּדֵי שֶׁיִּהְיֶה מִתְּחִלַּת שְׁנָתוֹ עַד שֶׁתַּעֲלֶה הַשֶּׁמֶשׁ שְׁמוֹנֶה שָׁעוֹת, וְנִמְצָא עוֹמֵד מִמִּטָּתוֹ קֹדֶם שֶׁתַּעֲלֶה הַשֶּׁמֶשׁ.

These **should be at the end of the night, in order that there will be eight hours from the beginning of his sleep until sunrise. He will thus rise from his bed before sunrise.**

HALAKHIC DISCUSSION

1. **Which is eight hours – שֶׁהוּא שְׁמוֹנֶה שָׁעוֹת**: Each person should follow this practice as much as his constitution allows him to do so (*Magen Avraham* on *Shulḥan Arukh*, *Oraḥ Ḥayyim* 238:1).

NOTES

a. Which will warm up the body.

b. This is the manner of eating while reclining (see *Hilkhot Berakhot* 7:1; *Hilkhot Ḥametz UMatza* 7:7–8).

HALAKHIC DISCUSSION

1. A person should not sleep face down or on his back – לֹא יִישַׁן אָדָם לֹא עַל פָּנָיו וְלֹא עַל עָרְפּוֹ: *Shulḥan Arukh, Even HaEzer* 23:3.

BACKGROUND

Quince – פְּרִישִׁין:

A quince

Halakha 5

לֹא יִישַׁן אָדָם לֹא עַל פָּנָיו וְלֹא עַל עָרְפּוֹ, אֶלָּא עַל צִדּוֹ: בִּתְחִלַּת הַלַּיְלָה עַל צַד שְׂמֹאל, וּבְסוֹף הַלַּיְלָה עַל צַד יָמִין.

A person should not sleep face down or on his back, but on his side:[a1] **At the start of the night on** his **left side, and on** his **right side at the end of the night.**

וְלֹא יִישַׁן סָמוּךְ לַאֲכִילָה, אֶלָּא יַמְתִּין אַחַר אֲכִילָה כְּמוֹ שָׁלֹשׁ אוֹ אַרְבַּע שָׁעוֹת. וְלֹא יִישַׁן בַּיּוֹם.

One should not sleep immediately after eating, but **rather he should wait about three or four hours after eating, and one should not sleep during the day.**

Halakha 6

דְּבָרִים הַמְשַׁלְשְׁלִין אֶת בְּנֵי מֵעַיִם, כְּגוֹן עֲנָבִים וּתְאֵנִים וְתוּתִים וְאַגָּסִים וַאֲבַטִּיחִים וּמְעֵי הַקִּשּׁוּאִים וּמְעֵי הַמְּלָפְפוֹנוֹת – אוֹכֵל אָדָם אוֹתָם בַּתְּחִלָּה קֹדֶם אֲכִילָה, וְלֹא יְעָרְבֵם עִם הַמָּזוֹן, אֶלָּא שׁוֹהֶה מְעַט עַד שֶׁיֵּצְאוּ מִבֶּטֶן הָעֶלְיוֹן, וְאוֹכֵל מְזוֹנוֹ.

Things that loosen the intestines, such as grapes, figs, strawberries, pears, melons, the insides of cucumbers[b] **and the insides of zucchini should be eaten by a person first, before the meal. He should not mix them together with the** rest of his **food, but wait a little until they have left the upper stomach**[c] **and** only then **eat his meal.**

וּדְבָרִים שֶׁהֵן מְאַמְּצִין אֶת בְּנֵי מֵעַיִם, כְּגוֹן רִמּוֹנִים וּפְרִישִׁין וְתַפּוּחִים וּקְרוּסְטְמֵלִין – אוֹכֵל אוֹתָם תֵּכֶף לִמְזוֹנוֹ, וְלֹא יַרְבֶּה מֵהֶן.

Foods which harden the intestines,[d] **such as pomegranates, quinces, apples, and wild pears should be eaten immediately after the meal, and** one should **not** consume **much of them.**

Halakha 7

כְּשֶׁיִּרְצֶה אָדָם לֶאֱכֹל בְּשַׂר עוֹף וּבְשַׂר בְּהֵמָה כְּאֶחָד – אוֹכֵל בַּתְּחִלָּה בְּשַׂר הָעוֹף. וְכֵן בֵּיצִים וּבְשַׂר עוֹף – אוֹכֵל בַּתְּחִלָּה בֵּיצִים.

When a person wishes to eat poultry and meat at one meal, he should **eat the poultry first.**[e] **Similarly,** if he wishes to eat **both eggs and poultry,** he should **eat** the **eggs first.**

בְּשַׂר בְּהֵמָה דַּקָּה וּבְשַׂר בְּהֵמָה גַּסָּה – אוֹכֵל בַּתְּחִלָּה בְּשַׂר הַדַּקָּה. לְעוֹלָם יַקְדִּים דָּבָר הַקַּל וּמְאַחֵר הַכָּבֵד.

If he wants both **meat of small domesticated animals and meat of large domesticated animals,** he should **eat the meat of the small domesticated animals first.** In sum, **the lighter** food should always be eaten **first, and the heavier** food **afterward.**

NOTES

a. See *Hilkhot Keriat Shema* 2:2; *Hilkhot Issurei Bia* 21:19.

b. Which contain its seeds.

c. So that they should not become mixed with the other foods even during the digestive stage.

d. And thus have a constipating effect.

e. Since it is easier to digest than meat.

Halakha 8

בִּימוֹת הַחַמָּה אוֹכֵל מַאֲכָלִים הַקָּרִים, וְלֹא יַרְבֶּה בִּתְבָלִין, וְאוֹכֵל אֶת הַחֹמֶץ. וּבִימוֹת הַגְּשָׁמִים אוֹכֵל אֳכָלִים הַחַמִּין, וּמַרְבֶּה בִּתְבָלִין, וְאוֹכֵל מְעַט מִן הַחַרְדָּל וּמִן הַחִלְתִּית.

In the summer one should **eat cold foods without many spices,**[a] **and eat vinegar. In the rainy season, one should eat warm foods, use many spices, and eat a little mustard and asafoetida.**[b]

וְעַל דֶּרֶךְ זוֹ הוֹלֵךְ וְעוֹשֶׂה בַּמְּקוֹמוֹת הַקָּרִים וּבַמְּקוֹמוֹת הַחַמִּים, בְּכָל מָקוֹם וּמָקוֹם כָּרָאוּי לוֹ.

One should consistently follow this path in both **cold places and warm places,** eating the **appropriate** food **for each and every place.**

Halakha 9

יֵשׁ מַאֲכָלוֹת שֶׁהֵן רָעִים בְּיוֹתֵר עַד מְאֹד, וְרָאוּי לָאָדָם שֶׁלֹּא לְאָכְלָן לְעוֹלָם, כְּגוֹן הַדָּגִים הַגְּדוֹלִים הַמְּלוּחִים הַיְשָׁנִים, וְהַגְּבִינָה הַמְּלֵחָה הַיְשָׁנָה, וְהַכְּמֵהִין וְהַפִּטְרִיּוֹת, וְהַבָּשָׂר הַמָּלִיחַ הַיָּשָׁן, וְיֵין מִגִּתּוֹ, וְתַבְשִׁיל שֶׁשָּׁהָה עַד שֶׁנָּדַף רֵיחוֹ. וְכֵן כָּל מַאֲכָל שֶׁרֵיחוֹ רַע אוֹ מַר בְּיוֹתֵר – הֲרֵי אֵלּוּ לַגּוּף כְּמוֹ סַם הַמָּוֶת.

There are foods that are extremely bad, and it is therefore **fitting for a person never to eat them, such as large, salted, aged fish; salted, aged cheese;**[c] **truffles and mushrooms; aged, salted meat; wine from its press;**[d] **a cooked dish that has been left** a long time **until it smells; and similarly, any food that has a foul smell or** which **is very bitter. These are like poison to the body.**

וְיֵשׁ מַאֲכָלוֹת שֶׁהֵן רָעִים, אֲבָל אֵינָם כְּמוֹ הָרִאשׁוֹנוֹת לָרַע. לְפִיכָךְ רָאוּי לָאָדָם שֶׁלֹּא לֶאֱכֹל מֵהֶן אֶלָּא מְעַט וְאַחַר יָמִים הַרְבֵּה, וְלֹא יַרְגִּיל עַצְמוֹ לִהְיוֹת מְזוֹנוֹ מֵהֶם אוֹ לְאָכְלָם עִם מְזוֹנוֹ תָּמִיד, כְּגוֹן דָּגִים גְּדוֹלִים, וּגְבִינָה, וְחָלָב שֶׁשָּׁהָה אַחַר שֶׁנֶּחֱלַב אַרְבַּע וְעֶשְׂרִים שָׁעוֹת, וּבְשַׂר שְׁוָרִים גְּדוֹלִים וּתְיָשִׁים גְּדוֹלִים, וְהַפּוֹל, וְהָעֲדָשִׁים, וְהַסַּפִּיר, וְלֶחֶם שְׂעוֹרִים, וְלֶחֶם מַצּוֹת, וְהַכְּרוּב, וְהֶחָצִיר, וְהַבְּצָלִים, וְהַשּׁוּמִים, וְהַחַרְדָּל, וְהַצְּנוֹן – כָּל אֵלּוּ מַאֲכָלוֹת רָעִים הֵן.

There are other **foods that are** also **bad, but they are not as bad as the first** group. **Therefore, a person should eat only a little of them and after** an interval of **many days.**[e] **He should not become accustomed for his meal** to consist **of them, or** even **eat them regularly with his** other **food.** These include, **for example, large fish; cheese; milk that has been left for more than twenty-four hours after it was milked; the meat of large oxen or large goats; beans; lentils; peas; barley bread; unleavened bread; cabbage; leeks; onions; garlic; mustard; and radish.**

אֵין רָאוּי לָאָדָם לֶאֱכֹל מֵאֵלּוּ אֶלָּא מְעַט עַד מְאֹד, וּבִימוֹת הַגְּשָׁמִים. אֲבָל שֶׁלֹּא בִּימוֹת הַגְּשָׁמִים לֹא יֹאכַל מֵהֶן כְּלָל. וְהַפּוֹל וְהָעֲדָשִׁים בִּלְבַד, אֵין רָאוּי לְאָכְלָן לֹא בִּימוֹת הַחַמָּה וְלֹא בִּימוֹת הַגְּשָׁמִים. וְהַדִּלּוּעִין, אוֹכְלִין מֵהֶן מְעַט בִּימוֹת הַחַמָּה.

All of these are bad foods. **A person should eat only an extremely small amount of such** foods, and even then, only **in the rainy season,**[f] whereas **in the summer he should not eat them at all. Beans and lentils alone should not be eaten either in the summer or in the rainy season.** As for **pumpkins, one may eat a little of them in the summer.**

NOTES

a. Which heat up the body.

b. Which are spicy and heat up the body.

c. Old foods that are prevented from going bad only by the salt they contain.

d. Wine that has not finished fermenting.

e. That is, he should eat them in small amounts and rarely.

f. Because digesting these foods strengthens and warms up the body (as stated in Halakha 8).

BACKGROUND

Mustard – הַחַרְדָּל:

Mustard plant

Asafoetida – הַחִלְתִּית:

Asafoetida plant

Halakha 10

וְיֵשׁ מַאֲכָלוֹת שֶׁהֵן רָעִים, וְאֵינָן כְּמוֹ אֵלּוּ, וְהֵם: עוֹף הַמַּיִם, וּבְנֵי יוֹנָה הַקְּטַנִּים, וְהַתְּמָרִים, וְלֶחֶם קָלוּי בְּשֶׁמֶן אוֹ לֶחֶם שֶׁנִּלּוֹשׁ בְּשֶׁמֶן, וְהַסֹּלֶת שֶׁנִּפּוּ אוֹתָהּ כָּל צָרְכָּהּ עַד שֶׁלֹּא נִשְׁאַר בָּהּ רֵיחַ מֻרְסָן, וְהַצִּיר, וְהַמֻּרְיָס –

There are yet other **foods that are** still **bad, but they are not as** harmful **as** either of **those** two groups presented above. **They are** as follows: **water fowl; young pigeons; dates; bread roasted in oil or bread kneaded in oil; flour that has been sifted as much as it requires, until no trace of bran is left in it;**[a] **and brine**[b] **and fish stew.**[c]

אֵין רָאוּי לְהַרְבּוֹת מֵאֲכִילַת אֵלּוּ. וְאָדָם שֶׁהוּא חָכָם וְכוֹבֵשׁ אֶת יִצְרוֹ וְלֹא יִמָּשֵׁךְ אַחַר תַּאֲוָתוֹ וְלֹא יֹאכַל מִכָּל הַנִּזְכָּרִים כְּלוּם אֶלָּא אִם נִצְרַךְ לָהֶם לִרְפוּאָה – הֲרֵי זֶה גִּבּוֹר.

One should not eat much of these foods. A man who is wise conquers his inclination, and is not drawn after his appetites and eats none of all those foods **listed above unless he needs them for a healing** purpose, **is a mighty** individual.

Halakha 11

לְעוֹלָם יִמְנַע אָדָם עַצְמוֹ מִפֵּרוֹת הָאִילָנוֹת, וְלֹא יַרְבֶּה מֵהֶן וַאֲפִלּוּ יְבֵשִׁים, וְאֵין צָרִיךְ לוֹמַר רְטֻבִּים. אֲבָל קֹדֶם שֶׁיִּתְבַּשְּׁלוּ כָּל צָרְכָּן – הֲרֵי הֵן לַגּוּף כַּחֲרָבוֹת.

A person should always withhold himself from fruits of trees. He should not eat much of them even if they are **dried, and needless to say** when they are **moist.**[d] **But** the worst is **when they are not fully ripened,** for then **they are like swords to the body.**[e]

וְכֵן הֶחָרוּבִין רָעִים לְעוֹלָם. וְכָל הַפֵּרוֹת הַחֲמוּצִין רָעִים, וְאֵין אוֹכְלִין מֵהֶן אֶלָּא מְעַט בִּימוֹת הַחַמָּה וּבִמְקוֹמוֹת הַחַמִּין. וְהַתְּאֵנִים וְהָעֲנָבִים וְהַשְּׁקֵדִים טוֹבִים לְעוֹלָם, בֵּין רְטֻבִּים בֵּין יְבֵשִׁים, וְאוֹכֵל אָדָם מֵהֶן כָּל צָרְכּוֹ. אֲבָל לֹא יַתְמִיד אֲכִילָתָן, אַף עַל פִּי שֶׁהֵן טוֹבִים מִכָּל פְּרִי הָאִילָנוֹת.

Carobs are also always bad. All pickled fruits are bad, and one should eat only a little of them in the summer and in warm places. Figs, grapes, and almonds are always good, whether they are moist or dried, and a person may eat as much **of them as he requires. However, he should not eat them regularly, even though they are the best of the fruits of trees.**

Halakha 12

הַדְּבַשׁ וְהַיַּיִן – רַע לִקְטַנִּים וְיָפֶה לַזְּקֵנִים, וְכָל שֶׁכֵּן בִּימוֹת הַגְּשָׁמִים. וְצָרִיךְ אָדָם לֶאֱכֹל בִּימוֹת הַחַמָּה שְׁנֵי שְׁלִישֵׁי מַה שֶּׁהוּא אוֹכֵל בִּימוֹת הַגְּשָׁמִים.

Honey and wine are harmful to the young and beneficial for adults, and they are **especially** good for adults **in the rainy season.** Generally speaking, **in the summer a person should eat two-thirds of what he eats in the rainy season.**[f]

NOTES

a. It has been completely cleaned from the husks of the wheat kernel.

b. Extracted from pickled, salted fish.

c. Made from fish innards.

d. Since these are even more harmful than dried fruits.

e. And are actively harmful.

f. In order that the body will not have to work as hard to digest the food, which might overheat it in the summer.

Halakha 13

לְעוֹלָם יִשְׁתַּדֵּל אָדָם שֶׁיִּהְיוּ מֵעָיו רָפִים כָּל יָמָיו, וְיִהְיֶה קָרוֹב לְשִׁלְשׁוּל מְעַט. וְזֶה כְּלָל גָּדוֹל בָּרְפוּאָה, שֶׁכָּל זְמַן שֶׁהָרְאִי נִמְנָע אוֹ יֵצֵא בְּקֹשִׁי – חֳלָאִים רַבִּים בָּאִים.

A person should always try to ensure that the contents of **his intestines are loose throughout his life, tending slightly toward diarrhea. This is a fundamental principle in medicine: Whenever one's stool is withheld or** if it **comes out** only **with difficulty,** this is an indication that **many diseases are coming.**

וּבַמֶּה יְרַפֶּה אָדָם מֵעָיו אִם נִתְאַמְּצוּ מְעַט? אִם הָיָה בָּחוּר – יֹאכַל בַּבֹּקֶר בַּבֹּקֶר מְלוּחִים שְׁלוּקִים מְתֻבָּלִים בְּשֶׁמֶן וּבְמֻרְיָס וּבְמֶלַח בְּלֹא פַּת, אוֹ יִשְׁתֶּה מֵי שֶׁלֶק שֶׁל תְּרָדִין אוֹ כְּרוּב בְּשֶׁמֶן וּמֶלַח וּמֻרְיָס.

How can a person heal his intestines if its contents **became slightly hard? If he is young, he should eat every morning** the leaves of **saltbushes,**[a] **boiled** and **seasoned with oil, fish stew, and salt, without bread, or drink boiled beet or cabbage juice,** seasoned **with oil, salt, and fish stew.**

וְאִם הָיָה זָקֵן – יִשְׁתֶּה דְּבַשׁ מָזוּג בְּמַיִם חַמִּין בַּבֹּקֶר, וְיִשְׁהֶה כְּמוֹ אַרְבַּע שָׁעוֹת, וְאַחַר כָּךְ יֹאכַל סְעוּדָתוֹ. יַעֲשֶׂה כֵּן יוֹם אַחַר יוֹם שְׁלֹשָׁה אוֹ אַרְבָּעָה יָמִים אִם צָרִיךְ לְכָךְ, עַד שֶׁיֵּרָפוּ מֵעָיו.

If he is elderly, he should drink honey diluted in hot water in the morning, wait approximately four hours, and then eat his meal. He should do this consecutively, for three or four days, if necessary, until his intestines heal.

Halakha 14

וְעוֹד כְּלָל אַחֵר אָמְרוּ בִּבְרִיאַת הַגּוּף: כָּל זְמַן שֶׁאָדָם מִתְעַמֵּל וְיָגֵעַ הַרְבֵּה, וְאֵינוֹ שָׂבֵעַ, וּמֵעָיו רָפִים – אֵין חֹלִי בָּא עָלָיו וְכֹחוֹ מִתְחַזֵּק, וַאֲפִלּוּ אָכַל מַאֲכָלוֹת הָרָעִים.

The Sages **stated another general rule with regard to the health of the body: As long as a person exercises, tiring out his** body,[b] **does not** eat until he is **satiated, and his intestines are loose, he will not become sick and he will grow in strength.** This is the case **even if he eats bad foods.**

Halakha 15

וְכָל מִי שֶׁהוּא יוֹשֵׁב לָבֶטַח וְאֵינוֹ מִתְעַמֵּל אוֹ מִי שֶׁמַּשְׁהֶה נְקָבָיו אוֹ מִי שֶׁמֵּעָיו קָשִׁים, אֲפִלּוּ אָכַל מַאֲכָלוֹת טוֹבִים וְשָׁמַר עַצְמוֹ עַל פִּי הָרְפוּאָה – כָּל יָמָיו יִהְיוּ מַכְאוֹבִים וְכֹחוֹ תָּשֵׁשׁ. וַאֲכִילָה גַּסָּה לְגוּף כָּל אָדָם כְּמוֹ סַם הַמָּוֶת, וְהִיא עִקָּר לְכָל הֶחֳלָאִים.

By contrast, **anyone who sits indolently and does not exercise, or one who delays relieving himself,**[c] **or whose intestines are hard, even if he eats good foods and takes care of himself in accordance with** the dictates of **medicine, all his days will be painful and his strength will ebb. Excessive eating is like a poison to anyone's body, and it is the main source of all illnesses.**

NOTES

a. A desert plant with wide, salty leaves.

b. See Halakha 2.

c. See Halakha 1.

רֹב הֶחֳלָאִים הַבָּאִים עַל הָאָדָם אֵינָן אֶלָּא אוֹ מִפְּנֵי מַאֲכָלִים רָעִים, אוֹ מִפְּנֵי שֶׁהוּא מְמַלֵּא בִּטְנוֹ וְאוֹכֵל אֲכִילָה גַּסָּה אֲפִלּוּ מִמַּאֲכָלִים טוֹבִים. הוּא שֶׁשְּׁלֹמֹה אוֹמֵר בְּחָכְמָתוֹ: "שֹׁמֵר פִּיו וּלְשׁוֹנוֹ שֹׁמֵר מִצָּרוֹת נַפְשׁוֹ" (משלי כא, כג), כְּלוֹמַר שׁוֹמֵר פִּיו מִלֶּאֱכֹל מַאֲכָל רַע אוֹ מִלִּשְׂבֹּעַ, וּלְשׁוֹנוֹ מִלְּדַבֵּר אֶלָּא בִּצְרָכָיו.

Most illnesses which come upon a person are either due to bad foods or because he fills his stomach and thus **engages in excessive eating, even of good foods. This is** the meaning of that **which Solomon said in his wisdom: "He who guards his mouth and his tongue guards himself from troubles"** (Proverbs 21:23). **That is,** he **"guards his mouth" from eating bad foods or satiating himself, and "his tongue" from speaking** about issues **other than his needs.**[a]

Halakha 16

דֶּרֶךְ הָרְחִיצָה – שֶׁיִּכָּנֵס אָדָם לַמֶּרְחָץ מִשִּׁבְעָה יָמִים לְשִׁבְעָה יָמִים. וְלֹא יִכָּנֵס סָמוּךְ לַאֲכִילָה, וְלֹא כְּשֶׁהוּא רָעֵב, אֶלָּא כְּשֶׁיַּתְחִיל הַמָּזוֹן לְהִתְאַכֵּל. וְרוֹחֵץ כָּל גּוּפוֹ בְּחַמִּין שֶׁאֵין הַגּוּף נִכְוֶה בָּהֶן, וְרֹאשׁוֹ בִּלְבַד בְּחַמִּין שֶׁהַגּוּף נִכְוֶה בָּהֶן,

The proper **manner of bathing** is **that a person should enter a bathhouse once a week. He should not enter soon after mealtime, nor when he is hungry, but when the food has begun to digest. He should wash his entire body in hot water that does not scald the body, and his head alone in hot water that does scald the body.**

וְאַחַר כָּךְ יִרְחַץ גּוּפוֹ בְּפוֹשְׁרִין, וְאַחַר כָּךְ בְּפוֹשְׁרִין מִן הַפּוֹשְׁרִין, עַד שֶׁיִּרְחַץ בְּצוֹנֵן. וְלֹא יַעֲבִיר עַל רֹאשׁוֹ כְּלָל לֹא פוֹשְׁרִין וְלֹא צוֹנֵן. וְלֹא יִרְחַץ בְּצוֹנֵן בִּימוֹת הַגְּשָׁמִים,

He should subsequently wash his body in lukewarm water, and then in gradually cooler water, until he washes himself **in cold water, but he should not put lukewarm or cold water on his head at all, nor wash in cold water in the rainy season.**[b]

וְלֹא יִרְחַץ עַד שֶׁיָּזִיעַ וְיִפָּרֵךְ כָּל גּוּפוֹ, וְלֹא יַאֲרִיךְ בַּמֶּרְחָץ, אֶלָּא כְּשֶׁיָּזִיעַ וְיִפָּרֵךְ גּוּפוֹ יִשְׁתַּטֵּף וְיֵצֵא.

One should not bathe until after he has sweated and his whole body is tired. One should also **not stay too long in the bathhouse. Rather, as soon as he is in a sweat and his body is tired, he should rinse himself and leave,** since after this point any more bathing can be harmful.

וּבוֹדֵק עַצְמוֹ קֹדֶם שֶׁיִּכָּנֵס לַמֶּרְחָץ וְאַחַר שֶׁיֵּצֵא, שֶׁמָּא הוּא צָרִיךְ לִנְקָבָיו. וְכֵן בּוֹדֵק אָדָם עַצְמוֹ תָּמִיד קֹדֶם אֲכִילָה וְאַחַר אֲכִילָה, וְקֹדֶם בְּעִילָה וְאַחַר בְּעִילָה, וְקֹדֶם שֶׁיִּיגַע וְיִתְעַמֵּל וְאַחַר שֶׁיִּיגַע וְיִתְעַמֵּל, וְקֹדֶם שֶׁיִּישַׁן וּכְשֶׁיֵּיעוֹר – הַכֹּל עֲשָׂרָה.

One should examine himself to see if he needs to attend to the call of nature **before entering the bath and after leaving it, in case he needs to relieve himself. Similarly, one should always examine himself before and after eating, before and after sexual intercourse, before and after exertion and exercise, before sleeping and when he gets up,** making **a total** of **ten** examinations.

Halakha 17

כְּשֶׁיֵּצֵא אָדָם מִן הַמֶּרְחָץ יִלְבַּשׁ בְּגָדָיו וִיכַסֶּה רֹאשׁוֹ בַּבַּיִת הַחִיצוֹן, כְּדֵי שֶׁלֹּא תִשְׁלֹט בּוֹ רוּחַ קָרָה, וַאֲפִלּוּ בִּימוֹת הַחַמָּה צָרִיךְ לְהִזָּהֵר.

When a person leaves the bathhouse, he should put on his clothes and cover his head in the outer vestibule of the bathhouse,[c] **so that he does not catch a chill. One must be careful** in this regard **even in the summer.**

NOTES

a. Since one should refrain from talking as much as possible (2:4).

b. So that he does not get too cold.

c. Where people get dressed (see *Hilkhot Tefillin UMezuza VeSefer Torah* 4:22).

וְיִשְׁהֶה אַחַר שֶׁיֵּצֵא עַד שֶׁתִּתְיַשֵּׁב נַפְשׁוֹ וְיָנוּחַ גּוּפוֹ וְתָסוּר הַחֲמִימוּת, וְאַחַר כָּךְ יֹאכַל. וְאִם יָשַׁן מְעַט כְּשֶׁיֵּצֵא מִן הַמֶּרְחָץ קֹדֶם אֲכִילָה – הֲרֵי זֶה יָפֶה עַד מְאֹד.

One should wait after leaving the bathhouse **until he regains his composure, his body has relaxed, and the warmth** from bathing **has receded, and then he should eat. If he takes a nap upon leaving the bathhouse, before eating, this is extremely beneficial.**

לֹא יִשְׁתֶּה אָדָם מַיִם קָרִים כְּשֶׁיֵּצֵא מִן הַמֶּרְחָץ, וְאֵין צָרִיךְ לוֹמַר שֶׁלֹּא יִשְׁתֶּה בַּמֶּרְחָץ. וְאִם צָמֵא כְּשֶׁיָּצָא וְאֵינוֹ יָכוֹל לִמְנֹעַ עַצְמוֹ – יְעָרֵב הַמַּיִם בְּיַיִן אוֹ בִּדְבַשׁ וְיִשְׁתֶּה. וְאִם סָךְ בְּשֶׁמֶן בַּמֶּרְחָץ בִּימוֹת הַגְּשָׁמִים אַחַר שֶׁיִּשְׁתַּטֵּף – הֲרֵי זֶה טוֹב.

A person should not drink cold water when he leaves the bathhouse, and needless to say he should not drink in the bathhouse itself. **If he is thirsty upon leaving** the bathhouse **and cannot restrain himself, he should mix the water with wine or honey, and** then **drink. If one rubs himself with oil in the bathhouse during the rainy season after he has rinsed himself off, this is beneficial.**

Halakha 18

לֹא יַרְגִּיל אָדָם עַצְמוֹ לְהַקִּיז דָּם תָּמִיד, וְלֹא יַקִּיז דָּם אֶלָּא אִם יִהְיֶה צָרִיךְ לוֹ בְּיוֹתֵר. וְלֹא יַקִּיז לֹא בִּימוֹת הַחַמָּה וְלֹא בִּימוֹת הַגְּשָׁמִים, אֶלָּא בְּיוֹמֵי נִיסָן וּמְעַט בְּיוֹמֵי תִּשְׁרֵי.

A person should not accustom himself to constant bloodletting.[a] **He should not let blood unless he has an extreme need** to do so. **He should not let** blood **in the summer or the rainy season, but in the days of** the month of **Nisan, and infrequently in the days of** the month of **Tishrei.**[b]

וּמֵאַחַר חֲמִשִּׁים שָׁנָה לֹא יַקִּיז כְּלָל. וְלֹא יַקִּיז אָדָם דָּם וְיִכָּנֵס לַמֶּרְחָץ בְּיוֹם אֶחָד, וְלֹא יַקִּיז וְיֵצֵא לַדֶּרֶךְ, וְלֹא בְּיוֹם שֶׁיָּבֹא מִן הַדֶּרֶךְ.

After one is **fifty years** old, **he should not let** blood **at all. And a person should not let** blood **and enter the bathhouse on the same day, or let** blood **and then leave on a journey, or** let blood **on the** same **day when he returns from a journey.**[c]

וְיֹאכַל וְיִשְׁתֶּה בְּיוֹם הַקָּזָה פָּחוֹת מִמַּה שֶּׁהוּא רָגִיל, וְיָנוּחַ בְּיוֹם הַהַקָּזָה, וְלֹא יִתְעַמֵּל וְלֹא יְטַיֵּל.

One should eat less than usual on the day of a bloodletting. He should rest on the day of a bloodletting, and not exercise or take a stroll.

Halakha 19

שִׁכְבַת זֶרַע הִיא כֹּחַ הַגּוּף וְחַיָּיו וּמְאוֹר הָעֵינַיִם. וְכָל זְמַן שֶׁתֵּצֵא בְּיוֹתֵר – הַגּוּף בָּלֶה וְכֹחוֹ כָּלֶה וְחַיָּיו אוֹבְדִים.

Semen[1] **is the strength and life** force **of the body and the light of the eyes. The more emission** of sperm, the more **the body wastes away, its strength dissipates, and one's life** force **is lost.**

הוּא שֶׁאָמַר שְׁלֹמֹה בְּחָכְמָתוֹ: "אַל תִּתֵּן לַנָּשִׁים חֵילֶךָ וּדְרָכֶיךָ לַמְחוֹת מְלָכִין" (משלי לא, ג).

This is the meaning of that **which Solomon said in his wisdom: "Do not give your strength to women, or your ways to that which destroys kings"**[d] (Proverbs 31:3).

HALAKHIC DISCUSSION

1. Semen – שִׁכְבַת זֶרַע: *Shulḥan Arukh, Oraḥ Ḥayyim* 240:14–15.

NOTES

a. As a medical procedure.

b. When the weather is mild.

c. Bloodletting is inadvisable when one's body is weak or if one cannot risk being weak afterward.

d. Do not let your conduct cause you to lose your future as a king.

HALAKHIC DISCUSSION

1. Nor on the day when he leaves on a journey – וְלֹא בְּיוֹם יְצִיאָה לַדֶּרֶךְ: This applies only if he will be walking on foot, but there is no need to refrain from bloodletting if one plans to ride or sit in a wagon (*Taz* on *Oraḥ Ḥayyim* 240:1).

NOTES

a. Since these are times when one is weak.

כָּל הַשָּׁטוּף בִּבְעִילָה – זִקְנָה קוֹפֶצֶת עָלָיו, וְכֹחוֹ תָּשֵׁשׁ, וְעֵינָיו כֵּהוֹת, וְרֵיחַ רַע נוֹדֵף מִפִּיו וּמִשֶּׁחְיו, וּשְׂעַר רֹאשׁוֹ וְגַבּוֹת עֵינָיו וְרִיסֵי עֵינָיו נוֹשֵׁר, וּשְׂעַר זְקָנוֹ וְשֶׁחְיו וּשְׂעַר רַגְלָיו רָבֶה, וְשִׁנָּיו נוֹפְלוֹת, וְהַרְבֵּה כְּאֵבִים חוּץ מֵאֵלּוּ בָּאִין עָלָיו.

Anyone who is steeped in promiscuity is overtaken by old age before his time: **His strength wanes; his eyes become dim; a foul odor wafts from his mouth and from his armpits; the hair of his head, his eyebrows, and eyelashes fall out,** while **the hair of his beard, his armpits, and legs increases; his teeth fall out, and many pains apart from these** also **come upon him.**

אָמְרוּ חַכְמֵי הָרוֹפְאִים: אֶחָד מֵאֶלֶף מֵת בִּשְׁאָר חֳלָאִים, וְהָאֶלֶף מֵרֹב הַתַּשְׁמִישׁ. לְפִיכָךְ צָרִיךְ אָדָם לְהִזָּהֵר בְּדָבָר זֶה אִם רָצָה לִחְיוֹת בְּטוֹבָה.

The scholarly physicians have said: One out of a thousand dies from any of the **other illnesses,** and the rest of **the thousand from excessive intercourse. Therefore, a person must take care in this regard if he wishes to live in good** health.

וְלֹא יִבְעֹל אֶלָּא כְּשֶׁיִּמְצָא גּוּפוֹ בָּרִיא וְחָזָק בְּיוֹתֵר, וְהוּא מִתְקַשֶּׁה הַרְבֵּה שֶׁלֹּא לְדַעְתּוֹ, וּמֵסִיחַ עַצְמוֹ לְדָבָר אַחֵר וְהַקִּשּׁוּי כְּשֶׁהָיָה, וְיִמְצָא כֹּבֶד מִמָּתְנָיו וּלְמַטָּה, וּכְאִלּוּ חוּטֵי הַבֵּיצִים נִמְשָׁכִים, וּבְשָׂרוֹ חַם – זֶה צָרִיךְ לִבְעֹל, וּרְפוּאָה לוֹ שֶׁיִּבְעֹל.

He should engage in intercourse only when the body is healthy and especially strong, when he has many involuntary erections, and the erection is still present even when he tries to **distract his** mind **by thinking of something else, and he experiences a heaviness from his thighs and below, as though the tendons of the testicles are being stretched, and his flesh is warm. This** man **needs to engage in intercourse, and it** is an act of **healing for him to have relations.**

לֹא יִבְעֹל אָדָם וְהוּא שָׂבֵעַ וְלֹא רָעֵב, אֶלָּא אַחַר שֶׁיִּתְאַכֵּל הַמָּזוֹן שֶׁבְּמֵעָיו. וְיִבְדֹּק נְקָבָיו קֹדֶם בְּעִילָה וְאַחַר בְּעִילָה.

A person should not engage in intercourse when he is either **full or hungry, but after the food in his intestines has been digested. He should examine** himself to see if he needs **to relieve himself before and after intercourse.**

וְלֹא יִבְעֹל מְעוּמָד, וְלֹא מְיוּשָּׁב, וְלֹא בְּבֵית הַמֶּרְחָץ, וְלֹא בְּיוֹם שֶׁנִּכְנַס לַמֶּרְחָץ, וְלֹא בְּיוֹם הַקָּזָה, וְלֹא בְּיוֹם יְצִיאָה לַדֶּרֶךְ אוֹ בִּיאָה מִן הַדֶּרֶךְ, לֹא לִפְנֵיהֶם וְלֹא לְאַחֲרֵיהֶם.

He should not engage in intercourse while standing or sitting, nor in the bathhouse, nor on a day when he goes to the bathhouse, nor on a day of bloodletting, nor on the day when he **leaves on a journey**[1] **or arrives from a journey, nor** on the day **before or after** those days.[a]

Halakha 20

כָּל הַמַּנְהִיג עַצְמוֹ בִּדְרָכִים אֵלּוּ שֶׁהוֹרִינוּ, אֲנִי עָרֵב לוֹ שֶׁאֵינוֹ בָּא לִידֵי חֹלִי כָּל יָמָיו, עַד שֶׁיַּזְקִין הַרְבֵּה וְיָמוּת וְאֵינוֹ צָרִיךְ לְרוֹפֵא, וְשֶׁיִּהְיֶה גּוּפוֹ שָׁלֵם וְעוֹמֵד עַל בֻּרְיוֹ כָּל יָמָיו,

Anyone who conducts himself in these ways that we have instructed, I guarantee that he will not become sick throughout his life, until he is very old and dies. He will not need a doctor, and his body will remain whole and retain its state of **health all his days.**

אֶלָּא אִם כֵּן הָיָה גּוּפוֹ רַע מִתְּחִלַּת בְּרִיָּתוֹ, אוֹ אִם הָיָה רָגִיל בְּמִנְהָג מִן הַמִּנְהָגוֹת הָרָעִים מִתְּחִלַּת מוֹלַדְתּוֹ, אוֹ אִם תָּבֹא מַכַּת דֶּבֶר אוֹ מַכַּת בַּצֹּרֶת לָעוֹלָם.

This is the case **unless his body was impaired from the start of its creation,**[a] **or if he was accustomed to one of the bad habits from his birth, or if a plague or a drought occurs in the world.**

Halakha 21

וְכָל הַמִּנְהָגוֹת הַטּוֹבִים הָאֵלּוּ שֶׁאָמַרְנוּ – אֵין רָאוּי לִנְהֹג בָּהֶן אֶלָּא הַבָּרִיא.

All of these beneficial habits that we have stated should be practiced only by a healthy person.

אֲבָל הַחוֹלֶה אוֹ מִי שֶׁאֶחָד מֵאֵבָרָיו חוֹלֶה אוֹ מִי שֶׁנָּהַג מִנְהָג רַע שָׁנִים רַבּוֹת – יֵשׁ לְכָל אֶחָד וְאֶחָד מֵהֶן דְּרָכִים אֲחֵרִים וּמִנְהָגוֹת כְּפִי חָלְיוֹ, כְּמוֹ שֶׁיִּתְבָּאֵר בְּסִפְרֵי הָרְפוּאוֹת. וְשִׁנּוּי וֶסֶת – תְּחִלַּת חֹלִי.

However, with regard to **an invalid, or someone who has a sick organ, or one who has followed a harmful practice** for **many years, each of these has different paths and practices** he should follow **in accordance with his malady, as clarified in the medical literature. And a change of regimen**[b] causes **the onset of diseases.**

Halakha 22

כָּל מָקוֹם שֶׁאֵין בּוֹ רוֹפֵא – אֶחָד הַבָּרִיא וְאֶחָד הַחוֹלֶה אֵין רָאוּי לוֹ לָזוּז מִכָּל הַדְּרָכִים שֶׁאָמַרְנוּ בְּפֶרֶק זֶה, שֶׁכָּל אֶחָד מֵהֶן לְאַחֲרִית טוֹבָה הוּא מֵבִיא.

In **any place that does not have a doctor, neither the healthy nor the sick should deviate from all the paths** and instructions **stated in this chapter,**[c] **for each of them leads to a beneficial result.**

Halakha 23

כָּל עִיר שֶׁאֵין בָּהּ עֲשָׂרָה דְּבָרִים הָאֵלּוּ – אֵין תַּלְמִיד חֲכָמִים רַשַּׁאי לָדוּר בְּתוֹכָהּ, וְאֵלּוּ הֵן: רוֹפֵא, וְאֻמָּן, וּבֵית הַמֶּרְחָץ, וּבֵית הַכִּסֵּא, וּמַיִם מְצוּיִין, כְּגוֹן נָהָר אוֹ מַעְיָן, וּבֵית הַכְּנֶסֶת, וּמְלַמֵּד תִּינוֹקוֹת, וְלַבְלָר, וְגַבַּאי צְדָקָה, וּבֵית דִּין מַכִּין וְחוֹבְשִׁין.

With regard to **any city that does not have these ten things, a Torah scholar is not permitted to reside there.**[d] **They are as follows: a doctor; a bloodletter; a bathhouse;** a public **bathroom; an available** source of **water, such as a river or spring; a synagogue; a teacher of young children;**[e] **a scribe; charity collectors; and a court that** has the authority to **flog and imprison** criminals.

NOTES

a. That is, he suffers from congenital defects.

b. From one's regular habits.

c. In the absence of any other recommendation, one should abide by the guidelines laid out here.

d. Because these things are essential for leading a proper life, and therefore a Torah scholar should be particular about them.

e. See also *Hilkhot Talmud Torah* 2:1.

פֶּרֶק חֲמִישִׁי

CHAPTER 5

The Conduct of a Torah Scholar

Halakha 1

כְּשֵׁם שֶׁהֶחָכָם נִכָּר בְּחָכְמָתוֹ וּבְדֵעוֹתָיו וְהוּא מֻבְדָּל בָּהֶן מִשְּׁאָר הָעָם, כָּךְ צָרִיךְ שֶׁיִּהְיֶה נִכָּר בְּמַעֲשָׂיו: בְּמַאֲכָלוֹ, וּבְמַשְׁקֵהוּ, וּבִבְעִילָתוֹ, וּבַעֲשִׂיַּת צְרָכָיו, וּבְדִבּוּרוֹ, וּבְהִלּוּכוֹ, וּבְמַלְבּוּשׁוֹ, וּבְכִלְכּוּל דְּבָרָיו, וּבְמַשָּׂאוֹ וּבְמַתָּנוֹ, וְיִהְיוּ כָּל הַמַּעֲשִׂים הָאֵלּוּ נָאִים וּמְתֻקָּנִים בְּיוֹתֵר.

כֵּיצַד? תַּלְמִיד חֲכָמִים לֹא יְהֵא גַּרְגְּרָן, אֶלָּא אוֹכֵל מַאֲכָל הָרָאוּי לְהַבְרוֹת גּוּפוֹ, וְלֹא יֹאכַל מִמֶּנּוּ אֲכִילָה גַּסָּה, וְלֹא יְהֵא רוֹדֵף לְמַלֹּאת בִּטְנוֹ כְּאֵלּוּ שֶׁמִּתְמַלְּאִין מִמַּאֲכָל וּמַשְׁקֶה עַד שֶׁתִּפַּח כְּרֵסָן, וַעֲלֵיהֶם מְפֹרָשׁ בַּקַּבָּלָה: "וְזֵרִיתִי פֶרֶשׁ עַל פְּנֵיכֶם פֶּרֶשׁ חַגֵּיכֶם" (מלאכי ב, ג),

Just as[1] **the wise** person **is distinctive*** **in his wisdom and his traits, and he stands apart from the rest of the people in these** aspects,[a] **so too he should be distinctive in his conduct: in his** manner of **eating, drinking, sexual intercourse, relieving himself, his speech, his** manner of **walking and dress,** his **management of his finances,**[b] **and in his business dealings. All of these actions should be exceptionally pleasing and correct.**

How so? A Torah scholar should not be a glutton. Rather, he should eat the appropriate food for the health of his body, without eating an excessive amount of it. He should not seek to fill his stomach, like those who stuff themselves with food and drink until their bellies almost **burst, regarding whom it is explicitly** stated **in the** sources of **tradition,** the books of the Prophets: **"And I will scatter dung**[c] **on your faces, the dung of your festivals"** (Malachi 2:3).

HALAKHIC DISCUSSION

1. **Just as – כְּשֵׁם:** Most of the halakhic rulings in this chapter are stated by the *Shulḥan Arukh* in a general manner as applying to all people, not specifically to a Torah scholar (see the appendix: "The Obligation to Wear a *Kippa*").

FROM THE LUBAVITCHER REBBE

*The wise person is distinctive – הֶחָכָם נִכָּר: The distinction of a wise individual with respect to regular people is expressed not only "in his wisdom and his traits," those realms in which people in general are superior to animals, but also in the daily actions that are common to man and beast, such as eating and drinking. Here, too, wise individuals differ from others – and not only in their preparations for them, or in their conduct after them. It can even be said that this is true of sleep itself. The reason why the Rambam did not specify sleep here is because, practically speaking, the only way to attain a distinguished form of sleep is through the actions that precede one's sleep (from the Rebbe's talk on Shabbat *Parashat Ḥayyei Sara* and *Parashat Toledot* 1985).

NOTES

a. It is evident from his wisdom and behavior that he is a distinguished person, who is different and special.

b. See Halakha 10.

c. Of which there is plenty, due to your overeating.

d. On which one is supposed to hold feasts and rejoice (see *Hilkhot Yom Tov* 6:17–18).

אָמְרוּ חֲכָמִים: אֵלּוּ בְּנֵי אָדָם שֶׁאוֹכְלִין וְשׁוֹתִין וְעוֹשִׂין כָּל יְמֵיהֶם כְּחַגִּים.

The Sages stated in explanation of this verse: **These are people who eat and drink and make all their days like festivals**[a] (see *Shabbat* 151b).

וְהֵם הָאוֹמְרִים: "אָכוֹל וְשָׁתוֹ כִּי מָחָר נָמוּת" (ישעיהו כב, יג), וְזֶה הוּא מַאֲכַל הָרְשָׁעִים. וְשֻׁלְחָנוֹת אֵלּוּ, הֵם שֶׁגִּנָּה הַכָּתוּב וְאָמַר: "כִּי כָּל שֻׁלְחָנוֹת מָלְאוּ קִיא צֹאָה בְּלִי מָקוֹם" (שם כח, ח).

Such people **say: "Eat and drink, for tomorrow we will die"**[b] (Isaiah 22:13). **This is the food of the wicked. It is these tables which the verse condemns, saying: "For all tables are full of vomit, excrement, with no room"**[c] (Isaiah 28:8).

אֲבָל הֶחָכָם אֵינוֹ אוֹכֵל אֶלָּא תַּבְשִׁיל אֶחָד אוֹ שְׁנַיִם, וְאוֹכֵל מִמֶּנּוּ כְּדֵי חַיָּיו, וְדַיּוֹ. הוּא שֶׁאָמַר שְׁלֹמֹה: "צַדִּיק אֹכֵל לְשֹׂבַע נַפְשׁוֹ" (משלי יג, כה).

The wise, however, eats only one dish or two, consuming only enough **of it for his** basic **sustenance, and that is sufficient for him.**[d] **This is** the meaning of that **which Solomon said: "The righteous eats to satisfy his soul"** (Proverbs 13:25).

Halakha 2

כְּשֶׁהֶחָכָם אוֹכֵל מְעַט זֶה הָרָאוּי לוֹ, לֹא יֹאכְלֶנּוּ אֶלָּא בְּבֵיתוֹ עַל שֻׁלְחָנוֹ. לֹא יֹאכַל בַּחֲנוּת וְלֹא בַּשּׁוּק אֶלָּא לְפִי צֹרֶךְ גָּדוֹל, כְּדֵי שֶׁלֹּא יִתְגַּנֶּה בִּפְנֵי הַבְּרִיּוֹת, וְלֹא יֹאכַל אֵצֶל עַמֵּי הָאָרֶץ, וְלֹא עַל אוֹתָן הַשֻּׁלְחָנוֹת הַמְלֵאִים "קִיא צוֹאָה".

When the wise person **eats that little which is fitting for him, he should eat it only in his** own **home, at** his own **table. He should not eat in a store or in the marketplace**[e] **unless there is a very pressing need, in order that he will not degrade himself before** other **people. He should not eat together with boorish** people, **nor at those tables that are filled with "vomit** and **excrement."**[f]

וְלֹא יַרְבֶּה סְעוּדוֹתָיו בְּכָל מָקוֹם, וַאֲפִלּוּ עִם הַחֲכָמִים. וְלֹא יֹאכַל בִּסְעוּדוֹת שֶׁיֵּשׁ בָּהֶן קִבּוּץ הַרְבֵּה.

Indeed, **he should not** eat **his meals frequently in any place** outside of his home, **not even** together **with the Sages, and he should not partake of meals at which there is a large gathering.**

וְאֵין רָאוּי לוֹ לֶאֱכֹל אֶלָּא בִּסְעוּדָה שֶׁל מִצְוָה בִּלְבַד, כְּגוֹן סְעוּדַת אֵרוּסִין וְנִשּׂוּאִין, וְהוּא שֶׁיִּהְיֶה תַּלְמִיד חֲכָמִים שֶׁנָּשָׂא בַּת תַּלְמִיד חֲכָמִים. וְהַצַּדִּיקִים הַחֲסִידִים הָרִאשׁוֹנִים לֹא אָכְלוּ מֵעוֹלָם מִסְּעוּדָה שֶׁאֵינָהּ שֶׁלָּהֶם.

It is fitting for him to eat only at a feast of a mitzva, such as a betrothal or wedding feast, provided that it is a Torah scholar marrying the daughter of a Torah scholar.[g] **The righteous and pious of the early** generations **never partook of a meal that was not their own**[h] (*Ḥullin* 7b).

Halakha 3

כְּשֶׁהֶחָכָם שׁוֹתֶה יַיִן – אֵינוֹ שׁוֹתֶה אֶלָּא כְּדֵי לִשְׁרוֹת אֲכִילָה שֶׁבְּמֵעָיו. וְכָל הַמִּשְׁתַּכֵּר – הֲרֵי זֶה חוֹטֵא וּמְגֻנֶּה וּמַפְסִיד חָכְמָתוֹ.

When a wise person **drinks wine, he drinks only enough** to ensure **that** the **food digests well in his stomach. Anyone who becomes drunk is a sinner, a reprehensible** individual, **and he forfeits his wisdom.**

NOTES

a. On which one is supposed to hold feasts and rejoice (see *Hilkhot Yom Tov* 6:17–18).

b. They seek any pleasure they can enjoy, while they can.

c. Such a meal is comparable to filth, since that will be the end state of the food eaten there; it will fulfill no useful purpose.

d. See 3:2, 4:2.

e. See *Hilkhot Edut* 11:5.

f. That is, together with people who are focused on eating for pleasure (see Halakha 1).

g. Which is a worthy, proper match (see *Hilkhot Issurei Bia* 21:32).

h. Because they did not wish to derive benefit from something that does not belong to them (see *Hilkhot Zekhiya UMattana* 12:17).

וְאִם נִשְׁתַּכֵּר בִּפְנֵי עַמֵּי הָאָרֶץ – הֲרֵי זֶה חִלֵּל אֶת הַשֵּׁם. וְאָסוּר לִשְׁתּוֹת בַּצָּהֳרַיִם וַאֲפִלּוּ מְעַט אֶלָּא אִם הָיָה בִּכְלַל הָאֲכִילָה, שֶׁהַשְּׁתִיָּה שֶׁבִּכְלַל הָאֲכִילָה אֵינָהּ מְשַׁכֶּרֶת, וְאֵין נִזְהָרִין אֶלָּא מִיַּיִן שֶׁלְּאַחַר הַמָּזוֹן.

If he gets drunk in the presence of the boorish, he has desecrated the name of God.[a] **It is prohibited to drink even a small quantity** of wine **in the afternoon**[b] **unless it is** imbibed **together with food, for drink that** is taken **together with food does not intoxicate. One need be careful only regarding wine that** is drunk **after the meal.**[c]

Halakha 4

אַף עַל פִּי שֶׁאִשְׁתּוֹ שֶׁל אָדָם מֻתֶּרֶת לוֹ תָּמִיד, רָאוּי לוֹ לְתַלְמִיד חֲכָמִים שֶׁיַּנְהִיג עַצְמוֹ בִּקְדֻשָּׁה, וְלֹא יְהֵא מָצוּי אֵצֶל אִשְׁתּוֹ כְּתַרְנְגוֹל, אֶלָּא מִלֵּילֵי שַׁבָּת לְלֵילֵי שַׁבָּת, אִם יֵשׁ בּוֹ כֹּחַ.

Even though a man's wife is always permitted to him, it is fitting for a Torah scholar[1] **to conduct himself with holiness. He should not be with his wife like a rooster.**[d] **Rather,** he should have relations only **from** one **night of Shabbat,** Friday night, **to the next,**[e] **if he** has the physical **stamina.**[f2]

וּכְשֶׁהוּא מְסַפֵּר עִמָּהּ – לֹא יְסַפֵּר לֹא בִּתְחִלַּת הַלַּיְלָה כְּשֶׁהוּא שָׂבֵעַ וּבִטְנוֹ מְלֵאָה, וְלֹא בְּסוֹף הַלַּיְלָה כְּשֶׁהוּא רָעֵב, אֶלָּא בְּאֶמְצַע הַלַּיְלָה כְּשֶׁיִּתְאַכֵּל הַמָּזוֹן שֶׁבְּמֵעָיו.

When he "speaks with her,"[g] **he should not speak** with her **at the beginning of the night,**[h3] **when he is satiated and his belly full, nor at the end of the night when he is hungry. Instead,** he should do so **in the middle of the night, when the food in his intestines has been digested.**

וְלֹא יָקֵל רֹאשׁוֹ בְּיוֹתֵר, וְלֹא יְנַבֵּל אֶת פִּיו בְּדִבְרֵי הֲבַאי, וַאֲפִלּוּ בֵּינוֹ לְבֵינָהּ. הֲרֵי הוּא אוֹמֵר בַּקַּבָּלָה: "מַגִּיד לְאָדָם מַה שֵּׂחוֹ" (עמוס ד, יג, ושם: ומגיד), אָמְרוּ חֲכָמִים: אֲפִלּוּ שִׂיחָה קַלָּה שֶׁבֵּין אִישׁ לְאִשְׁתּוֹ עָתִיד לִתֵּן עָלֶיהָ אֶת הַדִּין.

He should not be excessively frivolous, nor should he talk in a vulgar manner by uttering **worthless comments, even** in the intimate conversation **between him and her. For it is stated in the** sources of **tradition,** the books of the Prophets: **"Who tells man what his conversation is"** (Amos 4:13), and **the Sages said,** in explanation of this verse: **"One will be judged in the future even for the light conversation between a man and his wife"** (*Ḥagiga* 5b).

וְלֹא יִהְיוּ שְׁנֵיהֶם לֹא שִׁכּוֹרִים וְלֹא עַצְלָנִין וְלֹא עַצְבָנִין, וְלֹא אֶחָד מֵהֶן. וְלֹא תִּהְיֶה יְשֵׁנָה, וְלֹא יֶאֱנֹס אוֹתָהּ וְהִיא אֵינָהּ רוֹצָה, אֶלָּא בִּרְצוֹן שְׁנֵיהֶם וּבְשִׂמְחָתָן.

Both of them should not be drunk, or weary, or tense. This applies to both the husband and the wife, **or** even **one of them. She should not be asleep, nor should the man take her by force,**[i] **when she does not want** it. **Rather,** the relations should be conducted **with their mutual consent and when they are** in a state of **joy.**

HALAKHIC DISCUSSION

1. **It is fitting for a Torah scholar – רָאוּי לוֹ לְתַלְמִיד חֲכָמִים**: The later authorities state that nowadays anyone who studies or teaches Torah has the status of a Torah scholar with respect to the mitzva of conjugal relations, and therefore he should have intercourse with his wife once a week, every Friday night. Some authorities state that in our days one should have intercourse on a twice weekly basis (*Pitḥei Teshuva*, *Even HaEzer* 76:3; *Beur Halakha*, *Oraḥ Ḥayyim* 240:1).

2. **Rather, from one night of Shabbat to the next, if he has the stamina – אֶלָּא מִלֵּילֵי שַׁבָּת לְלֵילֵי שַׁבָּת אִם יֵשׁ בּוֹ כֹּחַ**: *Shulḥan Arukh*, *Even HaEzer* 76:2–3, *Oraḥ Ḥayyim* 240:1. The nights of Rosh Ḥodesh and festivals are also included in this law (*Magen Avraham*; for the frequency of conjugal relations for ordinary men, see *Hilkhot Ishut* 14:1, and in the "Halakhic Discussion" there). The later authorities state that a God-fearing man should not engage in intercourse on the first night of Passover, the night of Shavuot, the two nights of Rosh HaShana, or the night of Shemini Atzeret, unless it is the night of his wife's ritual immersion, when she sheds the status of a menstruating woman and becomes available to him (*Mishna Berura*).

3. **He should not speak with her at the beginning of the night – לֹא יְסַפֵּר לֹא בִּתְחִלַּת הַלַּיְלָה**: *Shulḥan Arukh*, *Even HaEzer* 25:2–3, 8–9, *Oraḥ Ḥayyim* 240:7–10. The *Shulḥan Arukh* explains that this is to prevent the man from hearing the sounds of other people and thinking about another woman. The later authorities state that these laws apply only to those who follow strict ascetic practices, or to someone who is concerned that he might indeed think about another woman, and there is also a kabbalistic teaching that one should engage in intercourse after midnight. If, however, a person realizes that his inclination is overpowering him and he might experience a seminal emission, he should not be particular in this regard (*Magen Avraham*).

NOTES

a. See *Hilkhot Yesodei HaTorah* 5:11.

b. Since this will cause him to lose the rest of the day.

c. Because wine drunk at that stage is intoxicating.

d. A creature that has sexual relations constantly (see *Hilkhot Issurei Bia* 21:11).

e. Which is the ideal time for Torah scholars to fulfill their conjugal obligations (*Hilkhot Ishut* 14:1).

f. If he is healthy and is able to do so (see *Hilkhot Ishut* 14:7).

g. A euphemism for intercourse.

h. See 4:19, *Hilkhot Ishut* 21:10.

i. See *Hilkhot Issurei Bia* 21:12.

יְסַפֵּר מְעַט וְיִשְׂחַק עִמָּהּ מְעַט, כְּדֵי שֶׁתִּתְיַשֵּׁב נַפְשָׁן, וְיִבְעַל בְּבוּשָׁה, לֹא בְּעַזּוּת, וְיִפְרֹשׁ מִיָּד.

He should converse and play with her a little, in order that she will be relaxed. He should then **engage in intercourse discreetly and not brazenly, and withdraw** from her **immediately** afterward.

Halakha 5

כָּל הַנּוֹהֵג מִנְהָג זֶה, לֹא דַּי לוֹ שֶׁקִּדֵּשׁ נַפְשׁוֹ וְטִהֵר עַצְמוֹ וְתִקֵּן דֵּעוֹתָיו, אֶלָּא שֶׁאִם הָיוּ לוֹ בָּנִים, הוֹוִין בָּנִים נָאִים וּבַיְשָׁנִין, רְאוּיִים לְחָכְמָה וְלַחֲסִידוּת.

Anyone who conducts himself in this manner, not only has he sanctified his soul, purified himself, and refined his traits, but if he has sons,[a] **they will be handsome and bashful sons, worthy of wisdom and piety.**[b]

וְכָל הַנּוֹהֵג בְּמִנְהֲגוֹת שְׁאָר הָעָם הַהוֹלְכִים בַּחֹשֶׁךְ – הוֹוִין לוֹ בָּנִים כְּמוֹ אוֹתָן הָעָם.

By contrast, **anyone who conducts himself in the ways of the rest of the people, who walk in darkness, will have children like those people.**[c]

Halakha 6

צְנִיעוּת גְּדוֹלָה נוֹהֲגִים תַּלְמִידֵי חֲכָמִים בְּעַצְמָן: לֹא יִתְבַּזּוּ וְלֹא יְגַלּוּ רֹאשָׁן וְלֹא גּוּפָן. וַאֲפִלּוּ בְּשָׁעָה שֶׁיִּכָּנְסוּ לְבֵית הַכִּסֵּא יְהֵא צָנוּעַ,

Torah scholars conduct themselves with exceptional modesty. They do not demean themselves and do not bare their heads or expose **their bodies.**[1] **Even when** a Torah scholar **enters a lavatory, he should be modest**[2] **and not uncover** himself from under **his clothes until he is seated.**

וְלֹא יְגַלֶּה בְּגָדָיו עַד שֶׁיֵּשֵׁב, וְלֹא יְקַנֵּחַ בְּיָמִין, וְיִתְרַחֵק מִכָּל אָדָם, וְיִכָּנֵס חֶדֶר בְּחֶדֶר לִפְנִים מִן הַמְּעָרָה, וְנִפְנֶה שָׁם. וְאִם נִפְנֶה אֲחוֹרֵי גָּדֵר – יַרְחִיק כְּדֵי שֶׁלֹּא יִשְׁמַע חֲבֵרוֹ קוֹלוֹ אִם נִתְעַטֵּשׁ.

He should not wipe himself in a lavatory **with his right hand.**[d3] **He should keep away from all** other **people and enter** one **chamber inside** another **chamber, within a cave,**[e] **and relieve himself there. If he relieves himself behind a fence, he should move far enough away that another** person **cannot hear the sound if he breaks wind.**

וְאִם נִפְנֶה בְּבִקְעָה – יַרְחִיק כְּדֵי שֶׁלֹּא יִרְאֶה חֲבֵרוֹ פֵּרוּעוֹ. וְלֹא יְדַבֵּר כְּשֶׁהוּא נִפְנֶה, אֲפִלּוּ לְצֹרֶךְ גָּדוֹל. וּכְדֶרֶךְ שֶׁנּוֹהֵג צְנִיעוּת בְּבֵית הַכִּסֵּא בַּיּוֹם, כָּךְ נוֹהֵג בַּלַּיְלָה.

If he relieves himself in an open field,[f] **he should move far enough away that another** person **cannot see his nakedness. He should not speak while relieving himself, even for a great need. Just as he conducts himself modestly in the lavatory by day, he should act likewise at night.**

וּלְעוֹלָם יְלַמֵּד אָדָם עַצְמוֹ לְהִפָּנוֹת שַׁחֲרִית וְעַרְבִית בִּלְבַד, כְּדֵי שֶׁלֹּא יִתְרַחֵק.

And a person should always train himself to relieve himself only in the morning and evening,[g] **so that he will not** have to **go far away.**

HALAKHIC DISCUSSION

1. **And do not bare their heads or expose their bodies – וְלֹא יְגַלּוּ רֹאשָׁן וְלֹא גּוּפָן:** *Shulḥan Arukh, Oraḥ Ḥayyim* 2:6. The *Shulḥan Arukh* states that a man should not walk four cubits with an uncovered head, and the later authorities add that it is an attribute of piety not to walk even less than that bareheaded (*Magen Avraham*), and one must also keep his head covered while sleeping (*Mishna Berura*). Likewise, one should not stand or sit with a bare head (*Shaarei Teshuva*; for more details, as well as the law of covering one's head while reciting sacred texts, see the appendix: "The Obligation to Wear a *Kippa*").

2. **Even when a Torah scholar enters a lavatory, he should be modest – בְּשָׁעָה שֶׁיִּכָּנְסוּ לְבֵית הַכִּסֵּא יְהֵא צָנוּעַ:** *Shulḥan Arukh, Oraḥ Ḥayyim* 3:2, 8, 10, 12.

3. **He should not wipe himself with his right hand – וְלֹא יְקַנֵּחַ בְּיָמִין:** Furthermore, he should not wipe himself with the middle finger of the left hand, because he wraps the strap of his phylacteries around it (*Magen Avraham*). As for a left-handed man, the later authorities dispute which hand he should use for wiping himself (see *Taz*; *Magen Avraham*; *Beur Halakha*).

NOTES

a. As a result of this intercourse.

b. Because he conceived them in sanctity.

c. Without any special character traits.

d. Since it is considered the more distinguished hand (see e.g., *Hilkhot Tefilla UVirkat Kohanim* 14:3; *Hilkhot Biat HaMikdash* 5:18).

e. So that there is an extra level of concealment.

f. Where there is nothing hiding his presence.

g. When there are not many people around, for if he relieves himself in the middle of the day, he will have to venture far off in order to preserve his modesty (see also *Hilkhot Maakhalot Asurot* 17:31).

Halakha 7

תַּלְמִיד חֲכָמִים לֹא יְהֵא צוֹעֵק וְצוֹוֵחַ בִּשְׁעַת דִּבּוּרוֹ כַּבְּהֵמוֹת וְכַחַיּוֹת וְלֹא יַגְבִּיהַּ קוֹלוֹ בְּיוֹתֵר, אֶלָּא דִּבּוּרוֹ בְּנַחַת עִם כָּל הַבְּרִיּוֹת. וּכְשֶׁיְּדַבֵּר בְּנַחַת, יִזָּהֵר שֶׁלֹּא יִתְרַחֵק עַד שֶׁיֵּרָאֶה כְּדִבְרֵי גַּסֵּי הָרוּחַ.

A Torah scholar should not shout or scream when speaking, like the animals and beasts, and he should not raise his voice too much. Rather, he should speak gently[a] **to all people.** At the same time, **when he speaks gently he should take care not to slow down** his speech so much **that it appears like the drawl of the arrogant.**

וּמַקְדִּים לִשְׁלוֹם כָּל הָאָדָם, כְּדֵי שֶׁתְּהֵא רוּחָן נוֹחָה הֵימֶנּוּ, וְדָן אֶת כָּל הָאָדָם לְכַף זְכוּת, מְסַפֵּר בְּשֶׁבַח חֲבֵרוֹ וְאֵינוֹ מְסַפֵּר בִּגְנוּתוֹ כְּלָל, אוֹהֵב שָׁלוֹם וְרוֹדֵף שָׁלוֹם.

He should be first in greeting all men, so that they will be pleased with him. He should judge every person favorably and **relate the praises of his fellow man, without relating anything derogatory about him. He should love peace and pursue peace.**

אִם רָאָה מָקוֹם שֶׁדְּבָרָיו מוֹעִילִין וְנִשְׁמָעִין – אוֹמֵר, וְאִם לָאו – שׁוֹתֵק. כֵּיצַד? לֹא יְרַצֶּה חֲבֵרוֹ בִּשְׁעַת כַּעֲסוֹ, וְלֹא יִשְׁאַל לוֹ עַל נִדְרוֹ בְּשָׁעָה שֶׁנָּדַר עַד שֶׁתִּתְקָרֵר דַּעְתּוֹ וְיָנוּחַ.

If he sees that on a particular **occasion his words will be effective and will be listened to,** he should **speak, but if not,** he should **remain silent. How so? He should not** try to **placate another while** he is in the throes of **his anger, nor question him about his vow**[b] **at the time that he took the vow,** but wait **until his mind cools** and he **calms down.**[c]

וְלֹא יְנַחֲמֶנּוּ בְּשָׁעָה שֶׁמֵּתוֹ מֻטָּל לְפָנָיו, מִפְּנֵי שֶׁהוּא בָּהוּל עַד שֶׁיִּקְבְּרֵהוּ, וְכֵן כָּל כַּיּוֹצֵא בָּאֵלּוּ. וְלֹא יֵרָאֶה לַחֲבֵרוֹ בִּשְׁעַת קַלְקָלָתוֹ, אֶלָּא יַעֲלִים עֵינוֹ מִמֶּנּוּ.

He should not attempt to **comfort** someone **when his dead is lying before him, because** his mind **is unsettled until he has buried** his dead.[d] **The same** applies **in all similar cases. He should not look at another at the hour of his disgrace,**[e] **but turn his focus away from him.**

וְלֹא יְשַׁנֶּה בְּדִבּוּרוֹ, וְלֹא יוֹסִיף וְלֹא יִגְרַע, אֶלָּא בְּדִבְרֵי שָׁלוֹם וְכַיּוֹצֵא בָּהֶן.

He should not deviate from the truth **when he speaks, or add or detract** from the facts, **except** when issuing **statements** intended to make **peace** between people[f] **and the like.**

כְּלָלוֹ שֶׁל דָּבָר – אֵינוֹ מְדַבֵּר אֶלָּא אוֹ בִּגְמִילוּת חֲסָדִים אוֹ בְּדִבְרֵי חָכְמָה וְכַיּוֹצֵא בָּהֶן. וְלֹא יְסַפֵּר עִם אִשָּׁה בַּשּׁוּק, אֲפִלּוּ הִיא אִשְׁתּוֹ אוֹ אֲחוֹתוֹ אוֹ בִּתּוֹ.

In sum, he should speak only with respect **to acts of kindness, or** when he is delivering **wise statements and the like. He should not speak to a woman in the marketplace, even** if **she is his wife or his sister or his daughter.**[g]

Halakha 8

לֹא יֵלֵךְ תַּלְמִיד חֲכָמִים בְּקוֹמָה זְקוּפָה וְגָרוֹן נָטוּי, כְּעִין שֶׁנֶּאֱמַר: "וַתֵּלַכְנָה נְטוּיוֹת גָּרוֹן וּמְשַׂקְּרוֹת עֵינָיִם" (ישעיהו ג, טז).

A Torah scholar should not walk with an upright posture[1] **and an outstretched neck, in the manner** that the verse **states: "And they walk with outstretched necks and winking eyes"**[h] (Isaiah 3:16).

HALAKHIC DISCUSSION

1. A Torah scholar should not walk with an upright posture – לֹא יֵלֵךְ תַּלְמִיד חֲכָמִים בְּקוֹמָה זְקוּפָה: *Shulḥan Arukh, Oraḥ Ḥayyim* 2:6.

NOTES

a. See also *Hilkhot Yesodei HaTorah* 5:11.

b. By asking him whether he regrets his vow and wishes to have it dissolved (for the manner of dissolving vows, see *Hilkhot Shevuot*, chap. 6).

c. From whatever upset him enough that he uttered the vow.

d. See also *Hilkhot Evel* 4:6.

e. When his friend is acting inappropriately, he should try to keep away from him, to avoid shaming him.

f. It is permitted to depart from the truth in order to restore peace between individuals who have quarreled (see also *Hilkhot Gezeila VaAveda* 14:13).

g. Since not everyone knows that they are family, it might look like he is behaving in an unseemly fashion.

h. This is from the prophet's rebuke of the haughty daughters of Zion.

וְלֹא יְהַלֵּךְ עָקֵב בְּצַד גּוּדָל בְּנַחַת כְּמוֹ הַנָּשִׁים וְגַסֵּי הָרוּחַ, כְּעֵין שֶׁנֶּאֱמַר: ״הָלוֹךְ וְטָפֹף תֵּלַכְנָה וּבְרַגְלֵיהֶן תְּעַכַּסְנָה״ (שם, ישעיה ג, טז; ושם: וּבְרַגְלֵיהֶם). וְלֹא יָרוּץ בִּרְשׁוּת הָרַבִּים וְיִנְהַג בְּשִׁגָּעוֹן, וְלֹא יִכְפֹּף קוֹמָתוֹ כְּבַעֲלֵי חֲטֹרֶת אֶלָּא מִסְתַּכֵּל לְמַטָּה כְּמִי שֶׁהוּא עוֹמֵד בִּתְפִלָּה, וּמְהַלֵּךְ בְּשָׁוֶה כְּאָדָם שֶׁהוּא טָרוּד בַּעֲסָקָיו.

He should also **not walk** in small steps, **heel to toe, like women, and the arrogant, in the manner that** the verse **states: "They walk with a mincing gait and strut their feet"** (Isaiah 3:16). **He should not run in the public domain and** thus **act in a crazy manner,**[a] **nor** be **bent over like a hunchback. Rather, he should look downward, like one who is standing in prayer.**[b] **He should walk at an even** speed, **like a person who is preoccupied with his affairs.**

גַּם בְּמַהֲלָכוֹ שֶׁל אָדָם נִכָּר אִם חָכָם בַּעַל דֵּעָה הוּא אוֹ שׁוֹטֶה וְסָכָל,

Even from a person's manner of **walk, it is evident whether he is a wise and thoughtful** person **or an imbecile and fool.**

וְכֵן אָמַר שְׁלֹמֹה בְּחָכְמָתוֹ: ״וְגַם בַּדֶּרֶךְ כְּשֶׁסָּכָל הֹלֵךְ לִבּוֹ חָסֵר וְאָמַר לַכֹּל סָכָל הוּא״ (קהלת י, ג) – מוֹדִיעַ לַכֹּל עַל עַצְמוֹ שֶׁהוּא סָכָל.

Solomon likewise stated in his wisdom: "Even while the fool walks on the way, his heart is lacking[c] **and says to everyone that he is a fool"** (Ecclesiastes 10:3). That is, **he** thereby **informs everyone about himself that he is a fool.**

Halakha 9

מַלְבּוּשׁ תַּלְמִיד חֲכָמִים – מַלְבּוּשׁ נָאֶה נָקִי, וְאָסוּר לוֹ שֶׁיִּמָּצֵא בְּבִגְדוֹ כֶּתֶם אוֹ שַׁמְנוּנִית וְכַיּוֹצֵא בָּהּ. וְלֹא יִלְבַּשׁ לֹא מַלְבּוּשׁ מְלָכִים, כְּגוֹן בִּגְדֵי זָהָב וְאַרְגָּמָן שֶׁהַכֹּל מִסְתַּכְּלִין בָּהֶם, וְלֹא מַלְבּוּשׁ עֲנִיִּים שֶׁהוּא מְבַזֶּה אֶת לוֹבְשָׁיו, אֶלָּא בְּגָדִים בֵּינוֹנִיִּים נָאִים.

The clothing of a Torah scholar should be pleasing, clean clothing. It is prohibited for a stain or any residue of **fat or something similar to be found on his garment.**[d] **He should not wear the apparel of kings, such as golden and purple garments, which everyone looks at,**[e] **nor the clothing of paupers, which demeans its wearers, but average, pleasing garments.**

וְלֹא יְהֵא בְּשָׂרוֹ נִרְאֶה מִתַּחַת מַדָּיו, כְּמוֹ בִּגְדֵי הַפִּשְׁתָּן הַקַּלִּים בְּיוֹתֵר שֶׁעוֹשִׂין בְּמִצְרַיִם. וְלֹא יִהְיוּ בְּגָדָיו סְחוּבִים עַל הָאָרֶץ כְּמוֹ בִּגְדֵי גַּסֵּי הָרוּחַ, אֶלָּא עַד עֲקֵבוֹ, וּבֵית יָד שֶׁלּוֹ עַד רָאשֵׁי אֶצְבְּעוֹתָיו.

His skin should not be visible through his cloak, such as when one wears **the extremely thin linen garments made in Egypt. His garments should not drag on the ground like the garments of the arrogant; rather,** they should extend **to his heel,**[f] **and his sleeve** should extend **to the ends of his fingers.**[g]

וְלֹא יְשַׁלְשֵׁל טַלִּיתוֹ, מִפְּנֵי שֶׁנִּרְאֶה כְּגַסּוּת רוּחַ, אֶלָּא בְּשַׁבָּת בִּלְבַד אִם אֵין לוֹ לְהַחֲלִיף. וְלֹא יִלְבַּשׁ מִנְעָלִים מְטֻלָּאִים בְּבֶגֶד טְלַאי עַל גַּבֵּי טְלַאי בִּימוֹת הַחַמָּה, אֲבָל בִּימוֹת הַגְּשָׁמִים מֻתָּר אִם הָיָה עָנִי.

He should not let his robe hang down,[h] **for that looks like** a mark of **arrogance, except on Shabbat alone,**[i] **if he has no substitute** attire. **He should not wear shoes that have been mended repeatedly with pieces of fabric, one patch over the other, in the summer, but** this **is permitted in the rainy season, if he is poor.**[j]

NOTES

a. Since it is unusual to run in public (see *Hilkhot Ḥovel UMazik* 6:9).

b. For one who is praying must direct his eyes downward, as though he were looking at the ground (see *Hilkhot Tefilla UVirkat Kohanim* 5:4).

c. He displays his ignorance.

d. Since this is demeaning to the wearer.

e. Because they are so flamboyant.

f. Covering the whole foot.

g. Covering the palms (see *Hilkhot Kelei HaMikdash* 8:17).

h. In such a manner that it has no folds, which is the style used by dignitaries and officials (see *Hilkhot Kelei HaMikdash* 8:4).

i. In honor of Shabbat (see also *Hilkhot Shabbat* 30:3).

j. Since he has to wear whatever shoes he has when it rains.

לֹא יֵצֵא מְבֻשָּׂם לַשּׁוּק, לֹא בִּבְגָדִים מְבֻשָּׂמִים וְלֹא יָשִׂים בֹּשֶׂם בִּשְׂעָרוֹ. אֲבָל אִם מָשַׁח בְּשָׂרוֹ בְּבֹשֶׂם כְּדֵי לְהַעֲבִיר אֶת הַזֻּהֲמָה – מֻתָּר.

He should not go out to the marketplace with his body **smeared with perfume,**[a] **nor with perfumed garments, nor with perfume in his hair. However, if he rubbed perfume on his skin in order to remove filth, it is permitted.**

וְכֵן לֹא יֵצֵא יְחִידִי בַּלַּיְלָה, אֶלָּא אִם הָיָה לוֹ זְמַן קָבוּעַ לָצֵאת בּוֹ לְתַלְמוּדוֹ. כָּל אֵלּוּ מִפְּנֵי הַחֲשָׁד.

Similarly, he should not go out alone at night, unless he has a fixed time when he goes out for his studies. All of these are **due to the** possible **suspicion** of sexual impropriety.

Halakha 10

תַּלְמִיד חֲכָמִים מְכַלְכֵּל דְּבָרָיו בְּמִשְׁפָּט, אוֹכֵל וְשׁוֹתֶה וְזָן אֶת אַנְשֵׁי בֵיתוֹ כְּפִי מָמוֹנוֹ וְהַצְלָחָתוֹ, וְלֹא יַטְרִיחַ עַל עַצְמוֹ יֶתֶר מִדַּי.

A Torah scholar manages his financial affairs prudently. He eats, drinks, and provides for the members of his household in accordance with his means, and the **success of his** endeavors, **without overextending himself.**[b]

צִוּוּ חֲכָמִים בְּדַרְכֵי אֶרֶץ שֶׁלֹּא יֹאכַל אָדָם בָּשָׂר אֶלָּא לְתֵאָבוֹן, שֶׁנֶּאֱמַר: "כִּי תְאַוֶּה נַפְשְׁךָ לֶאֱכֹל בָּשָׂר" (דברים יב, כ). דַּי לַבָּרִיא לְאָכְלוֹ מֵעֶרֶב שַׁבָּת לְעֶרֶב שַׁבָּת.

The Sages instructed us **on proper etiquette, that a person should eat meat only when he desires** to do so, **as it is stated: "Because your heart will desire to eat meat,** with all your heart's desire, you may eat meat" (Deuteronomy 12:20; *Ḥullin* 84a). **It is enough for a healthy** individual **to eat** meat once a week, **from one night of Shabbat to the next.**

וְאִם הָיָה עָשִׁיר כְּדֵי לֶאֱכֹל בָּשָׂר בְּכָל יוֹם – אוֹכֵל. צִוּוּ חֲכָמִים וְאָמְרוּ: לְעוֹלָם יֹאכַל אָדָם פָּחוֹת מִן הָרָאוּי לוֹ לְפִי מָמוֹנוֹ, וְיִלְבַּשׁ כָּרָאוּי לוֹ, וִיכַבֵּד אִשְׁתּוֹ וּבָנָיו יָתֵר מִן הָרָאוּי לוֹ.

If he is wealthy enough to eat meat every day, he may eat it. **The Sages** also **commanded and said: A person should always eat less than behooves him based on his finances,** and he should **dress as behooves him, and he should honor his wife and children more than behooves him** (*Ḥullin* 84b).

Halakha 11

דֶּרֶךְ בַּעֲלֵי דֵעָה שֶׁיִּקְבַּע לוֹ אָדָם מְלָאכָה הַמְפַרְנֶסֶת אוֹתוֹ תְּחִלָּה, וְאַחַר כָּךְ יִקְנֶה בֵּית דִּירָה, וְאַחַר כָּךְ יִשָּׂא אִשָּׁה, שֶׁנֶּאֱמַר:

It is the manner of those who act in accordance with the rational order of things **for a person to first establish for himself an occupation that will provide him with a livelihood, and then to purchase a place of residence, and** only **then to marry a wife, as it is stated:**

"וּמִי הָאִישׁ אֲשֶׁר נָטַע כֶּרֶם וְלֹא חִלְּלוֹ...אֲשֶׁר בָּנָה בַיִת חָדָשׁ וְלֹא חֲנָכוֹ...אֲשֶׁר אֵרַשׂ אִשָּׁה וְלֹא לְקָחָהּ" (דברים כ, ה–ז, בסדר שונה).

"Who is the man who planted a vineyard and did not celebrate it...who built a new house, and did not dedicate it...who betrothed a woman and has not married her" (Deuteronomy 20:5–7).[c]

NOTES

a. See also *Hilkhot Berakhot* 7:14.

b. He should not accustom himself to things he cannot afford.

c. These verses come from the Torah's commands regarding preparations for war. A priest must speak to the people and call upon anyone who has planted a vineyard, built a house, or betrothed a woman to return from the battlefield (see *Hilkhot Melakhim UMilḥemoteihem*, chap. 7). Although these three cases do not appear in the same order as the Rambam cites them here, the law is derived from the fact that the betrothal of a woman is stated last.

אֲבָל הַטִּפְּשִׁים מַתְחִילִין לִשָּׂא אִשָּׁה, וְאַחַר כָּךְ אִם תִּמְצָא יָדוֹ יִקְנֶה בַּיִת, וְאַחַר כָּךְ בְּסוֹף יָמָיו יְחַזֵּר לְבַקֵּשׁ אֻמָּנוּת אוֹ יִתְפַּרְנֵס מִן הַצְּדָקָה.

The fool, however, starts by marrying a woman, and then, if such a fool **has the means, he purchases a house, and subsequently, toward the end of his days, he will** begin to **search for a trade or** decide to **sustain himself from charity.**[a]

וְכֵן הוּא אוֹמֵר בַּקְּלָלוֹת: "אִשָּׁה תְאָרֵשׂ...בַּיִת תִּבְנֶה...כֶּרֶם תִּטַּע" (שם כח, ל).

It is similarly stated in the chapter of **the curses: "You will betroth a woman... you will build a house... you will plant a vineyard"** (Deuteronomy 28:30).

כְּלוֹמַר יִהְיוּ מַעֲשֶׂיךָ הֲפוּכִין, כְּדֵי שֶׁלֹּא תַּצְלִיחַ דְּרָכֶיךָ. וּבִבְרָכָה מַה הוּא אוֹמֵר? "וַיְהִי דָוִד לְכָל דְּרָכָו מַשְׂכִּיל וַיי עִמּוֹ" (שמואל א יח, יד).

That is, your endeavors will be in **the opposite** order than they should be, **so that you will not succeed in your ways.**[b] **But what does it state in** the case of **a blessing? "David was successful in all his ways, and the Lord was with him"** (I Samuel 18:14).

Halakha 12

וְאָסוּר לְאָדָם לְהַפְקִיר אוֹ לְהַקְדִּישׁ כָּל נְכָסָיו וְיַטְרִיחַ עַל הַבְּרִיּוֹת.

It is prohibited for a person to renounce ownership of all of his possessions, or to consecrate them all, **and** thereby **become a burden on** other **people.**[c]

וְלֹא יִמְכֹּר שָׂדֶה וְיִקְנֶה בַּיִת, וְלֹא בַּיִת וְיִקְנֶה מִטַּלְטְלִין אוֹ יַעֲשֶׂה סְחוֹרָה בִּדְמֵי בֵּיתוֹ.

One may not sell a field and buy a house,[d] or sell **a house and buy movable property, or** engage in **trade with** the **money** he received from the sale of **his house.**

אֲבָל מוֹכֵר הוּא מִטַּלְטְלִין וְקוֹנֶה שָׂדֶה. כְּלָלוֹ שֶׁל דָּבָר – יָשִׂים מְגַמָּתוֹ לְהַצְלִיחַ נְכָסָיו, לֹא לְהִתְנָאוֹת מְעַט לְפִי שָׁעָה אוֹ לֵהָנוֹת מְעַט וְיַפְסִיד הַרְבֵּה.

However, one may sell movable property and buy a field. The general rule is that **one's purpose should be to succeed in** the long-term management of **his property, rather than to embellish himself a little** in **a temporary** manner, **or to enjoy a slight pleasure but** later, as a result, he will **suffer a great reversal.**

Halakha 13

מַשָּׂאָן וּמַתָּנָן שֶׁל תַּלְמִידֵי חֲכָמִים בֶּאֱמֶת וּבֶאֱמוּנָה, אוֹמֵר עַל לָאו לָאו וְעַל הֵין הֵין, מְדַקְדֵּק עַל עַצְמוֹ בְּחֶשְׁבּוֹן, וְנוֹתֵן וּמְוַתֵּר לַאֲחֵרִים כְּשֶׁיִּקַּח מֵהֶן וְלֹא יְדַקְדֵּק עֲלֵיהֶן.

The business practices of a Torah scholar must be **conducted with honesty and** in good **faith.** He should **say "no"** when the appropriate response is **"no," and "yes"** when the right answer is **"yes."** He should be **particular with himself in** his **accounting,**[e] **but giving and yielding to others when he buys from them, without being particular with them.**

NOTES

a. If he is unable to take up a profession at that late stage.

b. The curse is that you will not act logically, which will inevitably lead to failure.

c. For if he has nothing, he will have to rely on others (see also *Hilkhot Arakhin VaḤaramin* 8:13).

d. Since a field yields greater income than a house.

e. To pay everything that he owes.

וְנוֹתֵן דְּמֵי הַלֶּקַח לְאַלְתַּר. וְאֵינוֹ נַעֲשֶׂה לֹא עָרֵב וְלֹא קַבְּלָן, וְלֹא יָבֹא בְּהַרְשָׁאָה.

He should **give the money of a purchase immediately.**[a] **He should not serve either as a guarantor or** as an **unconditional guarantor,**[b] **or come** to court **with authorization** to present a claim on behalf of another.[c]

מְחַיֵּב עַצְמוֹ בְּדִבְרֵי מֶקָּח וּמִמְכָּר בְּמָקוֹם שֶׁלֹּא חִיְּבָה אוֹתוֹ תּוֹרָה, כְּדֵי שֶׁיַּעֲמֹד בְּדִבּוּרוֹ וְלֹא יְשַׁנֵּהוּ.

He renders himself obligated in matters involving buying and selling, even **in cases where the Torah does not obligate him, in order to stand by his word and not deviate from it.**[d]

וְאִם נִתְחַיְּבוּ לוֹ אֲחֵרִים בַּדִּין – מַאֲרִיךְ לָהֶן וּמוֹחֵל לָהֶן, וּמַלְוֶה וְחוֹנֵן. וְלֹא יֵרֵד לְתוֹךְ אֻמָּנוּת חֲבֵרוֹ, וְלֹא יָצֵר לְאָדָם בָּעוֹלָם בְּחַיָּיו.

If others have been found legally obligated toward him, he is patient with them and forgives them. He lends items to those in need **and is gracious** toward them.[e] **He should not infringe upon the trade of another,**[f] **nor ever cause someone discomfort in his lifetime.**

כְּלָלוֹ שֶׁל דָּבָר – יִהְיֶה מִן הַנִּרְדָּפִין, לֹא מִן הָרוֹדְפִין, מִן הַנֶּעֱלָבִים וְלֹא מִן הָעוֹלְבִין. וְאָדָם שֶׁהוּא עוֹשֶׂה כָּל הַמַּעֲשִׂים הָאֵלּוּ וְכַיּוֹצֵא בָּהֶן, עָלָיו הַכָּתוּב אוֹמֵר: "וַיֹּאמֶר לִי עַבְדִּי אָתָּה יִשְׂרָאֵל אֲשֶׁר בְּךָ אֶתְפָּאָר" (ישעיהו מט, ג).

In sum, he should be among the pursued and not the pursuers, among those who are insulted, but not among those who insult others.[g] **A person who does all of these deeds and their ilk, the verse states regarding him: "He said to me: You are My servant, Israel, in whom I glory"**[h] (Isaiah 49:3).

NOTES

a. If he can afford to do so (*Hilkhot Yesodei HaTorah* 5:11).

b. They take it upon themselves to pay the debt of a third party, and thus they may lose out through no fault of their own (*Hilkhot Malveh VeLoveh* 25:5).

c. See *Hilkhot Sheluḥin VeShutafin* 3:5.

d. For example, if he said he would buy something, he will not retract, even though he is not legally bound to the commitment (*Hilkhot Mekhira* 7:8).

e. See Psalms 37:26.

f. By engaging in the same occupation in competition with him.

g. See also *Hilkhot Talmud Torah* 7:13.

h. Such conduct sanctifies God's name (*Hilkhot Yesodei HaTorah* 5:11).

פֶּרֶק שִׁשִּׁי

CHAPTER 6

The Mitzvot Involving the Love of One's Fellows

Halakhot 1–2:	Keeping away from the wicked and cleaving to the Sages
Halakhot 3–4:	Loving one's fellow and the convert
Halakhot 5–9:	The prohibition against hatred and the mitzva of reproof
Halakha 10:	Taking care not to harm orphans and widows

Halakha 1

דֶּרֶךְ בְּרִיָּתוֹ שֶׁל אָדָם לִהְיוֹת נִמְשָׁךְ בְּדֵעוֹתָיו וּבְמַעֲשָׂיו אַחַר רֵעָיו וַחֲבֵרָיו, וְנוֹהֵג בְּמִנְהַג אַנְשֵׁי מְדִינָתוֹ.

It is natural for a man to be influenced in his character and deeds by his colleagues and friends, and for him **to act in accordance with the customs of the inhabitants of his country.**

לְפִיכָךְ צָרִיךְ אָדָם לְהִתְחַבֵּר לַצַּדִּיקִים וְלֵישֵׁב אֵצֶל הַחֲכָמִים תָּמִיד כְּדֵי שֶׁיִּלְמַד מַעֲשֵׂיהֶם, וְיִתְרַחֵק מִן הָרְשָׁעִים הַהוֹלְכִים בַּחֹשֶׁךְ כְּדֵי שֶׁלֹּא יִלְמַד מִמַּעֲשֵׂיהֶם.

Accordingly, a person should associate with the righteous, and always sit with the wise, in order to learn from their deeds, and he should keep far from the wicked who walk in darkness, in order not to learn from their deeds.

הוּא שֶׁשְּׁלֹמֹה אוֹמֵר: "הוֹלֵךְ אֶת חֲכָמִים יֶחְכָּם וְרֹעֶה כְסִילִים יֵרוֹעַ" (משלי יג, כ), וְאוֹמֵר: "אַשְׁרֵי הָאִישׁ אֲשֶׁר לֹא הָלַךְ בַּעֲצַת רְשָׁעִים" וגו' (תהלים א, א).

This is the meaning of that **which Solomon states: "He who walks with the wise will become wise, and he who joins fools will be broken"**[a] (Proverbs 13:20), **and it states: "Happy is the man who has not walked in the counsel of the wicked..."** (Psalms 1:1).

וְכֵן אִם הָיָה בִּמְדִינָה שֶׁמִּנְהֲגוֹתֶיהָ רָעִים וְאֵין אֲנָשֶׁיהָ הוֹלְכִים בְּדֶרֶךְ יְשָׁרָה – יֵלֵךְ לְמָקוֹם שֶׁאֲנָשָׁיו צַדִּיקִים וְנוֹהֲגִים בְּדֶרֶךְ טוֹבִים.

Similarly, if he is in a country whose customs are evil and whose inhabitants do not follow the straight path, he should go to a place whose inhabitants are righteous[b] **and who conduct** themselves **in the ways of the good.**

NOTES

a. He will suffer from their company.

b. He should not live in close proximity to vile people (see also *Hilkhot Ishut* 13:15).

וְאִם הָיוּ כָּל הַמְּדִינוֹת שֶׁהוּא יוֹדְעָן וְשׁוֹמֵעַ שְׁמוּעָתָן נוֹהֲגִין בְּדֶרֶךְ לֹא טוֹבָה, כְּמוֹ זְמַנֵּנוּ, אוֹ שֶׁאֵינוֹ יָכוֹל לֵילֵךְ לִמְדִינָה שֶׁמִּנְהֲגוֹתֶיהָ טוֹבִים מִפְּנֵי הַגְּיָסוֹת אוֹ מִפְּנֵי הַחֹלִי – יֵשֵׁב לְבַדּוֹ יְחִידִי, כְּעִנְיַן שֶׁנֶּאֱמַר: "יֵשֵׁב בָּדָד וְיִדֹּם" (איכה ג, כח).

If all the countries with which he is familiar and about which he hears reports act in accordance with **a path** that is **not good, as** in **our times, or if he is unable to go to a place whose customs are good, due to** the presence of gentile **troops,**[a] **or due to illness, he should live alone**[b] **in seclusion, in the manner that it is stated: "Let him sit alone and be silent"** (Lamentations 3:28).

וְאִם הָיוּ רָעִים וְחַטָּאִים שֶׁאֵין מַנִּיחִין אוֹתוֹ לֵישֵׁב בַּמְּדִינָה אֶלָּא אִם כֵּן נִתְעָרֵב עִמָּהֶן וְנָהַג בְּמִנְהָגָן הָרַע – יֵצֵא לַמְּעָרוֹת וְלַחֲוָחִים וְלַמִּדְבָּרוֹת וְאַל יַנְהִיג עַצְמוֹ בְּדֶרֶךְ חַטָּאִים, כְּעִנְיַן שֶׁנֶּאֱמַר: "מִי יִתְּנֵנִי בַמִּדְבָּר מְלוֹן אֹרְחִים" וגו' (ירמיהו ט, א).

If they are so **wicked and sinful that they do not allow him to reside in the country unless he mingles with them and conducts** himself **in accordance with their evil customs, he should go out to caves, fortresses,**[c] **and deserts rather than conduct himself in the paths of sinners, in the manner that it is stated: "Would that I would be in the wilderness, in a wayfarers' lodging place,** and I would leave my people and go from them, for they are all adulterers, an assembly of traitors" (Jeremiah 9:1).

Halakha 2

מִצְוַת עֲשֵׂה לְהִדַּבֵּק בַּחֲכָמִים כְּדֵי לִלְמֹד מִמַּעֲשֵׂיהֶם, שֶׁנֶּאֱמַר: "וּבוֹ תִדְבָּק" (דברים י, כ) – וְכִי אֶפְשָׁר לָאָדָם לְהִדַּבֵּק בַּשְּׁכִינָה?

It is **a positive mitzva to cleave to the Sages**[d] **in order to learn from their deeds, as it is stated: "And to Him you shall cleave"** (Deuteronomy 10:20). **Now, is it possible for person to cleave to the Divine Presence?**

אֶלָּא כָּךְ אָמְרוּ חֲכָמִים בְּפֵרוּשׁ מִצְוָה זוֹ: הִדַּבֵּק בַּחֲכָמִים וְתַלְמִידֵיהֶם.

Rather, the Sages said the following, in explanation of this mitzva: One must **cleave to the wise and their disciples.**

לְפִיכָךְ צָרִיךְ אָדָם לְהִשְׁתַּדֵּל שֶׁיִּשָּׂא בַּת תַּלְמִיד חֲכָמִים, וְיַשִּׂיא בִּתּוֹ לְתַלְמִיד חֲכָמִים, וְלֶאֱכֹל וְלִשְׁתּוֹת עִם תַּלְמִידֵי חֲכָמִים, וְלַעֲשׂוֹת פְּרַקְמַטְיָא לְתַלְמִידֵי חֲכָמִים, וּלְהִתְחַבֵּר לָהֶם בְּכָל מִינֵי חִבּוּר, שֶׁנֶּאֱמַר: "וּלְדָבְקָה בוֹ" (שם יא, כב ועוד).

Therefore, one should make the effort to marry the daughter of a Torah scholar, and marry off one's daughter to a Torah scholar, eat and drink with Torah scholars, engage in trade with Torah scholars, and associate with them in every possible way, as it is stated: "And to cleave to Him" (Deuteronomy 11:22).[e]

וְכָךְ צִוּוּ חֲכָמִים וְאָמְרוּ: וֶהֱוֵי מִתְאַבֵּק בַּעֲפַר רַגְלֵיהֶם וְשׁוֹתֶה בַצָּמָא אֶת דִּבְרֵיהֶם.

The Sages thus commanded and said: "Sit in the dust at their feet, and with thirst, drink in their words" (*Avot* 1:4).

NOTES

a. Making it dangerous to travel.

b. Far from such people, so that he does not learn from their ways.

c. Protected places.

d. To maintain connections with them and stay close to them.

e. See *Ketubot* 111b.

Halakha 3

מִצְוָה עַל כָּל אָדָם לֶאֱהֹב אֶת כָּל אֶחָד וְאֶחָד מִיִּשְׂרָאֵל כְּגוּפוֹ, שֶׁנֶּאֱמַר: "וְאָהַבְתָּ לְרֵעֲךָ כָּמוֹךָ" (ויקרא יט, יח).

It is **a mitzva for each person to love every single** member **of Israel like himself, as it is stated: "You shall love your neighbor as yourself"** (Leviticus 19:18).

לְפִיכָךְ צָרִיךְ לְסַפֵּר בְּשִׁבְחוֹ וְלָחוּס עַל מָמוֹנוֹ כְּמוֹ שֶׁהוּא חָס עַל מָמוֹן עַצְמוֹ וְרוֹצֶה בִּכְבוֹד עַצְמוֹ. וְהַמִּתְכַּבֵּד בִּקְלוֹן חֲבֵרוֹ – אֵין לוֹ חֵלֶק לָעוֹלָם הַבָּא.

Accordingly, one should relate the praises of the other, **and be careful of his property,**[a] **just as he is careful about his own property and desires his own honor. One who attains veneration at** the expense of **the degradation of another has no share in the World to Come.**

Halakha 4

אַהֲבַת הַגֵּר שֶׁבָּא וְנִכְנַס תַּחַת כַּנְפֵי הַשְּׁכִינָה – שְׁתֵּי מִצְווֹת עֲשֵׂה: אַחַת מִפְּנֵי שֶׁהוּא בִּכְלַל רֵעִים, וְאַחַת מִפְּנֵי שֶׁהוּא גֵּר, וְהַתּוֹרָה אָמְרָה: "וַאֲהַבְתֶּם אֶת הַגֵּר" (דברים י, יט);

Loving a convert who has come under the wings of the Divine Presence[b] is the fulfillment **of two positive mitzvot: one, because he is included in** the category of all **fellow** Jews, **and** the other **one, because he is a convert and the Torah states: "You shall love the stranger"** (Deuteronomy 10:19).

צִוָּה עַל אַהֲבַת הַגֵּר כְּמוֹ שֶׁצִּוָּה עַל אַהֲבַת שְׁמוֹ, שֶׁנֶּאֱמַר: "וְאָהַבְתָּ אֵת יי אֱלֹהֶיךָ" (שם ו, ה; יא, א).

God **commanded** us **concerning the love of a convert** in the very same terms **as He commanded** us **concerning loving His name, as it is stated: "You shall love the Lord"** (Deuteronomy 6:5, 11:1).

הַקָּדוֹשׁ בָּרוּךְ הוּא עַצְמוֹ אוֹהֵב גֵּרִים, שֶׁנֶּאֱמַר: "וְאֹהֵב גֵּר" (שם י, יח).

The Holy One blessed be He Himself loves converts, as it is stated: "And He loves the stranger" (Deuteronomy 10:18).

Halakha 5

כָּל הַשּׂוֹנֵא אֶחָד מִיִּשְׂרָאֵל בְּלִבּוֹ – עָבַר בְּלֹא תַעֲשֶׂה, שֶׁנֶּאֱמַר: "לֹא תִשְׂנָא אֶת אָחִיךָ בִּלְבָבֶךָ" (ויקרא יט, יז).

Anyone who hates one member **of Israel in his heart**[c] **transgresses a prohibition, as it is stated: "You shall not hate your brother in your heart"** (Leviticus 19:17).

וְאֵין לוֹקִין עַל לָאו זֶה, לְפִי שֶׁאֵין בּוֹ מַעֲשֶׂה. וְלֹא הִזְהִירָה תּוֹרָה אֶלָּא עַל שִׂנְאָה שֶׁבַּלֵּב, אֲבָל הַמַּכֶּה אֶת חֲבֵרוֹ וְהַמְחָרֵף אֶת חֲבֵרוֹ, אַף עַל פִּי שֶׁאֵינוֹ רַשַּׁאי – אֵינוֹ עוֹבֵר מִשּׁוּם "לֹא תִשְׂנָא".

One is not flogged for violating **this prohibition because it does not involve an action.**[d] **Here, the Torah only warned against hatred in the heart, but one who strikes or taunts another, even though he is not allowed** to do so,[e] **does not violate the prohibition of "you shall not hate."**

NOTES

a. So that it is not damaged.

b. By accepting the obligation of the mitzvot and becoming a Jew (see *Hilkhot Issurei Bia* 13:4).

c. Even without this hatred having any practical effect.

d. One is liable to receive lashes only for a violation that involves an actual deed (see *Hilkhot Sanhedrin* 18:1–2).

e. See Halakha 8; *Hilkhot Ḥovel UMazik* 5:1.

Halakha 6

כְּשֶׁיֶּחֱטָא אִישׁ לְאִישׁ – לֹא יִשְׂטְמֶנּוּ וְיִשְׁתֹּק, כְּמוֹ שֶׁנֶּאֱמַר בָּרְשָׁעִים: "וְלֹא דִבֶּר אַבְשָׁלוֹם עִם אַמְנוֹן לְמֵרָע וְעַד טוֹב כִּי שָׂנֵא אַבְשָׁלוֹם אֶת אַמְנוֹן" (שמואל ב יג, כב),

When one person sins against another, the victim should **not despise him** in his heart **while remaining silent, in the manner that it is stated regarding the wicked: "Avshalom did not speak to Amnon, either good or bad, for Avshalom hated Amnon"** (II Samuel 13:22).

אֶלָּא מִצְוָה עָלָיו לְהוֹדִיעוֹ וְלוֹמַר לוֹ: 'לָמָּה עָשִׂיתָ לִי כָּךְ וְכָךְ, וְלָמָּה חָטָאתָ לִי בְּדָבָר פְּלוֹנִי?', שֶׁנֶּאֱמַר: "הוֹכֵחַ תּוֹכִיחַ אֶת עֲמִיתֶךָ" (ויקרא יט, יז).

Rather, it is a mitzva for him to inform him of his feelings **and say to him: "Why did you do this to me, and why did you sin against me in this way?" As it is stated: "You shall rebuke your neighbor"** (Leviticus 19:17).[a]

וְאִם חָזַר וּבִקֵּשׁ מִמֶּנּוּ לִמְחֹל לוֹ – צָרִיךְ לִמְחֹל. וְלֹא יְהֵא הַמּוֹחֵל אַכְזָרִי, שֶׁנֶּאֱמַר: "וַיִּתְפַּלֵּל אַבְרָהָם אֶל הָאֱלֹהִים" וגו' (בראשית כ, יז).

If that person **retracts and asks him to forgive him, he must** indeed **forgive** him. **The one who** is asked to **forgive should not be cruel,**[1] **as it is stated: "Abraham prayed to God..."** (Genesis 20:17).[b]

Halakha 7

הָרוֹאֶה חֲבֵרוֹ שֶׁחָטָא אוֹ שֶׁהוּא הוֹלֵךְ בְּדֶרֶךְ לֹא טוֹבָה – מִצְוָה לְהַחֲזִירוֹ לְמוּטָב, וּלְהוֹדִיעוֹ שֶׁהוּא חוֹטֵא עַל עַצְמוֹ בְּמַעֲשָׂיו הָרָעִים, שֶׁנֶּאֱמַר: "הוֹכֵחַ תּוֹכִיחַ אֶת עֲמִיתֶךָ" (ויקרא יט, יז).

If **one sees that another** Jew **has sinned**[2] **or that he is following a path** which is **not good,**[3] it **is a mitzva** for him to **restore him to the right** path,[c] **and to inform him that he is bringing evil upon himself through his bad deeds,**[d] **as it is stated: "You shall rebuke your neighbor"** (Leviticus 19:17).

הַמּוֹכִיחַ אֶת חֲבֵרוֹ, בֵּין בִּדְבָרִים שֶׁבֵּינוֹ לְבֵינוֹ בֵּין בִּדְבָרִים שֶׁבֵּינוֹ לְבֵין הַמָּקוֹם – צָרִיךְ לְהוֹכִיחוֹ בֵּינוֹ לְבֵין עַצְמוֹ, וִידַבֵּר לוֹ בְּנַחַת וּבְלָשׁוֹן רַכָּה, וְיוֹדִיעוֹ שֶׁאֵינוֹ אוֹמֵר לוֹ אֶלָּא לְטוֹבָתוֹ וְלַהֲבִיאוֹ לְחַיֵּי הָעוֹלָם הַבָּא.

One who rebukes another,[4] **whether involving matters between the two of them** or **whether involving matters between** that person **and the Omnipresent, should rebuke him in private. He should speak to him calmly and gently, informing him that he is only saying** this **to him for his own good, and to bring him to the life of the World to Come.**

HALAKHIC DISCUSSION

1. The one who is asked to forgive should not be cruel – וְלֹא יְהֵא הַמּוֹחֵל אַכְזָרִי: *Shulḥan Arukh, Oraḥ Ḥayyim* 606:1.

2. If one sees that another Jew has sinned – הָרוֹאֶה חֲבֵרוֹ שֶׁחָטָא: *Shulḥan Arukh, Oraḥ Ḥayyim* 608:2. The Rema states that one should not reprove people who unwittingly violate prohibitions that are not explicitly stated in the Torah (even if they are prohibited by Torah law), since it is better for them to be unwitting than intentional sinners (see *Hilkhot Shevitat Asor* 1:7). The later authorities add that this applies only in a case where one is sure that advice will not be accepted, but if he thinks they might mend their ways, he is obligated to reprove them (*Taz*; *Magen Avraham*), even if they are violating only rabbinic prohibitions (*Mishna Berura*). If it is a bad custom that is practiced by many in public, one should not reprove them, since they will presumably not accept it (*Beur Halakha*). The later authorities further state that all this applies only to something that is not explicit in the Torah; one must object to the violation of a prohibition that is expressly stated in the Torah even if one knows that the sinners will not listen to him, since all Jews are considered guarantors for one another, and one fulfills his role as a guarantor only by protesting the sin (*Shulḥan Arukh HaRav*).

3. Following a path which is not good – הוֹלֵךְ בְּדֶרֶךְ לֹא טוֹבָה: The mitzva of reproof applies only to the occasional transgressor; there is no obligation to rebuke someone who has entirely removed the yoke of Heaven from upon himself, such as one who desecrates Shabbat in public (*Beur Halakha*).

4. Another – חֲבֵרוֹ: One is only obligated to reprove close friends, not others, who might come to hate him as a result (*Magen Avraham*).

NOTES

a. This is the continuation of the verse: "You shall not hate your brother in your heart." That is, rather than continuing to bear hatred for what your brother did to you, you should rebuke him.

b. Abraham prayed for the recovery of the Philistine king Avimelekh and forgave him for taking his wife Sarah, after the king had requested his forgiveness.

c. Which he would accomplish by forsaking his sin (see *Hilkhot Teshuva* 4:1).

d. See *Hilkhot Teshuva* 5:2.

אִם קִבֵּל מִמֶּנּוּ – מוּטָב, וְאִם לָאו – יוֹכִיחַ פַּעַם שְׁנִיָּה וּשְׁלִישִׁית. וְכֵן תָּמִיד חַיָּב לְהוֹכִיחַ, עַד שֶׁיַּכֵּהוּ הַחוֹטֵא וְיֹאמַר לוֹ: 'אֵינִי שׁוֹמֵעַ'.

If his colleague **accepts** the rebuke **from him, it is good; if not,** he should **rebuke him a second and a third time.**[1] **In fact, one is always obligated to** keep **rebuking until the sinner strikes him**[2] **and says to him: "I am not listening."**[a]

וְכָל שֶׁאֶפְשָׁר בְּיָדוֹ לִמְחוֹת וְאֵינוֹ מְמַחֶה – הוּא נִתְפָּשׂ בַּעֲוֹן אֵלּוּ כֻּלָּם שֶׁאֶפְשָׁר לוֹ לִמְחוֹת בָּהֶן.

Anyone who has **the capability to** effectively **protest** a person's sinful conduct **and does not protest is held accountable for the transgressions of all the** people **whom he could have rebuked.**

Halakha 8

הַמּוֹכִיחַ אֶת חֲבֵרוֹ תְּחִלָּה – לֹא יְדַבֵּר לוֹ קָשׁוֹת עַד שֶׁיַּכְלִימֶנּוּ, שֶׁנֶּאֱמַר: "וְלֹא תִשָּׂא עָלָיו חֵטְא" (ויקרא יט, יז).

One who rebukes another should initially not speak to him so **harshly that** the other **is embarrassed** by his comments, **as it is stated: "And you shall not bear a sin because of him"** (Leviticus 19:17).

כָּךְ אָמְרוּ חֲכָמִים: יָכוֹל אַתָּה מוֹכִיחוֹ וּפָנָיו מִשְׁתַּנּוֹת? תַּלְמוּד לוֹמַר: "וְלֹא תִשָּׂא עָלָיו חֵטְא". מִכָּאן שֶׁאָסוּר לָאָדָם לְהַכְלִים אֶת יִשְׂרָאֵל, וְכָל שֶׁכֵּן בָּרַבִּים.

In this regard, **the Sages said the following:** One **might** have thought that **you** should continue **rebuking him** even if **his face changes;**[b] therefore, **the verse states: "And you shall not bear a sin because of him"**[c] (*Arakhin* 16b). **From here** it is derived **that it is prohibited for a person to embarrass** a fellow **Jew, all the more so** by rebuking him **in public.**

אַף עַל פִּי שֶׁהַמַּכְלִים אֶת חֲבֵרוֹ אֵינוֹ לוֹקֶה, עָוֹן גָּדוֹל הוּא. כָּךְ אָמְרוּ חֲכָמִים: הַמַּלְבִּין פְּנֵי חֲבֵרוֹ בָּרַבִּים – אֵין לוֹ חֵלֶק לָעוֹלָם הַבָּא.

Even though one who embarrasses another is not flogged, it is a grave transgression. The Sages said the following: "One who humiliates another in public[d] **has no share in the World to Come"** (*Sanhedrin* 99a).

לְפִיכָךְ צָרִיךְ אָדָם לְהִזָּהֵר בְּדָבָר זֶה, שֶׁלֹּא יַבְיִשׁ חֲבֵרוֹ בָּרַבִּים, בֵּין קָטָן בֵּין גָּדוֹל,

Therefore, a person must be careful in this regard, not to embarrass another in public, whether he is of **minor or great stature.**

וְלֹא יִקְרָא לוֹ בְּשֵׁם שֶׁהוּא בּוֹשׁ מִמֶּנּוּ, וְלֹא יְסַפֵּר לְפָנָיו דָּבָר שֶׁהוּא בּוֹשׁ מִמֶּנּוּ.

Likewise, he should **not call him by a name that shames him,**[e] **or relate in his presence a matter of which he is ashamed.**

בַּמֶּה דְּבָרִים אֲמוּרִים? בְּדִבְרִים שֶׁבֵּין אָדָם לַחֲבֵרוֹ.

In what case **is this statement said? In matters that are between** one **person and another.**

אֲבָל בְּדִבְרֵי שָׁמַיִם, אִם לֹא חָזַר בּוֹ בַּסֵּתֶר – מַכְלִימִים אוֹתוֹ בָּרַבִּים, וּמְפַרְסְמִין חֶטְאוֹ, וּמְחָרְפִים אוֹתוֹ בְּפָנָיו, וּמְבַזִּים וּמְקַלְּלִים, עַד שֶׁיַּחֲזֹר לְמוּטָב, כְּמוֹ שֶׁעָשׂוּ כָּל הַנְּבִיאִים בְּיִשְׂרָאֵל.

However, in matters involving **Heaven, if** the sinner **does not retract** after being reproved **in private, he** should be **publicly shamed**[3] **and his sin publicized. He may be taunted to his face, scorned and cursed until he returns to** the **right** path, **as was done by all the prophets of Israel.**[f]

HALAKHIC DISCUSSION

1. **A second and a third time – פַּעַם שְׁנִיָּה וּשְׁלִישִׁית:** If one is required to reprove many sinners, and one knows that they will not accept the reproof, he should do so only once (Rema).

2. **Until the sinner strikes him – עַד שֶׁיַּכֵּהוּ הַחוֹטֵא:** The later authorities state that it is enough to keep rebuking someone until the sinner castigates him. One need not rebuke another if doing so will endanger the rebuker (*Mishna Berura*).

3. **Publicly shamed – מַכְלִימִים אוֹתוֹ בָּרַבִּים:** The later authorities state that if the person sinned in private, one should rebuke him in private, when the opportunity arises, but if he sinned publicly, he should be rebuked immediately, to prevent the desecration of God's name (*Magen Avraham*).

NOTES

a. I will not accept what you are telling me.

b. Due to his pain and humiliation.

c. In other words, the one giving rebuke may not sin by embarrassing the other person.

d. See *Hilkhot Teshuva* 3:14.

e. An insulting nickname.

f. They did not hold back from rebuking Israel publicly and in the harshest terms.

Halakha 9

מִי שֶׁחָטָא עָלָיו חֲבֵרוֹ, וְלֹא רָצָה לְהוֹכִיחוֹ וְלֹא לְדַבֵּר לוֹ כְּלוּם מִפְּנֵי שֶׁהָיָה הַחוֹטֵא הֶדְיוֹט בְּיוֹתֵר אוֹ שֶׁהָיְתָה דַּעְתּוֹ מְשֻׁבֶּשֶׁת, וּמָחַל לוֹ בְּלִבּוֹ וְלֹא שְׂטָמוֹ וְלֹא הוֹכִיחוֹ – הֲרֵי זוֹ מִדַּת חֲסִידוּת. לֹא הִקְפִּידָה תּוֹרָה אֶלָּא עַל הַמַּשְׂטֵמָה.

If a person was sinned against by another, and he does not wish to reprove him or say anything to him because the sinner is very dim-witted,[a] **or because he is mentally disturbed, and he forgives him in his heart and does not despise him while** also **not rebuking him, this is an attribute of piety. The Torah is particular only about one who despises** another.[b]

Halakha 10

חַיָּב אָדָם לְהִזָּהֵר בִּיתוֹמִים וְאַלְמָנוֹת, מִפְּנֵי שֶׁנַּפְשָׁן שְׁפָלָה לִמְאֹד וְרוּחָן נְמוּכָה, אַף עַל פִּי שֶׁהֵן בַּעֲלֵי מָמוֹן. אֲפִלּוּ אַלְמְנָתוֹ שֶׁל מֶלֶךְ וִיתוֹמָיו שֶׁל מֶלֶךְ – מֻזְהָרִין אָנוּ עֲלֵיהֶן, שֶׁנֶּאֱמַר: "כָּל אַלְמָנָה וְיָתוֹם לֹא תְעַנּוּן" (שמות כב, כא).

A person is obligated to be very careful with regard to orphans and widows[c] **because they are extremely downtrodden, and their spirits are lowly.** This applies **even if they have** plenty of **money. Even** in the case of **a king's widow and the orphans of a king,**[d] **we are warned** against mistreating **them, as it is stated: "You shall not afflict any widow or orphan"** (Exodus 22:21).

וְהֵיאַךְ נוֹהֲגִין עִמָּהֶן? לֹא יְדַבֵּר אֲלֵיהֶם אֶלָּא רַכּוֹת, וְלֹא יִנְהֹג בָּהֶם אֶלָּא מִנְהַג כָּבוֹד, וְלֹא יַכְאִיב גּוּפָן בַּעֲבוֹדָה וְלֹא לִבָּן בִּדְבָרִים, וְיָחוּס עַל מָמוֹנָם יָתֵר מִמָּמוֹן עַצְמוֹ.

How should one treat them? One should speak to them only softly, and treat them only in a respectful manner. One should not make their bodies suffer with labor, nor their hearts with harsh **words, and one should have more concern for their property than for his own property.**

כָּל הַמַּקְנִיטָן אוֹ הִכְעִיסָן אוֹ הִכְאִיב לִבָּן אוֹ רָדָה בָּהֶן אוֹ אִבֵּד מָמוֹנָם – הֲרֵי זֶה עוֹבֵר בְּלֹא תַעֲשֶׂה, וְכָל שֶׁכֵּן הַמַּכֶּה אוֹתָן אוֹ הַמְקַלְּלָן. וְלָאו זֶה, אַף עַל פִּי שֶׁאֵין לוֹקִין עָלָיו – הֲרֵי עָנְשׁוֹ מְפֹרָשׁ בַּתּוֹרָה: "וְחָרָה אַפִּי וְהָרַגְתִּי אֶתְכֶם בֶּחָרֶב" (שמות כב, כג).

Anyone who angers or annoys them, hurts their feelings, subjugates them,[e] **or causes them financial loss violates a prohibition, all the more so one who strikes or curses them. Even though one is not flogged for** violating **this prohibition, its punishment is explicit in the Torah: "My wrath will be enflamed and I will kill you with the sword"** (Exodus 22:23).

בְּרִית כָּרַת לָהֶם מִי שֶׁאָמַר וְהָיָה הָעוֹלָם, שֶׁכָּל זְמַן שֶׁהֵן צוֹעֲקִין מֵחָמָס – הֵן נַעֲנִין, שֶׁנֶּאֱמַר: "כִּי אִם צָעֹק יִצְעַק אֵלַי שָׁמֹעַ אֶשְׁמַע צַעֲקָתוֹ" (שם כב, כב).

The One who spoke and the world came into being enacted a covenant with them[f] **that whenever they cry out** to Him **due to oppression they will be answered, as it is stated: "If you afflict him, then when he cries out to Me, I will hear his cry"** (Exodus 22:22).

בַּמֶּה דְּבָרִים אֲמוּרִים? בִּזְמַן שֶׁעִנָּה אוֹתָם לְצָרְכֵי עַצְמוֹ. אֲבָל אִם עִנָּה אוֹתָם הָרַב כְּדֵי לְלַמְּדָם תּוֹרָה אוֹ אֻמָּנוּת אוֹ לְהוֹלִיכָם בְּדֶרֶךְ יְשָׁרָה – הֲרֵי זֶה מֻתָּר.

In what case **is this statement said? When one made them suffer for his own purposes. If, however, a teacher made them suffer in order to teach them Torah,**[g] **or a craft, or to lead them on the straight path, this is permitted.**

NOTES

a. He is so lacking in intelligence that he does not understand the implications of what he has done.

b. The main point is that one must not harbor bad feelings against another, and he must rebuke him if that is what it takes to remove the hatred from his heart.

c. Not to oppress them (see *Hilkhot Yom Tov* 6:18; *Hilkhot Megilla* 2:17).

d. Who do not require any financial assistance.

e. By making them perform hard and painful labor.

f. That is, God made a promise to orphans and widows.

g. A rabbi has permission to strike his students (see *Hilkhot Talmud Torah* 2:2; *Hilkhot Rotze'aḥ UShmirat HaNefesh* 5:6).

Even so, he should not treat them in the same manner as he **treats all others, but make exceptions for them and lead them gently, with great compassion and honor, "for the Lord will fight their battle"** (Proverbs 22:23). This applies to **both those orphaned from a father and those orphaned from a mother.**

וְאַף עַל פִּי כֵן, לֹא יִנְהֹג בָּהֶם מִנְהַג כָּל אָדָם, אֶלָּא יַעֲשֶׂה לָהֶם הֶפְרֵשׁ וִינַהֲלֵם בְּנַחַת וּבְרַחֲמִים גְּדוֹלִים וְכָבוֹד, "כִּי יי יָרִיב רִיבָם" (משלי כב, כג). אֶחָד יָתוֹם מֵאָב וְאֶחָד יָתוֹם מֵאֵם.

Until when are they called orphans with regard to this mitzva? **Until they no longer need to rely on an adult to raise them and care for them; rather, they can provide for all their own needs by themselves, like all other adults.**

וְעַד אֵימָתַי נִקְרָאִין יְתוֹמִים לְעִנְיָן זֶה? עַד שֶׁלֹּא יִהְיוּ צְרִיכִין לְאָדָם גָּדוֹל לְהִסָּמֵךְ לוֹ לְאַמְּנָם וּלְהִטַּפֵּל בָּהֶן, אֶלָּא יִהְיֶה עוֹשֶׂה כָּל צְרָכֵי עַצְמוֹ לְעַצְמוֹ כִּשְׁאָר כָּל הַגְּדוֹלִים.

פֶּרֶק שְׁבִיעִי
CHAPTER 7

Prohibitions Against Harming Others

Halakhot 1–6:	Gossip, slander, and defamation
Halakhot 7–8:	Taking revenge and bearing a grudge

Halakha 1

הַמְרַגֵּל בַּחֲבֵרוֹ – עוֹבֵר בְּלֹא תַעֲשֶׂה, שֶׁנֶּאֱמַר: "לֹא תֵלֵךְ רָכִיל בְּעַמֶּיךָ" (ויקרא יט, טז).

One who gossips[1] **about another violates a prohibition, as it is stated: "You shall not go as a gossip among your people"** (Leviticus 19:16).

וְאַף עַל פִּי שֶׁאֵין לוֹקִין עַל לָאו זֶה, עָוֹן גָּדוֹל הוּא, וְגוֹרֵם לַהֲרֹג נְפָשׁוֹת רַבּוֹת מִיִּשְׂרָאֵל, לְכָךְ נִסְמַךְ לוֹ: "לֹא תַעֲמֹד עַל דַּם רֵעֶךָ" (שם). צֵא וּלְמַד מָה אֵרַע לְדוֹאֵג הָאֲדוֹמִי.

Even though one is not flogged for violating **this prohibition,**[a] **it is a severe transgression and can cause the death of many Jews. Therefore,** the warning: **"You shall not stand by the blood of your neighbor" is placed alongside it,** in the same verse. **Go and learn what occurred** on account **of Doeg the Edomite.**[b]

Halakha 2

אֵי זֶה הוּא רָכִיל? זֶה שֶׁהוּא טוֹעֵן דְּבָרִים, וְהוֹלֵךְ מִזֶּה לָזֶה וְאוֹמֵר: 'כָּךְ וְכָךְ אָמַר פְּלוֹנִי', 'כָּךְ וְכָךְ שָׁמַעְתִּי עַל פְּלוֹנִי'. אַף עַל פִּי שֶׁהוּא אוֹמֵר אֱמֶת, הֲרֵי זֶה מַחֲרִיב אֶת הָעוֹלָם.

Who is a gossiper? This is one who stores up[c] **information**[2] and then **goes from one person to another, saying: "So-and-so said this,"** or, **"I heard this about so-and-so." Even if he is speaking the truth, he** thereby **destroys the world.**[d]

יֵשׁ עָוֹן גָּדוֹל מִזֶּה עַד מְאֹד, וְהוּא בִּכְלַל לָאו זֶה, וְהוּא לָשׁוֹן הָרַע, וְהוּא הַמְסַפֵּר בִּגְנוּת חֲבֵרוֹ, אַף עַל פִּי שֶׁאָמַר אֱמֶת. אֲבָל הָאוֹמֵר שֶׁקֶר – מוֹצִיא שֵׁם רַע עַל חֲבֵרוֹ נִקְרָא.

There is a far more serious transgression than that, which is included in this prohibition, and that is slander [*lashon hara*], **which** is violated by **one who relates negative** reports **about another.**[e] This is the case **even if he is speaking the truth. However, one who speaks lies is called a defamer** [*motzi shem ra*] **of another** person.[f]

HALAKHIC DISCUSSION

1. One who gossips – הַמְרַגֵּל: Most of the halakhot of slander and gossip are not dealt with in the *Shulḥan Arukh*, but they are discussed in great depth in the eponymous work *Ḥafetz Ḥayyim*, and in this chapter we will mention a few of the detailed laws that appear there.

2. This is one who stores up information – זֶה שֶׁהוּא טוֹעֵן דְּבָרִים: This includes written as well as verbal means of communication (*Ḥafetz Ḥayyim*, *Hilkhot Lashon Hara* 1:8).

NOTES

a. For it is a prohibition that does not involve an action (see 6:5).

b. Doeg informed King Saul that David had received assistance from Ahimelekh the priest, as a result of which Saul executed all the priests in the city of Nov (I Samuel, chap. 22).

c. A gossiper [*rokhel*] resembles a peddler who stores up merchandise and then goes around from one place to another.

d. Since it will likely lead to strife between people.

e. Publicizing bad deeds that he has done.

f. See *Hilkhot Naara Betula* 3:1.

אֲבָל בַּעַל לָשׁוֹן הָרַע זֶה שֶׁיּוֹשֵׁב וְאוֹמֵר: 'כָּךְ וְכָךְ עָשָׂה פְּלוֹנִי, וְכָךְ וְכָךְ הָיוּ אֲבוֹתָיו, וְכָךְ וְכָךְ שָׁמַעְתִּי עָלָיו', וְאוֹמֵר דְּבָרִים שֶׁל גְּנַאי. עַל זֶה הַכָּתוּב אוֹמֵר: "יַכְרֵת ה׳ כָּל שִׂפְתֵי חֲלָקוֹת לָשׁוֹן מְדַבֶּרֶת גְּדֹלוֹת" (תהלים יב, ד).

By contrast, a slanderer[a] is one who sits and says: "So-and-so did such-and-such, and his ancestors were like such-and-such, and I heard such-and-such about him," while saying derogatory things. With regard to this transgression, the verse states: "May the Lord cut off all flattering lips,[b] and the tongue that boasts" (Psalms 12:4).

אֲבָל בַּעַל לָשׁוֹן הָרַע זֶה שֶׁיּוֹשֵׁב וְאוֹמֵר כָּךְ עָשָׂה אִישׁ פְּלוֹנִי. אָמַר אַבְרָהָם: לֹא כֵן אֶלָּא קָשֶׁה הָרִאשׁוֹן מִן הַשֵּׁנִי, שֶׁהָרִאשׁוֹן הוּא תְּלִיתָאִי וְהוֹרֵג נְפָשׁוֹת וְהַשֵּׁנִי תִּנְיָן וְאֵינוֹ הוֹרֵג אֶלָּא עַצְמוֹ (ראה בבלי ערכין טו, ב). בִּינָה זֹאת.

"But a slanderer is one who sits and says: Such was done by this man." Avraham says: Not so; rather, the first type of speech, gossip, is worse than the second, for the first is "third speech," that is, damaging talk about a third party, whereas the second type, slander, is "second speech," it involves only two people,[c] and therefore he kills only himself (see *Arakhin* 15b). Understand this.

Halakha 3

אָמְרוּ חֲכָמִים: שָׁלֹשׁ עֲבֵרוֹת נִפְרָעִין מִן הָאָדָם בָּעוֹלָם הַזֶּה, וְאֵין לוֹ חֵלֶק לָעוֹלָם הַבָּא: עֲבוֹדָה זָרָה וְגִלּוּי עֲרָיוֹת וּשְׁפִיכוּת דָּמִים, וְלָשׁוֹן הָרַע כְּנֶגֶד כֻּלָּם. וְעוֹד אָמְרוּ חֲכָמִים: כָּל הַמְסַפֵּר בִּלְשׁוֹן הָרַע כְּאִלּוּ כָּפַר בָּעִקָּר, שֶׁנֶּאֱמַר: "אֲשֶׁר אָמְרוּ לִלְשֹׁנֵנוּ נַגְבִּיר שְׂפָתֵינוּ אִתָּנוּ מִי אָדוֹן לָנוּ" (תהלים יב, ה). וְעוֹד אָמְרוּ חֲכָמִים: שְׁלֹשָׁה לָשׁוֹן הָרַע הוֹרֶגֶת: הָאוֹמְרוֹ, וְהַמְקַבְּלוֹ, וְזֶה שֶׁאוֹמְרִין עָלָיו. וְהַמְקַבְּלוֹ יָתֵר מִן הָאוֹמְרוֹ.

The Sages said: There are three transgressions regarding which punishment is exacted from a person in this world and he also has no share in the World to Come: idol worship; forbidden sexual relations; and bloodshed, and yet slander is equal in severity to all of them.[d] The Sages also said: Anyone who speaks slander is considered as though he denied the fundamental of belief in God, as it is stated: "Those who say: With our tongue we will prevail; our lips are our own. Who is master over us?" (Psalms 12:5). And the Sages further said that slander kills three: the one who says it; the one who accepts it as true; and the one about whom it is stated.[e] And it affects the one who accepts it more than the one who says it (*Arakhin* 15b).[f1]

Halakha 4

וְיֵשׁ שָׁם דְּבָרִים שֶׁהֵן אֲבַק לָשׁוֹן הָרַע. כֵּיצַד? 'מִי יֹאמַר לִפְלוֹנִי שֶׁיִּהְיֶה כְּמוֹת שֶׁהוּא עַתָּה?', אוֹ שֶׁיֹּאמַר: 'שִׁתְקוּ מִפְּלוֹנִי, אֵינִי רוֹצֶה לְהוֹדִיעַ מָה אֵרַע וּמֶה הָיָה', וְכַיּוֹצֵא בִּדְבָרִים הָאֵלּוּ.

There are also certain statements that are called "a hint of slander."[g] How so? For example, if one says: "Who would possibly tell so-and-so that he should continue behaving as he is now," or if he says: "Be silent about so-and-so; I do not want to inform you of what happened and what his behavior was," and similar comments.

HALAKHIC DISCUSSION

1. **And it affects the one who accepts it more than the one who says it – וְהַמְקַבְּלוֹ יָתֵר מִן הָאוֹמְרוֹ:** Just as it is prohibited to speak slander, it is likewise prohibited to accept it. However, one may listen to such reports if he thinks that he will be able to appease the teller, or if relating them will help that person calm down and cause him not to relate them to anyone else. Likewise, it is permitted to investigate and listen to slander about matters that concern oneself, for example if one wishes to enter into a partnership with a certain person and needs to know if he is trustworthy. Even so, one should not accept and believe such reports unconditionally, but only take them into account in his decision-making (*Ḥafetz Ḥayyim, Hilkhot Lashon Hara* 6:2, 4; see there for more details on when one may accept slander).

NOTES

a. Who speaks the truth, unlike a defamer.

b. The lips of all those who utter prohibited statements.

c. One who hears gossip that conveys what someone is planning to do to him might feel threatened and retaliate, leading to a further escalation, whereas a bad report about someone else's sinful behavior does not affect the listener himself (*Kesef Mishne*).

d. See *Hilkhot Teshuva* 3:6.

e. It harms all parties involved.

f. He is treated more severely, since if he had not accepted the slander, no harm would have resulted.

g. When one avoids actually relating what someone did in plain terms (see *Hilkhot Issurei Bia* 22:19).

וְכֵן הַמְסַפֵּר בְּטוֹבַת חֲבֵרוֹ בִּפְנֵי שׂוֹנְאָיו הֲרֵי זֶה אֲבַק לָשׁוֹן הָרַע, שֶׁזֶּה גּוֹרֵם לָהֶם שֶׁיְּסַפְּרוּ בִּגְנוּתוֹ. וְעַל עִנְיָן זֶה אָמַר שְׁלֹמֹה: "מְבָרֵךְ רֵעֵהוּ בְּקוֹל גָּדוֹל בַּבֹּקֶר הַשְׁכֵּים קְלָלָה תֵּחָשֶׁב לוֹ" (משלי כז, יד), שֶׁמִּתּוֹךְ טוֹבָתוֹ בָּא לִידֵי רָעָתוֹ.

Similarly, when one speaks favorably about another in the presence of his enemies,[1] **this is also "a hint of slander," for it will cause them to talk disparagingly about him. In this regard, Solomon said: "He who blesses his friend in a loud voice early in the morning, it will be considered a curse to him"**[a] (Proverbs 27:14), **since from the praise** spoken about **him,** someone may **come to** speak about **him** in a **derogatory** manner.

וְכֵן הַמְסַפֵּר בְּלָשׁוֹן הָרַע דֶּרֶךְ שְׂחוֹק וְדֶרֶךְ קַלּוּת רֹאשׁ, כְּלוֹמַר שֶׁאֵינוֹ מְדַבֵּר בְּשִׂנְאָה. הוּא שֶׁשְּׁלֹמֹה אוֹמֵר: "כְּמִתְלַהְלֵהַּ הַיֹּרֶה זִקִּים חִצִּים וָמָוֶת, כֵּן אִישׁ רִמָּה אֶת רֵעֵהוּ וְאָמַר הֲלֹא מְשַׂחֵק אָנִי" (משלי כו, יח–יט). וְכֵן הַמְסַפֵּר בְּלָשׁוֹן הָרַע דֶּרֶךְ רְמִיּוּת, וְהוּא שֶׁיְּסַפֵּר לְתֻמּוֹ כְּאִלּוּ אֵינוֹ יוֹדֵעַ שֶׁדָּבָר זֶה לָשׁוֹן הָרַע הוּא, אֶלָּא כְּשֶׁמְּמַחִין בּוֹ אוֹמֵר: 'אֵינִי יוֹדֵעַ שֶׁאֵלּוּ מַעֲשָׂיו שֶׁל פְּלוֹנִי' אוֹ 'שֶׁזֶּה לָשׁוֹן הָרַע'.

The same applies to **one who relates slander in a manner of jest and frivolity, as though to say that he is not speaking with hatred.**[b] **This is** the meaning of that **which Solomon says: "Like the prankster who shoots firebrands, arrows, and death, so is a man who deceives his friend and says: Am I not joking?"** (Proverbs 26:18–19). **The same** is true of **one who speaks slander in a sly manner, which** means **that he relates it innocently, as though he does not know that it is slander,**[c] and **when** people **object to him** saying such things, **he says: "I did not know that these deeds** were committed **by so-and-so,"** or, "I did not know **that this is slander."**

Halakha 5

אֶחָד הַמְסַפֵּר בְּלָשׁוֹן הָרַע בִּפְנֵי חֲבֵרוֹ אוֹ שֶׁלֹּא בְּפָנָיו. וְהַמְסַפֵּר דְּבָרִים שֶׁגּוֹרְמִין אִם נִשְׁמְעוּ אִישׁ מִפִּי אִישׁ לְהַזִּיק חֲבֵרוֹ בְּגוּפוֹ אוֹ בְּמָמוֹנוֹ, וַאֲפִלּוּ לְהָצֵר לוֹ אוֹ לְהַפְחִידוֹ – הֲרֵי זֶה לָשׁוֹן הָרַע.

It is the same **whether one speaks slander in the presence of** the person involved **or away from his presence. If one relates information that, were it to be passed from one person to another, would cause bodily or monetary harm to** the **person**[2] who is the subject of the comments, **or even** merely **upset him or frighten him, this is slander.**

וְאִם נֶאֶמְרוּ דְּבָרִים אֵלּוּ בִּפְנֵי שְׁלֹשָׁה – כְּבָר נִשְׁמַע הַדָּבָר וְנוֹדַע, וְאִם סִפֵּר הַדָּבָר אֶחָד מִן הַשְּׁלֹשָׁה פַּעַם אַחֶרֶת – אֵין בּוֹ מִשּׁוּם לָשׁוֹן הָרַע. וְהוּא שֶׁלֹּא יִתְכַּוֵּן לְהַעֲבִיר הַקּוֹל וּלְגַלּוֹתוֹ יָתֵר.

If such statements were issued in the presence of three people, it may be assumed that **the matter has already been heard and is public knowledge.**[d3] Accordingly, **if one of** those **three** people **relates the matter another time, it does not constitute slander, provided that he does not intend to spread the rumor and publicize it further.**

HALAKHIC DISCUSSION

1. **In the presence of his enemies – בִּפְנֵי שׂוֹנְאָיו:** It is also prohibited to speak favorably about someone in public, since it is likely that there will be someone there who will be jealous and proceed to say negative things about him. It is permitted, however, to praise someone who is well known to be a good, righteous individual. One may also speak highly of someone with whom his listeners are unfamiliar, since there is no reason to think that this will lead them to disparage him (*Ḥafetz Ḥayyim*, *Hilkhot Lashon Hara* 9:2–3).

2. **One relates information that… would cause bodily or monetary harm to that person – וְהַמְסַפֵּר דְּבָרִים שֶׁגּוֹרְמִין...לְהַזִּיק חֲבֵרוֹ בְּגוּפוֹ אוֹ בְּמָמוֹנוֹ:** It is permitted to relate slander for a constructive purpose, for example if one informs a person's relatives or students that he has bad character flaws so that they will keep away from him, or by telling the truth about a prospective business partner or suitor and the like (*Ḥafetz Ḥayyim*, *Hilkhot Lashon Hara* 4:10–11; see the rest of that section, and also section 10, which details the conditions that must be met for it to be permitted to relate slander).

3. If such statements were issued in the presence of three people, it may be assumed that the matter has already been heard and is public knowledge – **וְאִם נֶאֶמְרוּ דְּבָרִים אֵלּוּ בִּפְנֵי שְׁלֹשָׁה כְּבָר נִשְׁמַע הַדָּבָר וְנוֹדַע:** The Rambam's ruling is based on the statement of the Gemara (*Bava Batra* 39a–b) that anything said in the presence of three people does not constitute slander. Some of the early authorities maintain that this leniency applies only to reports that are not derogatory (*Tosafot*). Others interpret the Gemara differently, as saying that anything a person reveals about himself in the presence of three people may be conveyed by them to others (Rashi, *Arakhin* 16a) even if it is derogatory (Rashbam, *Bava Batra* 39a; see *Ḥafetz Ḥayyim*, *Hilkhot Lashon Hara* 2:2–3, and in *Be'er Mayim Ḥayyim* there).

If the speaker warns his listeners not to reveal what he is telling them, or if one of them is a God-fearing person who does not wish to be tainted by slander at all, or if he is related to the object of the slander, or a good friend of his, they should not repeat what they have heard. Furthermore, they may relate the information only in the same city where they heard it, but not elsewhere (*Ḥafetz Ḥayyim*, *Hilkhot Lashon Hara* 2:5–7).

NOTES

a. This verse teaches that speaking good about a person can sometimes be like a curse.

b. He does not mean it seriously.

c. Or that he does not know who he is talking about.

d. And therefore one who spreads it further is causing no harm.

Halakha 6

כָּל אֵלּוּ הֵם בַּעֲלֵי לָשׁוֹן הָרָע שֶׁאָסוּר לָדוּר בִּשְׁכוּנָתָם, וְכָל שֶׁכֵּן לֵישֵׁב עִמָּהֶן וְלִשְׁמֹעַ דִּבְרֵיהֶם. וְלֹא נֶחְתַּם גְּזַר דִּין עַל אֲבוֹתֵינוּ בַּמִּדְבָּר אֶלָּא עַל לָשׁוֹן הָרָע בִּלְבַד.

All these are slanderers, in whose neighborhood it is prohibited to reside;[a] **all the more so,** one may not **sit with them and listen to their comments. The sentence** upon **our ancestors in the wilderness,** that they would not entire the Land of Israel, **was sealed only for** the sin **of slander.**[b]

Halakha 7

הַנּוֹקֵם אֶת חֲבֵרוֹ – עוֹבֵר בְּלֹא תַעֲשֶׂה, שֶׁנֶּאֱמַר: "לֹא תִקֹּם" (ויקרא יט, יח). וְאַף עַל פִּי שֶׁאֵינוֹ לוֹקֶה, דַּעַת רָעָה הִיא עַד מְאֹד,

One who takes revenge against another violates a prohibition, as it is stated: "You shall not take vengeance" (Leviticus 19:18). **Even though one is not flogged** for this sin,[c] **it is an extremely bad trait.**

אֶלָּא רָאוּי לָאָדָם לִהְיוֹת מַעֲבִיר עַל כָּל דִּבְרֵי הָעוֹלָם, שֶׁהַכֹּל אֵצֶל הַמְּבִינִים דִּבְרֵי הֶבֶל וַהֲבַאי וְאֵינָם כְּדַאי לִנְקֹם עֲלֵיהֶם.

Instead, a person should be the type of individual **who is forgiving with respect to all worldly matters, since for people of understanding,** they are **all vanity and emptiness, unworthy of vengeance.**[d]

כֵּיצַד הִיא הַנְּקִימָה? אָמַר לוֹ חֲבֵרוֹ: 'הַשְׁאִילֵנִי קַרְדֻּמְּךָ', אָמַר לוֹ: 'אֵינִי מַשְׁאִילָךְ'. לְמָחָר צָרַךְ לִשְׁאֹל מִמֶּנּוּ, אָמַר לוֹ: 'הַשְׁאִילֵנִי קַרְדֻּמְּךָ', אָמַר לוֹ: 'אֵינִי מַשְׁאִילָךְ כְּדֶרֶךְ שֶׁלֹּא הִשְׁאַלְתַּנִי כְּשֶׁשָּׁאַלְתִּי מִמְּךָ' –

How is taking **revenge** performed in practice? For example, one person **said to another, "Lend me your ax,"** and **he replied, "I will not lend** it **to you." On the following day,** the one who refused the request **needs to borrow an ax from his colleague,** and thus **he** in turn **says to him, "Lend me your ax." He retorts: "I will not lend** it **to you, in the same manner that you did not lend** your ax **to me."**

הֲרֵי זֶה נוֹקֵם. אֶלָּא כְּשֶׁיָּבֹא לוֹ לִשְׁאֹל, יִתֵּן בְּלֵב שָׁלֵם, וְלֹא יִגְמֹל לוֹ כַּאֲשֶׁר גְּמָלוֹ, וְכֵן כָּל כַּיּוֹצֵא בָּאֵלּוּ.

This person **is taking revenge. Rather, when he comes to ask him to borrow** the ax, **he should give** it to him **wholeheartedly, without retaliating against him in the same manner that** the other **treated him. The same** applies **in all similar** cases.

וְכֵן אָמַר דָּוִד בְּדֵעוֹתָיו הַטּוֹבוֹת: "אִם גָּמַלְתִּי שׁוֹלְמִי רָע וָאֲחַלְּצָה צוֹרְרִי רֵיקָם" וכו' (תהלים ז, ה).

Thus King David proclaimed, invoking his fine traits:[e] **"If I have repaid my friend with evil, or despoiled my enemy without cause…"** (Psalms 7:5).

Halakha 8

וְכֵן כָּל הַנּוֹטֵר לְאֶחָד מִיִּשְׂרָאֵל – עוֹבֵר בְּלֹא תַעֲשֶׂה, שֶׁנֶּאֱמַר: "וְלֹא תִטֹּר אֶת בְּנֵי עַמֶּךָ" (ויקרא יט, יח).

Similarly, anyone who bears a grudge against another Jew[f] **violates a prohibition, as it is stated: "You shall not bear any grudge against members of your people"** (Leviticus 19:18).

NOTES

a. In case one learns from their ways (see 6:1; *Hilkhot Tumat Tzaraat* 16:10).

b. Because the children of Israel believed the spies' negative reports about the Land (Numbers, chap. 13–14).

c. Since it does not involve an action (as stated in Halakha 1).

d. Wise individuals realize that these squabbles are worthless and do not justify acts of revenge.

e. David is praying to God to forgive him in merit of his good character traits, one of which is that he does not repay those who have wronged him in kind.

f. And keeps in mind how he was mistreated by him.

כֵּיצַד? רְאוּבֵן שֶׁאָמַר לְשִׁמְעוֹן: 'שְׂכֹר לִי בַּיִת זֶה' אוֹ 'הַשְׁאִילֵנִי שׁוֹר זֶה', וְלֹא רָצָה שִׁמְעוֹן. לְיָמִים צָרַךְ שִׁמְעוֹן לִרְאוּבֵן לִשְׁאֹל מִמֶּנּוּ אוֹ לִשְׂכֹּר, וְאָמַר לוֹ רְאוּבֵן: 'הֵא לְךָ, הֲרֵינִי מַשְׁאִילְךָ וְאֵינִי כְּמוֹתְךָ, וְלֹא אֲשַׁלֵּם לְךָ כְּמַעֲשֶׂיךָ', הָעוֹשֶׂה כָּזֶה – עָבַר בְּ'לֹא תִטֹּר'.

How so? For example, **Reuben asked Simeon:** "Will you **rent this house to me?" or: "Lend this ox to me," and Simeon was unwilling** to do so. **A few days later, Simeon needed to borrow or rent something from Reuben, and Reuben said to him: "Take it. I am lending it to you; I am not** mean-spirited **like you, and I will not pay you back in the same manner as you acted." One who acts like this has violated** the prohibition of "**you shall not bear a grudge.**"

אֶלָּא יִמְחֶה הַדָּבָר מִלִּבּוֹ וְלֹא יִטְּרֶנּוּ, שֶׁכָּל זְמַן שֶׁהוּא נוֹטֵר אֶת הַדָּבָר וְזוֹכְרוֹ, שֶׁמָּא יָבֹא לִנְקֹם. לְפִיכָךְ הִקְפִּידָה תּוֹרָה עַל הַנְּטִירָה, עַד שֶׁיִּמְחֶה הֶעָוֹן מִלִּבּוֹ כְּלָל וְלֹא יִזְכְּרֶנּוּ.

Instead, he should wipe the whole **thing from his heart and not bear it** in mind, **for as long as he bears the matter** in mind **and recalls it, he might come to take revenge.**[a] **Therefore, the Torah is particular about bearing a grudge,** to the extent **that one must wipe the transgression from his heart entirely, and not recall it** at all.

וְזוֹ הִיא הַדֵּעָה הַנְּכוֹנָה שֶׁאֶפְשָׁר שֶׁיִּתְקַיֵּם בָּהּ יִשּׁוּב הָאָרֶץ וּמַשָּׂא וּמַתָּן שֶׁל בְּנֵי אָדָם זֶה עִם זֶה.

This is the proper character **trait through which a civilized society, and trade between people, can be maintained.**

בְּרִיךְ רַחֲמָנָא דְּסַיְּעַן

Blessed is the Merciful One, who has assisted us.

NOTES

a. Which is an even greater sin, "an extremely bad trait" (Halakha 7).

b. Which is an even greater sin, "an extremely bad trait" (Halakha 7).

הִלְכוֹת
תַּלְמוּד תּוֹרָה

The Halakhot (Laws) of Torah Study

יֵשׁ בִּכְלָלָן שְׁתֵּי מִצְוֹות עֲשֵׂה: רִאשׁוֹנָה – לִלְמֹד תּוֹרָה. שְׁנִיָּה – לְכַבֵּד מְלַמְּדֶיהָ וְיוֹדְעֶיהָ.
וּבֵאוּר שְׁתֵּי מִצְוֹות אֵלּוּ בִּפְרָקִים אֵלּוּ.

These halakhot include two positive mitzvot:

1) To study Torah 2) To honor its teachers and its scholars

These two mitzvot will be explained in the following chapters.

Hilkhot Talmud Torah: Parallels to the mitzvot

The mitzva	*Sefer HaMitzvot*	The mitzva in *Hilkhot Talmud Torah*
To study Torah	Positive mitzva 11	1:1–3
To honor its teachers and scholars	Positive mitzva 209	6:1

Introduction to *Hilkhot Talmud Torah*

The obligation and mitzva of Torah study appears in the Torah and is expounded upon in both the Mishna and the Talmud. While there are indeed many statements of the Sages that expound on the value, importance, and methods of Torah study, these various teachings are scattered throughout the Mishna and Talmud. It was the Rambam who first forged a comprehensive, systematic corpus addressing all aspects of Torah study – from the overarching definitions of the general obligation to study Torah, to the details of the order and methods of the study itself. He also provides pedagogical guidance from the perspective of the student, whether a child or an adult, as well as from the perspective of the teacher. Within this section of laws, not only does the Rambam present Torah study as a way of life, and an integral component of a person's endeavors, but he also discusses the social structures that sustain Torah study. As such, he deals with the obligations of teachers and their social standing, the obligation to honor and revere Torah scholars, as well as defining how society as a whole should safeguard those who study and teach Torah.

Even though the later authorities were certainly conversant with the Rambam's *Hilkhot Talmud Torah*, few developed these halakhot beyond what the Rambam provides. As such, to a large extent, the Rambam's work remains pivotal for the study of this topic, not only in order to gain a complete picture regarding the value and essence of Torah study, but also in order to analyze the many detailed laws regarding it.

Contents

Chapters 5–7: Honoring Torah Scholars

Chapter 5: Honoring One's Teacher

Halakha 1:	The importance of honoring one's teacher
Halakhot 2–4:	Issuing rulings in the presence of one's teacher
Halakhot 5–9:	How to honor one's teacher
Halakhot 9–10:	Honoring Torah scholars who are not one's preeminent teacher, and other Torah scholars
Halakhot 11–13:	A Torah scholar forgoing honor due to him, and the obligation of honoring students

Chapter 6: Honoring Torah Scholars

Halakhot 1–8:	Standing before a Torah scholar
Halakha 9:	Standing before an elder
Halakha 10:	Exemption from taxes, and additional benefits
Halakhot 11–13:	Disgracing Torah scholars, and ostracism for doing so
Halakha 14:	The reasons for which one is ostracized

Chapter 7: Ostracism and Excommunication

Halakha 1:	Ostracizing Torah scholars
Halakhot 2–6:	Laws of ostracism and excommunication
Halakhot 7–12:	Revoking ostracism
Halakha 13:	Considerations regarding imposing and revoking ostracism; a sage's conduct when ostracized

פֶּרֶק רִאשׁוֹן

CHAPTER 1

The Obligation of Torah Study

Halakha 1

נָשִׁים וַעֲבָדִים פְּטוּרִים מִתַּלְמוּד תּוֹרָה.

Women and slaves are exempt from the mitzva of **Torah study.**[1] The exemption of women from this mitzva is derived from the verse cited later in this Halakha: "You shall teach them to your sons" – which explicitly excludes daughters.[a] Similarly, slaves are also exempt, as they are absolved from any mitzvot from which women are exempt.[b]

אֲבָל קָטָן – אָבִיו חַיָּב לְלַמְּדוֹ תּוֹרָה, שֶׁנֶּאֱמַר: "וְלִמַּדְתֶּם אֹתָם אֶת בְּנֵיכֶם לְדַבֵּר בָּם" (דברים יא, יט). וְאֵין הָאִשָּׁה חַיֶּבֶת לְלַמֵּד אֶת בְּנָהּ, שֶׁכָּל הַחַיָּב לִלְמֹד חַיָּב לְלַמֵּד.

However, a minor son is included in the mitzva, as **his father is obligated to teach him Torah,**[2] **as it is stated: "You shall teach them to your sons, to speak of them"** (Deuteronomy 11:19). **A woman is not obligated to teach her son,**[3] as the rule is that **anyone who is obligated to study, is obligated to teach.** Therefore, anyone who is not obligated to study is also not obligated to teach.

NOTES

a. See Halakha 13.

b. See, for example, *Hilkhot Keriat Shema* 4:1.

HALAKHIC DISCUSSION

1. **Women and slaves are exempt from Torah study – נָשִׁים וַעֲבָדִים פְּטוּרִים מִתַּלְמוּד תּוֹרָה:** With regard to slaves, not only are they exempt from the mitzva, but there is also a prohibition against teaching Torah to them (*Hilkhot Avadim* 8:18; *Shulḥan Arukh, Yoreh De'a* 267:71).

2. **A minor son, his father is obligated to teach him Torah – קָטָן אָבִיו חַיָּב לְלַמְּדוֹ תּוֹרָה:** *Shulḥan Arukh, Yoreh De'a* 245:1.

3. **A woman is not obligated to teach her son – וְאֵין הָאִשָּׁה חַיֶּבֶת לְלַמֵּד אֶת בְּנָהּ:** Nevertheless, should a woman assist her son or husband, thereby facilitating their Torah study, she acquires a share in the reward accrued from their learning (Rema, *Yoreh De'a* 246:6).

Halakha 2

כְּשֵׁם שֶׁאָדָם חַיָּב לְלַמֵּד אֶת בְּנוֹ, כָּךְ הוּא חַיָּב לְלַמֵּד אֶת בֶּן בְּנוֹ, שֶׁנֶּאֱמַר: "וְהוֹדַעְתָּם לְבָנֶיךָ וְלִבְנֵי בָנֶיךָ" (דברים ד, ט).

Just as a person is obligated to teach his son,[1] **so too, he is obligated to teach his grandson, as it is stated: "And you shall impart them to your sons and to your sons' sons"** (Deuteronomy 4:9).

וְלֹא בְּנוֹ וּבֶן בְּנוֹ בִּלְבַד, אֶלָּא מִצְוָה עַל כָּל חָכָם וְחָכָם מִיִּשְׂרָאֵל לְלַמֵּד אֶת כָּל הַתַּלְמִידִים אַף עַל פִּי שֶׁאֵינָם בָּנָיו, שֶׁנֶּאֱמַר: "וְשִׁנַּנְתָּם לְבָנֶיךָ" (שם ו, ז), מִפִּי הַשְּׁמוּעָה לָמְדוּ: "בָּנֶיךָ" – אֵלּוּ תַּלְמִידֶיךָ, שֶׁהַתַּלְמִידִים קְרוּיִים בָּנִים, שֶׁנֶּאֱמַר: "וַיֵּצְאוּ בְנֵי הַנְּבִיאִים" (מלכים ב ב, ג).

The obligation to teach is **not only** with regard to **one's son and grandson, rather it is a mitzva** incumbent on **each and every sage of the Jewish people to teach all students, even though they are not his sons, as it is stated: "You shall inculcate them in your sons"** (Deuteronomy 6:7), **and** the Sages **learned, on the basis of the** Oral **tradition: "Your sons," these are your students, for students are called sons, as it is stated: "The sons of the prophets"** (II Kings 2:3) in reference to their students.

אִם כֵּן, לָמָּה נִצְטַוָּה עַל בְּנוֹ וּבֶן בְּנוֹ? לְהַקְדִּים בְּנוֹ לְבֶן בְּנוֹ, וּבֶן בְּנוֹ לְבֶן חֲבֵרוֹ.

If so, why is a person explicitly **commanded with regard to** teaching **his son and his grandson?** In order **to grant precedence to** teaching **his son over his grandson, and to his grandson over another's son.**[2]

Halakha 3

וְחַיָּב לִשְׂכֹּר מְלַמֵּד לִבְנוֹ וּלְלַמְּדוֹ, וְאֵינוֹ חַיָּב לְלַמֵּד בֶּן חֲבֵרוֹ אֶלָּא בְּחִנָּם.

A father **is obligated** to ensure that his son studies Torah to the extent that, if necessary, he must even pay **to hire a teacher to teach his son.**[a][3] In contrast, although **one is obligated to teach another's son,** that is **only when** doing so **doesn't involve any cost;** one is not obligated to spend money in order to hire a teacher for him.

מִי שֶׁלֹּא לִמְּדוֹ אָבִיו – חַיָּב לְלַמֵּד אֶת עַצְמוֹ כְּשֶׁיַּכִּיר, שֶׁנֶּאֱמַר: "וּלְמַדְתֶּם אֹתָם וּשְׁמַרְתֶּם לַעֲשֹׂתָם" (דברים ה, א).

Someone who was not taught by his father[4] **is obligated to teach himself, once he recognizes** that he is obligated in studying Torah, **as it is stated: "And you shall study them, and you shall take care to perform them"** (Deuteronomy 5:1) which teaches that one needs to study in order to perform the mitzvot.

וְכֵן אַתָּה מוֹצֵא בְּכָל מָקוֹם שֶׁהַתַּלְמוּד קוֹדֵם לְמַעֲשֶׂה, מִפְּנֵי שֶׁהַתַּלְמוּד מֵבִיא לִידֵי מַעֲשֶׂה, וְאֵין הַמַּעֲשֶׂה מֵבִיא לִידֵי תַּלְמוּד.

And similarly, you find in every place that studying Torah **takes precedence over the practice** of the mitzvot, as it is more important[b] **due to** the fact **that the study** of Torah **leads** one **to** engage in its **practice,*** since only by studying does one know how to perform the mitzvot, **whereas** engaging in **its practice does not lead** one **to study.**

HALAKHIC DISCUSSION

1. Just as a person is obligated to teach his son – כְּשֵׁם שֶׁאָדָם חַיָּב לְלַמֵּד אֶת בְּנוֹ: *Shulḥan Arukh, Yoreh De'a* 245:3.

2. To grant precedence to teaching his son over his grandson, and to his grandson over another's son – לְהַקְדִּים בְּנוֹ לְבֶן בְּנוֹ וּבֶן בְּנוֹ לְבֶן חֲבֵרוֹ: One's progeny takes precedence over students who are unrelated, with nearer descendants being accorded priority over those more distantly related (*Shulḥan Arukh HaRav, Hilkhot Talmud Torah* 1:8; *Arukh HaShulḥan*).

3. One is obligated to hire a teacher to teach his son – וְחַיָּב לִשְׂכֹּר מְלַמֵּד לִבְנוֹ וּלְלַמְּדוֹ: *Shulḥan Arukh, Yoreh De'a* 245:4. A father can be compelled to employ a teacher for his son. If the father is not present in the city, but possesses assets there, and there is no viable means to apprise him of his obligation, then a teacher may be employed by utilizing those assets as remuneration (Rema). The later commentaries write that a father is likewise duty-bound to procure a teacher for his grandson (*Shakh*. See also *Shulḥan Arukh HaRav, Talmud Torah* 1:8 and *Arukh HaShulḥan* which discuss the obligation to hire a teacher for one's other relatives).

4. Someone who was not taught by his father – מִי שֶׁלֹּא לִמְּדוֹ אָבִיו: *Shulḥan Arukh, Yoreh De'a* 245:1.

FROM THE LUBAVITCHER REBBE

*Studying takes precedence over practice, due to the fact that studying leads to its practice – שֶׁהַתַּלְמוּד קוֹדֵם לְמַעֲשֶׂה, מִפְּנֵי שֶׁהַתַּלְמוּד מֵבִיא לִידֵי מַעֲשֶׂה: The implication here is not that the sole rationale for the obligation to study Torah is its conduciveness to the observance of mitzvot. This is evident from the Rambam's ruling that one is obligated, from the very onset of one's studies, to engage even in topics that are devoid of practical application. Rather, since numerous sources underscore the primacy of Torah study over the performance of mitzvot due to the former's capacity to engender the latter, it follows that study is, in fact, more important than practice. Consequently, it follows that anyone who is obligated to perform the mitzvot is certainly obligated to study Torah (*Torat Menaḥem, Hitvaaduyot, Ḥukkat* 5744; *Likkutei Siḥot* 36, p. 18).

NOTES

a. See Halakha 7.

b. See 3:3.

Halakha 4

הָיָה הוּא לִלְמֹד תּוֹרָה, וְיֵשׁ לוֹ בֵּן לִלְמֹד תּוֹרָה – הוּא קוֹדֵם לִבְנוֹ.

If a person needs **to study Torah himself, but he has a son** who also needs **to study Torah,**[1] and he has insufficient resources to enable both of them to study, then **he takes precedence over his son,** due to the principle that one must give precedence to the fulfillment of one's own mitzvot over the fulfillment of other's mitzvot.[a]

וְאִם הָיָה בְּנוֹ נָבוֹן וּמַשְׂכִּיל מַה שֶּׁיִּלְמַד יוֹתֵר מִמֶּנּוּ – בְּנוֹ קוֹדֵם. וְאַף עַל פִּי שֶׁבְּנוֹ קוֹדֵם – לֹא יִבָּטֵל הוּא, שֶׁכְּשֵׁם שֶׁמִּצְוָה עָלָיו לְלַמֵּד אֶת בְּנוֹ, כָּךְ הוּא מְצֻוֶּה לְלַמֵּד אֶת עַצְמוֹ.

However, if his son is wise, and he comprehends what he studies to a greater degree than the father, then **the son takes precedence. However, even though his son takes precedence,** the father himself **should not cease** from studying, rather he should study as much as he is able, **as just as there is a mitzva upon him to teach his son, so too he is commanded to teach himself.**

Halakha 5

לְעוֹלָם יִלְמַד אָדָם תּוֹרָה וְאַחַר כָּךְ יִשָּׂא אִשָּׁה, שֶׁאִם נָשָׂא אִשָּׁה תְּחִלָּה – אֵין דַּעְתּוֹ פְּנוּיָה לִלְמֹד. וְאִם הָיָה יִצְרוֹ מִתְגַּבֵּר עָלָיו עַד שֶׁנִּמְצָא שֶׁאֵין לִבּוֹ פָּנוּי – יִשָּׂא אִשָּׁה, וְאַחַר כָּךְ יִלְמַד תּוֹרָה.

A person should always first **study Torah, and** only **afterward marry a woman,**[2] **because were he to first marry a woman,** he would then be concerned with supporting his home, and so **his mind would not be free to** be fully engaged in the **study** of Torah. **However, if his desires overwhelm him to the extent that his heart is not free** to be fully engaged in the study of Torah, then **he should** first **get married to a woman,** and then **afterward he should study Torah.**

Halakha 6

מֵאֵימָתַי מַתְחִיל אָבִיו לְלַמְּדוֹ תּוֹרָה? מִשֶּׁיַּתְחִיל לְדַבֵּר מְלַמְּדוֹ: "תּוֹרָה צִוָּה לָנוּ מֹשֶׁה מוֹרָשָׁה" וגו' (דברים לג, ד), וּפָסוּק רִאשׁוֹן מִפָּרָשַׁת 'שְׁמַע'.

From when should a father begin to teach his son **Torah?**[3] **From when** his son **begins to speak,** the father **should teach him**[4] the verse: **"Torah, Moses commanded us, a heritage** of the assembly of Jacob" (Deuteronomy 33:4) **and** the **first verse of the** first **portion of the Shema,** in order to implant within his heart faith in the importance of the Torah and the unity of God,

וְאַחַר כָּךְ מְלַמְּדוֹ מְעַט מְעַט, פְּסוּקִים פְּסוּקִים, עַד שֶׁיִּהְיֶה בֶּן שֵׁשׁ אוֹ בֶּן שֶׁבַע, לְפִי בָּרְיוֹ, מוֹלִיכוֹ אֵצֶל מְלַמֵּד הַתִּינוֹקוֹת.

and afterward he should continue to **teach him** additional verses, **little by little, verse by verse, until he reaches the age of six or seven, depending on his physical strength,**[b] at which point **he should take him to a teacher of young children** to continue his studying with him.

HALAKHIC DISCUSSION

1. If a person needs to study Torah himself, but he has a son who also needs to study Torah – הָיָה הוּא לִלְמֹד תּוֹרָה, וְיֵשׁ לוֹ בֵּן לִלְמֹד תּוֹרָה: *Shulḥan Arukh, Yoreh De'a* 245:2.

2. A person should always study Torah, and afterward marry a woman – לְעוֹלָם יִלְמַד אָדָם תּוֹרָה וְאַחַר כָּךְ יִשָּׂא אִשָּׁה: *Shulḥan Arukh, Yoreh De'a* 246:2.

3. From when should a father begin to teach his son Torah? – מֵאֵימָתַי מַתְחִיל אָבִיו לְלַמְּדוֹ תּוֹרָה: *Shulḥan Arukh, Yoreh De'a* 245:5.

4. From when his son begins to speak, he should teach him – מִשֶּׁיַּתְחִיל לְדַבֵּר מְלַמְּדוֹ: When a child reaches the age of three, one should teach him the letters of the Torah, in order that he will become familiar with them and be able to read the Torah himself (Rema).

NOTES

a. See above, Halakha 1.

b. See 2:2.

Halakha 7

הָיָה מִנְהַג הַמְּדִינָה לִקַּח מְלַמֵּד הַתִּינוֹקוֹת שָׂכָר – נוֹתֵן לוֹ שְׂכָרוֹ. וְחַיָּב לְלַמְּדוֹ בְּשָׂכָר עַד שֶׁיִּקְרָא תּוֹרָה שֶׁבִּכְתָב כֻּלָּהּ. מָקוֹם שֶׁנָּהֲגוּ לְלַמֵּד תּוֹרָה שֶׁבִּכְתָב בְּשָׂכָר – מֻתָּר לְלַמֵּד בְּשָׂכָר.

If **the regional custom is for a teacher of young children to take payment,**[1] then **one gives him payment.** The father **is obligated to pay for his son to be taught until** the son **has read the entirety of the Written Torah,**[2] the whole of Tanakh. In **a locale where** teachers **are accustomed to take payment for teaching the Written Torah**[3] **it is permitted to teach for payment.**

אֲבָל תּוֹרָה שֶׁבְּעַל פֶּה – אָסוּר לְלַמְּדָהּ בְּשָׂכָר, שֶׁנֶּאֱמַר: "רְאֵה לִמַּדְתִּי אֶתְכֶם חֻקִּים וּמִשְׁפָּטִים כַּאֲשֶׁר צִוַּנִי יי אֱלֹהָי" וגו' (דברים ד, ה) – מָה אֲנִי בְּחִנָּם לָמַדְתִּי, אַף אַתֶּם בְּחִנָּם לְמַדְתֶּם מִמֶּנִּי. וְכֵן כְּשֶׁתְּלַמְּדוּ לְדוֹרוֹת – בְּחִנָּם, כְּמוֹ שֶׁלְּמַדְתֶּם מִמֶּנִּי.

However, it is forbidden to teach the Oral Torah for payment,[4] **as it is stated** by Moses in his speech to the Jewish people: **"See, I have taught you statutes and ordinances, as the Lord my God commanded me…"** (Deuteronomy 4:5) from which the Sages derive: **"Just as I,** Moses, **studied** Torah from God **without charge, so too,** when **you studied from me,** it was done **free of charge, and similarly, when you teach** Torah **in future generations,** do so **free of charge, just as when you studied from me."**

לֹא מָצָא מִי שֶׁיְּלַמְּדוֹ בְּחִנָּם – יְלַמֵּד בְּשָׂכָר, שֶׁנֶּאֱמַר: "אֱמֶת קְנֵה" (משלי כג, כג). יָכוֹל יְלַמֵּד לַאֲחֵרִים בְּשָׂכָר? תַּלְמוּד לוֹמַר: "וְאַל תִּמְכֹּר" (שם). הָא לָמַדְתָּ שֶׁאָסוּר לוֹ לְלַמֵּד בְּשָׂכָר, אַף עַל פִּי שֶׁלִּמְּדוֹ רַבּוֹ בְּשָׂכָר.

If, nevertheless, a father **cannot find someone to teach** Torah to his son **for no charge,** then **he should pay for his son to be taught, as it is stated: "Acquire truth"** (Proverbs 23:23). One **might** have thought, based on this verse, **that one** who was taught by a teacher who took payment **may** therefore **teach others for payment.** To counter this, **the verse** continues, to **state: "And do not sell** it." **You learn** from **this that it is forbidden to teach for payment, even if one's teacher taught him for payment.**

HALAKHIC DISCUSSION

1. **If the regional custom is for a teacher of young children to take payment** – הָיָה מִנְהַג הַמְּדִינָה לִקַּח מְלַמֵּד הַתִּינוֹקוֹת שָׂכָר: *Shulḥan Arukh, Yoreh De'a* 245:6.

2. **Until he has read the entirety of the Written Torah** – עַד שֶׁיִּקְרָא תּוֹרָה שֶׁבִּכְתָב כֻּלָּהּ: If the father possesses the financial means, he also bears the responsibility to pay for his son's education in Mishna, Talmud, halakha, and *aggada* (*Shulḥan Arukh*). The later commentaries deliberate as to whether the father's duty extends solely to the Written Torah, encompassing the whole of Tanakh, or if he is also obligated to ensure his son's comprehensive study of the Oral Torah (see *Arukh HaShulḥan*). The authorities discuss the fact that, in practice, individuals often neglect to ensure their sons' thorough study of the Written Torah, often excluding the Prophets and Writings. While some argue that this deviation indeed contradicts the halakha (Baḥ), others justify it, citing a variety of reasons (see *Shakh* to *Shulḥan Arukh, Yoreh De'a* 245:5, *Shulḥan Arukh HaRav, Talmud Torah* 1:6).

3. **A locale where they are accustomed to take payment for teaching the Written Torah** – מָקוֹם שֶׁנָּהֲגוּ לְלַמֵּד תּוֹרָה שֶׁבִּכְתָב בְּשָׂכָר: *Shulḥan Arukh, Yoreh De'a* 246:5.

4. **However, it is forbidden to teach the Oral Torah for payment** – אֲבָל תּוֹרָה שֶׁבְּעַל פֶּה אָסוּר לְלַמְּדָהּ בְּשָׂכָר: The *Shulḥan Arukh* stipulates that in a community where it is customary to receive payment for teaching the Oral Torah, such remuneration is permissible. This allowance applies under the condition that the teacher lacks alternative sources of income, or accepts payment to enable his full dedication to teaching without resorting to additional employment for financial support. The Rema adds that it is permissible to receive payment for teaching rabbinic decrees.

Halakha 8

כָּל אִישׁ מִיִּשְׂרָאֵל חַיָּב בְּתַלְמוּד תּוֹרָה, בֵּין עָנִי בֵּין עָשִׁיר, בֵּין שָׁלֵם בְּגוּפוֹ בֵּין בַּעַל יִסּוּרִין, בֵּין בָּחוּר בֵּין שֶׁהָיָה זָקֵן גָּדוֹל שֶׁתָּשַׁשׁ כֹּחוֹ.

Every Jewish man is obligated in the mitzva of **studying Torah.**[1] This is true **whether he is poor or rich, whether he** is healthy and **whole in his body or a person** who suffers **afflictions, whether he is a young man or a very elderly person whose strength has waned.**

אֲפִלּוּ עָנִי הַמְחַזֵּר עַל הַפְּתָחִים, וַאֲפִלּוּ בַּעַל אִשָּׁה וּבָנִים – חַיָּב לִקְבֹּעַ לוֹ זְמַן לְתַלְמוּד תּוֹרָה בַּיּוֹם וּבַלַּיְלָה, שֶׁנֶּאֱמַר: "וְהָגִיתָ בּוֹ יוֹמָם וָלַיְלָה" (יהושע א, ח).

Even a poor person who goes around to beg for money and food **at** people's **doors, and even a man who has a wife and children** whom he is obligated to support[a] **is obligated to fix for himself a time for studying Torah,** every day, a time **during the day and** a time **during the night,**[2] **as it is stated:** "This book of the Torah shall not depart from your mouth, **and you shall ponder it day and night"** (Joshua 1:8).

Halakha 9

גְּדוֹלֵי חַכְמֵי יִשְׂרָאֵל הָיָה מֵהֶם חוֹטְבֵי עֵצִים, וּמֵהֶם שׁוֹאֲבֵי מַיִם, וּמֵהֶם סוּמִין, וְאַף עַל פִּי כֵן הָיוּ עוֹסְקִין בַּתּוֹרָה בַּיּוֹם וּבַלַּיְלָה. וְהֵם מִכְּלַל מַעְתִּיקֵי הַשְּׁמוּעָה אִישׁ מִפִּי אִישׁ מִפִּי מֹשֶׁה רַבֵּנוּ.

Among the greatest sages of the Jewish people, there were those who were **hewers of wood and** those who were **drawers of water, and** those who were **blind, and nevertheless,** despite the strain of their circumstances, **they engaged in the study of Torah day and night. And** moreover, **these** sages **were among the transmitters of the** Oral **Tradition** that was transmitted **from person to person** in a chain of tradition **from Moses, our teacher** (see the introduction to the *Mishne Torah*).

Halakha 10

עַד אֵימָתַי חַיָּב אָדָם לִלְמֹד תּוֹרָה? עַד יוֹם מוֹתוֹ, שֶׁנֶּאֱמַר: "וּפֶן יָסוּרוּ מִלְּבָבְךָ כֹּל יְמֵי חַיֶּיךָ" (דברים ד, ט), וְכָל זְמַן שֶׁלֹּא יַעֲסֹק בְּלִמּוּד הוּא שׁוֹכֵחַ.

Until when is a person obligated[3] **to study Torah? Until the day of his death, as it is stated** concerning words of Torah: **"And lest they move from your heart all the days of your life"** (Deuteronomy 4:9), instructing that the words of Torah should not be forgotten, **and whenever a person is not engaged in studying, he forgets.**[4]

NOTES

a. See above, Halakha 5.

HALAKHIC DISCUSSION

1. **Every Jewish man is obligated in the mitzva of studying Torah** – כָּל אִישׁ מִיִּשְׂרָאֵל חַיָּב בְּתַלְמוּד תּוֹרָה: *Shulḥan Arukh, Yoreh De'a* 246:1. An individual who is unable to engage in Torah study, whether due to a lack of skill, or due to the weight of various responsibilities, should instead support others in their study of Torah (*Shulḥan Arukh*). One who supports others in their studies is regarded as if he had engaged in study himself (Rema). Moreover, one who does study Torah himself should nevertheless also try to provide support to others who study (*Arukh HaShulḥan*).

2. **He is obligated to fix for himself a time for studying Torah, during the day and during the night** – חַיָּב לִקְבֹּעַ לוֹ זְמַן לְתַלְמוּד תּוֹרָה בַּיּוֹם וּבַלַּיְלָה: In exigent circumstances, if an individual recites the Shema in the morning and evening, he has discharged his obligation of Torah study (Rema and *Arukh HaShulḥan*. However, the Birkei Yosef disagrees and writes that doing so fulfills the obligation derived from the verse "This book of the Torah shall not depart from your mouth," but it does not completely satisfy the mitzvah of Torah study).

3. **Until when is a person obligated** – עַד אֵימָתַי חַיָּב: *Shulḥan Arukh, Yoreh De'a* 246:3.

4. **And whenever a person is not engaged in studying, he forgets** – וְכָל זְמַן שֶׁלֹּא יַעֲסֹק בְּלִמּוּד הוּא שׁוֹכֵחַ: The *Shulḥan Arukh HaRav* (*Talmud Torah* 2) goes to great lengths to explain the prohibition against forgetting even a single detail of one's Torah study when one has forgotten due to inadequate review of the material. It describes a mode of study that would enable any person to study in such a way that the material will be organized, with fluency and retention, to the best of his abilities and the strength of his memory, regardless of the quantity of Torah studied, be it small or extensive.

Halakha 11

וְחַיָּב לְשַׁלֵּשׁ אֶת זְמַן לְמִידָתוֹ: שְׁלִישׁ בַּתּוֹרָה שֶׁבִּכְתָב, וּשְׁלִישׁ בַּתּוֹרָה שֶׁבְּעַל פֶּה, וּשְׁלִישׁ יָבִין וְיַשְׂכִּיל אַחֲרִית דָּבָר מֵרֵאשִׁיתוֹ, וְיוֹצִיא דָּבָר מִדָּבָר, וִידַמֶּה דָּבָר לְדָבָר, וְיָדִין בַּמִּדּוֹת שֶׁהַתּוֹרָה נִדְרֶשֶׁת בָּהֶן עַד שֶׁיֵּדַע הֵיאַךְ הוּא עִקַּר הַמִּדּוֹת, וְהֵיאַךְ יוֹצִיא הָאָסוּר וְהַמֻּתָּר וְכַיּוֹצֵא בָּהֶן מִדְּבָרִים שֶׁלָּמַד מִפִּי הַשְּׁמוּעָה. וְעִנְיָן זֶה הוּא הַנִּקְרָא תַּלְמוּד.

A person is obligated to divide his study time into three:[1] **a third for** the study of **the Written Torah, a third for the Oral Torah, and** in the final **third, he will** use his time to **understand and abstract the ultimate** halakhic **conclusion from its original source, and he will infer** one **matter from** another **matter, and compare one matter to** another **matter, and he will examine the hermeneutical principles** of biblical exegesis received from the Sages **until he knows the essence of those principles, and how that which is forbidden and that which is permitted, and similar matters, are derived from the material that he studied from the** Oral **tradition. This** latter **process is referred to as "Talmud."**

Halakha 12

כֵּיצַד? הָיָה בַּעַל אֻמָּנוּת, וְהָיָה עוֹסֵק בִּמְלָאכָה שָׁלֹשׁ שָׁעוֹת בַּיּוֹם וּבַתּוֹרָה תֵּשַׁע – אוֹתָן הַתֵּשַׁע, קוֹרֵא בְּשָׁלֹשׁ מֵהֶן בַּתּוֹרָה שֶׁבִּכְתָב, וּבְשָׁלֹשׁ בַּתּוֹרָה שֶׁבְּעַל פֶּה, וּבְשָׁלֹשׁ מִתְבּוֹנֵן בְּדַעְתּוֹ לְהָבִין דָּבָר מִדָּבָר.

How should this obligation to split one's study into three be accomplished?[2] If a person **is a craftsman who is engaged in work for three hours a day and** in the study of **the Torah for nine hours,**[a] then during **those nine hours, he reads the Written Torah for three of those** hours, **and for** another **three** hours he studies **the Oral Torah, and for** the remaining **three** hours **he contemplates in order to understand** how to derive **one matter from another.**

וְדִבְרֵי קַבָּלָה בִּכְלַל תּוֹרָה שֶׁבִּכְתָב הֵן, וּפֵרוּשָׁן בִּכְלַל תּוֹרָה שֶׁבְּעַל פֶּה. וְהָעִנְיָנוֹת הַנִּקְרָאִין פַּרְדֵּס בִּכְלַל הַתַּלְמוּד.

The texts of the tradition, i.e., Prophets and Writings, **are included in the Written Torah,** whereas **their explanations are included in the Oral Torah. The subject matters referred to as "*Pardes*,"** the contemplation of the existence of God and his greatness,[b] **are included in "Talmud,"**[3]* as this also involves understanding how these matters are derived from their source in the Torah.

בַּמֶּה דְּבָרִים אֲמוּרִים? בִּתְחִלַּת תַּלְמוּדוֹ שֶׁל אָדָם.

In what case **is this statement,** about how to divide up one's study, **said?** Only **in the initial** stage **of a person's study,** when he is still not fully versed in the Written and Oral Torah.

HALAKHIC DISCUSSION

1. **A person is obligated to divide his study time into three** – וְחַיָּב לְשַׁלֵּשׁ זְמַן לְמִידָתוֹ: *Shulḥan Arukh, Yoreh De'a* 246:4. Some authorities argue that this obligation can be fulfilled through the study of the Babylonian Talmud, as it incorporates references to the Written Torah, Mishna, and the logic arguments the Rambam refers to as "Talmud" (Rema). While this practice is indeed the common custom, a person should, in addition, ensure they gain a comprehensive knowledge of the Written Torah and Mishna. Homeowners who are constrained by time should prioritize the study of practical halakha over the Talmud to ensure proficiency in the essential practical halakhot (*Arukh HaShulḥan*). The *Shulḥan Arukh HaRav* (*Talmud Torah* 2:2) states that the intention of dividing one's study time into three is not that one should split the time into three portions of equal length. Rather, the intention is to allocate adequate time to each area of study in parallel – Written Torah, Mishna, and Talmud – to ensure comprehensive coverage of each one.

2. **How should this be accomplished** – כֵּיצַד: *Shulḥan Arukh, Yoreh De'a* 246:4.

3. **The subject matters referred to as "*Pardes*" are included in "Talmud"** – וְהָעִנְיָנוֹת הַנִּקְרָאִין פַּרְדֵּס בִּכְלַל הַתַּלְמוּד: Concerning who is fitting to study such matters, see the "Halakhic Discussion" on *Hilkhot Yesodei HaTorah* 4:13.

NOTES

a. See 3:9–10 concerning the importance of engaging in earning a livelihood in addition to one's Torah study.

b. See *Hilkhot Yesodei HaTorah* 4:13.

FROM THE LUBAVITCHER REBBE

*The subject matters referred to as "*Pardes*" are included in the Talmud – וְהָעִנְיָנוֹת הַנִּקְרָאִין פַּרְדֵּס בִּכְלַל הַתַּלְמוּד: This ruling serves as the foundation for the Admor HaZaken's assertion that the study of Kabbala, the mystical tradition, falls within the domain of the "Talmud" portion of one's learning (*Shulḥan Arukh HaRav, Hilkhot Talmud Torah*, conclusion of 1). Nevertheless, in *Likkutei Torah*, he specifies that the study of mystical texts such as the *Zohar* and the writings of the Ari are to be included in the Written Torah portion of one's learning. The resolution of this apparent contradiction is that when these subjects are studied at a foundational level, they fall under the category of the Written Torah; however, when pursued with depth and breadth, they become part of the "Talmud" segment of study (*Siḥot Motzaei Zot Ḥanukah* 5746, *Likkutei Siḥot* 30, page 172).

אֲבָל כְּשֶׁיַּגְדִּיל בְּחָכְמָה וְלֹא יְהֵא צָרִיךְ לֹא לִלְמֹד תּוֹרָה שֶׁבִּכְתָב וְלֹא לַעֲסֹק תָּמִיד בַּתּוֹרָה שֶׁבְּעַל פֶּה – יִקְרָא בְּעִתִּים מְזֻמָּנִים תּוֹרָה שֶׁבִּכְתָב וְדִבְרֵי הַשְּׁמוּעָה כְּדֵי שֶׁלֹּא יִשְׁכַּח דָּבָר מִדִּבְרֵי דִּינֵי תּוֹרָה, וְיִפְנֶה כָּל יָמָיו לַתַּלְמוּד בִּלְבַד, לְפִי רֹחַב לִבּוֹ וְיִשּׁוּב דַּעְתּוֹ.

However, once he grows in his wisdom and knowledge, to the extent that **he will no** longer **need neither to study the Written Torah, nor to constantly engage in the Oral Torah,** then **at assigned times he should read the Written Torah and the words of the** Oral **tradition,** to the extent that is necessary **in order not to forget** any **matter from the matters of the laws of the Torah, and he should focus all** the rest of **his days on the exclusive study of "the Talmud"**[1] to the extent of his ability, **as per his heart's capacity and his mind's composure.**

Halakha 13

אִשָּׁה שֶׁלָּמְדָה תּוֹרָה – יֵשׁ לָהּ שָׂכָר, אֲבָל אֵינוֹ כִּשְׂכַר הָאִישׁ, מִפְּנֵי שֶׁלֹּא נִצְטַוַּת, וְכָל הָעוֹשֶׂה דָּבָר שֶׁאֵינוֹ מְצֻוֶּה עָלָיו, אֵין שְׂכָרוֹ כִּשְׂכַר הַמְצֻוֶּה שֶׁעָשָׂה, אֶלָּא פָּחוֹת מִמֶּנּוּ.

If **a women studies Torah,**[2] **she receives reward** for doing so, as she is permitted to perform and rewarded for performing mitzvot even when she is not obligated to do them,[a] **however,** her reward **is not comparable to the reward** that **a man** receives for studying Torah, **because she is not commanded** in the mitzva, **and** the rule is that when **anyone does something concerning which they are not commanded** to do, **their reward is not comparable to the reward of one who did something** that **they are commanded** to do; **rather,** they receive **less than them.**

וְאַף עַל פִּי שֶׁיֵּשׁ לָהּ שָׂכָר, צִוּוּ חֲכָמִים שֶׁלֹּא יְלַמֵּד אָדָם אֶת בִּתּוֹ תּוֹרָה, מִפְּנֵי שֶׁרֹב הַנָּשִׁים אֵין דַּעְתָּן מְכֻוֶּנֶת לְהִתְלַמֵּד, וְהֵן מוֹצִיאִין דִּבְרֵי תוֹרָה לְדִבְרֵי הֲבַאי לְפִי עֲנִיּוּת דַּעְתָּן. אָמְרוּ חֲכָמִים: כָּל הַמְלַמֵּד אֶת בִּתּוֹ תּוֹרָה, כְּאִלּוּ לִמְּדָהּ תִּפְלוּת.

Even though a woman **does** receive **reward** for studying Torah, nevertheless, **the Sages instructed that a person should not teach his daughter Torah,**[3] **due to** the fact **that** in the case of **most women, their minds are not** sufficiently **focused to be able to study, and** so when they study, they misunderstand the material and thereby **transfer the words of Torah into insubstantial matters, due to their poor understanding. The Sages stated: Anyone who teaches his daughter Torah, it is as if he has taught her nonsense.**[b]

בַּמֶּה דְּבָרִים אֲמוּרִים? בַּתּוֹרָה שֶׁבְּעַל פֶּה. אֲבָל תּוֹרָה שֶׁבִּכְתָב – לֹא יְלַמֵּד אוֹתָהּ לְכַתְּחִלָּה, וְאִם לִמְּדָהּ – אֵינוֹ כִּמְלַמְּדָהּ תִּפְלוּת.

In what case is this statement said? Concerning the Oral Torah, which can be easily misunderstood. **However,** with regard to the **Written Torah, a person should not teach her *ab initio*, but if he taught her, then it is not** considered **as though he taught her nonsense.**

HALAKHIC DISCUSSION

1. And he should focus all of his days on the exclusive study of "Talmud" – וְיִפְנֶה כָּל יָמָיו לַתַּלְמוּד בִּלְבַד: *Shulḥan Arukh HaRav* (*Talmud Torah* 2:2) states that such a person should dedicate his time to delving deeply into talmudic study, aiming to comprehend the underlying rationale of the halakhot, and even to derive and formulate new ones, to the best of his abilities. Furthermore, he should engage in the study of *aggada* in order to extract from them ethical insights, and deepen his understanding of God, as the majority of the Torah's mystical wisdom is encapsulated within the *aggada*.

2. If a women studies Torah – אִשָּׁה שֶׁלָּמְדָה תּוֹרָה: *Shulḥan Arukh, Yoreh De'a* 246:6.

3. The Sages instructed that a person should not teach his daughter Torah – צִוּוּ חֲכָמִים שֶׁלֹּא יְלַמֵּד אָדָם אֶת בִּתּוֹ תּוֹרָה: Nevertheless, a woman is obligated to study the practical laws that are relevant to her (Rema. See appendix: "Torah Study for Women").

NOTES

a. See *Hilkhot Tzitzit* 3:9.

b. Or, according to some commentaries, as though he taught her scandalous matters.

פֶּרֶק שֵׁנִי

CHAPTER 2

The Program of Study for Children

Halakhot 1–4:	Teachers for young children, their appointment, and their teaching methods
Halakhot 5–7:	Maintaining the quality of teaching

Halakha 1

Teachers of young children should be appointed in each and every province[1] **and each and every district. Any city that does not** ensure that its **young children learn in school, should be excommunicated**[a] **until they appoint a teacher for its young children. And if they do not appoint one, the city** forfeits it right to exist and so **should be destroyed, for the world endures only through the breath of young children** studying Torah **in school.**

מוֹשִׁיבִין מְלַמְּדֵי תִּינוֹקוֹת בְּכָל מְדִינָה וּמְדִינָה וּבְכָל פֶּלֶךְ וָפֶלֶךְ. וְכָל עִיר שֶׁאֵין בָּהּ תִּינוֹקוֹת שֶׁל בֵּית רַבָּן – מַחֲרִימִין אֶת אַנְשֵׁי הָעִיר עַד שֶׁמּוֹשִׁיבִין מְלַמֵּד תִּינוֹקוֹת. וְאִם לֹא הוֹשִׁיבוּ – מַחֲרִיבִין אֶת הָעִיר, שֶׁאֵין הָעוֹלָם מִתְקַיֵּם אֶלָּא בְּהֶבֶל פִּיהֶם שֶׁל תִּינוֹקוֹת שֶׁל בֵּית רַבָּן.

HALAKHIC DISCUSSION

1. Teachers of young children should be appointed in each and every province – מוֹשִׁיבִין מְלַמְּדֵי תִּינוֹקוֹת בְּכָל מְדִינָה: *Shulḥan Arukh, Yoreh De'a* 245:7. It is the custom of Jewish communities to maintain, through communal funds, a school for Torah study in which orphans and children of the poor can study (*Arukh HaShulḥan*; see also *Shulḥan Arukh HaRav, Hilkhot Talmud Torah* 1:3).

NOTES

a. See Chapter 7 for the meaning of this punishment.

BACKGROUND

Teachers of young children – מְלַמְּדֵי תִּינוֹקוֹת:

Early color photograph from Russia of a Jewish teacher of young children

Halakha 2

מַכְנִיסִין אֶת הַתִּינוֹקוֹת לְהִתְלַמֵּד כְּבֶן שֵׁשׁ כְּבֶן שֶׁבַע, לְפִי כֹּחַ הַבֵּן וּבִנְיַן גּוּפוֹ. וּפָחוֹת מִבֶּן שֵׁשׁ אֵין מַכְנִיסִין אוֹתוֹ. וּמַכֶּה אוֹתָן הַמְלַמֵּד לְהַטִּיל עֲלֵיהֶן אֵימָה, וְאֵינוֹ מַכֶּה אוֹתָן מַכַּת אוֹיֵב מוּסַר אַכְזָרִי. לְפִיכָךְ לֹא יַכֶּה אוֹתָן בְּשׁוֹטִים וְלֹא בְּמַקְלוֹת, אֶלָּא בִּרְצוּעָה קְטַנָּה.

Young children are to be **brought** under a teacher's instruction **to study when they are around six or seven years old,**[1] **depending on the child's strength and physical development.**[a] **They should not be brought before the age of six. The teacher may strike them**[2] **in order to instill fear within them,**[b] **but** when doing so **he may not strike them in the manner of an enemy, of a cruel person.**[c] **As such, he should not strike them with whips or sticks, rather only with a small strap.**

וּמְלַמְּדָן כָּל הַיּוֹם כֻּלּוֹ וּמִקְצָת מִן הַלַּיְלָה, כְּדֵי לְחַנְּכָן לִלְמֹד בַּיּוֹם וּבַלַּיְלָה. וְלֹא יִבָּטְלוּ הַתִּינוֹקוֹת כְּלָל, חוּץ מֵעַרְבֵי שַׁבָּתוֹת וְעַרְבֵי יָמִים טוֹבִים בְּסוֹף הַיּוֹם, וּבְיָמִים טוֹבִים.

He should sit and teach them the entire day and part of the night in order to train them to study both **during the day and night.**[d] **The young children should not cease** studying, **except toward the end of the day on the eve of Shabbat and the eve of festivals,** shortly before they begin, **and on festivals** themselves.

אֲבָל בְּשַׁבָּת – אֵין קוֹרִין לְכַתְּחִלָּה, אֲבָל שׁוֹנִין לָרִאשׁוֹן. וְאֵין מְבַטְּלִין הַתִּינוֹקוֹת, וַאֲפִלּוּ לְבִנְיַן בֵּית הַמִּקְדָּשׁ.

However, on Shabbat they should study, **but they should not read new material for the first time,** since doing so could impinge upon the restful atmosphere of the day; **rather, they should review** material that they have already studied, even if they are reviewing for **the first time.** The Torah study of **young children** is so important that it is **not to be disrupted** for anything, **even for the building of the Temple,** as through their studying the world endures.[e]

Halakha 3

מְלַמֵּד תִּינוֹקוֹת שֶׁהוּא מַנִּיחַ אֶת הַתִּינוֹקוֹת וְיוֹצֵא, אוֹ שֶׁהוּא עוֹשֶׂה מְלָאכָה אַחֶרֶת עִמָּהֶן, אוֹ שֶׁהוּא מִתְרַשֵּׁל בְּתַלְמוּדָן – הֲרֵי הוּא בִּכְלַל "אָרוּר עֹשֶׂה מְלֶאכֶת יי רְמִיָּה" (ירמיהו מח, י).

A teacher of young children who leaves the young children alone,[3] and does not constantly oversee their studying, **or engages in other work** while he is **with them, or is negligent** in some other way **in teaching them;**[4] not teaching them sufficiently, or teaching them with errors,[f] **is included in the curse: "Cursed is the one who performs the labor of the Lord deceitfully"** (Jeremiah 48:10), as he did not faithfully fulfill his responsibility to teach God's Torah.

לְפִיכָךְ אֵין רָאוּי לְהוֹשִׁיב מְלַמֵּד אֶלָּא בַּעַל יִרְאָה, מָהִיר לִקְרוֹת וּלְדַקְדֵּק.

Therefore, only someone who is God-fearing, and efficient in teaching children **to read** the Torah, **and to do so with precision, should be appointed as a teacher.**

HALAKHIC DISCUSSION

1. Young children are to be brought under a teacher's instruction to study when they are around six or seven years old – מַכְנִיסִין אֶת הַתִּינוֹקוֹת לְהִתְלַמֵּד כְּבֶן שֵׁשׁ כְּבֶן שֶׁבַע: *Shulḥan Arukh, Yoreh De'a* 245:8.

2. The teacher may strike them – וּמַכֶּה אוֹתָן הַמְלַמֵּד: *Shulḥan Arukh, Yoreh De'a* 245:10–14.

3. A teacher of young children who leaves the young children alone – מְלַמֵּד תִּינוֹקוֹת שֶׁהוּא מַנִּיחַ אֶת הַתִּינוֹקוֹת וְיוֹצֵא: *Shulḥan Arukh, Yoreh De'a* 245:17.

4. Or is negligent in some other way in teaching them – אוֹ שֶׁהוּא מִתְרַשֵּׁל בְּתַלְמוּדָן: It is forbidden for a teacher to do things that will impair his ability to teach properly, such as staying up too late at night, or to overly abstain from or overindulge in eating and drinking (Rema; see *Hilkhot Deot* 3:4 in the Halakhic Discussion there).

NOTES

a. See *Halakha* 1:6.

b. See *Hilkhot Rotze'aḥ UShmirat HaNefesh* 5:6.

c. The phrasing is borrowed from Jeremiah 30:14.

d. See *Halakha* 1:8.

e. See *Halakha* 1; *Hilkhot Beit HaBeḥira* 1:12.

f. See also *Hilkhot Sekhirut* 10:7.

NOTES

a. See *Hilkhot Issurei Bia* 22:13.

Halakha 4

וּמִי שֶׁאֵין לוֹ אִשָּׁה – לֹא יְלַמֵּד תִּינוֹקוֹת, מִפְּנֵי אִמּוֹתֵיהֶן שֶׁהֵן בָּאִין אֵצֶל בְּנֵיהֶן. וְכֵן הָאִשָּׁה לֹא תְּלַמֵּד תִּינוֹקוֹת, מִפְּנֵי אֲבוֹתֵיהֶן שֶׁהֵן בָּאִין אֵצֶל הַבָּנִים.

One who does not have a wife should not teach young children,[1] **due to** the fact that **their mothers come to** visit **their sons** and so there is a concern the teacher will be tempted by them. **Similarly, a woman should not teach young children**[2] **due to** the fact that **their fathers come** to visit **their sons,** and so there is a concern that a father might become secluded with her.[a]

Halakha 5

עֶשְׂרִים וַחֲמִשָּׁה תִּינוֹקוֹת לְמֵדִים אֵצֶל מְלַמֵּד אֶחָד. הָיוּ יָתֵר עַל חֲמִשָּׁה וְעֶשְׂרִים: עַד אַרְבָּעִים – מוֹשִׁיבִין עִמּוֹ אַחֵר לְסַיְּעוֹ בְּלִמּוּדָן; הָיוּ יָתֵר עַל אַרְבָּעִים – מַעֲמִידִין לָהֶם שְׁנֵי מְלַמְּדֵי תִּינוֹקוֹת.

A maximum of **twenty-five young children may study under one teacher.**[3] If **there are more than twenty-five** students:[4] If there **up to forty** students, **another** person **is appointed to assist** the teacher **in teaching them;**[5] if **there are over forty** students, **two teachers are appointed for them** and they are split into two groups.

Halakha 6

מוֹלִיכִין אֶת הַקָּטָן מִמְּלַמֵּד לִמְלַמֵּד אַחֵר שֶׁהוּא מָהִיר מִמֶּנּוּ, בֵּין בְּמִקְרָא בֵּין בְּדִקְדּוּק.

A young child may be transferred[6] **from one teacher to another teacher** only **if** the latter **is more efficient** than the former **both in** teaching the **reading** of the Torah **and in** doing so with **precision,** such that transferring him will be to the child's advantage.

HALAKHIC DISCUSSION

1. **One who does not have a wife should not teach young children – וּמִי שֶׁאֵין לוֹ אִשָּׁה לֹא יְלַמֵּד תִּינוֹקוֹת:** *Shulḥan Arukh, Yoreh De'a* 245:20–21, *Even HaEzer* 22:20. There is no requirement that a married teacher's wife be present at the school, rather, as long as she is at home, the husband can teach in his school (*Hilkhot Issurei Bia* 22:13; *Shulḥan Arukh*). Despite this ruling, the custom developed for single men to teach children. The later authorities justify this practice since nowadays women do not regularly bring their sons to school. Nevertheless, it certainly remains a pious practice that, if at all possible, young Jewish children should be taught only by married male teachers (*Tzitz Eliezer* 6:40 in *Kuntres Issurei Yiḥud* 26).

2. **A woman should not teach young children – הָאִשָּׁה לֹא תְּלַמֵּד תִּינוֹקוֹת:** Some authorities prohibit even a married woman from teaching unless her husband is present with her (Taz). Others, however, permit it on condition that her husband is present in the same city and is aware of her whereabouts (*Ḥelkat Meḥokek* and *Beit Shmuel*; see also *Iggerot Moshe, Even HaEzer* 4:65). Nevertheless, it was common practice for women to teach even when their husbands were not present in the same city. Some authorities justified this practice, explaining that these restrictions do not apply to the modern situation, where women do not teach in their private homes, but rather in schools where there are many people present and fathers do not regularly visit. As such, in most cases, there is no concern of a female teacher being secluded with one of the fathers (*Shevet HaLevi* 10:235; see further *Mishne Halakhot* 6:225, which prohibits a woman from teaching older unmarried students).

3. **A maximum of twenty-five young children may study under one teacher – עֶשְׂרִים וַחֲמִשָּׁה תִּינוֹקוֹת לְמֵדִים אֵצֶל מְלַמֵּד אֶחָד:** *Shulḥan Arukh, Yoreh De'a* 245:15. Authorities differ as to whether there is an obligation to hire a teacher in a city that does not have twenty-five children (Rema). However, in a case where it is not possible to send the students to a teacher in a nearby city, then according to all opinions, the city must hire a teacher to ensure the children will be taught (*Arukh HaShulḥan*).

4. **If there are more than twenty-five students – הָיוּ יָתֵר עַל חֲמִשָּׁה וְעֶשְׂרִים:** Other early authorities write that up to forty students may study under one teacher, even without an assistant, and that when there are forty to fifty students, an assistant must be added. Once there are more than fifty students, two teachers are required (Rosh). Notwithstanding all these figures, it appears that in determining the maximum number of students per class, the characteristics of the teacher, the students, and the style of study must also be considered (*Shakh*). Some later authorities write that in later generations, in which the intellect and concentration of people have become diminished, class sizes should be smaller (*Pitḥei Teshuva*).

5. **Another person is appointed to assist the teacher in teaching them – מוֹשִׁיבִין עִמּוֹ אַחֵר לְסַיְּעוֹ בְּלִמּוּדָן:** The teacher can select the assistant himself, but the community must pay his wages (Rema).

6. **A young child may be transferred – מוֹלִיכִין אֶת הַקָּטָן:** *Shulḥan Arukh, Yoreh De'a* 245:16.

בַּמֶּה דְּבָרִים אֲמוּרִים? בְּשֶׁהָיוּ שְׁנֵיהֶן בְּעִיר אַחַת וְלֹא הָיָה הַנָּהָר מַפְסִיק בֵּינֵיהֶן. אֲבָל מֵעִיר לְעִיר, אוֹ מִצַּד הַנָּהָר לְצִדּוֹ אֲפִלּוּ בְּאוֹתָהּ הָעִיר – אֵין מוֹלִיכִין אֶת הַקָּטָן, אֶלָּא אִם כֵּן הָיָה בִּנְיָן בָּרִיא עַל גַּבֵּי הַנָּהָר, בִּנְיָן שֶׁאֵינוֹ רָאוּי לִפֹּל בִּמְהֵרָה.

In what case is this statement said? When there is no danger to the child in traveling to the new teacher, such as when **both are** located **in the same city and they are not separated by a river. However,** if transferring to a new teacher would involve traveling **from** one **city to** another **city, or from one side of a river to the other side, even if** both sides are **in the same city,** then **a child is not to be transferred unless there is a sturdy structure,** a bridge, **over the river, that is unlikely to collapse quickly.**

Halakha 7

אֶחָד מִבְּנֵי מָבוֹי שֶׁבִּקֵּשׁ לְהֵעָשׂוֹת מְלַמֵּד, אֲפִלּוּ אֶחָד מִבְּנֵי הֶחָצֵר – אֵין יְכוֹלִין שְׁכֵנָיו לִמְחוֹת בְּיָדוֹ.

If **a resident of an alleyway wishes to become a teacher**[1] and open a school in the alleyway, and **even** if **a resident of a courtyard** wishes to do so in his courtyard, then despite the disturbance that it may cause to the other residents, **his neighbors cannot object.** This is because it is permitted to do so, as explained at the end of this *Halakha.*[a]

וְכֵן מְלַמֵּד תִּינוֹקוֹת שֶׁבָּא חֲבֵרוֹ וּפָתַח בֵּית לְלַמֵּד תִּינוֹקוֹת בְּצִדּוֹ כְּדֵי שֶׁיָּבֹאוּ תִּינוֹקוֹת אֲחֵרִים לוֹ, אוֹ כְּדֵי שֶׁיָּבֹאוּ מִתִּינוֹקוֹת שֶׁל זֶה אֵצֶל זֶה – אֵינוֹ יָכוֹל לִמְחוֹת בְּיָדוֹ, שֶׁנֶּאֱמַר: "יי חָפֵץ לְמַעַן צִדְקוֹ יַגְדִּיל תּוֹרָה וְיַאְדִּיר" (ישעיהו מב, כא).

Similarly, if there is already **one teacher of young children,** and **another** teacher **comes and opens up a school for teaching young children nearby,** whether **in order to bring other young children to him or** even **in order to** encourage the **young children who are** studying **with this** first teacher **to come to this** new teacher, the first **cannot object,**[b] **as it is stated: "The Lord is desirous of him because of his righteousness; he will make the Torah great and glorious"** (Isaiah 42:21), and therefore, any increase in the number of teachers teaching Torah is considered a positive thing, and is permitted.

HALAKHIC DISCUSSION

1. If a resident of an alleyway wishes to become a teacher – אֶחָד מִבְּנֵי מָבוֹי שֶׁבִּקֵּשׁ לְהֵעָשׂוֹת מְלַמֵּד: *Shulḥan Arukh, Yoreh De'a* 245:22.

NOTES

a. See also *Hilkhot Shekhenim* 6:12.

b. See *Hilkhot Shekhenim* 6:8.

פֶּרֶק שְׁלִישִׁי

CHAPTER 3

The Appropriate Way to Engage in the Study of Torah

Halakha 1

בִּשְׁלֹשָׁה כְּתָרִים נִכְתְּרוּ יִשְׂרָאֵל: כֶּתֶר תּוֹרָה וְכֶתֶר כְּהֻנָּה וְכֶתֶר מַלְכוּת. כֶּתֶר כְּהֻנָּה – זָכָה בּוֹ אַהֲרֹן, שֶׁנֶּאֱמַר: ״וְהָיְתָה לּוֹ וּלְזַרְעוֹ אַחֲרָיו בְּרִית כְּהֻנַּת עוֹלָם״ (במדבר כה, יג).

The Jewish people were crowned with three crowns,[1] three levels of virtue: **the crown of Torah, the crown of priesthood, and the crown of kingship. Aaron,** brother of Moses, **merited the crown of priesthood, as it is stated: "It shall be for him, and for his descendants after him, a covenant of an eternal priesthood"** (Numbers 25:13).

כֶּתֶר מַלְכוּת – זָכָה בּוֹ דָּוִד, שֶׁנֶּאֱמַר: ״זַרְעוֹ לְעוֹלָם יִהְיֶה וְכִסְאוֹ כַשֶּׁמֶשׁ נֶגְדִּי״ (תהלים פט, לז).

King **David merited the crown of kingship, as it is stated: "His seed will endure forever, and his throne will be as the sun before Me"** (Psalms 89:37). These two crowns are an inheritance exclusively for Aaron and David's descendants.[a]

תּוֹרָה – הֲרֵי מֻנַּחַת וְעוֹמֶדֶת וּמוּכֶנֶת לַכֹּל, שֶׁנֶּאֱמַר: ״תּוֹרָה צִוָּה לָנוּ מֹשֶׁה מוֹרָשָׁה קְהִלַּת יַעֲקֹב״ (דברים לג, ד) – כָּל מִי שֶׁיִּרְצֶה יָבֹא וְיִטֹּל.

The crown of Torah, however, **lies ready and prepared for each Jew** to take it, **as it is stated: "Torah, Moses commanded us, a heritage of the assembly of Jacob"** (Deuteronomy 33:4), meaning it is an inheritance for all of Israel and not just for a particular tribe or family.[b] **Whoever desires it, may come and take it.**

HALAKHIC DISCUSSION

1. The Jewish people were crowned with three crowns – בִּשְׁלֹשָׁה כְּתָרִים נִכְתְּרוּ יִשְׂרָאֵל: *Tur, Yoreh De'a* 246.

NOTES

a. See *Hilkhot Kelei HaMikdash* 4:1–2, *Hilkhot Melakhim UMilḥemoteihem* 1:7.

b. See *Hilkhot Melakhim UMilḥemoteihem* 8:10.

שֶׁמָּא תֹּאמַר שֶׁאוֹתָן הַכְּתָרִים גְּדוֹלִים מִכֶּתֶר תּוֹרָה? הֲרֵי הוּא אוֹמֵר: "בִּי מְלָכִים יִמְלֹכוּ וְרוֹזְנִים יְחֹקְקוּ צֶדֶק, בִּי שָׂרִים יָשֹׂרוּ" (משלי ח, טו–טז). הָא לָמַדְתָּ שֶׁכֶּתֶר הַתּוֹרָה גָּדוֹל מִכֶּתֶר כְּהֻנָּה וְכֶתֶר מַלְכוּת.

Perhaps you might **say that those other crowns are greater than the crown of Torah? But the verse states** that Wisdom declares: **"Through me, kings reign, and princes legislate justice. Through me, rulers rule, and nobles, all righteous judges"** (Proverbs 8:15–16). This indicates that sovereignty and authority themselves depend upon wisdom, which is the Torah. **Consequently, you have learned that the crown of Torah is greater than both of them.**

Halakha 2

אָמְרוּ חֲכָמִים: מַמְזֵר תַּלְמִיד חֲכָמִים קוֹדֵם לְכֹהֵן גָּדוֹל עַם הָאָרֶץ, שֶׁנֶּאֱמַר: "יְקָרָה הִיא מִפְּנִינִים" (משלי ג, טו) – יְקָרָה הִיא מִכֹּהֵן גָּדוֹל שֶׁנִּכְנָס לִפְנַי לִפְנִים.

The Sages said: A son born from an incestuous or adulterous relationship [*mamzer*] **who is a Torah scholar takes precedence over an ignorant High Priest,** even though in terms of their lineage, the High Priest is more important,[a] **as it is stated: "She,** the Torah, **is more precious than pearls** [*peninim*]" (Proverbs 3:15), from which it can be derived that the Torah is more precious **than a High Priest who enters the Holy of Holies** [*lifnai velifnim*] once a year on Yom Kippur.[b]

Halakha 3

אֵין לְךָ מִצְוָה בְּכָל הַמִּצְוֹת כֻּלָּן שֶׁהִיא שְׁקוּלָה כְּנֶגֶד תַּלְמוּד תּוֹרָה, אֶלָּא תַּלְמוּד תּוֹרָה כְּנֶגֶד כָּל הַמִּצְוֹת כֻּלָּן, שֶׁהַתַּלְמוּד מֵבִיא לִידֵי מַעֲשֶׂה. לְפִיכָךְ הַתַּלְמוּד קוֹדֵם לְמַעֲשֶׂה בְּכָל מָקוֹם.

Of all the mitzvot, there is none that is equal in value **to the study of Torah. Moreover, the study of Torah is equivalent to all the mitzvot** combined,[1] **because study leads to practice.** Therefore, all the mitzvot depend on Torah study.[c] **Therefore,** the mitzva to **study** Torah **takes precedence over** the **practice** of other mitzvot, **in every case.**

Halakha 4

הָיָה לְפָנָיו עֲשִׂיַּת מִצְוָה וְתַלְמוּד תּוֹרָה: אִם אֶפְשָׁר לַמִּצְוָה לְהֵעָשׂוֹת עַל יְדֵי אֲחֵרִים – לֹא יַפְסִיק תַּלְמוּדוֹ;

If **one is faced with** the opportunity to perform **a mitzva** or to engage in **Torah study, if it is possible for the mitzva to be performed by others** who are not studying, **he should not interrupt his Torah study,** rather that mitzva should be performed by someone else. In this way both the study of Torah and that mitzva will be fulfilled.

וְאִם לָאו – יַעֲשֶׂה הַמִּצְוָה וְיַחֲזֹר לְתוֹרָתוֹ.

If not, he should perform the mitzva and then return to his studies. If he does not do so, not only will the mitzva go unfulfilled, but he will have also undermined his Torah study, as it will no longer be considered "study that leads to practice."[d]

HALAKHIC DISCUSSION

1. The study of Torah is equivalent to all the mitzvot combined – תַּלְמוּד תּוֹרָה כְּנֶגֶד כָּל הַמִּצְווֹת: *Shulḥan Arukh, Yoreh De'a* 246:18.

NOTES

a. See also *Hilkhot Mattenot Aniyyim* 8:17–18.

b. This interpretation is based on a play on words, that the word *peninim* (pearls) is spelled as though it reads *peniyim*, which suggests the idea of something innermost, thereby alluding to the Holy of Holies, which is referred to as *lifnai velifnim* (comment of Rav Yosef Kapaḥ at the end of *Horayot*).

c. See above 1:3.

d. See Halakha 3.

Halakha 5

תְּחִלַּת דִּינוֹ שֶׁל אָדָם אֵינוֹ נִדּוֹן אֶלָּא עַל הַתַּלְמוּד, וְאַחַר כָּךְ עַל שְׁאָר מַעֲשָׂיו.

A person's judgment in heaven, after one dies, **begins exclusively with him being judged concerning his** Torah **study,**[1] **and** only **afterward** are **the rest of his deeds** examined.

לְפִיכָךְ אָמְרוּ חֲכָמִים: לְעוֹלָם יַעֲסֹק אָדָם בַּתּוֹרָה אֲפִלּוּ שֶׁלֹּא לִשְׁמָהּ, שֶׁמִּתּוֹךְ שֶׁלֹּא לִשְׁמָהּ בָּא לִשְׁמָהּ.

Therefore, the Sages said: "A person should always engage in Torah study, **even when he does so for ulterior motives,** i.e., not out of a love of God, but in order to receive reward,[a] **because through** study **for ulterior motives, he will come to** study Torah **for its own sake"** (*Pesaḥim* 50b). By constantly engaging in Torah, one will become wise and understand that it is fitting to study Torah for its own sake and not for another benefit.[b]

Halakha 6

מִי שֶׁנְּשָׂאוֹ לִבּוֹ לְקַיֵּם מִצְוָה זוֹ כָּרָאוּי לָהּ וְלִהְיוֹת מֻכְתָּר בְּכִתְרָהּ שֶׁל תּוֹרָה – לֹא יַסִּיחַ דַּעְתּוֹ לִדְבָרִים אֲחֵרִים, וְלֹא יָשִׂים עַל לִבּוֹ שֶׁיִּקְנֶה תּוֹרָה עִם הָעֹשֶׁר וְהַכָּבוֹד כְּאֶחָד. כָּךְ הוּא דַּרְכָּהּ שֶׁל תּוֹרָה: פַּת בְּמֶלַח תֹּאכֵל, וְעַל הָאָרֶץ תִּישַׁן, וְחַיֵּי צַעַר תִּחְיֶה, וּבַתּוֹרָה תִּהְיֶה עָמֵל.

One whose heart motivates him to properly fulfill this mitzva, and to be crowned with the crown of Torah, should not divert his attention to other matters, nor should one imagine that he will be able to acquire Torah together with wealth and honor, simultaneously.[2] **For this is the way of the Torah: You will eat bread with salt, sleep on the ground, and live a life of suffering while toiling in Torah.**[c]

וְלֹא עָלֶיךָ הַמְּלָאכָה לִגְמֹר, וְלֹא אַתָּה בֶן חוֹרִין לִבָּטֵל. אֲבָל אִם הִרְבִּיתָ תּוֹרָה – הִרְבִּיתָ שָׂכָר. וְהַשָּׂכָר לְפִי הַצַּעַר.

It is not upon you to complete the study of the entire Torah, **but nor are you free to cease** from studying it. **If you increase the** amount of **Torah** study, **you will** receive **increased reward, and the** greatness of the **reward is proportional to the suffering** and toil one exerted for it.

Halakha 7

שֶׁמָּא תֹּאמַר: עַד שֶׁאֲקַבֵּץ מָמוֹן וְאֶחֱזֹר אֶקְרָא, עַד שֶׁאֶקְנֶה מַה שֶּׁאֲנִי צָרִיךְ וְאֶפְנֶה מֵעֲסָקַי וְאֶחֱזֹר אֶקְרָא.

Perhaps you will say: Only **once I have amassed wealth,** then **I will return and read** Torah. Or: Only **once I have acquired** all the material goods **that I need** for life, at which point **I will become free of my occupations,** then **I will return and read** Torah.

אִם תַּעֲלֶה מַחֲשָׁבָה זוֹ עַל לִבְּךָ, אֵין אַתָּה זוֹכֶה לְכִתְרָהּ שֶׁל תּוֹרָה לְעוֹלָם. אֶלָּא עֲשֵׂה תּוֹרָתְךָ קֶבַע וּמְלַאכְתְּךָ עֲרַאי, וְאַל תֹּאמַר: לִכְשֶׁאֶפָּנֶה אֶשְׁנֶה, שֶׁמָּא לֹא תִּפָּנֶה.

If this thought arises in your heart, you will never merit the crown of Torah, as you will always end up pushing aside Torah for other things. **Rather, make your Torah study** your **permanent** and primary value and focus, **and your labor** a **transient** endeavor.[3] **And do not say: When I become free, I will study, for perhaps you will never become free.**

HALAKHIC DISCUSSION

1. A person's judgment in heaven, after one dies, begins exclusively with him being judged concerning his Torah study – **תְּחִלַּת דִּינוֹ שֶׁל אָדָם אֵינוֹ נִדּוֹן אֶלָּא עַל הַתַּלְמוּד**: *Shulḥan Arukh, Yoreh De'a* 246:19–20.

2. Nor should one imagine that he will be able to acquire Torah together with wealth and honor, simultaneously – **וְלֹא יָשִׂים עַל לִבּוֹ שֶׁיִּקְנֶה תּוֹרָה עִם הָעֹשֶׁר וְהַכָּבוֹד כְּאֶחָד**: *Shulḥan Arukh, Yoreh De'a* 246:21.

3. Make your Torah study your permanent and primary value and focus and your labor a transient endeavor – **עֲשֵׂה תּוֹרָתְךָ קֶבַע וּמְלַאכְתְּךָ עֲרַאי**: *Shulḥan Arukh, Yoreh De'a* 246:21.

NOTES

a. See *Hilkhot Teshuva* 10:4–5.

b. See also *Hilkhot Teshuva* 10:5.

c. See further Halakhot 7–8.

Halakha 8

כָּתוּב בַּתּוֹרָה: "לֹא בַשָּׁמַיִם הִיא... וְלֹא מֵעֵבֶר לַיָּם הִיא" (דברים ל, יב–יג): "לֹא בַשָּׁמַיִם הִיא" – לֹא בְּגַסֵּי הָרוּחַ הִיא מְצוּיָה;

It is written in the Torah, about Torah: **"It is not in the heavens[1] ... it is not across the sea ...** rather, the matter is very near to you, in your mouth and in your heart, to perform it" (Deuteronomy 30:12–14). **"It is not in the heavens"** teaches that Torah **is not found among the arrogant** whose heads are in the heavens.

"וְלֹא מֵעֵבֶר לַיָּם הִיא" – לֹא בִּמְהַלְּכֵי מֵעֵבֶר לַיָּם הִיא. לְפִיכָךְ אָמְרוּ חֲכָמִים: לֹא כָּל הַמַּרְבֶּה סְחוֹרָה מַחְכִּים. וְצִוּוּ וְאָמְרוּ: הֱוֵי מְמַעֵט עֵסֶק וַעֲסֹק בַּתּוֹרָה.

"It is not across the sea" teaches that **it is not** found **among those who travel across the sea** for business. **Therefore, the Sages said: "Not everyone who engages extensively in business becomes wise,"** because they are unable to engage fully in Torah (*Avot* 2:5). **And** the Sages **instructed and said: "Minimize your involvement in business and occupy yourself with Torah** study" (*Avot* 4:10). For it is fitting not to pursue wealth, but rather to be satisfied with one's portion.[a]

Halakha 9

דִּבְרֵי תוֹרָה נִמְשְׁלוּ בַּמַּיִם, שֶׁנֶּאֱמַר: "הוֹי כָּל צָמֵא לְכוּ לַמַּיִם" (ישעיהו נה, א),

The words of Torah are analogized to water,[2] as it is stated: "Ho, everyone thirsty, go to water" (Isaiah 55:1). The prophet urged the people to go and hear the words of God, which are the words of the Torah.

לוֹמַר לְךָ: מָה הַמַּיִם אֵין מִתְכַּנְּסִין בְּמָקוֹם מִדְרוֹן אֶלָּא נִזְחָלִין מֵעָלָיו וּמִתְקַבְּצִין בְּמָקוֹם אֲשִׁבְרָן, כָּךְ דִּבְרֵי תוֹרָה אֵינָן נִמְצָאִין בְּגַסֵּי הָרוּחַ וְלֹא בְּלֵב כָּל גְּבַהּ לֵב, אֶלָּא בְּדַכָּא וּשְׁפַל רוּחַ, שֶׁמִּתְאַבֵּק בַּעֲפַר רַגְלֵי הַחֲכָמִים וּמֵסִיר הַתַּאֲווֹת וְתַעֲנוּגֵי הַזְּמַן מִלִּבּוֹ,

This analogy is **to tell you: Just as water does not gather in a sloping place, but rather flows off it and collects in a depression, so too the words of Torah are not found among the arrogant, nor in the heart of any haughty person, but rather in one who is humble and lowly, who is** even willing to **become covered in dust** by sitting **in the dirt** on the ground **at the feet of the Sages** in order to study from them,[b] **and who removes lust and transient pleasures from his heart.[3]**

וְעוֹשֶׂה מְלָאכָה בְּכָל יוֹם מְעַט כְּדֵי חַיָּיו אִם לֹא הָיָה לוֹ מַה יֹּאכַל, וּשְׁאָר יוֹמוֹ וְלֵילוֹ עוֹסֵק בַּתּוֹרָה.

Rather, he does a small amount of work each day, just **sufficient to subsist, when** otherwise **he would have nothing to eat, and the rest of his day and night he engages in Torah** study.

NOTES

a. See *Hilkhot Deot* 2:7.

b. See *Hilkhot Deot* 6:2.

HALAKHIC DISCUSSION

1. It is written in the Torah. It is not in the heavens – כָּתוּב בַּתּוֹרָה, לֹא בַשָּׁמַיִם הִיא: *Tur, Yoreh De'a* 246.

2. The words of Torah are analogized to water – דִּבְרֵי תוֹרָה נִמְשְׁלוּ בַּמַּיִם: *Tur, Yoreh De'a* 246.

3. And who removes lust and transient pleasures from his heart – וּמֵסִיר הַתַּאֲווֹת וְתַעֲנוּגֵי הַזְּמַן מִלִּבּוֹ: *Shulḥan Arukh, Yoreh De'a* 246:21.

Halakha 10

כָּל הַמֵּשִׂים עַל לִבּוֹ שֶׁיַּעֲסֹק בַּתּוֹרָה וְלֹא יַעֲשֶׂה מְלָאכָה וְיִתְפַּרְנֵס מִן הַצְּדָקָה – הֲרֵי זֶה חִלֵּל אֶת הַשֵּׁם, וּבִזָּה אֶת הַתּוֹרָה, וְכִבָּה מְאוֹר הַדָּת,

Whoever sets his heart on engaging exclusively **in Torah** study[1] **and not working, but** rather **finances himself from charity,** by doing so **he has desecrated the Name** of God, **scorned the Torah, and extinguished the light of the religion,** as by doing so he suggests that the study of Torah is like any mundane occupation from which one earns a living.

וְגָרַם רָעָה לְעַצְמוֹ, וְנָטַל חַיָּיו מִן הָעוֹלָם הַבָּא, לְפִי שֶׁאָסוּר לֵהָנוֹת בְּדִבְרֵי תוֹרָה בָּעוֹלָם הַזֶּה.§ אָמְרוּ חֲכָמִים: כָּל הַנֶּהֱנֶה מִדִּבְרֵי תוֹרָה – נָטַל חַיָּיו מִן הָעוֹלָם.

In addition, **he brings harm upon himself, and has removed his life from the World** to Come, **for it is forbidden to derive benefit from the words of Torah in this world. The Sages said: "Whoever derives benefit from the words of Torah** has thereby **removed his life from the World** to Come" (*Avot* 4:5).

וְעוֹד צִוּוּ וְאָמְרוּ: לֹא תַּעֲשֵׂם עֲטָרָה לְהִתְגַּדֵּל בָּהֶם וְלֹא קַרְדֹּם לַחְפֹּר בָּהֶם. וְעוֹד צִוּוּ וְאָמְרוּ: אֱהֹב אֶת הַמְּלָאכָה וּשְׂנָא אֶת הָרַבָּנוּת, וְכָל תּוֹרָה שֶׁאֵין עִמָּהּ מְלָאכָה סוֹפָהּ בְּטֵלָה, וְסוֹף אָדָם זֶה שֶׁיְּהֵא מְלַסְטֵם אֶת הַבְּרִיּוֹת.

They further instructed and said: "Do not make the Torah **a crown to glorify yourself with, nor a spade to dig with"**[a] (*Avot* 4:5). **They further instructed and said: "Love work and despise** being in **positions of authority** as a means of income" (*Avot* 4:10). **Any Torah that is not accompanied by work will ultimately be negated** due to the inability to support oneself. The **end for such a person is that he will** come to **rob people** in order to finance himself.

Halakha 11

מַעֲלָה גְּדוֹלָה הִיא לְמִי שֶׁהוּא מִתְפַּרְנֵס מִמַּעֲשֵׂה יָדָיו, וּמִדַּת חֲסִידִים הָרִאשׁוֹנִים הִיא,

It is a great virtue for one who finances himself from the work of his hands without relying on support from others, **and it was the trait of the pious of the first** generations of the Sages.[b]

וּבָזֶה זוֹכֶה לְכָל כָּבוֹד וְטוֹבָה שֶׁבָּעוֹלָם הַזֶּה וְלָעוֹלָם הַבָּא, שֶׁנֶּאֱמַר: "יְגִיעַ כַּפֶּיךָ כִּי תֹאכֵל אַשְׁרֶיךָ וְטוֹב לָךְ" (תהלים קכח, ב): "אַשְׁרֶיךָ" בָּעוֹלָם הַזֶּה, "וְטוֹב לָךְ" לָעוֹלָם הַבָּא, שֶׁכֻּלּוֹ טוֹב.

Through this, he merits all the honor and goodness in this world and in the World to Come, as it is stated: "When you eat of the labor of your hands, you are happy, and it is good for you" (Psalms 128:2), which the Sages expounded[c] as meaning: **"you are happy" in this world,** as you have the financial means to support yourself, **"and it is good for you" in the World to Come, which is** a world that is **entirely good,** and is when a person receives the rewards for his mitzvot.[d]

HALAKHIC DISCUSSION

1. **Whoever sets his heart on engaging exclusively in Torah study – כָּל הַמֵּשִׂים עַל לִבּוֹ שֶׁיַּעֲסֹק בַּתּוֹרָה**: *Tur, Yoreh De'a* 246; *Shulḥan Arukh, Yoreh De'a* 246:21. The Rema cites this halakha of the Rambam and qualifies that it applies only to an able-bodied individual capable of supporting himself. However, for the elderly or ill, it is permissible to derive benefit from their Torah study by having others provide for their needs. The Rema further adds that some authorities permitted receiving financial support for Torah study even for a healthy person. Consequently, it became customary in Jewish communities for the city's rabbi to receive a salary from the residents, thereby enabling him to devote himself fully to his duties without the indignity of seeking employment. This dispensation is to be exercised only when necessary, and it is certainly forbidden for a wealthy person to receive communal funds for serving as a rabbi or studying Torah. It is a trait of piety to eschew deriving any livelihood from Torah study, though this is not expected of every individual. The aforementioned dispensation pertains specifically to a fixed salary, but it is prohibited for a Torah scholar to accept gifts from people on account of his Torah study, except for modest gifts customarily offered to esteemed individuals, even when they are not great Torah scholars (see the appendix: "Earning a Livelihood from Torah Study").

NOTES

a. That is, do not make it a means of achieving material benefits.

b. See above, 1:9.

c. *Avot* 4:1.

d. See *Hilkhot Teshuva* 8:1.

Halakha 12

אֵין דִּבְרֵי תוֹרָה מִתְקַיְּמִין בְּמִי שֶׁמְּרַפֶּה עַצְמוֹ עֲלֵיהֶן, וְלֹא בְּאֵלּוּ שֶׁלּוֹמְדִין מִתּוֹךְ עִדּוּן וּמִתּוֹךְ אֲכִילָה וּשְׁתִיָּה, אֶלָּא בְּמִי שֶׁמֵּמִית עַצְמוֹ עֲלֵיהֶן וּמְצַעֵר גּוּפוֹ תָּמִיד, וְלֹא יִתֵּן שְׁנַת לְעֵינָיו, לְעַפְעַפָּיו תְּנוּמָה.

The words of Torah are not retained by one who engages in them lackadaisically,[1] **nor by those who study amidst luxury and while eating and drinking. Rather,** only **by one who kills himself,** i.e., completely exerts himself, **over them, and constantly afflicts his body, and does not allow sleep to his eyes nor slumber to his eyelids.**[a]

אָמְרוּ חֲכָמִים דֶּרֶךְ רֶמֶז: "זֹאת הַתּוֹרָה אָדָם כִּי יָמוּת בְּאֹהֶל" (במדבר יט, יד) – אֵין הַתּוֹרָה מִתְקַיֶּמֶת אֶלָּא בְּמִי שֶׁמֵּמִית עַצְמוֹ בְּאָהֳלֵי הַחָכְמָה.

The Sages expressed this idea through a homiletical interpretation of the verse: **"This is the Torah: When a man dies in a tent..."** (Numbers 19:14). Although the verse plainly refers to the laws of ritual impurity, the Sages interpreted it to teach that **the Torah is only retained by one who kills himself,** as it were, **in the tents of wisdom,** i.e., the study hall.

וְכָךְ אָמַר שְׁלֹמֹה בְּחָכְמָתוֹ: "הִתְרַפִּיתָ בְּיוֹם צָרָה צַר כֹּחֶכָה" (משלי כד, י).

And this is what King **Solomon said, in his wisdom: "If you falter on a day of trouble, your strength will be curbed"** (Proverbs 24:10), which teaches that if one falters, is lackadaisical, in their study of Torah, then their strength, i.e., their Torah, will not be retained.

וְעוֹד אָמַר: "אַף חָכְמָתִי עָמְדָה לִּי" (קהלת ב, ט) – חָכְמָה שֶׁלָּמַדְתִּי בְּאַף, עָמְדָה לִי.

And he also said: "Also [*af*] my wisdom stood by me" (Ecclesiastes 2:9). The word "*af*" can mean "also," which is its meaning in the plain interpretations of the verse, but it can also refer to something done with tremendous exertion. The Sages interpreted the verse homiletically using this latter meaning, such that the verse teaches that **the wisdom,** the Torah, **that I studied through exertion,** it is only that Torah that **stood by me** and was retained.

אָמְרוּ חֲכָמִים: בְּרִית כְּרוּתָה, שֶׁכָּל הַיָּגֵעַ בְּתוֹרָתוֹ בְּבֵית הַכְּנֶסֶת – לֹא בִּמְהֵרָה הוּא מְשַׁכֵּחַ, וְכָל הַיָּגֵעַ בְּתַלְמוּדוֹ בִּצְנִעָה – מַחְכִּים, שֶׁנֶּאֱמַר: "וְאֶת צְנוּעִים חָכְמָה" (משלי יא, ב). וְכָל הַמַּשְׁמִיעַ קוֹלוֹ בִּשְׁעַת תַּלְמוּדוֹ – תַּלְמוּדוֹ מִתְקַיֵּם בְּיָדוֹ, אֲבָל הַקּוֹרֵא בְּלַחַשׁ – בִּמְהֵרָה הוּא שׁוֹכֵחַ.

The Sages said: "A covenant was forged:[b] **Whoever toils in his Torah** study **in the synagogue will not forget it quickly. And whoever toils in his** Torah **study privately will become wise, as it is stated: 'And wisdom is with the humble'** (Proverbs 11:2). **And whoever makes his voice audible while studying, his study will be retained by him; however, one who reads quietly will quickly forget"** (Jerusalem Talmud, *Berakhot* 5:1).

NOTES

a. The phrasing is based on Psalms 132:4.

b. That is, a binding divine promise was made.

HALAKHIC DISCUSSION

1. The words of Torah are not retained by one who engages in them lackadaisically – אֵין דִּבְרֵי תוֹרָה מִתְקַיְּמִין בְּמִי שֶׁמְּרַפֶּה עַצְמוֹ עֲלֵיהֶן: *Shulḥan Arukh, Yoreh De'a* 246:21–22.

Halakha 13

אַף עַל פִּי שֶׁמִּצְוָה לִלְמֹד בַּיּוֹם וּבַלַּיְלָה, אֵין אָדָם לָמֵד רֹב חָכְמָתוֹ אֶלָּא בַּלַּיְלָה. לְפִיכָךְ מִי שֶׁרָצָה לִזְכּוֹת בְּכֶתֶר הַתּוֹרָה – יִזָּהֵר בְּכָל לֵילוֹתָיו, וְלֹא יְאַבֵּד אֲפִלּוּ אַחַת מֵהֶן בְּשֵׁנָה וַאֲכִילָה וּשְׁתִיָּה וְשִׂיחָה וְכַיּוֹצֵא בָּהֶן, אֶלָּא בְּתַלְמוּד תּוֹרָה וְדִבְרֵי חָכְמָה.

Even though it is a mitzva to study Torah **during** both **the day and night** (as stated in 1:8), **a person does not gain most of his wisdom except at night.**[1] **Therefore, one who wishes to merit the crown of the Torah* should be careful with all his nights, and not waste even one of them with sleeping, eating, drinking, idle conversation and things similar to them, but rather with the study of Torah and words of wisdom.**[2]

אָמְרוּ חֲכָמִים: אֵין גָּרְנָהּ שֶׁל תּוֹרָה אֶלָּא לַיְלָה, שֶׁנֶּאֱמַר: "קוּמִי רֹנִּי בַלַּיְלָה" (איכה ב, יט).

The Sages said: The threshing floor of Torah, where one's Torah is gathered and processed, **is only the night, as it is stated,** in reference to the Torah which is referred to as a songful cry [*rina*]: **"Arise, cry out [*roni*] at night"** (Lamentations 2:19).

וְכָל הָעוֹסֵק בַּתּוֹרָה בַּלַּיְלָה – חוּט שֶׁל חֶסֶד נִמְשָׁךְ עָלָיו בַּיּוֹם, שֶׁנֶּאֱמַר: "יוֹמָם יְצַוֶּה יי חַסְדּוֹ וּבַלַּיְלָה שִׁירֹה עִמִּי תְּפִלָּה לְאֵל חַיָּי" (תהלים מב, ט).

And for whoever **engages in Torah at night,** a **thread of kindness,** a special Divine grace that will radiate his face, **is drawn over him by day, as it is stated: "The Lord commands His kindness by day. His song remains with me by night, a prayer to the Almighty God of my life"** (Psalms 42:9). The blessing at the beginning of the verse is bestowed upon the one who sings God's song, his Torah, at night.

וְכָל בַּיִת שֶׁאֵין דִּבְרֵי תוֹרָה נִשְׁמָעִים בּוֹ בַּלַּיְלָה – אֵשׁ אוֹכַלְתּוֹ. "דְּבַר יי בָּזָה" (במדבר טו, לא) – זֶה שֶׁלֹּא הִשְׁגִּיחַ עַל דִּבְרֵי תוֹרָה כָּל עִקָּר.

And any home where words of Torah are not heard at night – a fire will consume it. The verse states: "It is the Lord that he blasphemes and that person shall be excised from among his people, **because he scorned the word of the Lord"** (Numbers 15:30–31), **this refers to one who did not pay careful attention to the words of Torah at all.**

וְכֵן כָּל שֶׁאֶפְשָׁר לוֹ לַעֲסֹק בַּתּוֹרָה וְאֵינוֹ עוֹסֵק, אוֹ שֶׁקָּרָא וְשָׁנָה וּפֵרַשׁ לְהַבְלֵי עוֹלָם וְהִנִּיחַ תַּלְמוּדוֹ וּזְנָחוֹ – הֲרֵי זֶה בִּכְלַל בּוֹזֶה דְּבַר יי. אָמְרוּ חֲכָמִים: כָּל הַמְבַטֵּל אֶת הַתּוֹרָה מֵעֹשֶׁר – סוֹפוֹ לְבַטְּלָהּ מֵעֹנִי, וְכָל הַמְקַיֵּם אֶת הַתּוֹרָה מֵעֹנִי – סוֹפוֹ לְקַיְּמָהּ מֵעֹשֶׁר.

Similarly, anyone who is able to engage in Torah yet does not engage, or one who read the Written Torah **and studied** the Oral Torah **and** then **turned aside to the vanities of the world and left his study and abandoned it, he is** also **included in** the verse **"he scorned the word of the Lord." The Sages said: Whoever neglects the Torah due to** the distractions of **wealth** will be punished and **will ultimately** be forced to **neglect it due to** the strains of **poverty, and whoever upholds Torah despite poverty** will be rewarded and **will ultimately uphold it along with wealth** (*Avot* 4:9).

HALAKHIC DISCUSSION

1. **A person does not gain most of his wisdom except at night** – אֵין אָדָם לָמֵד רֹב חָכְמָתוֹ אֶלָּא בַּלַּיְלָה: *Shulḥan Arukh, Yoreh De'a* 246:23–26. From the 15th of Av onward, when the length of the nights begins to increase, one should increase the amount of one's nightly Torah study (Rema).

2. **But rather with Torah study and words of wisdom** – אֶלָּא בְּתַלְמוּד תּוֹרָה וְדִבְרֵי חָכְמָה: The Rema (in his comment to *Shulḥan Arukh, Yoreh De'a* 246:4) writes that an individual should focus exclusively on studying the Written Torah, Mishna, Talmud, and later halakhic works and refrain from engaging in the study of other areas of wisdom, unless one studies them only incidentally. Even then, this is only to be done after one has already gained knowledge of the laws of the permitted and prohibited. Furthermore, this permission is conditional on the material not being heretical (see further *Hilkhot Yesodei HaTorah* 4:13 and the Halakhic Discussion there).

FROM THE LUBAVITCHER REBBE

***One who wishes to merit the crown of the Torah** – מִי שֶׁרָצָה לִזְכּוֹת בְּכֶתֶר הַתּוֹרָה: The phrase "the crown of Torah" can refer to two distinct ideas: a) the Torah serving as the crown of an individual, and b) the lofty part, the crown, of the Torah itself.

Earlier, in Halakha 6, the Rambam deals with one who wants "to be crowned with the crown of Torah," which is the first idea. The Torah crowns the individual and becomes part of the entirety of the person's being. However, in this Halakha, the Rambam is dealing with the second idea, and therefore changes his language and writes: "to merit the crown" and not "to be crowned," and also refers here to "the crown of the Torah," adding the definite article to "Torah" so that it refers to the crown of the Torah itself, and not just the person's crown of Torah.

One can explain that this second idea, "the crown of the Torah," refers to the fundamental essence of the Torah. That when one studies Torah, one not only cleaves to the Torah, but to God, the Giver of the Torah. Therefore, the Rambam also mentions here the engagement in "words of wisdom," alluding to the *Pardes*, the inner meanings and depth of the Torah, which lead one to sense one's connection to God.

The reason for studying specifically at night is not only because it is easier to concentrate then, but because night is a time suitable for arousing a sense of self-nullification and humility, and only through study stemming from such a feeling can one cleave to the holiness of the Torah. (*Torat Menaḥem, Hitvaaduyot, Va'etḥanan* 5745; *Likkutei Siḥot* 34, p. 41).

זֶה מְפֹרָשׁ הוּא בַּתּוֹרָה, הֲרֵי הוּא אוֹמֵר: "תַּחַת אֲשֶׁר לֹא עָבַדְתָּ אֶת יי אֱלֹהֶיךָ בְּשִׂמְחָה וּבְטוּב לֵבָב מֵרֹב כֹּל, וְעָבַדְתָּ אֶת אֹיְבֶיךָ אֲשֶׁר יְשַׁלְּחֶנּוּ יי בָּךְ בְּרָעָב וּבְצָמָא וּבְעֵירֹם וּבְחֹסֶר כֹּל וְנָתַן עֹל בַּרְזֶל" וגו' (דברים כח, מז–מח),

This matter **is explicitly** stated **in the Torah, as it says: "Because you did not serve the Lord your God with joy and with gladness of heart, due to the abundance of everything, you will serve your enemies, whom the Lord will dispatch against you, in hunger, and in thirst, and in nakedness, and in the lack of everything, and he will place an iron yoke** on your neck, until he destroys you" (Deuteronomy 28:47–48), indicating that one who fails to serve God out of abundance will forfeit that abundance.

וְאוֹמֵר: "לְמַעַן עַנֹּתְךָ וּלְמַעַן נַסֹּתֶךָ לְהֵיטִבְךָ בְּאַחֲרִיתֶךָ" (שם ח, טז).

And it says: "In order to afflict you, and in order to test you, to do good for you in your future" (Deuteronomy 8:16), indicating that any affliction is only to test if one will remain committed to God, and so if one does, then that affliction will be taken away and replaced with the bestowal of goodness.

פֶּרֶק רְבִיעִי

CHAPTER 4

Studying within a Study Hall

Halakha 1

אֵין מְלַמְּדִין דִּבְרֵי תּוֹרָה אֶלָּא לְתַלְמִיד הָגוּן, נָאֶה בְּמַעֲשָׂיו, אוֹ לְתָם. אֲבָל אִם הָיָה הוֹלֵךְ בְּדֶרֶךְ לֹא טוֹבָה – מַחֲזִירִין אוֹתוֹ לְמוּטָב וּמַנְהִיגִין אוֹתוֹ בְּדֶרֶךְ יְשָׁרָה וּבוֹדְקִין אוֹתוֹ, וְאַחַר כָּךְ מַכְנִיסִין אוֹתוֹ לְבֵית הַמִּדְרָשׁ וּמְלַמְּדִין אוֹתוֹ.

Torah is only to be taught to a worthy student,[1] who has good character traits, and **who is refined in his deeds, or to a simple person,** whose behavior is unknown. **However, if** a person **is following a bad path,** then he should not be taught straightaway, rather, first **he should be redirected back toward good** conduct[2] **and guided onto a path of righteousness. Then he is checked** to see if he is worthy to be taught, and if he is, then **afterward he is brought into the study hall and taught.**

אָמְרוּ חֲכָמִים: כָּל הַשּׁוֹנֶה לְתַלְמִיד שֶׁאֵינוֹ הָגוּן, כְּאִלּוּ זָרַק אֶבֶן לְמַרְקוּלִיס, שֶׁנֶּאֱמַר: "כִּצְרוֹר אֶבֶן בְּמַרְגֵּמָה כֵּן נוֹתֵן לִכְסִיל כָּבוֹד" (משלי כו, ח), וְאֵין כָּבוֹד אֶלָּא תּוֹרָה, שֶׁנֶּאֱמַר: "כָּבוֹד חֲכָמִים יִנְחָלוּ" (שם ג, לה).

The Sages said: "Whoever teaches Torah **to a student who is not worthy, it is as though he threw a stone at Markulis,**[a] **as it is stated: 'Like a pebble in a place for thrown stones, so is he who gives honor to a fool'** (Proverbs 26:8)" (*Ḥullin* 133b). The honor referred to in the verse is the Torah taught to an unworthy student, as the word **honor is used only** as a reference **to Torah, as it is stated: "The wise will inherit honor"** (Proverbs 3:35) and the Torah is the inheritance of the wise, who follow a path of righteousness.[b]

HALAKHIC DISCUSSION

1. Torah is only to be taught to a worthy student – אֵין מְלַמְּדִין דִּבְרֵי תּוֹרָה אֶלָּא לְתַלְמִיד הָגוּן: *Shulḥan Arukh, Yoreh De'a* 246:7–8. The *Arukh HaShulḥan* opines that the unworthy student referred to in this context is one who studies Torah in order to be able to engage in sophistry against the Torah. However, a student who has some other ulterior motive may be taught, since it is assumed that he will ultimately come to learn for its own sake (see above, 3:5).

2. He should be redirected back toward good conduct – מַחֲזִירִין אוֹתוֹ לְמוּטָב: Some later authorities suggest that even if it proves impossible to redirect an unworthy student back toward righteous conduct, should he nonetheless persist in his demand to continue learning, he should not be rejected outright (see *Shulḥan Arukh HaRav, Hilkhot Talmud Torah* 4:3, 4:17 and the *Kuntres Aḥaron* glosses there, 1).

NOTES

a. Markulis was an idol, and this was the way in which he was worshipped. See *Hilkhot Avoda Zara* 3:2; see there regarding the possible identification of Markulis as Mercury.

b. See *Hilkhot Deot* 1:4–5.

וְכֵן הָרַב שֶׁאֵינוֹ הוֹלֵךְ בְּדֶרֶךְ טוֹבָה, אַף עַל פִּי שֶׁחָכָם גָּדוֹל הוּא וְכָל הָעָם צְרִיכִין לוֹ – אֵין מִתְלַמְּדִין מִמֶּנּוּ עַד שֶׁיַּחֲזֹר לְמוּטָב, שֶׁנֶּאֱמַר: "כִּי שִׂפְתֵי כֹהֵן יִשְׁמְרוּ דַעַת וְתוֹרָה יְבַקְשׁוּ מִפִּיהוּ כִּי מַלְאַךְ יי צְבָאוֹת הוּא" (מלאכי ב, ז).

And similarly, a teacher who does not follow a good path, even though he is a great scholar and the whole nation needs him as a source of Torah knowledge, **one should not study under him until he returns back to good** conduct, **as it is stated: "For the lips of the priest will safeguard knowledge, and they will seek Torah from his mouth, as he is a messenger of the Lord of hosts"** (Malachi 2:7).

אָמְרוּ חֲכָמִים: אִם דּוֹמֶה הָרַב לְמַלְאַךְ יי צְבָאוֹת – תּוֹרָה יְבַקְשׁוּ מִפִּיהוּ, וְאִם לָאו – אַל יְבַקְשׁוּ תּוֹרָה מִפִּיהוּ.

In exposition of this verse, the Sages said: **If the teacher is,** in terms of his conduct, **comparable to an angel of the Lord of Hosts,** then **one should seek Torah from his mouth. But if he is not,** then **one should not seek Torah from his mouth.**

Halakha 2

כֵּיצַד מְלַמְּדִין? הָרַב יוֹשֵׁב בָּרֹאשׁ, וְהַתַּלְמִידִים לְפָנָיו מֻקָּפִין עֲטָרָה, כְּדֵי שֶׁיִּהוּ כֻּלָּן רוֹאִין אֶת הָרַב וְשׁוֹמְעִין דְּבָרָיו. וְלֹא יֵשֵׁב הָרַב עַל הַכִּסֵּא וְתַלְמִידָיו עַל הַקַּרְקַע, אֶלָּא אוֹ הַכֹּל עַל הָאָרֶץ אוֹ הַכֹּל עַל הַכִּסְאוֹת.

How should teachers **teach?**[1] **The teacher sits up front, and the students sit in front of him, surrounding** him in a circular **crown** formation, **such that they are all** able **to see the teacher and hear his words. The teacher should not sit on a chair while the students are on the floor,**[2] **rather either they should all be on the floor or they should all be on chairs.**

וּבָרִאשׁוֹנָה הָיָה הָרַב יוֹשֵׁב וְהַתַּלְמִידִים עוֹמְדִים, וּמִקֹּדֶם חֻרְבַּן בַּיִת שֵׁנִי נָהֲגוּ הַכֹּל לְלַמֵּד לַתַּלְמִידִים וְהֵן יוֹשְׁבִין.

Initially, in ancient times, **the teacher would sit and the students would stand, however,** already **before the destruction of the Second Temple,** under the Sages' direction, **everyone became accustomed to teach their students while they** were all **sitting,** so that they would not become fatigued.

Halakha 3

אִם הָיָה הָרַב מְלַמֵּד מִפִּיו לַתַּלְמִידִים – מְלַמֵּד. וְאִם הָיָה מְלַמֵּד עַל יְדֵי מְתֻרְגְּמָן – הַמְתֻרְגְּמָן עוֹמֵד בֵּינוֹ וּבֵין הַתַּלְמִידִים, וְהָרַב אוֹמֵר לַמְתֻרְגְּמָן, וְהַמְתֻרְגְּמָן מַשְׁמִיעַ לְכָל הַתַּלְמִידִים.

If the teacher wishes to **teach his students** by himself, directly **from his mouth, he** may **teach** like that. **But if he teaches through a disseminator,**[3] whose function is to broadcast the teacher's words to the many students, **the disseminator stands between him and the students, and the teacher says to the disseminator** that which he wishes to teach, **and then the disseminator vocalizes** those teachings **for all the students** to hear.

HALAKHIC DISCUSSION

1. How should teachers teach? – כֵּיצַד מְלַמְּדִין: *Shulḥan Arukh, Yoreh De'a* 246:9.

2. The teacher should not sit on a chair while the students are on the floor – וְלֹא יֵשֵׁב הָרַב עַל הַכִּסֵּא וְתַלְמִידָיו עַל הַקַּרְקַע: The Rema writes that this law applies only to students who have received ordination, and as such their teachers should afford them the honor of sitting on the same level as them.

3. But if he teaches through a disseminator – וְאִם הָיָה מְלַמֵּד עַל יְדֵי מְתֻרְגְּמָן: The laws concerning a teacher who teachers through a disseminator are not brought in the *Shulḥan Arukh*, as it is uncommon to do this nowadays (Rema, *Yoreh De'a* 246:9).

וּכְשֶׁהֵן שׁוֹאֲלִין לַמְתַרְגֵּם, הוּא שׁוֹאֵל לָרַב, וְהָרַב מֵשִׁיב לַמְתַרְגֵּם, וְהַמְתַרְגֵּם מֵשִׁיב לַשּׁוֹאֵל. וְלֹא יַגְבִּיהַּ הָרַב קוֹלוֹ יָתֵר מִקּוֹל הַמְתַרְגֵּם, וְלֹא יַגְבִּיהַּ הַמְתַרְגֵּם קוֹלוֹ בְּעֵת שֶׁשּׁוֹאֵל אֶת הָרַב יָתֵר מִקּוֹל הָרַב.

And when the students ask **the disseminator** questions, **he asks the teacher, and** then **the teacher tells** the answer **to the disseminator, and the disseminator responds to the one who asked. The teacher should not raise his voice more** loudly **than the voice of the disseminator,** out of respect for the disseminator, **nor should the disseminator raise his voice when asking the teacher more than the voice of the teacher,** out of respect for the teacher.[a]

אֵין הַתֻּרְגְּמָן רַשַּׁאי לֹא לִפְחוֹת וְלֹא לְהוֹסִיף וְלֹא לְשַׁנּוֹת, אֶלָּא אִם כֵּן הָיָה הַתֻּרְגְּמָן אָבִיו שֶׁל חָכָם אוֹ רַבּוֹ.

The disseminator is not permitted to omit, add, or change anything that the teacher said, rather he should relate everything precisely as it was said to him, **unless** the disseminator **is the sage's father or his teacher,** in which case, since the disseminator is greater, he may change things as he sees fit.

אָמַר הָרַב לַתֻּרְגְּמָן: 'כָּךְ אָמַר לִי רַבִּי' אוֹ 'כָּךְ אָמַר לִי אַבָּא מָארִי' – כְּשֶׁאוֹמֵר הַתֻּרְגְּמָן הַדְּבָרִים לָעָם, אוֹמְרָן בְּשֵׁם הֶחָכָם, וּמַזְכִּיר שְׁמוֹ שֶׁל אֲבִי הָרַב אוֹ שֶׁל רַבּוֹ, וְאוֹמֵר: 'כָּךְ אָמַר רַבָּנָא פְּלוֹנִי',

If **the teacher says to the disseminator: "This is what my teacher said to me" or "This is what my father and master said to me,"** then, even though the teacher didn't explicitly mention his father's or teacher's name when citing them, **when the disseminator relays these matters to the people, he should state them using the name of the sage** who originally said them, explicitly **mentioning the name of the teacher's father or his teacher, and say: "This is what our Master So-and-so said."**

אַף עַל פִּי שֶׁלֹּא הִזְכִּיר הֶחָכָם שְׁמוֹ, שֶׁאָסוּר לוֹ לִקְרוֹת לְרַבּוֹ אוֹ לְאָבִיו בִּשְׁמוֹ.

He does so **even though the teacher did not mention the name of the sage,** because he only omitted his name **as it is forbidden to call one's teacher or father by name,**[b] and that prohibition does not apply to the disseminator himself if he is neither a son nor student of that sage.

GLOSSES OF THE RAAVAD

"אֵין הַתֻּרְגְּמָן רַשַּׁאי לֹא לִפְחוֹת וְלֹא לְהוֹסִיף וְלֹא לְשַׁנּוֹת אֶלָּא אִם הָיָה תֻּרְגְּמָן אָבִיו שֶׁל חָכָם אוֹ רַבּוֹ." אָמַר אַבְרָהָם: דָּבָר זֶה מִקְרֶה חָדָשׁ. וְהוּא רַב שֶׁעָמַד תֻּרְגְּמָן לְר' שִׁילָא בְּמַסֶּכֶת יוֹמָא (כ,ב),

"The disseminator is not permitted to omit, add, or change, unless he is the sage's father or his teacher." Avraham says: This matter is based on a very **exceptional occurrence,** which is when **Rav,** having arrived in a place where he was unknown, **rose** to serve as **disseminator before Rav Sheila,** as related **in Tractate** *Yoma* (20b).

וְשָׁנָה וְהוֹסִיף שֶׁהָיָה גָּדוֹל מִמֶּנּוּ

Rav then **changed and added** to Rav Sheila's teaching, **for he was greater than** Rav Sheila in wisdom. Since this was such a unique and exceptional case, the Rambam should not have cited it.

NOTES

a. In a similar vein, see *Hilkhot Tefilla* 12:11.

b. See 5:5; *Hilkhot Mamrim* 6:3.

Halakha 4

הָרַב שֶׁלִּמֵּד וְלֹא הֵבִינוּ הַתַּלְמִידִים – לֹא יִכְעֹס עֲלֵיהֶם וְיִרְגַּז, אֶלָּא חוֹזֵר וְשׁוֹנֶה הַדָּבָר אֲפִלּוּ כַּמָּה פְּעָמִים, עַד שֶׁיָּבִינוּ עֹמֶק הַהֲלָכָה.

If a teacher teaches and the students do not understand[1] the matter, **he should not get angry with them, nor be furious, but rather he should continue to review the matter, even several times, until they comprehend the depth of the law.** This in accordance with the basic obligation of a teacher to ensure that his students understand the law and its rationale well.

וְכֵן לֹא יֹאמַר הַתַּלְמִיד: 'הֵבַנְתִּי' וְהוּא לֹא הֵבִין, אֶלָּא חוֹזֵר וְשׁוֹאֵל אֲפִלּוּ כַּמָּה פְּעָמִים. וְאִם כָּעַס עָלָיו רַבּוֹ וְרָגַז, יֹאמַר לוֹ: 'רַבִּי, תּוֹרָה הִיא, וְלִלְמֹד אֲנִי צָרִיךְ, וְדַעְתִּי קְצָרָה'.

Similarly, the student should not say: "I understand," when, in fact, **he does not understand, but rather he should continue to ask** for clarification **even** if he needs to do so **several times. If his teacher becomes angry with him, or is furious** with him, the student **should say to** the teacher: **"My teacher, this is Torah, and I need to learn** it, **but my intellect is limited** and I have not grasped the matter."

Halakha 5

לֹא יִהְיֶה הַתַּלְמִיד בּוֹשׁ מֵחֲבֵרָיו שֶׁלָּמְדוּ מִפַּעַם רִאשׁוֹנָה אוֹ שְׁנִיָּה וְהוּא לֹא לָמַד אֶלָּא אַחַר כַּמָּה פְּעָמִים,

A student should not be embarrassed before his peers[2] **who** are able to **learn** more quickly than him, successfully understanding the material already **after the first or second time** they study it, **while he does not** succeed in **learning** it **until after several repetitions.**

שֶׁאִם נִתְבַּיֵּשׁ מִדָּבָר זֶה, נִמְצָא נִכְנָס וְיוֹצֵא לְבֵית הַמִּדְרָשׁ וְהוּא אֵינוֹ לָמֵד כְּלוּם.

For if he is embarrassed by this, and therefore claims he understands when in truth he does not, **he will end up coming and going from the study hall without** actually **learning anything.**

לְפִיכָךְ אָמְרוּ חֲכָמִים הָרִאשׁוֹנִים: אֵין הַבַּיְשָׁן לָמֵד, וְלֹא הַקַּפְּדָן מְלַמֵּד.

Therefore, the earlier Sages said: "One who is shy does not learn, because he is embarrassed to ask questions when he doesn't understand, **and one who is fastidious cannot teach,** because he easily becomes angry at his students and so they will claim they understand when they don't, in order to avoid the teacher's wrath" (*Avot* 2:6).

בַּמֶּה דְּבָרִים אֲמוּרִים? בִּזְמַן שֶׁלֹּא הֵבִינוּ הַתַּלְמִידִים הַדָּבָר מִפְּנֵי עָמְקוֹ אוֹ מִפְּנֵי דַּעְתָּן שֶׁהִיא קְצָרָה.

In which case is this **statement,** that a teacher should not become angry at his students, **said? When the students do not understand the matter due to its depth** and complexity **or their limited intellect.**

HALAKHIC DISCUSSION

1. If a teacher teaches and the students do not understand – הָרַב שֶׁלִּמֵּד וְלֹא הֵבִינוּ הַתַּלְמִידִים: *Shulḥan Arukh, Yoreh De'a* 246:10.

2. A student should not be embarrassed before his peers – לֹא יִהְיֶה הַתַּלְמִיד בּוֹשׁ מֵחֲבֵרָיו: *Shulḥan Arukh, Yoreh De'a* 246:11.

HALAKHIC DISCUSSION

1. Students should not ask a teacher questions immediately upon his entering the study hall – אֵין שׁוֹאֲלִין אֶת הָרַב כְּשֶׁיִּכָּנֵס לְבֵית הַמִּדְרָשׁ: *Shulḥan Arukh, Yoreh De'a* 246:12.

NOTES

a. See 3:12.

אֲבָל אִם נִכָּר לָרַב שֶׁהֵן מִתְרַשְּׁלִין בְּדִבְרֵי תּוֹרָה וּמִתְרַפִּין עֲלֵיהֶן וּלְפִיכָךְ לֹא הֵבִינוּ – חַיָּב לִרְגּוֹ עֲלֵיהֶן וּלְהַכְלִימָן בִּדְבָרִים כְּדֵי לְחַדְּדָן,

But if it is apparent to the teacher that the reason the students do not understand is because **they are being negligent in** their efforts to understand **the words of Torah, and lackadaisical in** their approach to **them,**[a] **and therefore they do not understand** them, then the teacher **is obligated to become angry with them, and shame them with words** of rebuke for their behavior, **in order to sharpen them,** by making them carefully analyze the matter until they understand it well.

וּבְעִנְיָן זֶה אָמְרוּ חֲכָמִים: זְרֹק מָרָה בַּתַּלְמִידִים. לְפִיכָךְ אֵין רָאוּי לָרַב לִנְהֹג קַלּוּת רֹאשׁ בִּפְנֵי הַתַּלְמִידִים, וְלֹא לִשְׂחֹק בִּפְנֵיהֶם, וְלֹא לֶאֱכֹל וְלִשְׁתּוֹת עִמָּהֶם, כְּדֵי שֶׁתִּהְיֶה אֵימָתוֹ עֲלֵיהֶן וְיִלְמְדוּ מִמֶּנּוּ בִּמְהֵרָה.

It was **regarding this** that **the Sages said: "Cast fear upon the students"** (*Ketubot* 103b). **Therefore, it is not proper for a teacher to act frivolously in the presence of** his **students, nor to laugh in their presence, nor to eat and drink with them, in order that his awe will be upon them and** then **they will learn from him quickly.**

Halakha 6

אֵין שׁוֹאֲלִין אֶת הָרַב כְּשֶׁיִּכָּנֵס לְבֵית הַמִּדְרָשׁ עַד שֶׁתִּתְיַשֵּׁב דַּעְתּוֹ עָלָיו, וְאֵין הַתַּלְמִיד שׁוֹאֵל כְּשֶׁיִּכָּנֵס עַד שֶׁיֵּשֵׁב וְיָנוּחַ, וְאֵין שׁוֹאֲלִין שְׁנַיִם כְּאֶחָד.

Students **should not ask a teacher** questions immediately **upon** his **entering the study hall,**[1] rather they should wait **until** the teacher's **mind is settled. Nor should a student ask** questions immediately **upon entering** the study hall, rather only **once he has sat down and rested.** Also, students **should not ask two** questions **at once.** These principles are meant to ensure that the questions will be relevant, and the answers will be given with deliberation and consideration.

וְאֵין שׁוֹאֲלִין אֶת הָרַב מֵעִנְיָן אַחֵר, אֶלָּא מֵאוֹתוֹ הָעִנְיָן שֶׁהֵן עוֹסְקִין בּוֹ, כְּדֵי שֶׁלֹּא יִתְבַּיֵּשׁ.

Students **should not ask a teacher about a topic other than the one they are currently engaged in, so that he will not be embarrassed** if he is not familiar enough with the material to be able to answer.

וְיֵשׁ לָרַב לְהַטְעוֹת אֶת הַתַּלְמִידִים בִּשְׁאֵלוֹתָיו וּבַמַּעֲשִׂים שֶׁעוֹשֶׂה בִּפְנֵיהֶם כְּדֵי לְחַדְּדָן, וּכְדֵי שֶׁיֵּדַע אִם זוֹכְרִים הֵם מַה שֶּׁלִּמְּדָם אוֹ אֵינָם זוֹכְרִים.

A teacher has the right **to mislead** his **students with his questions, and with actions** he performs **before them** which appear to contradict what he has taught them, **in order to sharpen them,** by forcing them to think about how to resolve these questions with what they have been taught by him, **and in order to know if they remember what he taught them or not.**

וְאֵין צָרִיךְ לוֹמַר שֶׁיֵּשׁ לוֹ רְשׁוּת לִשְׁאֹל אוֹתָן בְּעִנְיָן אַחֵר שֶׁאֵינָן עוֹסְקִין בּוֹ, כְּדֵי לְזָרְזָן.

Needless to say, a teacher **has the authority to ask** his students questions regarding **a topic other than the one they are engaged in, in order to motivate them** to go and study other topics.

Halakha 7

אֵין שׁוֹאֲלִין מְעוֹמֵד, וְאֵין מְשִׁיבִין מְעוֹמֵד, וְלֹא מִגָּבוֹהַּ, וְלֹא מֵרָחוֹק, וְלֹא מֵאֲחוֹרֵי הַזְּקֵנִים. וְאֵין שׁוֹאֲלִין הָרַב אֶלָּא בָּעִנְיָן, וְאֵין שׁוֹאֲלִין אֶלָּא מִיִּרְאָה. וְלֹא יִשְׁאַל בָּעִנְיָן יָתֵר מִשָּׁלֹשׁ הֲלָכוֹת.

Students **should not ask questions of their teacher while standing,**[1] **nor should they answer** questions **while standing,** nor should they ask or answer **from a high place, nor from a distant place, nor from behind the elders** who sit between them and the teacher; rather, they should move forward so that they are directly before the teacher. Students **should only ask the teacher about the topic** they are currently engaged in,[2] **and they should ask with reverence. On the topic** being studied a student **should not ask** about **more than three laws** at a time.

Halakha 8

שְׁנַיִם שֶׁשָּׁאֲלוּ: שָׁאַל אֶחָד בָּעִנְיָן וְשָׁאַל אֶחָד שֶׁלֹּא בָּעִנְיָן – נִזְקָקִין לָעִנְיָן; מַעֲשֶׂה וְשֶׁאֵינוֹ מַעֲשֶׂה – נִזְקָקִין לְמַעֲשֶׂה;

If **two people ask** questions[3] of a teacher, **one** of whom **asks** appropriately **about the topic**[4] being studied, **and** the other **one asks about** something which is **not the topic** being studied, then the teacher **should deal with the** question on **topic,** as it is more relevant. Similarly, whenever two people ask questions, the teacher should deal with the more important question first. As such, if one question concerns **a matter of practical** halakha **and** the other concerns something which is **not a matter of practical** halakha, then **he should deal with** the question about **the matter of practical** halakha.

הֲלָכָה וּמִדְרָשׁ – נִזְקָקִין לַהֲלָכָה; מִדְרָשׁ וְהַגָּדָה – נִזְקָקִין לַמִּדְרָשׁ;

If one concerns **a law** of the Torah, and the other **an exegetical derivation** of a verse of the Torah, in order to derive from it a law, then **he should deal with** the question about **the law.** If one concerns **an exegetical derivation,** and the other **an *aggada*,** an ethical teaching derived from verses or learned from parables and events, then **he should deal with** the question about **the exegetical derivation.**

הַגָּדָה וְקַל וָחֹמֶר – נִזְקָקִין לְקַל וָחֹמֶר; קַל וָחֹמֶר וּגְזֵרָה שָׁוָה – נִזְקָקִין לְקַל וָחֹמֶר.

If one concerns **an *aggada*,** and the other **an *a fortiori*** inference, then **he should deal with** the question about **the *a fortiori*** inference.[5] If one concerns **an *a fortiori*** inference, and the other **a verbal analogy,** in which two sections of the Torah are compared due to a similar word appearing in both sections, then **he should deal with** the question about **the *a fortiori*** inference.

HALAKHIC DISCUSSION

1. **Students should not ask questions of their teacher while standing – אֵין שׁוֹאֲלִין מְעוֹמֵד:** *Shulḥan Arukh, Yoreh De'a* 246:13. Some authorities rule that when asking about a matter of law, one must stand (Rema. See *Shakh* who questions this ruling, and *Arukh HaShulḥan* who explains it).

2. **Students should only ask the teacher about the topic they are currently engaged in – וְאֵין שׁוֹאֲלִין הָרַב אֶלָּא בָּעִנְיָן:** This limitation refers to the very specific topic that they are studying. For example, if they are engaged in a certain topic in the laws of Shabbat, then they should not ask about other topics, even if those topics are also part of the laws of Shabbat (*Arukh HaShulḥan*).

3. **If two people ask questions – שְׁנַיִם שֶׁשָּׁאֲלוּ:** *Shulḥan Arukh, Yoreh De'ah* 246:14–15.

4. **One of whom asks appropriately about the topic – שָׁאַל אֶחָד בָּעִנְיָן:** A student who asks about the laws of Passover during the thirty days before Passover is considered to be asking on topic (*Taz*).

5. **If one concerns an *aggada*, and the other concerns an *a fortiori* inference, then he should deal with the question about the *a fortiori* inference – הַגָּדָה וְקַל וָחֹמֶר נִזְקָקִין לְקַל וָחֹמֶר:** There is a variant text of this halakha that states that attention should be paid to the question on the *aggada* (*Shakh*).

הָיוּ הַשּׁוֹאֲלִים אֶחָד חָכָם וְאֶחָד תַּלְמִיד – נִזְקָקִין לֶחָכָם; תַּלְמִיד וְעַם הָאָרֶץ – נִזְקָקִין לַתַּלְמִיד; שְׁנֵיהֶם חֲכָמִים, שְׁנֵיהֶם תַּלְמִידִים, שְׁנֵיהֶם עַמֵּי הָאָרֶץ, שָׁאֲלוּ שְׁנֵיהֶם בִּשְׁתֵּי הֲלָכוֹת אוֹ בִּשְׁתֵּי שְׁאֵלוֹת, שְׁתֵּי תְּשׁוּבוֹת, שְׁתֵּי מַעֲשִׂים – הָרְשׁוּת בְּיַד הַתֻּרְגְּמָן מֵעַתָּה.

If, of **the** two **questioners, one is a sage and one is a student,** then **he should deal with** the question of **the sage.**[1] If one is **a student and** one is **an ignoramus,** then **he should deal with** the question of **the student.** If **both are sages,** or **both are students,** or **both are ignoramuses,** and **they both ask concerning two** different **laws, or** they ask concerning **two questions** that have previously been raised, **or** that concern **two practical matters,** then **at that point the disseminator has the option** to choose which question should be addressed, since he is the one who will then address the question to the teacher.[a]

Halakha 9

אֵין יְשֵׁנִים בְּבֵית הַמִּדְרָשׁ. וְכָל הַמִּתְנַמְנֵם בְּבֵית הַמִּדְרָשׁ – חָכְמָתוֹ נַעֲשֵׂית קְרָעִים קְרָעִים, וְכֵן אָמַר שְׁלֹמֹה בְּחָכְמָתוֹ: "וּקְרָעִים תַּלְבִּישׁ נוּמָה" (משלי כג, כא).

One should not sleep in a study hall.[2] **Anyone who dozes off in a study hall, his wisdom becomes torn to shreds,** and he will not be able to remember an entire halakha, **and so Solomon said in his wisdom: "And slumber will clothe you in tatters"** (Proverbs 23:21), meaning that one who is lazy and sleeps will end up wearing tattered garments. The verse is taken as an analogy for one who sleeps in the study hall; that his clothes, his study, will be torn to tatters.

וְאֵין מְשִׂיחִין בְּבֵית הַמִּדְרָשׁ אֶלָּא בְּדִבְרֵי תוֹרָה בִּלְבַד. אֲפִלּוּ מִי שֶׁנִּתְעַטֵּשׁ, אֵין אוֹמְרִין לוֹ 'רְפוּאָה' בְּבֵית הַמִּדְרָשׁ, וְאֵין צָרִיךְ לוֹמַר שְׁאָר הַדְּבָרִים. וּקְדֻשַּׁת בֵּית הַמִּדְרָשׁ חֲמוּרָה מִקְּדֻשַּׁת בָּתֵּי כְּנֵסִיּוֹת.

Within the study hall, one should converse only on matters of Torah. Even if someone sneezes,[3] **one should not say to him:** "Good **health" in a study hall and, needless to say,** one should not talk about **other matters. The sanctity of a study hall is more stringent than the sanctity of synagogues** due to the frequency of study there.[b]

HALAKHIC DISCUSSION

1. One is a sage and one is a student, then he should deal with the question of the sage – אֶחָד חָכָם וְאֶחָד תַּלְמִיד נִזְקָקִין לֶחָכָם: A Torah scholar who is a *mamzer* (one born from an incestuous or adulterous union, whose lineage is considered tainted) takes precedence over a kohen who is an ignoramus (Rema; and see the Shakh, who details in which matters a kohen should take precedence, and when a scholar who is not a kohen should take precedence).

2. One should not sleep in a study hall – אֵין יְשֵׁנִים בְּבֵית הַמִּדְרָשׁ: *Shulḥan Arukh, Yoreh De'a* 246:16–17. The Shakh notes that, according to the letter of the law, it is permitted to take a casual nap in the study hall, as codified in the *Shulḥan Arukh* (*Oraḥ Ḥayyim* 151:3). Nevertheless, out of piety, one should refrain from that as well. The *Arukh HaShulḥan* adds that during a lecture or study session, even a casual nap or dozing is forbidden; the *Shulḥan Arukh's* statement regarding a casual nap only applies when no lectures or study is taking place.

3. Even if someone sneezes – אֲפִלּוּ מִי שֶׁנִּתְעַטֵּשׁ: Some later authorities contend that in contemporary times, it is permissible to bless someone who sneezes with: "Good health," as nowadays people are anyway not vigilant about refraining from casual conversation within the study hall (*Derisha*, *Arukh HaShulchan*). However, others advise against such leniency, arguing that even allowing one to say: "Good health" will lead people to engage even more in idle conversation (*Taz*).

NOTES

a. See above, Halakha 3.

b. As such, a study hall should not be converted into a synagogue. See *Hilkhot Tefilla* 11:14; 8:3.

פֶּרֶק חֲמִישִׁי

CHAPTER 5

Honoring One's Teacher

Halakha 1:	The importance of honoring one's teacher
Halakhot 2–4:	Issuing rulings in the presence of one's teacher
Halakhot 5–9:	How to honor one's teacher
Halakhot 9–10:	Honoring Torah scholars who are not one's preeminent teacher, and other Torah scholars
Halakhot 11–13:	A Torah scholar forgoing honor due to him, and the obligation of honoring students

Halakha 1

כְּשֵׁם שֶׁאָדָם מְצֻוֶּה בִּכְבוֹד אָבִיו וּבְיִרְאָתוֹ, כָּךְ הוּא חַיָּב בִּכְבוֹד רַבּוֹ וְיִרְאָתוֹ. וְרַבּוֹ יָתֵר מֵאָבִיו, שֶׁאָבִיו הֱבִיאוֹ לְחַיֵּי הָעוֹלָם הַזֶּה, וְרַבּוֹ שֶׁלִּמְּדוֹ חָכְמָה מְבִיאוֹ לְחַיֵּי הָעוֹלָם הַבָּא.

Just as a person is commanded to honor and revere his father and mother,[a] **so too, he is obligated to honor and revere his teacher. His teacher** even **takes precedence over his father**[1] with regard to all obligations of honor and reverence,[b] **as his father brought him into this world, while his teacher, who teaches him** the **wisdom** of the Torah, **brings him into the World to Come.**

רָאָה אֲבֵדַת אָבִיו וַאֲבֵדַת רַבּוֹ – שֶׁל רַבּוֹ קוֹדֶמֶת לְשֶׁל אָבִיו. אָבִיו וְרַבּוֹ נוֹשְׂאִים בְּמַשָּׂא – מַנִּיחַ אֶת שֶׁל רַבּוֹ וְאַחַר כָּךְ שֶׁל אָבִיו.

If one saw his father's lost object, and at the same time also saw **his teacher's** lost object,[2] **his teacher's takes precedence over his father's,**[3] meaning that he should first retrieve and return his teacher's lost object, and only afterward return his father's. **If his father and his teacher were** both **carrying burdens, he must first** help **put down his teacher's** burden, **and then his father's.**

HALAKHIC DISCUSSION

1. His teacher takes precedence over his father – וְרַבּוֹ יָתֵר מֵאָבִיו: *Shulḥan Arukh, Yoreh De'a* 242:1.

2. If one saw his father's lost object and his teacher's lost object – רָאָה אֲבֵדַת אָבִיו וַאֲבֵדַת רַבּוֹ: *Shulḥan Arukh, Yoreh De'a* 242:34.

3. His teacher's takes precedence over his father's – שֶׁל רַבּוֹ קוֹדֶמֶת לְשֶׁל אָבִיו: Some say that if his father had hired the teacher to teach him, he should prioritize his father over the teacher (Rema).

NOTES

a. *Hilkhot Mamrim* Chapter 6.

b. All of the halakhot in this section regarding obligations to one's teacher apply only to one's preeminent teacher. See below, Halakha 9.

אָבִיו וְרַבּוֹ שְׁבוּיִים בַּשִּׁבְיָה – פּוֹדֶה אֶת רַבּוֹ וְאַחַר כָּךְ פּוֹדֶה אֶת אָבִיו. וְאִם הָיָה אָבִיו תַּלְמִיד חֲכָמִים – פּוֹדֶה אֶת אָבִיו תְּחִלָּה.

If his father and his teacher were both **taken captive, he must redeem his teacher first and** only **then redeem his father. But if his father is** also **a Torah scholar, he must redeem his father first.**[1] Due to the distress of captivity and his status as a Torah scholar, he should redeem his father first and only then redeem his teacher.[a]

וְכֵן אִם הָיָה אָבִיו חָכָם, אַף עַל פִּי שֶׁאֵינוֹ שָׁקוּל כְּנֶגֶד רַבּוֹ – מֵשִׁיב אֲבֵדָתוֹ, וְאַחַר כָּךְ מֵשִׁיב אֲבֵדַת רַבּוֹ.

Similarly, if his father is a sage, a higher-level designation than Torah scholar, **even if he is not equivalent** in stature **to his teacher, he must return his father's lost object first**[2] **and then his teacher's.** Because of respect for his father's Torah, he returns his lost object first.[b]

וְאֵין לְךָ כָּבוֹד גָּדוֹל מִכְּבוֹד הָרַב וְלֹא מוֹרָא יָתֵר מִמּוֹרָא הָרַב. אָמְרוּ חֲכָמִים: מוֹרָא רַבְּךָ כְּמוֹרָא שָׁמַיִם. לְפִיכָךְ אָמְרוּ: כָּל הַחוֹלֵק עַל רַבּוֹ – כְּחוֹלֵק עַל הַשְּׁכִינָה, שֶׁנֶּאֱמַר: "בְּהַצֹּתָם עַל יי" (במדבר כו, ט),

There is no greater honor than the honor due to one's teacher, nor any **greater reverence than the reverence due to one's teacher,** and **the Sages said: "The reverence due to your teacher is like the fear of Heaven." Therefore, they** also **said: "Whoever disagrees with his teacher's** ruling, **it is as if he disagrees with the Divine Presence,"**[3] **as it is stated** about the assembly of Koraḥ, who disputed Moshe's leadership: **"When they incited against the Lord" (Numbers 26:9).**

וְכָל הָעוֹשֶׂה מְרִיבָה עִם רַבּוֹ – כְּעוֹשֶׂה עִם הַשְּׁכִינָה, שֶׁנֶּאֱמַר: "אֲשֶׁר רָבוּ בְנֵי יִשְׂרָאֵל אֶת יי" (שם כ, יג), וְכָל הַמִּתְרַעֵם עַל רַבּוֹ – כְּמִתְרַעֵם עַל הַשְּׁכִינָה, שֶׁנֶּאֱמַר: "לֹא עָלֵינוּ תְלֻנֹּתֵיכֶם כִּי עַל יי" (שמות טז, ח),

Whoever quarrels with his teacher, it is as if he quarrels with the Divine Presence, as it is stated about the sin of the Waters of Dispute, when the children of Israel quarreled with Moshe over the lack of water:[c] **"Where the children of Israel quarreled with the Lord" (Numbers 20:13). And whoever expresses resentment toward his teacher, it is as if he expresses resentment toward the Divine Presence, as it is stated** by Moshe to the children of Israel after they complained about the lack of food:[d] **"Your complaints are not against us, but against the Lord" (Exodus 16:8).**

וְכָל הַמְהַרְהֵר אַחַר רַבּוֹ – כִּמְהַרְהֵר אַחַר הַשְּׁכִינָה, שֶׁנֶּאֱמַר: "וַיְדַבֵּר הָעָם בֵּאלֹהִים וּבְמֹשֶׁה" (במדבר כא, ה).

Whoever suspects his teacher[4] of wrongdoing, **it is as if he suspects the Divine Presence, as it is stated** after the people grew impatient with the journey around the land of Edom and complained: **"The people spoke against God and against Moses" (Numbers 21:5).**

NOTES

a. See *Hilkhot Mattenot Aniyyim* 8:17–18.

b. See *Hilkhot Gezeila VaAveda* 12:2, which discusses a case where it is not possible to return both (*Yad Peshuta*).

c. See Numbers 20:3: "The people quarreled with Moses."

d. See Numbers 16:3: "They assembled against Moses and against Aaron."

HALAKHIC DISCUSSION

1. **If his father is also a Torah scholar, he must redeem his father first** – וְאִם הָיָה אָבִיו תַּלְמִיד חֲכָמִים פּוֹדֶה אֶת אָבִיו תְּחִלָּה: Regarding redemption from captivity, one should prioritize his father if he is a Torah scholar, even if he is not as knowledgeable as his teacher (*Shulḥan Arukh* and Rema), due to the potential danger to life entailed in the situation (*Kesef Mishne*). Similarly, regarding unloading a burden, one should prioritize his father even if he is not as knowledgeable as his teacher (*Shulḥan Arukh* and Rema), due to the physical distress and potential danger (*Taz* and *Leḥem Mishne*).

2. **If his father is a sage, although he is not equivalent in stature to his teacher, he must return his father's lost object first** – הָיָה אָבִיו חָכָם אַף עַל פִּי שֶׁאֵינוֹ שָׁקוּל כְּנֶגֶד רַבּוֹ מֵשִׁיב אֲבֵדָתוֹ: The *Shulḥan Arukh* and Rema state that he should return his father's lost object first only if his father is equal in stature to his teacher (and see *Kesef Mishne*, who explains that this is, in fact, Rambam's view as well (*Hilkhot Gezeila VaAveida* 12:2), and that there is a scribal error in the text; see also *Arukh HaShulḥan*. Our in-line commentary above offers a different resolution of the Rambam's opinion).

3. **Whoever disagrees with his teacher, it is as if he disagrees with the Divine Presence** – כָּל הַחוֹלֵק עַל רַבּוֹ כְּחוֹלֵק עַל הַשְּׁכִינָה: *Shulḥan Arukh, Yoreh De'a* 242:2.

4. **Whoever suspects his teacher** – וְכָל הַמְהַרְהֵר אַחַר רַבּוֹ: The halakhic authorities state that this prohibition applies only if he states his opinion verbally and expresses disparaging remarks about him (*Birkei Yosef*, cited in *Ben Ish Ḥai, Ki Tetze* 3).

Halakha 2

אֵי זֶה הוּא חוֹלֵק עַל רַבּוֹ? זֶה שֶׁקּוֹבֵעַ לוֹ מִדְרָשׁ וְיוֹשֵׁב וְדוֹרֵשׁ וּמְלַמֵּד שֶׁלֹּא בִּרְשׁוּת רַבּוֹ וְרַבּוֹ קַיָּם, וְאַף עַל פִּי שֶׁרַבּוֹ בִּמְדִינָה אַחֶרֶת. וְאָסוּר לְאָדָם לְהוֹרוֹת בִּפְנֵי רַבּוֹ לְעוֹלָם, וְכָל הַמּוֹרֶה הֲלָכָה בִּפְנֵי רַבּוֹ – חַיָּב מִיתָה.

Who is included in the category of one who is **disagreeing with his teacher?**[1] **This refers to one who establishes a study hall** where he teaches regularly, **and sits and expounds and teaches, without the permission of his teacher, while his teacher is still alive, even if he is in another country. It is always forbidden for a person to issue halakhic rulings in the presence of his teacher,**[2] even without establishing a permanent study hall, for this would be considered insolent, **and anyone who does issue a halakhic ruling in the presence of his teacher,**[3] meaning within his geographic sphere of influence, **is liable** to receive **the death penalty.**[4]

Halakha 3

הָיָה בֵּינוֹ וּבֵין רַבּוֹ שְׁנֵים עָשָׂר מִיל, וְשָׁאַל לוֹ אָדָם דְּבַר הֲלָכָה – מֻתָּר לְהָשִׁיב. וּלְהַפְרִישׁ מִן הָאִסּוּר – אֲפִלּוּ בִּפְנֵי רַבּוֹ מֻתָּר לְהוֹרוֹת.

If there is a distance of twelve *mil*, approximately twelve kilometers, **between him and his teacher,** which is a large distance that defines him as outside his teacher's domain,[a] **and someone asks him** about **a matter of halakha, he is permitted to respond,**[5] as long as this happened incidentally. **But if** he needs to give a halakhic ruling **to** warn someone that he is about to do something forbidden, and thereby **distance** him **from** violating a **prohibition, he is permitted to rule even in his teacher's presence.**[6]

HALAKHIC DISCUSSION

1. **Who is included in the category of one who is disagreeing with his teacher – אֵי זֶה הוּא חוֹלֵק עַל רַבּוֹ:** *Shulḥan Arukh, Yoreh De'a* 242:3–4. A student is permitted to dispute his teacher's ruling or instruction if he has textual proof or logical evidence that he is correct in doing so (Rema). However, if his teacher insists that his position is correct, it is forbidden for the student to rule differently until his teacher admits he is correct (*Arukh HaShulḥan*). Some say that as long as one is a full-fledged student, he may never dispute his teacher or contradict his ruling; he may do so only once he reaches his teacher's level of knowledge, or approaches it (*She'elat Yaavetz* 1:5). It is also forbidden for one to issue halakhic rulings if there is someone greater than himself in his city, even if that scholar is not his teacher, until he reaches the age of forty (Rema, *Yoreh De'a* 242:31). According to some, he must wait until forty years pass from the beginning of his studies (*Shakh*).

2. **One who establishes a study hall… issues halakhic rulings in the presence of his teacher – זֶה שֶׁקּוֹבֵעַ לוֹ מִדְרָשׁ...לְהוֹרוֹת בִּפְנֵי רַבּוֹ:** The authorities disagree on whether the prohibition applies only to one who issues halakhic rulings, or even to one who establishes his own study hall without ruling on halakha, since by doing so he is essentially disputing his teacher's authority (see *Shakh*).

3. **Issue a halakhic ruling in the presence of his teacher – הַמּוֹרֶה הֲלָכָה בִּפְנֵי רַבּוֹ:** The Rema says that this prohibition applies specifically to one's preeminent teacher (in accordance with the Rambam's ruling; see below, Halakha 9. See also the Halakhic Discussion on Halakha 3, which quotes others who say that it applies even if he is not his preeminent teacher). He also states that, according to some, this applies even to a disciple-colleague, if the ruling is given directly in front of his teacher. The *Shulḥan Arukh* (*Yoreh De'a* 242:12) states that the prohibition extends even to ruling on halakhic matters for members of the student's household (but see *Pitḥei Teshuva*, which quotes others who permit this). Nevertheless, he may personally follow his own rulings, if he has attained the ability to issue rulings (*Arukh HaShulḥan*). Some authorities state that it is proper to rule only after consulting a book, and not to rely on memory, for the books that have been accepted by the Jewish people have the status of teachers, and hence, one may not rule in their presence (*Pitḥei Teshuva*; *Birkei Yosef*), but others disagree (*Arukh HaShulḥan*).

4. **Is liable to receive the death penalty – חַיָּב מִיתָה:** The *Shulḥan Arukh* mentions several limitations to this prohibition: A student may answer those who ask him which opinion the halakha follows, with regard to a particular dispute. It is also permitted to rule according to a well-known, simple ruling that does not involve any unusual circumstances. Also, some permit ruling in one's teacher's presence according to previous decisions written in books, as long as he does not compare one case to another and issue an original ruling (*Yoreh De'a*, 242:7–9). Some permit ruling without permission, according to a decision recorded in the *Shulḥan Arukh* (*Ben Ish Ḥai*, *Ki Tetze* 4).

5. **If there is a distance of twelve *mil* between him and his teacher… he is permitted to respond – הָיָה בֵּינוֹ וּבֵין רַבּוֹ שְׁנֵים עָשָׂר מִיל...מֻתָּר לְהָשִׁיב:** *Shulḥan Arukh, Yoreh De'a* 242:4. The *Shulḥan Arukh* quotes the Rambam, and states that some say that a disciple-colleague is forbidden to rule within twelve *mil*, but permitted if he is farther than this distance from the teacher, while for a full-fledged student, it is forbidden to rule even outside of the twelve-*mil* radius (according to this view, there is no distinction, such as the Rambam makes, between incidental or permanent rulings; *Shakh*). Some say that according to this view, if the teacher does not regularly go to that location, it is permitted for the student to issue rulings if he is farther than twelve *mil* from his teacher (Rema).

6. **To distance him from violating a prohibition, he is permitted to rule even in his teacher's presence – וּלְהַפְרִישׁ מִן הָאִסּוּר אֲפִלּוּ בִּפְנֵי רַבּוֹ מֻתָּר לְהוֹרוֹת:** *Shulḥan Arukh, Yoreh De'a* 244:11.

NOTES

a. See also *Hilkhot Sanhedrin* 20:9.

NOTES

a. See above, Halakha 2.

כֵּיצַד? כְּגוֹן שֶׁרָאָה אָדָם עוֹשֶׂה דָּבָר הָאָסוּר, מִפְּנֵי שֶׁלֹּא יָדַע בְּאִסּוּרוֹ אוֹ מִפְּנֵי רִשְׁעוֹ – יֵשׁ לוֹ לְהַפְרִישׁוֹ וְלוֹמַר לוֹ: 'דָּבָר זֶה אָסוּר', וַאֲפִלּוּ בִּפְנֵי רַבּוֹ, וְאַף עַל פִּי שֶׁלֹּא נָתַן לוֹ רַבּוֹ רְשׁוּת, שֶׁכָּל מָקוֹם שֶׁיֵּשׁ חִלּוּל הַשֵּׁם – אֵין חוֹלְקִין כָּבוֹד לָרַב.

How so? For example, if he saw someone doing something forbidden, either because he did not know it was prohibited or due to his wickedness, he may distance him from the prohibition by issuing a warning, **and say to him: "This matter is prohibited," even in the presence of his teacher, and even though his teacher did not grant him permission** to do so, **for whenever there is a desecration of God's name,** such as through a sinful act, **one does not defer honor to a teacher.**

בַּמֶּה דְּבָרִים אֲמוּרִים? בְּדָבָר שֶׁנִּקְרָה נִקְרָה. אֲבָל לִקְבֹּעַ עַצְמוֹ לְהוֹרָאָה וְלֵישֵׁב וּלְהוֹרוֹת לְכָל שׁוֹאֵל, אֲפִלּוּ הוּא בְּסוֹף הָעוֹלָם וְרַבּוֹ בְּסוֹף הָעוֹלָם – אָסוּר לוֹ לְהוֹרוֹת עַד שֶׁיָּמוּת רַבּוֹ, אֶלָּא אִם כֵּן נָטַל רְשׁוּת מֵרַבּוֹ.

In what case **is this statement said? Regarding something that happened incidentally. However,** if the student were **to establish himself** as a permanent authority, viewed as having jurisdiction **to rule, and** were to **sit and instruct anyone who asks, even if he is at one end of the world and his teacher is at the other end,**[a] **it is** nevertheless **forbidden for him to rule until his teacher dies, unless he received permission from his teacher.**[1]

וְלֹא כָּל מִי שֶׁמֵּת רַבּוֹ מֻתָּר לוֹ לֵישֵׁב וּלְהוֹרוֹת בַּתּוֹרָה, אֶלָּא אִם כֵּן הָיָה תַּלְמִיד שֶׁהִגִּיעַ לְהוֹרָיָה.

And not everyone whose teacher dies is then **permitted to sit and** publicly **teach Torah;**[2] **only a student who has attained the ability to issue rulings,** meaning one who understands the ways of halakha, and rules with a settled mind, and fear of Heaven.

Halakha 4

וְכָל תַּלְמִיד שֶׁלֹּא הִגִּיעַ לְהוֹרָאָה וּמוֹרֶה – הֲרֵי זֶה שׁוֹטֶה רָשָׁע וְגַס רוּחַ, וְעָלָיו נֶאֱמַר: "כִּי רַבִּים חֲלָלִים הִפִּילָה" (משלי ז, כו).

Any student who has not attained the ability to issue rulings and nevertheless does **issue rulings**[3] **is considered a foolish, wicked, and arrogant person, and about him, it is stated: "For many slain has she felled" (Proverbs 7:26).** Because of his arrogance, he rules incorrectly and causes others to stumble into sin.

HALAKHIC DISCUSSION

1. Unless he received permission from his teacher – אֶלָּא אִם כֵּן נָטַל רְשׁוּת מֵרַבּוֹ: Even if he received permission from his teacher, it is forbidden for him to rule within twelve *mil* of him (Rema, *Yoreh De'a* 242:4), but some permit this (see *Shakh* 242:4, 13). If one has several preeminent teachers, it is forbidden to rule until he receives permission from all of them (*Shulḥan Arukh*). But some say that if he received permission from one of them, he is permitted to rule provided he is farther than twelve *mil* from all of them (Rema).

2. Not everyone whose teacher dies is then permitted to sit and publicly teach Torah – וְלֹא כָּל מִי שֶׁמֵּת רַבּוֹ מֻתָּר לוֹ לֵישֵׁב וּלְהוֹרוֹת בַּתּוֹרָה: Rema, *Yoreh De'a* 242:12.

3. Any student who has not attained the ability to issue rulings and nevertheless does issue rulings – וְכָל תַּלְמִיד שֶׁלֹּא הִגִּיעַ לְהוֹרָאָה וּמוֹרֶה: *Shulḥan Arukh*, *Yoreh De'a* 242:13.

Similarly, a Torah scholar who has attained the ability to issue rulings,[1] but does not issue rulings[2] when necessary, is guilty of withholding Torah from the people and metaphorically placing stumbling blocks before the blind, and about him, it is stated in the continuation of the above verse: "...and considerable are all her killed" (Proverbs 7:26). Even though he did not actively cause them to stumble, the result of his refusal to rule is that people stumble into sin.[a]

וְכֵן חָכָם שֶׁהִגִּיעַ לְהוֹרָיָה וְאֵינוֹ מוֹרֶה – הֲרֵי זֶה מוֹנֵעַ תּוֹרָה וְנוֹתֵן מִכְשׁוֹלוֹת לִפְנֵי הָעִוְרִים, וְעָלָיו נֶאֱמַר: "וַעֲצֻמִים כָּל הֲרֻגֶיהָ" (שם).

Concerning insignificant students who have not amassed sufficient Torah knowledge as is fitting,[3] and in spite of this, seek greatness before the ignorant masses and the people of their city, because they want those people to think they are great and knowledgeable in Torah, and they jump and sit at the head of public assemblies to judge and instruct Israel, these irresponsible and arrogant students increase controversies, and they are the ones who destroy the world, extinguish the light of Torah, and ruin the vineyard of the Lord of Hosts. About them, King Solomon said in his wisdom: "Catch for us the foxes, little foxes that ruin the vineyards" (Song of Songs 2:15).

אֵלּוּ הַתַּלְמִידִים הַקְּטַנִּים שֶׁלֹּא הִרְבּוּ תּוֹרָה כָּרָאוּי, וְהֵם מְבַקְּשִׁים לְהִתְגַּדֵּל בִּפְנֵי עַמֵּי הָאָרֶץ וּבֵין אַנְשֵׁי עִירָם וְקוֹפְצִים וְיוֹשְׁבִים בָּרֹאשׁ לָדִין וּלְהוֹרוֹת בְּיִשְׂרָאֵל – הֵם הַמַּרְבִּים אֶת הַמַּחֲלוֹקוֹת, וְהֵם הַמַּחֲרִיבִים אֶת הָעוֹלָם, וְהַמְכַבִּים נֵרָהּ שֶׁל תּוֹרָה, וְהַמְחַבְּלִים כֶּרֶם יי צְבָאוֹת, וַעֲלֵיהֶם אָמַר שְׁלֹמֹה בְּחָכְמָתוֹ: "אֶחֱזוּ לָנוּ שֻׁעָלִים שֻׁעָלִים קְטַנִּים מְחַבְּלִים כְּרָמִים וּכְרָמֵינוּ סְמָדַר" (שיר השירים ב, טו).

Halakha 5

It is forbidden for a student to call his teacher by his first name,[4] even if he is not in his presence. He also should not mention his teacher's name in his presence, even to refer to others who have the same name as his teacher, just as he does with his father's name if he needs to refer to others with the same name;[b] rather, he must change their names, meaning refer to them by monikers, titles, or nicknames, even after their death.

אָסוּר לוֹ לְתַלְמִיד לִקְרוֹת לְרַבּוֹ בִּשְׁמוֹ, וַאֲפִלּוּ שֶׁלֹּא בְּפָנָיו. וְלֹא יַזְכִּיר שְׁמוֹ בְּפָנָיו, וַאֲפִלּוּ לִקְרוֹת לַאֲחֵרִים שֶׁשְּׁמָם כְּשֵׁם רַבּוֹ, כְּדֶרֶךְ שֶׁעוֹשֶׂה בְּשֵׁם אָבִיו, אֶלָּא יְשַׁנֶּה שְׁמָם, וַאֲפִלּוּ לְאַחַר מוֹתָם.

HALAKHIC DISCUSSION

2. A Torah scholar who has attained the ability to issue rulings but does not issue rulings – וְכֵן חָכָם שֶׁהִגִּיעַ לְהוֹרָיָה וְאֵינוֹ מוֹרֶה: *Shulḥan Arukh, Yoreh De'a* 242:14.

3. Insignificant students who have not amassed sufficient Torah knowledge as is fitting – אֵלּוּ הַתַּלְמִידִים הַקְּטַנִּים שֶׁלֹּא הִרְבּוּ תּוֹרָה כָּרָאוּי: *Shulḥan Arukh, Yoreh De'a* 242:13.

4. To call his teacher by his first name – לִקְרוֹת לְרַבּוֹ: *Shulḥan Arukh, Yoreh De'a* 242:15–16. The Rema (242:15:1) writes that in a case where one's father is his preeminent teacher, he should call him "Rabbi," but if not, he should call him "Father." However, the later authorities state that today, the custom is not to call one's father "Rabbi" (*Shakh*). The Rema also states that the prohibition against mentioning one's teacher's name applies only if he uses his name without clarification, but it is permitted to say "My master and teacher, Rabbi So-and-so."

HALAKHIC DISCUSSION

1. Attained the ability to issue rulings – שֶׁהִגִּיעַ לְהוֹרָיָה: It has become customary in our times to grant rabbinical ordination to students so that everyone knows they have attained the ability to issue rulings, and do so with their teacher's permission. But if someone's teacher died, or he doesn't have a single preeminent teacher, he doesn't need ordination. One can also be granted specialized authorization specifically for arranging bills of divorce. (In the case of one who was not granted this authorization, and is not known by the public to be an expert in this area, but nevertheless arranged divorces or conducted *ḥalitza* rituals to enable a woman whose husband died to be freed of her levirate bonds, some authorities are stringent and do not accept the validity of the divorces and *ḥalitza* ceremonies that he arranged, while others are lenient after the fact. In practice, one should be lenient only in a case where it is not possible to conduct a new divorce procedure, and thus the stringency would prevent the woman from being able to remarry - see Hema, *Yoreh De'a* **242**:14 and see also *Arukh HaShulḥan*.) It is customary that one granted ordination is viewed as somewhat subordinate to the one who granted him ordination, even if he is not actually his teacher, if he received ordination only from him. But if he received ordination from multiple rabbis, including one rabbi who isn't his teacher, he is not subordinate to that rabbi (Rema and *Shulḥan Arukh*, *Yoreh De'a* 242:6). The Rema (*Yoreh De'a* 242:31) records various principles regarding halakhic rulings: A Torah scholar cannot permit something based on his own reasoning after his colleague has prohibited it, unless he persuades the colleague that he was mistaken. However, he can permit it if it is clear, based on an unambiguous tradition, that his colleague was mistaken, or if his colleague erred regarding a matter that has been unequivocally decided. Therefore, one may ask a Torah scholar about something another scholar already ruled to prohibit, as long as he informs the second scholar about the first ruling. Similarly, if a scholar permitted something in a certain case and his ruling was accepted, another scholar cannot prohibit it based on his own reasoning (the *Shakh* disagrees and permits this). The *Shulḥan Arukh* rules that a scholar cannot permit something unusual that appears to the masses as if he permitted a prohibition. However, if he explains the reasoning, or provides proofs from written sources, it is permitted (*Shakh*). For additional principles of ruling in cases of doubts and disputes, see Rema, *Ḥoshen Mishpat* 25:2.

NOTES

a. See also *Hilkhot Sanhedrin* 20:8.

b. *Hilkhot Mamrim* 6:3.

וְהוּא שֶׁיִּהְיֶה הַשֵּׁם פֶּלִא, שֶׁכָּל הַשּׁוֹמֵעַ יֵדַע שֶׁהוּא פְּלוֹנִי.

However, this applies only **if the name is unique,** i.e., rare and distinctive, **such that anyone who hears it will know that it refers to so-and-so,** and therefore using it would constitute disrespect for his father or teacher. If it is a common name, he is permitted to use it for others when not in the presence of his father or teacher.

וְלֹא יִתֵּן שָׁלוֹם לְרַבּוֹ אוֹ יַחֲזִיר לוֹ שָׁלוֹם כְּדֶרֶךְ שֶׁנּוֹתְנִין הָרֵעִים וּמַחֲזִירִין זֶה לָזֶה, אֶלָּא שׁוֹחֶה לְפָנָיו וְאוֹמֵר לוֹ בְּיִרְאָה וְכָבוֹד: 'שָׁלוֹם עָלֶיךָ רַבִּי'. וְאִם נָתַן לוֹ רַבּוֹ שָׁלוֹם – יַחֲזִיר לוֹ: 'שָׁלוֹם עָלֶיךָ רַבִּי וּמָרִי'.

He also must not greet his teacher or return his greeting in the same casual **manner that friends greet and return greetings to each other. Rather, he should bow before him** in submission **and say to him with awe and respect: "Peace be upon you, my teacher."**[1] **And if his teacher greets him, he should return: "Peace be upon you, my teacher and master."**[2]

Halakha 6

וְכֵן לֹא יַחֲלֹץ תְּפִלָּיו בִּפְנֵי רַבּוֹ, וְלֹא יָסֵב, אֶלָּא יוֹשֵׁב כְּיוֹשֵׁב לִפְנֵי הַמֶּלֶךְ. וְלֹא יִתְפַּלֵּל לִפְנֵי רַבּוֹ, וְלֹא לְאַחַר רַבּוֹ, וְלֹא בְּצַד רַבּוֹ, וְאֵין צָרִיךְ לוֹמַר שֶׁאָסוּר לוֹ לְהַלֵּךְ בְּצִדּוֹ,

Similarly, he should not remove his phylacteries in front of his teacher,[3] as this shows a lack of respect, **nor recline** to eat in a lounging posture,[a] which would be arrogant, **but rather** he should **sit as one** does when **sitting before a king.**[4] **He should not pray in front of his teacher,**[5] **behind his teacher,**[6] **or at the side of his teacher, and needless to say, it is forbidden for him to walk at his side,** as all these acts show arrogance.

אֶלָּא יִתְרַחֵק לְאַחַר רַבּוֹ, וְלֹא יִהְיֶה מְכֻוָּן כְּנֶגֶד אֲחוֹרָיו, וְאַחַר כָּךְ יִתְפַּלֵּל. וְלֹא יִכָּנֵס עִם רַבּוֹ לַמֶּרְחָץ. לֹא יֵשֵׁב בִּמְקוֹם רַבּוֹ, וְלֹא יַכְרִיעַ דְּבָרָיו בְּפָנָיו, וְלֹא יִסְתֹּר אֶת דְּבָרָיו,

Rather, he should position himself at a distance behind his teacher, not directly behind him, and then he may pray. He should also not enter a bathhouse[7] **together with his teacher,** as this is disrespectful.[b] **He should not sit in the place** where **his teacher** regularly sits, **challenge his words in his presence, or contradict his statements.**[8] On a matter that is subject to reasoning, it is forbidden to say otherwise than what his teacher said.[c]

HALAKHIC DISCUSSION

1. Bow before him and say to him… Peace be upon you, my teacher – שׁוֹחֶה לְפָנָיו וְאוֹמֵר לוֹ...שָׁלוֹם עָלֶיךָ רַבִּי: This is the common practice, though some say the student should not greet his teacher at all (Rema).

2. Peace be upon you, my teacher and master – שָׁלוֹם עָלֶיךָ רַבִּי וּמָרִי: The later authorities write that it is common to address an important person in Hebrew using the plural form of the verb (similar to the distinction in ancient English, which is still used in modern French), and therefore this certainly applies when speaking to one's teacher; only if the teacher is his father or brother may he address him in the singular (*Arukh HaShulḥan*). Some say that, when addressing or writing to an important person repeatedly, one need not be strict about calling him "the Rabbi" every time; there is no problem using the pronoun "you" some of the time (*Taz* 242:14, citing *Baḥ*).

3. He should not remove his phylacteries in front of his teacher – לֹא יַחֲלֹץ תְּפִלָּיו בִּפְנֵי רַבּוֹ: *Shulḥan Arukh, Yoreh De'a* 242:16.

4. He should not… recline… but rather sit as one does when sitting before a king – וְלֹא יָסֵב אֶלָּא יוֹשֵׁב כְּיוֹשֵׁב לִפְנֵי הַמֶּלֶךְ: If he is the one leading Grace after Meals, he should ask permission from his teacher first, and then from the others (Rema).

5. He should not pray in front of his teacher – וְלֹא יִתְפַּלֵּל לִפְנֵי רַבּוֹ: However, if he is more than four cubits away from his teacher, this is permitted (*Shulḥan Arukh*). However, the authorities disagree as to whether it is permitted to pray farther than four cubits away with one's back to the teacher (*Shakh*).

6. Behind his teacher – וְלֹא לְאַחַר רַבּוֹ: This applies when praying individually, but when praying with the congregation it is permitted to pray behind one's teacher (*Shakh*).

7. Should also not enter a bathhouse – וְלֹא יִכָּנֵס עִם רַבּוֹ לַמֶּרְחָץ: He may, however, enter a bathhouse with his teacher if the teacher needs his assistance (*Shulḥan Arukh*). Also, if the bathhouse is one in which the people are not completely undressed, but rather wear minimal garments, he may enter with his teacher. If the student is in the bathhouse and the teacher enters, the student is not obligated to leave (Rema).

8. Should not… contradict his statements – וְלֹא יִסְתֹּר אֶת דְּבָרָיו: Even if he is not in his teacher's presence (*Taz*), and even regarding matters unrelated to Torah study (*Ben Ish Ḥai, Ki Tetze* 8).

NOTES

a. See *Hilkhot Ḥametz UMatza* 7:8.

b. See *Hilkhot Issurei Bia* 21:16.

c. See Responsa of the Rambam, 264.

וְלֹא יֵשֵׁב לְפָנָיו עַד שֶׁיֹּאמַר לוֹ: 'שֵׁב', וְלֹא יַעֲמֹד מִלְּפָנָיו עַד שֶׁיֹּאמַר לוֹ: 'עֲמֹד', אוֹ עַד שֶׁיִּטֹּל רְשׁוּת לַעֲמֹד. וּכְשֶׁיִּפָּטֵר מֵרַבּוֹ – לֹא יַחֲזִיר לוֹ אֲחוֹרָיו, אֶלָּא נִרְתָּע לַאֲחוֹרָיו וּפָנָיו כְּנֶגֶד פָּנָיו.

He should not sit in front of his teacher **until he tells him: "Sit," and he should not stand up from before him until he tells him: "Stand," or until he asks permission to stand. When taking leave of his teacher,**[1] **he should not turn his back to him, but rather** should **walk away backward** while **facing him.**[a]

Halakha 7

וְחַיָּב לַעֲמֹד מִפְּנֵי רַבּוֹ מִשֶּׁיִּרְאֶנּוּ מֵרָחוֹק מְלֹא עֵינָיו, עַד שֶׁיִּתְכַּסֶּה מִמֶּנּוּ וְלֹא יִרְאֶה קוֹמָתוֹ, וְאַחַר כָּךְ יֵשֵׁב. וְחַיָּב אָדָם לְהַקְבִּיל אֶת פְּנֵי רַבּוֹ בָּרֶגֶל.

One is obligated to stand before his teacher[2] **from** the moment **when he** first **sees him** coming, **from a distance, to the full extent of the sight of his eyes,**[3] meaning as long as he sees him,[b] **until he is out of sight and can no longer see his** teacher's **full height, and then he may sit. A person is obligated to** visit and **greet his teacher on the pilgrimage festivals,**[4] for greeting one's teacher is considered akin to welcoming the Divine Presence, and it is therefore in a sense like going on the pilgrimage.

Halakha 8

אֵין חוֹלְקִין כָּבוֹד לְתַלְמִיד בִּפְנֵי הָרַב, אֶלָּא אִם כֵּן הָיָה דֶּרֶךְ רַבּוֹ לַחֲלֹק לוֹ כָּבוֹד. וְכָל מְלָאכוֹת שֶׁהָעֶבֶד עוֹשֶׂה לְרַבּוֹ – תַּלְמִיד עוֹשֶׂה לְרַבּוֹ.

One does not show honor to a student in the presence of his teacher[5] **unless the teacher is accustomed to show him honor.**[6] **A student must perform for his teacher all the tasks** of service and assistance **that a servant** generally **performs for his master.**

וְאִם הָיָה בְּמָקוֹם שֶׁאֵין מַכִּירִין אוֹתוֹ וְלֹא הָיוּ לוֹ תְּפִלִּין, וְחָשׁ שֶׁמָּא יֹאמְרוּ: 'עֶבֶד הוּא' – אֵינוֹ נוֹעֵל לוֹ מִנְעָלוֹ וְלֹא חוֹלְצוֹ.

However, **if he is in a place where he is not known, and he does not have phylacteries** on, which might cause people to conclude that he is a Canaanite slave, since he is serving the rabbi, and slaves do not wear phylacteries,[c] **and he is concerned that people might say: "He is a slave,"** which would detract from his lineage, **he should not remove his** teacher's **shoes for him, nor put them on,** as these are tasks specific to a Canaanite slave.[d]

וְכָל הַמּוֹנֵעַ תַּלְמִידוֹ מִלְּשַׁמְּשׁוֹ – מוֹנֵעַ מִמֶּנּוּ חֶסֶד, וּפוֹרֵק מִמֶּנּוּ יִרְאַת שָׁמַיִם. וְכָל תַּלְמִיד שֶׁמְּזַלְזֵל בְּדָבָר מִכָּל כְּבוֹד רַבּוֹ – גּוֹרֵם לַשְּׁכִינָה שֶׁתִּסְתַּלֵּק מִיִּשְׂרָאֵל.

One who prevents his student from serving him withholds kindness from him and removes the **fear of Heaven from him.** Conversely, **any student who treats lightly any aspect of the honor due to his teacher causes the Divine Presence to depart from Israel.**

HALAKHIC DISCUSSION

1. When taking leave of his teacher – וּכְשֶׁיִּפָּטֵר מֵרַבּוֹ: One who received permission from his teacher to depart but then remained in the city overnight must return to the teacher and again request permission to leave, unless he had told his teacher originally that he intended to spend the night and leave only afterward (Rema).

2. One is obligated to stand before his teacher – וְחַיָּב לַעֲמֹד מִפְּנֵי רַבּוֹ: *Shulḥan Arukh*, *Yoreh De'a* 242:16, 244:9. However, he need not stand if he is in one domain and his teacher in another, such as if he is sitting on the ground and the teacher is standing above, in a building, or if his rabbi went up to read from the Torah, since the platform the rabbi stands on is considered a separate domain (*Shulḥan Arukh* and Rema 242:18), or if his teacher is in his regular place, because a student need not stand in that circumstance (*Arukh HaShulḥan*).

3. From when he sees him from a distance, to the full extent of the sight of his eyes – מִשֶּׁיִּרְאֶנּוּ מֵרָחוֹק מְלֹא עֵינָיו: The *Shulḥan Arukh* states that this rule applies only to one's preeminent teacher, or to a great scholar who is extraordinarily wise (*Yoreh De'a* 244:10; see also below, 6:6).

4. A person is obligated to greet his teacher on the pilgrimage festivals – וְחַיָּב אָדָם לְהַקְבִּיל אֶת פְּנֵי רַבּוֹ בָּרֶגֶל: On Shabbat and Rosh Ḥodesh there is a mitzva, but not an obligation, to do this. A woman is equivalent to a man with regard to this halakha (*Magen Avraham*, *Oraḥ Ḥayyim* 301:7).

5. One does not show honor to a student in the presence of his teacher – אֵין חוֹלְקִין כָּבוֹד לְתַלְמִיד בִּפְנֵי הָרַב: *Shulḥan Arukh*, *Yoreh De'a* 242:19–21. It is forbidden for a person to stand up in honor of his father or teacher in front of a rabbi who is the teacher of both of them, unless that rabbi shows them honor (Rema), or unless the rabbi takes pride in the fact that others show honor to his students (*Shakh*).

6. The teacher is accustomed to show him honor – הָיָה דֶּרֶךְ רַבּוֹ לַחֲלֹק לוֹ כָּבוֹד: The teacher need not stand before his student, even if the student is a great Torah scholar (*Shakh*).

NOTES

a. See *Hilkhot Beit HaBeḥira* 7:4; *Hilkhot Tefilla* 9:2.

b. See below, 6:6.

c. *Hilkhot Tefillin* 4:13; *Hilkhot Keriat Shema* 4:1; see also *Hilkhot Avadim* 8:17.

d. *Hilkhot Avadim* 1:7.

Halakha 9

רָאָה אֶת רַבּוֹ עוֹבֵר עַל דִּבְרֵי תוֹרָה – אוֹמֵר לוֹ: ׳לִמַּדְתָּנוּ רַבֵּנוּ כָּךְ וְכָךְ?׳. וְכָל זְמַן שֶׁמַּזְכִּיר שְׁמוּעָה בְּפָנָיו, אוֹמֵר לוֹ: ׳כָּךְ לִמַּדְתָּנוּ רַבֵּנוּ׳. וְלֹא יֹאמַר דָּבָר שֶׁלֹּא שָׁמַע מֵרַבּוֹ עַד שֶׁיַּזְכִּיר שֵׁם אוֹמְרוֹ.

If one saw his teacher transgressing the words of the Torah,[1] **he** should **say to him: "Did you not teach us such-and-such, Rabbi?"** as if asking him a question, and not as a rebuke.[a] Also, **whenever recounting a teaching in his** teacher's **presence, he** should **say to him: "So did our Rabbi teach us."** If he is recounting **something** to others, that **he did not hear from his teacher, he should not say** it **unless he mentions the name of the one who said it,** lest the people mistakenly attribute the words to his teacher.

וּכְשֶׁיָּמוּת רַבּוֹ – קוֹרֵעַ כָּל בְּגָדָיו עַד שֶׁהוּא מְגַלֶּה אֶת לִבּוֹ, וְאֵינוֹ מְאַחֶה לְעוֹלָם.בַּמֶּה דְּבָרִים אֲמוּרִים? בְּרַבּוֹ מֻבְהָק, שֶׁלָּמַד מִמֶּנּוּ רֹב חָכְמָתוֹ. אֲבָל אִם לֹא לָמַד מִמֶּנּוּ רֹב חָכְמָתוֹ – הֲרֵי זֶה תַּלְמִיד חָבֵר, וְאֵינוֹ חַיָּב בִּכְבוֹדוֹ בְּכָל הַדְּבָרִים הָאֵלּוּ,

When his teacher dies,[2] **he** should **rend**[3] **all his garments until his heart is exposed,**[4] as is done when one mourning for one's father or mother,[b] **and** may **never sew them back together** in a way that makes the garment appear whole again.[c] **In what case is this statement said?**[5] **Regarding one's preeminent teacher, from whom he learned most of his wisdom.**[6] **However, if he did not learn most of his wisdom from him, he is** considered **a "disciple-colleague,"**[7] **and is not obligated to accord him all these honors.**[8]

HALAKHIC DISCUSSION

1. **If one saw his teacher transgressing the words of the Torah** – רָאָה אֶת רַבּוֹ עוֹבֵר עַל דִּבְרֵי תוֹרָה: *Shulḥan Arukh, Yoreh De'a* 242:22–27. He must protest even if the rabbi wishes to violate only a rabbinical prohibition. If he sees his teacher about to violate a biblical prohibition, he should ask him about it before he acts, but if he is about to violate a rabbinical prohibition, he should let him act first and then ask him about it (Rema).

2. **When his teacher dies** – וּכְשֶׁיָּמוּת רַבּוֹ: If his teacher dies and is laid out before him, it is forbidden for him to eat meat and drink wine, like one whose deceased relative is laid out unburied before him (*Shulḥan Arukh, Yoreh De'a* 242:27). One must mourn for one's teacher by uncovering a shoulder (one of the mourning customs that used to be observed for a father or mother), and follow all mourning laws for part of the day of death or part of the "day of tidings" (the day he heard of the death; *Shulḥan Arukh, Yoreh De'a* 242:25. See also *Hilkhot Evel* 9:12). The *Shulḥan Arukh* also states that he can uncover his right shoulder, left shoulder, or both, but the Rema (240:17) writes that today we do not observe the practice of uncovering the shoulder at all. And when mentioning his teacher within twelve months of his passing, he must say, "May I be an atonement for his resting soul," as one does for a parent (*Shulḥan Arukh, Yoreh De'a* 242:28).

NOTES

a. See *Hilkhot Mamrim* 6:11.

b. *Hilkhot Evel* 8:3, 9:5.

c. See *Hilkhot Evel* 9:1–3.

HALAKHIC DISCUSSION

3. **Rend** – קוֹרֵעַ: Even for "distant tidings" (when one hears about the death after thirty days have passed) he must rend his garments for his teacher just as he would for his parent (*Shulḥan Arukh, Yoreh De'a* 242:26).

4. **Until his heart is exposed** – עַד שֶׁהוּא מְגַלֶּה אֶת לִבּוֹ: The *Shulḥan Arukh* (*Yoreh De'a* 242:25, 340:8) cites this opinion of the Rambam, that one should rend his clothes for his preeminent teacher until he uncovers his heart, but adds that some say he should rend them only a handbreadth.

5. **In what case is this statement said?** – בַּמֶּה דְּבָרִים אֲמוּרִים: *Shulḥan Arukh, Yoreh De'a* 242:30.

6. **Regarding one's preeminent teacher, from whom he learned most of his wisdom** – בְּרַבּוֹ מֻבְהָק שֶׁלָּמַד מִמֶּנּוּ רֹב חָכְמָתוֹ: This applies whether he taught him scripture, Mishna, or Talmud (*Shulḥan Arukh*). However, the Rema writes that the main consideration in defining one's preeminent teacher is the one who taught him halakhic rulings and analysis, and set him on the path of truth and uprightness, not one who taught him the method of casuistry and fine distinctions (which were prevalent in the Rema's time). See also *Arukh HaShulḥan*, which gives other criteria for defining one's preeminent teacher.

7. **However, if he did not learn most of his wisdom from him, he is considered a "disciple-colleague"** – אֲבָל אִם לֹא לָמַד מִמֶּנּוּ רֹב חָכְמָתוֹ הֲרֵי זֶה תַּלְמִיד חָבֵר: A "disciple-colleague" is a student who has achieved greatness in Torah and has become a peer to his teacher, and is close to being as great as his teacher. Some define a "disciple-colleague" as any student whose teacher is not defined as his preeminent one, from whom he learned most of his wisdom (Rema 242:4).

8. **And is not obligated to accord him all these honors** – וְאֵינוֹ חַיָּב בִּכְבוֹדוֹ בְּכָל הַדְּבָרִים הָאֵלּוּ: The *Shulḥan Arukh* (*Yoreh De'a* 242:4) cites an opinion that holds that a disciple-colleague is forbidden to issue halakhic rulings within twelve *mil* of his teacher. The Rema, though, permits it, writing that some forbid it only if he is in his teacher's immediate presence, or if the questioner had already honored the teacher by saying they would ask his opinion, or if the senior rabbi is the most wise and elderly scholar in that city.

אֲבָל עוֹמֵד מִלְּפָנָיו, וְקוֹרֵעַ עָלָיו כְּשֵׁם שֶׁהוּא קוֹרֵעַ עַל כָּל הַמֵּתִים שֶׁהוּא מִתְאַבֵּל עֲלֵיהֶן. אֲפִלּוּ לֹא לָמַד מִמֶּנּוּ אֶלָּא דָּבָר אֶחָד, בֵּין קָטָן בֵּין גָּדוֹל – עוֹמֵד מִלְּפָנָיו וְקוֹרֵעַ עָלָיו.

However, a disciple-colleague **does stand before** a senior teacher-colleague,[a] **and rend** his clothes **for him**[1] when he dies, **as he would rend for any** other **deceased relative,**[2] **over** whom **he is mourning** for whom the rending is less than for a father or mother.[b] **Even if he learned from** a teacher **only one thing,**[3] **whether minor or major, he** is obligated to **stand before him and rend** his clothes **for him**[4] when he dies, as a disciple-colleague.

Halakha 10

וְכָל תַּלְמִיד חֲכָמִים שֶׁדֵּעוֹתָיו מְכֻוָּנוֹת, אֵינוֹ מְדַבֵּר בִּפְנֵי מִי שֶׁהוּא גָּדוֹל מִמֶּנּוּ בְּחָכְמָה, אַף עַל פִּי שֶׁלֹּא לָמַד מִמֶּנּוּ כְּלוּם.

Any Torah scholar whose character traits are proper[5] and refined[c] **does not speak in front of one who is greater than him in wisdom, even if he has not learned anything** directly **from him.**[6] This is not based on the halakha of honoring one's teacher; it is merely appropriate conduct.

Halakha 11

הָרַב הַמֻּבְהָק שֶׁרָצָה לִמְחֹל עַל כְּבוֹדוֹ בְּכָל הַדְּבָרִים הָאֵלּוּ אוֹ בְּאֶחָד מֵהֶן, לְכָל תַּלְמִידָיו אוֹ לְאֶחָד מֵהֶן – הָרְשׁוּת בְּיָדוֹ. וְאַף עַל פִּי שֶׁמָּחַל – חַיָּב הַתַּלְמִיד לְהַדְּרוֹ, וַאֲפִלּוּ בְּשָׁעָה שֶׁמָּחַל.

If one's **preeminent teacher wishes to relinquish** the honor due him,[7] with regard **to all the matters** enumerated in this chapter **or one of them, for all his students or for one of them, he has the authority** to do so. **But even if he has relinquished** the honor due him, **the student is** nonetheless **obligated to revere him** and honor him like any Torah scholar,[d] **even at the time when he was relinquishing** his honor.

Halakha 12

כְּשֵׁם שֶׁהַתַּלְמִידִים חַיָּבִין בִּכְבוֹד הָרַב, כָּךְ הָרַב צָרִיךְ לְכַבֵּד אֶת תַּלְמִידָיו וּלְקָרְבָן. כָּךְ אָמְרוּ חֲכָמִים: יְהִי כְבוֹד תַּלְמִידְךָ חָבִיב עָלֶיךָ כְּשֶׁל חֲבֵרְךָ. וְצָרִיךְ אָדָם לְהִזָּהֵר בְּתַלְמִידָיו וּלְאָהֳבָן, שֶׁהֵם הַבָּנִים הַמְהַנִּין בָּעוֹלָם הַזֶּה וְלָעוֹלָם הַבָּא.

Just as students are obligated to honor their teacher, so too the teacher must honor his students and draw them close. The Sages said: "Let the honor of your student be as beloved to you as that of your colleague."[e8] **A person must be careful regarding his students and love them, for they are the sons who bring** him **delight in this world and the World to Come.**[f]

NOTES

a. See below, 6:1.

b. See *Hilkhot Evel* 8:2.

c. See *Hilkhot Deot* 1:4.

d. See below, 6:1.

e. Mishna *Avot* 4:1.

f. See above, 1:2.

HALAKHIC DISCUSSION

1. Rend his clothes for him – וְקוֹרֵעַ עָלָיו: *Shulḥan Arukh, Yoreh De'a* 242:30, 340:8.

2. As he would rend for any other deceased relative – כְּשֵׁם שֶׁהוּא קוֹרֵעַ עַל כָּל הַמֵּתִים: Some say that even for a teacher who is not one's preeminent teacher, the rent should not be re-sewn (Rema 340:8).

3. Even if he learned from him only one thing – אֲפִלּוּ לֹא לָמַד מִמֶּנּוּ אֶלָּא דָּבָר אֶחָד: *Shulḥan Arukh, Yoreh De'a* 242:30.

4. He is obligated to stand before him and rend his clothes for him – עוֹמֵד מִלְּפָנָיו וְקוֹרֵעַ עָלָיו: Torah scholars in many areas have observed the custom of rending a handbreadth for each other, even if they were equals in greatness and did not learn from one another (*Shulḥan Arukh, Yoreh De'a* 340:7). But Ashkenazic communities were lenient in this matter, and did not rend for a scholar who was not their direct teacher. Therefore, they did not practice rending for a colleague who was learning with them in a group, or for one who enlightened them on one matter, as this is only a stringency dependent on custom (Rema 242:7–8; see also the Shakh, who questions why they did not rend even for a great scholar from whose innovative teachings they had benefited).

5. Any Torah scholar whose character traits are proper – וְכָל תַּלְמִיד חֲכָמִים שֶׁדֵּעוֹתָיו מְכֻוָּנוֹת: *Shulḥan Arukh, Yoreh De'a* 242:31.

6. Even if he has not learned anything directly from him – אַף עַל פִּי שֶׁלֹּא לָמַד מִמֶּנּוּ כְּלוּם: The Rema details various cases when one may issue halakhic rulings in a city where there is a Torah scholar greater than him who is not his teacher, as well as situations where a Torah scholar may permit something his colleague has prohibited.

7. If one's preeminent teacher wishes to relinquish the honor due him – הָרַב הַמֻּבְהָק שֶׁרָצָה לִמְחֹל עַל כְּבוֹדוֹ: *Shulḥan Arukh, Yoreh De'a* 242:32.

8. Let the honor of your student be as beloved to you as that of your colleague – יְהִי כְבוֹד תַּלְמִידְךָ חָבִיב עָלֶיךָ כְּשֶׁל חֲבֵרְךָ: *Shulḥan Arukh, Yoreh De'a* 242:33.

Halakha 13

הַתַּלְמִידִים מוֹסִיפִין חָכְמַת הָרַב וּמַרְחִיבִין לִבּוֹ. אָמְרוּ חֲכָמִים: הַרְבֵּה חָכְמָה לָמַדְתִּי, מֵחֲבֵרַי יָתֵר מֵרַבּוֹתַי, וּמִתַּלְמִידַי יָתֵר מִכֻּלָּם. וּכְשֵׁם שֶׁעֵץ קָטָן מַדְלִיק אֶת הַגָּדוֹל, כָּךְ תַּלְמִיד קָטָן מְחַדֵּד אֶת הָרַב, עַד שֶׁיּוֹצִיא מִמֶּנּוּ בִּשְׁאֵלוֹתָיו חָכְמָה מְפֹאָרָה.

The students add to the teacher's wisdom and broaden his mind.[1] They aid in his learning and develop his intellect. **The Sages said: "I have learned much wisdom, from my colleagues more than from my teachers, and from my students, more than from all of them."**[a] **Just as a small** piece of **wood kindles a large one, so too a young student sharpens** the mind of **the teacher, as he draws forth from him impressive wisdom through his questions.** Because of his students' questions, the teacher is compelled to clarify his words and expound them correctly.

HALAKHIC DISCUSSION

1. The students add to the teacher's wisdom and broaden his mind – הַתַּלְמִידִים מוֹסִיפִין חָכְמַת הָרַב וּמַרְחִיבִין לִבּוֹ: *Tur, Yoreh De'a* 242.

NOTES

a. *Taanit* 7a; *Makkot* 10a.

פֶּרֶק שִׁשִּׁי

CHAPTER 6

Honoring Torah Scholars

Halakha 1

כָּל תַּלְמִיד חֲכָמִים - מִצְוָה לְהַדְּרוֹ, וְאַף עַל פִּי שֶׁאֵינוֹ רַבּוֹ, שֶׁנֶּאֱמַר: "מִפְּנֵי שֵׂיבָה תָּקוּם וְהָדַרְתָּ פְּנֵי זָקֵן" (ויקרא יט, לב) - זֶה שֶׁקָּנָה חָכְמָה.

It is a mitzva to honor every Torah scholar[1] and stand before him, **even if he is not one's own teacher, as it is stated: "You shall rise before the graybeard, and show deference before the elderly** [*zaken*]**" (Leviticus 19:32); this** is interpreted as an acronym that **refers to one who has acquired** [*zeh kana*] **wisdom,** making it a reference to a Torah scholar.

וּמֵאֵימָתַי חַיָּבִין לַעֲמֹד מִפְּנֵי הֶחָכָם? מִשֶּׁיִּקְרַב מִמֶּנּוּ בְּאַרְבַּע אַמּוֹת, עַד שֶׁיַּעֲבֹר מִכְּנֶגֶד פָּנָיו.

And from when is one obligated to rise before the Torah scholar? From when he approaches within four cubits, making it evident that he is standing in honor of that scholar, **until he passes from before him** and is no longer directly opposite him.[a]

Halakha 2

אֵין עוֹמְדִין מִפָּנָיו לֹא בְּבֵית הַמֶּרְחָץ וְלֹא בְּבֵית הַכִּסֵּא, שֶׁנֶּאֱמַר: "תָּקוּם וְהָדַרְתָּ" (ויקרא יט, לב) - קִימָה שֶׁיֵּשׁ בָּהּ הִדּוּר.

One should not stand before a Torah scholar **in the bathhouse or in the bathroom,**[2] since standing in these places would not be respectable and thus would not show honor, **as it is stated: "You shall rise... and show deference** before the elderly" **(Leviticus 19:32),** meaning **standing that entails honor.**

HALAKHIC DISCUSSION

1. Every Torah scholar – כָּל תַּלְמִיד חֲכָמִים: *Shulḥan Arukh, Yoreh De'a* 244:1–2. It is a mitzva to honor a Talmud scholar, even if he is a minor who has not yet reached the age of mitzvot (*Shakh* and *Taz*).

2. One should not stand before a Torah scholar in the bathhouse or in the bathroom – אֵין עוֹמְדִין מִפָּנָיו לֹא בְּבֵית הַמֶּרְחָץ וְלֹא בְּבֵית הַכִּסֵּא: *Shulḥan Arukh, Yoreh De'a* 244:4–5. However, in the outer room of the bathhouse (where people are dressed), one must stand (Rema).

NOTES

a. See further elaboration below, Halakha 6.

וְאֵין בַּעֲלֵי אֻמָּנִיּוֹת חַיָּבִין לַעֲמֹד מִפְּנֵי תַּלְמִידֵי חֲכָמִים בְּשָׁעָה שֶׁעֲסוּקִין בִּמְלַאכְתָּן, שֶׁנֶּאֱמַר: "תָּקוּם וְהָדַרְתָּ" – מַה הִדּוּר שֶׁאֵין בּוֹ חֶסְרוֹן כִּיס, אַף קִימָה שֶׁאֵין בָּהּ חֶסְרוֹן כִּיס.

Craftsmen are not obligated to stand before Torah scholars while they are engaged in their work,[1] as this would interrupt them from their work, which would cause a monetary loss, **as it is stated: "You shall rise… and show deference"; just as showing deference does not entail a monetary loss, so too the** type of **standing** that is commanded **does not involve a monetary loss.**

וּמִנַּיִן שֶׁלֹּא יַעֲצִים עֵינָיו מִן הֶחָכָם כְּדֵי שֶׁלֹּא יִרְאֵהוּ עַד שֶׁלֹּא יַעֲמֹד מִפָּנָיו? תַּלְמוּד לוֹמַר: "וְיָרֵאתָ מֵּאֱלֹהֶיךָ" (שם), הָא כָּל דָּבָר שֶׁהוּא מָסוּר לַלֵּב נֶאֱמַר בּוֹ: "וְיָרֵאתָ מֵּאֱלֹהֶיךָ".

And from where is it derived **that one should not close his eyes so as not to see** the Torah scholar,[2] and thus avoid the obligation **to stand before him? The** continuation of the above **verse states: "You shall fear your God." About any matter that is entrusted to** a person's **heart,** such as this situation, where it is impossible to know whether he saw from the beginning or did not see, and only the person himself knows about it, **the Torah states: "You shall fear your God."**

Halakha 3

אֵין רָאוּי לֶחָכָם שֶׁיַּטְרִיחַ אֶת הָעָם וִיכַוֵּן עַצְמוֹ לָהֶן כְּדֵי שֶׁיַּעַמְדוּ מִפָּנָיו, אֶלָּא יֵלֵךְ בְּדֶרֶךְ קְצָרָה, וּמִתְכַּוֵּן שֶׁלֹּא יִרְאֶה אוֹתוֹ אֶחָד כְּדֵי שֶׁלֹּא יַטְרִיחוֹ לַעֲמֹד. וְהַחֲכָמִים הָיוּ מַקִּיפִין וְהוֹלְכִין בַּדֶּרֶךְ הַחִיצוֹנָה שֶׁאֵין מַכִּירֵיהֶן מְצוּיִין שָׁם, כְּדֵי שֶׁלֹּא יַטְרִיחוּ.

If there is another possibility, **it is not appropriate for a Torah scholar to trouble the people**[3] **and direct himself to** walk among **them** intentionally, **so that they** will be obligated to **stand before him. Rather, he should walk the shortest** possible **route, intending for no one to see him, so that he will not trouble** anyone to have **to stand. The Sages would** even inconvenience themselves and **walk around on an outer path** farther away, **where their acquaintances were not present, so as not to trouble them,** as it is a pious act to inconvenience oneself rather than others.

Halakha 4

רוֹכֵב – הֲרֵי הוּא כִּמְהַלֵּךְ, וּכְשֵׁם שֶׁעוֹמְדִין מִפְּנֵי הַמְהַלֵּךְ, כָּךְ עוֹמְדִין מִפְּנֵי הָרוֹכֵב.

If a Torah scholar **is** not walking on foot, but is **riding** an animal, he **is** considered **as if he is walking;**[4] **just as one** is obligated to **stand before** a Torah scholar who **is walking, so too he** must **stand before** one who is **riding.**

Halakha 5

שְׁלֹשָׁה שֶׁהָיוּ מְהַלְּכִין בַּדֶּרֶךְ – הָרַב בְּאֶמְצַע, גָּדוֹל מִימִינוֹ, קָטָן מִשְּׂמֹאלוֹ.

If **three** people, a Torah scholar and two others who were accompanying him, **were walking on the road,**[5] they honor him in his walking in this manner: **The teacher** should walk **in the middle,** with **the greater** of the two others walking **to his right, and the lesser** one **to his left.**[6]

HALAKHIC DISCUSSION

1. Craftsmen are not obligated to stand… while they are engaged in their work – וְאֵין בַּעֲלֵי אֻמָּנִיּוֹת חַיָּבִין לַעֲמֹד...בְּשָׁעָה שֶׁעֲסוּקִין בִּמְלַאכְתָּן: If he is engaged in work for which he is being paid by others, it is forbidden for him to be stringent upon himself and stand (*Shulḥan Arukh*). However, when one is engaged in Torah study, he must stand before a Torah scholar (*Shulḥan Arukh, Yoreh De'a* 244:11).

2. From where is it derived that one should not close his eyes so as not to see the Torah scholar – וּמִנַּיִן שֶׁלֹּא יַעֲצִים עֵינָיו מִן הֶחָכָם: *Shulḥan Arukh, Yoreh De'a* 244:3.

3. It is not appropriate for a Torah scholar to trouble the people – אֵין רָאוּי לֶחָכָם שֶׁיַּטְרִיחַ אֶת הָעָם: *Shulḥan Arukh, Yoreh De'a* 244:6. This applies only in a situation where the people are sitting on the ground, and it is a great exertion to stand up. But if they are sitting on benches, so that it would not be difficult to stand, this concern does not apply, provided that the Torah scholar did not intentionally pass in front of them so that they would stand before him (*Shakh*).

4. If a Torah scholar is riding an animal, he is considered as if he is walking – רוֹכֵב הֲרֵי הוּא כִּמְהַלֵּךְ: *Shulḥan Arukh, Yoreh De'a* 242:16; 244:2.

5. If three people were walking on the road – שְׁלֹשָׁה שֶׁהָיוּ מְהַלְּכִין בַּדֶּרֶךְ: *Shulḥan Arukh, Yoreh De'a* 242:17. However, one does not need to demonstrate honor while traveling on the road if each is going his own way and they are not in one group, or if they are in a place of danger (*Hilkhot Berakhot* 7:12; Rema).

6. The greater of the two to his right, and the lesser one to his left – גָּדוֹל מִימִינוֹ קָטָן מִשְּׂמֹאלוֹ: It is forbidden to walk within four cubits of one's teacher (see above, 5:6). When walking on the road, the students should walk to the sides of the rabbi and a bit behind him, at a distance of more than four cubits (*Shakh*).

Halakha 6

הָרוֹאֶה חָכָם – אֵינוֹ עוֹמֵד מִלְּפָנָיו עַד שֶׁיַּגִּיעַ לוֹ לְאַרְבַּע אַמּוֹת, וְכֵיוָן שֶׁעָבַר – יוֹשֵׁב. רָאָה אַב בֵּית דִּין – עוֹמֵד מִלְּפָנָיו מִשֶּׁיִּרְאֶנּוּ מֵרָחוֹק מְלֹא עֵינָיו, וְאֵינוֹ יוֹשֵׁב עַד שֶׁיַּעֲבֹר מֵאַחֲרָיו אַרְבַּע אַמּוֹת. רָאָה אֶת הַנָּשִׂיא – עוֹמֵד מִלְּפָנָיו מְלֹא עֵינָיו, וְאֵינוֹ יוֹשֵׁב עַד שֶׁיֵּשֵׁב בִּמְקוֹמוֹ אוֹ עַד שֶׁיִּתְכַּסֶּה מֵעֵינָיו.

One who sees a Torah scholar[1] **does not** need to **stand before him until he approaches him within four cubits,** as noted above,[a] **and once** the Torah scholar **has passed** him and is more than four cubits away, **he** may **sit down. One who sees the deputy** *Nasi* of the Sanhedrin[b] must **stand before him from when he sees him from afar, to the full extent of his vision, and he** may **not sit down until** the deputy *Nasi* **has passed him** and is more than **four cubits** away. **One who sees the** *Nasi* must **stand before him to the full extent of his vision,** similar to the law regarding one's preeminent teacher,[c] **and not sit down until** the *Nasi* **has sat in his place, or until he is out of sight.**

וְהַנָּשִׂיא שֶׁמָּחַל עַל כְּבוֹדוֹ – כְּבוֹדוֹ מָחוּל. כְּשֶׁהַנָּשִׂיא נִכְנָס – כָּל הָעָם עוֹמְדִין, וְאֵינָן יוֹשְׁבִין עַד שֶׁיֹּאמַר לָהֶם: 'שְׁבוּ'. כְּשֶׁאַב בֵּית דִּין נִכְנָס – עוֹשִׂין לוֹ שְׁתֵּי שׁוּרוֹת עוֹמְדִין מִכָּאן וּמִכָּאן, עַד שֶׁנִּכְנָס וְיֵשֵׁב בִּמְקוֹמוֹ, וּשְׁאָר הָעָם יוֹשְׁבִין בִּמְקוֹמָן.

If the *Nasi* **relinquished** the honor due him, agreeing to not be treated with as much honor,[d] **his honor is relinquished.**[2] **When the** *Nasi* **enters** the study hall, **all the people stand, and they do not sit down until he tells them: "Sit." When the deputy** *Nasi* **enters,**[3] **they** should **form two rows** by **standing,** some **on this** side **and** some **on that** side, **until he has entered and sat in his place,** and then **the rest of the people** between whom he has passed may **sit in their places.**

Halakha 7

חָכָם שֶׁנִּכְנָס – כָּל שֶׁיַּגִּיעַ לוֹ בְּאַרְבַּע אַמּוֹת עוֹמֵד מִלְּפָנָיו, אֶחָד עוֹמֵד וְאֶחָד יוֹשֵׁב, עַד שֶׁנִּכְנָס וְיֵשֵׁב בִּמְקוֹמוֹ.

When **a Torah scholar enters** the study hall, **when he passes within four cubits of** someone, that person must **stand before him,** so that **one stands** as the scholar approaches **and one sits** after the scholar has passed him, **until** the scholar **has entered and sat in his place.**

בְּנֵי חֲכָמִים וְתַלְמִידֵי חֲכָמִים, בִּזְמַן שֶׁהָרַבִּים צְרִיכִין לָהֶם – מְקַפְּצִין עַל רָאשֵׁי הָעָם וְנִכְנָסִין לִמְקוֹמָן.

Regarding **the children of Torah scholars, and** their **students, if the public needs them** in the study hall and therefore they need to enter, **they** may step over the people who are already seated, making it appear that they are **leaping over the heads of the people,** which may seem disrespectful, **and go to their places.** The seated people do not need to stand before them.

וְאֵין שֶׁבַח לְתַלְמִיד חֲכָמִים שֶׁיִּכָּנֵס בָּאַחֲרוֹנָה. יָצָא לְצֹרֶךְ – חוֹזֵר לִמְקוֹמוֹ.

It is not praiseworthy for a Torah scholar to enter last, as he should be among the first to come to the study hall. **If he went out for a purpose, he returns to his place.**

HALAKHIC DISCUSSION

1. One who sees a Torah scholar – הָרוֹאֶה חָכָם: *Shulḥan Arukh, Yoreh De'a* 244:9–17.

2. If the *Nasi* relinquished the honor due him, his honor is relinquished – וְהַנָּשִׂיא שֶׁמָּחַל עַל כְּבוֹדוֹ כְּבוֹדוֹ מָחוּל: Similarly, any other Torah scholars who have relinquished the honor due to them, their honor is relinquished. Nevertheless, there is a mitzva to honor them and rise somewhat before them (*Shulḥan Arukh*; see also above, 5:11).

3. When the deputy *Nasi* enters – כְּשֶׁאַב בֵּית דִּין נִכְנָס: This law does not apply to the president of a court in the present era (*Shakh*, 244:11).

NOTES

a. Halakha 1.

b. See *Hilkhot Sanhedrin* 1:3.

c. See above, 5:7.

d. See above, 5:11.

בְּנֵי חֲכָמִים: בִּזְמַן שֶׁיֵּשׁ בָּהֶן דַּעַת לִשְׁמֹעַ – הוֹפְכִין פְּנֵיהֶם כְּלַפֵּי אֲבִיהֶם; אֵין בָּהֶם דַּעַת לִשְׁמֹעַ – הוֹפְכִין פְּנֵיהֶם כְּלַפֵּי הָעָם.

The children of Torah scholars, if they have the intellectual **ability to listen** and understand, **they turn their faces toward their fathers,** facing them as the other students do. But **if they do not have the** intellectual **ability to listen** and understand, **they turn their faces toward the people,** to demonstrate that they are sitting there out of respect for their fathers, but not as students.

Halakha 8

תַּלְמִיד שֶׁהוּא יוֹשֵׁב לִפְנֵי רַבּוֹ תָּמִיד – אֵינוֹ רַשַּׁאי לַעֲמֹד מִלְּפָנָיו אֶלָּא שַׁחֲרִית וְעַרְבִית בִּלְבַד, שֶׁלֹּא יְהֵא כְּבוֹדוֹ מְרֻבֶּה מִכְּבוֹד שָׁמַיִם.

A student who constantly sits before his teacher is permitted to stand before him only once **in the morning and** once in **the evening,**[1] **lest** the teacher's **honor be greater than the honor of Heaven.** Since they accept the yoke of the kingdom of Heaven twice a day, in the recitation of the *Shema*,[a] it was established that students should likewise stand for their teachers only twice a day.

Halakha 9

מִי שֶׁהוּא זָקֵן מֻפְלָג בְּזִקְנָה, אַף עַל פִּי שֶׁאֵינוֹ חָכָם – עוֹמְדִין לְפָנָיו. וַאֲפִלּוּ הֶחָכָם שֶׁהוּא יֶלֶד עוֹמֵד בִּפְנֵי הַזָּקֵן הַמֻּפְלָג בְּזִקְנָה, וְאֵינוֹ חַיָּב לַעֲמֹד מְלֹא קוֹמָתוֹ, אֶלָּא כְּדֵי לְהַדְּרוֹ.

In the case of **one who is an extremely old person, very advanced in age,**[2] **we must stand before him even if he is not a Torah scholar.**[3] **Even a Torah scholar who is** great in scholarship, but **young,**[4] must **stand before the extremely old person** who is **very advanced in age.** However, **he is not obligated to stand up to his full height, but rather** it is sufficient that he rises up a little, in a way that it is evident that he is doing this **to honor him.**[5]

וַאֲפִלּוּ זָקֵן גּוֹי – מְהַדְּרִין אוֹתוֹ בִּדְבָרִים וְנוֹתְנִין לוֹ יָד לְסָמְכוֹ, שֶׁנֶּאֱמַר: "מִפְּנֵי שֵׂיבָה תָּקוּם" (ויקרא יט, לב) – כָּל שֵׂיבָה בְּמַשְׁמָע.

We must **honor even an old gentile with** honorable **speech** and words of praise, **and give him a hand to lean on** as a way of honoring him, **as it is stated: "You shall rise before the greybeard" (Leviticus 19:32),** an expression that **includes any old person.**

Halakha 10

תַּלְמִידֵי חֲכָמִים אֵינָן יוֹצְאִין לַעֲשׂוֹת בְּעַצְמָן עִם כָּל הַקָּהָל בְּבִנְיָן וַחֲפִירָה שֶׁל מְדִינָה וְכַיּוֹצֵא בָּהֶן, כְּדֵי שֶׁלֹּא יִתְבַּזּוּ בִּפְנֵי עַמֵּי הָאָרֶץ. וְאֵין גּוֹבִין מֵהֶן לְבִנְיַן הַחוֹמוֹת וְתִקּוּן הַשְּׁעָרִים וּשְׂכַר הַשּׁוֹמְרִים וְכַיּוֹצֵא בָּהֶן,

Torah scholars[6] **do not go out to personally participate**[7] **with the entire community in building and digging of the city and** things **like this, so that they not be degraded in the eyes of the uneducated people** who might then consider the Torah scholars equal to themselves in status.[b] **They also are not taxed for building the** city **walls, or the repair of the gates, or the wages of the guards and similar** matters, since their learning protects them and they therefore do not require or benefit from the additional security.[c]

HALAKHIC DISCUSSION

1. A student who constantly sits before his teacher is permitted to stand before him only once in the morning and once in the evening – תַּלְמִיד שֶׁהוּא יוֹשֵׁב לִפְנֵי רַבּוֹ תָּמִיד...אֶלָּא שַׁחֲרִית וְעַרְבִית בִּלְבַד: *Shulḥan Arukh, Yoreh De'a* 242:16. Some say that this law applies only when he is in his teacher's home, but in front of others, who do not know that he has already stood before him, he is obligated to stand (Rema).

2. One who is an extremely old person, very advanced in age – מִי שֶׁהוּא זָקֵן מֻפְלָג בְּזִקְנָה: These laws apply to a person at least seventy years old (*Shulḥan Arukh, Yoreh De'a* 244:1).

3. Even if he is not a Torah scholar – אַף עַל פִּי שֶׁאֵינוֹ חָכָם: This applies if he is an ignoramus, provided that he is not wicked (Rema).

4. Even a Torah scholar who is young – וַאֲפִלּוּ הֶחָכָם שֶׁהוּא יֶלֶד: *Shulḥan Arukh, Yoreh De'a* 244:7.

5. He is not obligated to stand up to his full height, but rather… it is evident that he is doing this to honor him – וְאֵינוֹ חַיָּב לַעֲמֹד מְלֹא קוֹמָתוֹ אֶלָּא כְּדֵי לְהַדְּרוֹ: This applies specifically to a Torah scholar. However, one who is not a Torah scholar, or is not more learned than the old person, is obligated to stand up to his full height before the old person (*Taz*, *Shakh*).

6. Torah scholars – תַּלְמִידֵי חֲכָמִים: *Shulḥan Arukh, Yoreh De'a* 243:1–5.

7. Do not go out to personally participate – אֵינָן יוֹצְאִין לַעֲשׂוֹת בְּעַצְמָן: They are also not obligated to hire others to do this work in their place. But if the townspeople hire workers to do things necessary for their livelihood, such as digging wells for drinking water and the like, Torah scholars must participate equally (*Shulḥan Arukh*).

NOTES

a. *Hilkhot Keriat Shema* 1:1–2.

b. However, when they collect money from all citizens for some communal need, they collect equally from Torah scholars (*Hilkhot Shekhenim* 6:6).

c. See *Hilkhot Shekhenim* 6:4–6.

וְלֹא לִתְשׁוּרַת הַמֶּלֶךְ, וְאֵין מְחַיְּבִין אוֹתָם לִתֵּן הַמַּס, בֵּין מַס שֶׁהוּא קָצוּב עַל בְּנֵי הָעִיר בֵּין מַס שֶׁהוּא קָצוּב עַל כָּל אִישׁ וְאִישׁ, שֶׁנֶּאֱמַר: "גַּם כִּי יִתְנוּ בַגּוֹיִם עַתָּה אֲקַבְּצֵם וַיָּחֵלּוּ מְּעָט מִמַּשָּׂא מֶלֶךְ וְשָׂרִים" (הושע ח, י, ושם: שָׂרִים).

They also are **not** taxed **for** a **gift** that the public is obligated to give to **the king, and they are not obligated to contribute** toward **the tax, whether** it is **a tax that is fixed for** all **the residents of the city or a tax that is fixed on every individual,**[1] **as it is stated: "Even as they give tribute among the nations, now I will gather them, and they will begin to be diminished from the burden of king and princes"** (Hosea 8:10). The Sages derived from this verse that those who "give," meaning learn the laws, will "begin to be diminished," i.e., be exempt from the "burden of the king and princes," the tax payments.

וְכֵן אִם הָיְתָה סְחוֹרָה לְתַלְמִיד חֲכָמִים – מַנִּיחִין אוֹתוֹ לִמְכֹּר תְּחִלָּה, וְאֵין מַנִּיחִין אֶחָד מִבְּנֵי הַשּׁוּק לִמְכֹּר עַד שֶׁיִּמְכֹּר הוּא. וְכֵן אִם הָיָה לוֹ דִּין וְהָיָה עוֹמֵד בִּכְלַל בַּעֲלֵי דִּינִין הַרְבֵּה – מַקְדִּימִין אוֹתוֹ וּמוֹשִׁיבִין אוֹתוֹ.

Similarly, if a Torah scholar has merchandise to sell, **they** must **let him sell it first,** meaning give him the exclusive rights to sell that merchandise until he has sold everything; **they do not allow one of the** other vendors **from the marketplace to sell** that same type of merchandise **until he has sold** his.[2] **Also, if he has a** court case requiring **judgment, and he is standing among many litigants** waiting to be judged,[a] **they** must **give him priority. Also, he** is allowed **to sit,** although usually the litigants stand.[b]

Halakha 11

עָוֹן גָּדוֹל הוּא לְבַזּוֹת אֶת הַחֲכָמִים אוֹ לְשָׂנְאָתָן. לֹא חָרְבָה יְרוּשָׁלַיִם עַד שֶׁבִּזּוּ בָּהּ תַּלְמִידֵי חֲכָמִים, שֶׁנֶּאֱמַר: "וַיִּהְיוּ מַלְעִבִים בְּמַלְאֲכֵי הָאֱלֹהִים וּבוֹזִים דְּבָרָיו וּמִתַּעְתְּעִים בִּנְבִאָיו" (דברי הימים ב לו, טז), כְּלוֹמַר בּוֹזִים מְלַמְּדֵי דְּבָרָיו. וְכֵן זֶה שֶׁאָמְרָה תּוֹרָה: "אִם בְּחֻקֹּתַי תִּמְאָסוּ" (ויקרא כו, טו, ושם: וְאִם) – מְלַמְּדֵי חֻקּוֹתַי תִּמְאָסוּ.

It is a great sin to disgrace or to hate Torah scholars.[3] In fact, **Jerusalem was not destroyed until disrespect was shown to the Torah scholars within it, as it is stated: "They would insult the messengers of God, scorn His words, and scoff at His prophets"** (II Chronicles 36:16),[c] **meaning that they scorned the teachers of His words. This is** also the meaning of **what the Torah said: "If you despise My statutes"** (Leviticus 26:15), **meaning you despise the teachers of My statutes.**

וְכָל הַמְבַזֶּה אֶת הַחֲכָמִים – אֵין לוֹ חֵלֶק לָעוֹלָם הַבָּא, וַהֲרֵי זֶה בִּכְלַל "כִּי דְבַר ה׳ בָּזָה" (במדבר טו, לא).

Anyone who despises the Sages has no share in the World to Come, and is included in the statement: **"Because he has scorned the word of the Lord" (Numbers 15:31).** One's attitude toward Torah scholars is parallel to one's attitude toward the word of God itself, since Torah scholars teach the words of God, the Torah.

HALAKHIC DISCUSSION

1. **They are not obligated to contribute toward the tax... or a tax that is fixed on every individual** – **וְאֵין מְחַיְּבִין אוֹתָם לִתֵּן...בֵּין מַס שֶׁהוּא קָצוּב עַל כָּל אִישׁ וְאִישׁ**: The community must pay all the taxes imposed on a Torah scholar, regardless of his financial situation, even if the government has ordered him to pay personally (*Shulḥan Arukh* and Rema). These laws apply only to Torah scholars whose Torah is their profession. One who is involved a little in a craft or a business for his livelihood, but not enough to become wealthy, and whenever he is free he studies Torah, is defined as one whose Torah is his profession (*Shulḥan Arukh*). He must also be known as a Torah scholar in his generation, who is capable of discussing and understanding the Torah, and is fully competent in most areas of the Talmud and its commentaries and the rulings of the geonim. Today, there is no one considered a Torah scholar with regard to these laws, but nevertheless, in some places it is customary to exempt any Torah scholar from taxes, and in other places they are not exempt (Rema).

2. **They do not allow any other one of the vendors from the marketplace to sell the same type of merchandise until he has sold his** – **וְאֵין מַנִּיחִין אֶחָד מִבְּנֵי הַשּׁוּק לִמְכֹּר עַד שֶׁיִּמְכֹּר הוּא**: But in a marketplace where there are also gentile merchants, who will not respect these rules, one should not prevent other Jews from selling their merchandise immediately (*Shulḥan Arukh*).

3. **It is a great sin to disgrace... Torah scholars** – **עָוֹן גָּדוֹל הוּא לְבַזּוֹת אֶת הַחֲכָמִים**: *Shulḥan Arukh, Yoreh De'a* 343:6. It is also prohibited to be served by one who teaches halakha or Talmud (Rema). But if the person performs this service on his own, it is permitted (*Shiyurei Berakhah*).

NOTES

a. For the standard order of precedence in court cases, see *Hilkhot Sanhedrin* 21:6.

b. See *Hilkhot Sanhedrin* 21:3–4.

c. This verse is part of a passage enumerating the sins of the king of Judah, his officers, and the people. It explains why the wrath of God rose against Israel, until He brought the king of Babylonia to destroy the Temple and Jerusalem.

Halakha 12

אַף עַל פִּי שֶׁהַמְבַזֶּה אֶת הַחֲכָמִים אֵין לוֹ חֵלֶק, אִם בָּאוּ עֵדִים שֶׁבִּזָּהוּ, אֲפִלּוּ בִּדְבָרִים – חַיָּב נִדּוּי. וּמְנַדִּין אוֹתוֹ בֵּית דִּין בָּרַבִּים, וְקוֹנְסִין אוֹתוֹ לִיטְרָא זָהָב בְּכָל מָקוֹם, וְנוֹתְנִין אוֹתָהּ לֶחָכָם.

Even though one who disgraces Torah scholars has no portion in the World to Come, **if witnesses come** and testify in court **that he insulted** a Torah scholar, **even** merely **with words, he is** also **liable** to receive the punishment of **ostracism.**[a][1] In such a case, **the court publicly ostracizes** the offender **and fines him a *litra* of gold**[b] **in every place,**[c] since this is technically not a fine, but compensation for his humiliation, **and gives** the money **to the Torah scholar.**[2]

וְהַמְבַזֶּה אֶת הֶחָכָם בִּדְבָרִים, אֲפִלּוּ לְאַחַר מִיתָה – מְנַדִּין אוֹתוֹ בֵּית דִּין, וְהֵם מַתִּירִין אוֹתוֹ כְּשֶׁיַּחֲזֹר בִּתְשׁוּבָה. אֲבָל אִם הָיָה הֶחָכָם חַי – אֵין מַתִּירִין לוֹ עַד שֶׁיְּרַצֶּה זֶה שֶׁנִּדּוּהוּ בִּשְׁבִילוֹ. וְכֵן הֶחָכָם עַצְמוֹ מְנַדֶּה לִכְבוֹדוֹ לְעַם הָאָרֶץ שֶׁהִפְקִיר בּוֹ, וְאֵינוֹ צָרִיךְ לֹא עֵדִים וְלֹא הַתְרָאָה,

If one insulted a Torah scholar verbally, even after his death, the court ostracizes him, and they **revoke** the ostracism only **when he repents. However, if the** insulted **Torah scholar is alive, they do not revoke** the ostracism **until he** not only repents but also **appeases this** Torah scholar whom he insulted[d] and **because of whom** the court **ostracized him. A Torah scholar himself** is also empowered to **ostracize, for the sake of his honor,**[3] **an ignorant person who treats him with contempt, and** to do so **he does not require witnesses and** does not need to **warn** the offender first.[4]

וְאֵין מַתִּירִין לוֹ עַד שֶׁיְּרַצֶּה אֶת הֶחָכָם. וְאִם מֵת הֶחָכָם – בָּאִין שְׁלֹשָׁה וּמַתִּירִין לוֹ. וְאִם רָצָה הֶחָכָם לִמְחֹל לוֹ וְלֹא נִדָּהוּ – הָרְשׁוּת בְּיָדוֹ.

In such a case, the court **does not revoke** his ostracism **until he appeases the Torah scholar** whom he insulted, **and if the Torah scholar** has **died,** he needs **three** people to **come and revoke** the ostracism. **But if the Torah scholar wants to** waive his honor,[e] ignore the insolence, and **forgive him, and** hence chooses **not to ostracize him, he has the authority** to do so.

NOTES

a. See chapter 7 for details of ostracism and excommunication.

b. A large sum, as compensation for the humiliation he caused to the Torah scholar (see *Hilkhot Ḥovel UMazik* 3:5–6).

c. Even outside of the Land of Israel, where fines are usually not imposed. See *Hilkhot Sanhedrin* 5:8–9.

d. Some understand this to mean that the Torah scholar must assent to having the offender's ostracism revoked.

e. See below 7:13; *Hilkhot Sanhedrin* 26:6.

HALAKHIC DISCUSSION

1. Even though one who disgraces Torah scholars has no portion in the World to Come… he is liable to receive the punishment of ostracism – אַף עַל פִּי שֶׁהַמְבַזֶּה אֶת הַחֲכָמִים אֵין לוֹ חֵלֶק...חַיָּב נִדּוּי: *Shulḥan Arukh, Yoreh De'a* 243:7–8.

2. Fines him a *litra* of gold in every place and gives the money to the Torah scholar – וְקוֹנְסִין אוֹתוֹ לִיטְרָא זָהָב בְּכָל מָקוֹם וְנוֹתְנִין אוֹתָהּ לֶחָכָם: Today, there is no one defined as a Torah scholar for this purpose. Hence, the court fines one who humiliates a Torah scholar according to their discretion, taking into account the identities of the offender and the victim. One should not fine a person who despised a Torah scholar if the Torah scholar was the one who started the quarrel and thereby caused himself to be despised. Nevertheless, even in this case, one should not be insolent toward the Torah scholar or respond to him impudently (Rema).

3. A Torah scholar himself is also empowered to ostracize for the sake of his honor – וְכֵן הֶחָכָם עַצְמוֹ מְנַדֶּה לִכְבוֹדוֹ: There are differing opinions as to whether, in our era, a Torah scholar is allowed to ostracize someone for the sake of his honor (Rema, *Yoreh De'a* 243:8).

4. He does not require witnesses and does not need to warn the offender first – וְאֵינוֹ צָרִיךְ לֹא עֵדִים וְלֹא הַתְרָאָה: The *Shulḥan Arukh* states that one who transgresses a prohibition (see below, Halakha 14) is ostracized immediately, but if someone is to be ostracized for a monetary matter (because he refuses to appear before a court or to pay his debt), the court must first warn him three times, on a consecutive Monday, Thursday, and Monday (*Hilkhot Sanhedrin* 25:8, 25:11; *Shulḥan Arukh, Yoreh De'a* 334:1, *Ḥoshen Mishpat* 11:1, 19:3).

Halakha 13

הָרַב שֶׁנִּדָּה לִכְבוֹדוֹ – חַיָּבִין כָּל תַּלְמִידָיו לִנְהֹג נִדּוּי בִּמְנֻדֶּה. אֲבָל תַּלְמִיד שֶׁנִּדָּה לִכְבוֹד עַצְמוֹ – אֵין הָרַב חַיָּב לִנְהֹג בּוֹ נִדּוּי, אֲבָל כָּל הָעָם חַיָּבִין לִנְהֹג בּוֹ נִדּוּי.

If a rabbi ostracizes someone **for the sake of his honor, all his students are obligated**[1] **to observe the** terms of the **ostracism**[a] **toward the one who was ostracized,** as they are obligated to protect the honor of their teacher. **But** if **a student ostracized** someone **for the sake of his own honor,**[2] **the rabbi is not obligated to observe** the terms of the **ostracism,**[3] **but all the** other **people** in the community **are obligated to observe** the terms of the **ostracism,** as they are obligated to protect the honor of Torah scholars.

וְכֵן מְנֻדֶּה לַנָּשִׂיא – מְנֻדֶּה לְכָל יִשְׂרָאֵל, מְנֻדֶּה לְכָל יִשְׂרָאֵל – אֵינוֹ מְנֻדֶּה לַנָּשִׂיא; מְנֻדֶּה לְעִירוֹ – מְנֻדֶּה לְעִיר אַחֶרֶת, מְנֻדֶּה לְעִיר אַחֶרֶת – אֵינוֹ מְנֻדֶּה לְעִירוֹ.

Similarly, one who was **ostracized on behalf of the** ***Nasi***[4] is considered **ostracized** for **all** the people of **Israel,** as they are all obligated to protect the honor of the *Nasi*. However, **one** who was **ostracized** on behalf of **all the people of Israel is not** considered **ostracized for the** ***Nasi*****. One** who was **ostracized** on behalf of **his city,** for the sake of honor of the Torah scholars of the city, **is** considered **ostracized** for the people of **another city,** but **one** who was **ostracized** on behalf of **another city, is not** considered **ostracized** for the people of **his city.**

Halakha 14

בַּמֶּה דְּבָרִים אֲמוּרִים? בְּמִי שֶׁנִּדּוּהוּ מִפְּנֵי שֶׁבִּזָּה תַּלְמִידֵי חֲכָמִים. אֲבָל מִי שֶׁנִּדּוּהוּ עַל שְׁאָר דְּבָרִים שֶׁחַיָּבִין עֲלֵיהֶם נִדּוּי, אֲפִלּוּ נִדָּהוּ קָטָן שֶׁבְּיִשְׂרָאֵל – חַיָּב הַנָּשִׂיא וְכָל יִשְׂרָאֵל לִנְהֹג בּוֹ נִדּוּי עַד שֶׁיַּחֲזֹר בִּתְשׁוּבָה מִדָּבָר שֶׁנִּדּוּהוּ בִּשְׁבִילוֹ וְיַתִּירוּ לוֹ.

In what case **is this statement said?**[5] **In** the case **of one who was ostracized because he disgraced a Torah scholar. But** in the case **of one who was ostracized due to other matters for which one is liable to receive ostracism, even if he was ostracized by** a scholar of the **lowest** stature **among** the people of **Israel, the** ***Nasi*** **and all** the people of **Israel are obligated to observe** the terms **of ostracism toward him until he repents of the matter for which they ostracized him and they revoke** the ostracism for **him.**

NOTES

a. See below, Chapter 7.

HALAKHIC DISCUSSION

1. **If a rabbi ostracizes someone for the sake of his honor, all his students are obligated** – הָרַב שֶׁנִּדָּה לִכְבוֹדוֹ חַיָּבִין כָּל תַּלְמִידָיו: *Shulḥan Arukh, Yoreh De'a* 334:15. However, other Torah scholars are not obligated to observe the terms of the ostracism (Rema), although some disagree with this ruling (*Shakh*).

2. **If a student ostracized someone for the sake of his own honor** – תַּלְמִיד שֶׁנִּדָּה לִכְבוֹד עַצְמוֹ: It is forbidden for a student to ostracize someone for the sake of his own honor in the presence of his rabbi, unless his rabbi grants him honor (*Shulḥan Arukh*).

3. **The rabbi is not obligated to observe the terms of the ostracism** – אֵין הָרַב חַיָּב לִנְהֹג בּוֹ נִדּוּי: Similarly, other Torah scholars, even those lesser than the student, are not obligated to observe the terms of the ostracism (Rema), but others say that anyone who is not greater than the student is obligated to observe the terms of the ostracism toward the one ostracized by the student. But all this applies only if the student is a Torah scholar worthy of ostracizing someone for the sake of his honor (*Shakh*).

4. **Similarly, one who was ostracized on behalf of the** ***Nasi*** – וְכֵן מְנֻדֶּה לַנָּשִׂיא: *Shulḥan Arukh, Yoreh De'a* 334:20–21.

5. **In what case is this statement said** – בַּמֶּה דְּבָרִים אֲמוּרִים: *Shulḥan Arukh, Yoreh De'a* 334:17.

עַל אַרְבָּעָה וְעֶשְׂרִים דְּבָרִים מְנַדִּין אֶת הָאָדָם, בֵּין אִישׁ בֵּין אִשָּׁה, וְאֵלּוּ הֵן: א) הַמְבַזֶּה אֶת הֶחָכָם, וַאֲפִלּוּ לְאַחַר מוֹתוֹ. ב) הַמְבַזֶּה שְׁלִיחַ בֵּית דִּין. ג) הַקּוֹרֵא לַחֲבֵרוֹ עֶבֶד. ד) הַמְזַלְזֵל בְּדָבָר אֶחָד מִדִּבְרֵי סוֹפְרִים, וְאֵין צָרִיךְ לוֹמַר בְּדִבְרֵי תּוֹרָה. ה) מִי שֶׁשָּׁלְחוּ לוֹ בֵּית דִּין וְקָבְעוּ לוֹ זְמַן וְלֹא בָּא. ו) מִי שֶׁלֹּא קִבֵּל עָלָיו אֶת הַדִּין – מְנַדִּין אוֹתוֹ עַד שֶׁיִּתֵּן.

A person, whether a man or a woman, may be ostracized for twenty-four matters,[1] and they are: 1) One who disgraces a Torah scholar,[a] even after his death; 2) One who disgraces an emissary of the court;[b] 3) One who calls another Jew a slave;[c] 4) One who treats any rabbinic law lightly,[2] and all the more so a Torah law; 5) One to whom the court sent a summons **and set a time** for him to appear before them **but he did not come;[d] 6) One who refused to accept the verdict** of a court,[e] **the court ostracizes him until he complies;**

ז) מִי שֶׁיֵּשׁ בִּרְשׁוּתוֹ דָּבָר הַמַּזִּיק כְּגוֹן כֶּלֶב רַע אוֹ סֻלָּם רָעוּעַ – מְנַדִּין אוֹתוֹ עַד שֶׁיָּסִיר הֶזֵּקוֹ. ח) הַמּוֹכֵר קַרְקַע שֶׁלּוֹ לְגוֹי – מְנַדִּין אוֹתוֹ עַד שֶׁיְּקַבֵּל עָלָיו כָּל אֹנֶס שֶׁיָּבֹא מִן הַגּוֹי לְיִשְׂרָאֵל חֲבֵרוֹ בַּעַל הַמֶּצֶר. ט) הַמֵּעִיד עַל יִשְׂרְאֵלִי בְּעַרְכָּאוֹת שֶׁל גּוֹיִם וְהוֹצִיא מִמֶּנּוּ בְּעֵדוּתוֹ מָמוֹן שֶׁלֹּא כְּדִין יִשְׂרָאֵל – מְנַדִּין אוֹתוֹ עַד שֶׁיְּשַׁלֵּם.

7) One who owns a dangerous thing such as a vicious dog[f] or a dilapidated ladder,[g] they ostracize him until he removes the danger; 8) One who sells his land to a gentile,[h] they ostracize him until he accepts upon himself all damage that may be caused by the gentile to his Jewish neighbor who owns the field **bordering** on his; **9) One who testifies against a Jew in a gentile court[i]** and thereby **causes him, through his testimony, to lose money against** the ruling of **Jewish law** in this case, **they ostracize him until he pays** for the loss;

י) טַבָּח כֹּהֵן שֶׁאֵינוֹ מַפְרִישׁ הַמַּתָּנוֹת וְנוֹתְנָן לְכֹהֵן אַחֵר – מְנַדִּין אוֹתוֹ עַד שֶׁיִּתֵּן. יא) הַמְחַלֵּל יוֹם טוֹב שֵׁנִי שֶׁל גָּלֻיּוֹת, אַף עַל פִּי שֶׁהוּא מִנְהָג. יב) הָעוֹשֶׂה מְלָאכָה בְּעֶרֶב הַפֶּסַח אַחַר חֲצוֹת. יג) הַמַּזְכִּיר שֵׁם שָׁמַיִם לְבַטָּלָה אוֹ לִשְׁבוּעָה בְּדִבְרֵי הֲבַאי. יד) הַמֵּבִיא אֶת הָרַבִּים לִידֵי חִלּוּל הַשֵּׁם.

10) A priest who is a **butcher, who does not separate the** priestly **gifts** from the meat he sells **and give them to another priest** as is required,[j] **they ostracize him until he gives** the priestly gifts; **11) One who desecrates the second day of a festival** observed **in the Diaspora,[k] even though this is** only **a custom; 12) One who does work on the eve of Passover after midday;[l] 13) One who invokes the name of Heaven in vain,[m] or in an oath with words of exaggeration; 14) One who causes the public to desecrate God's name;**

NOTES

a. See above, Halakhot 12–14.

b. *Hilkhot Sanhedrin* 25:5.

c. See *Hilkhot Teshuva* 3:14.

d. *Hilkhot Sanhedrin* 25:8.

e. *Hilkhot Malve VeLoveh* 22:3; *Hilkhot Toen VeNitan* 1:5; *Hilkhot Sanhedrin* 5:17, 25:11.

f. *Hilkhot Nizkei Mamon* 5:9.

g. *Hilkhot Rotze'aḥ UShmirat HaNefesh* 11:4.

h. *Hilkhot Shekhenim* 12:7.

i. *Hilkhot Sanhedrin* 26:7.

j. *Hilkhot Bikkurim* 9:9.

k. *Hilkhot Yom Tov* 1:22.

l. *Hilkhot Yom Tov* 8:17.

m. *Hilkhot Shevuot* 12:9–11.

HALAKHIC DISCUSSION

1. A person…may be ostracized for twenty-four matters – עַל אַרְבָּעָה וְעֶשְׂרִים דְּבָרִים מְנַדִּין אֶת הָאָדָם: *Shulḥan Arukh, Yoreh De'a* 334:43. To ostracize someone, it is not necessary for the court to receive clear testimony and evidence. Rather, it is sufficient for someone, even a woman or a minor, to make a definitive claim, if it seems reasonable to the court that the accusation is true (Rema). The *Shulḥan Arukh* (*Yoreh De'a* 334:44) adds additional cases for which one may be ostracized, and Torah scholars or community leaders are also permitted to impose ostracism or excommunication on one who transgresses their decrees (see the *Beur HaGola* at the end of the section, which lists a number of bans issued by various sages, and also see further elaboration in the appendix: "Ostracism and Excommunication"). It is customary that when a person transgresses the community's ordinance, they are not ostracized until the leaders of the community first publicly announce the impending ostracism (*Shulḥan Arukh, Yoreh De'a* 334:22).

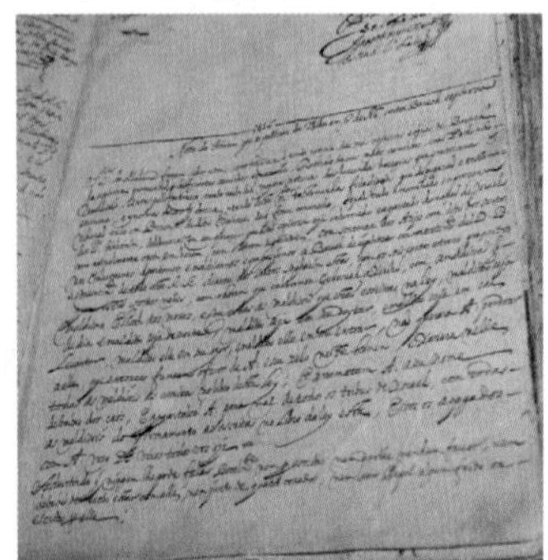

Letter from the leaders of the Amsterdam Jewish community announcing the ostracism of Benedict Spinoza, 1656

2. One who treats any rabbinic law lightly – הַמְזַלְזֵל בְּדָבָר אֶחָד מִדִּבְרֵי סוֹפְרִים: One who transgresses a rabbinic prohibition is liable to receive lashes. Some say that one is liable to be ostracized if they uproot a rabbinic prohibition regarding a matter that is fundamentally rabbinic in nature, but if one transgresses a rabbinic prohibition in a matter that is based on Torah law, they are liable to receive lashes for rebelliousness, and are not ostracized (*Shakh*).

טו) הַמֵּבִיא אֶת הָרַבִּים לִידֵי אֲכִילַת קָדָשִׁים בַּחוּץ. טז) הַמְחַשֵּׁב שָׁנִים וְקוֹבֵעַ חֳדָשִׁים בְּחוּצָה לָאָרֶץ. יז) הַמַּכְשִׁיל אֶת הָעִוֵּר. יח) הַמְעַכֵּב אֶת הָרַבִּים מִלַּעֲשׂוֹת מִצְוָה. יט) טַבָּח שֶׁיָּצְאָת טְרֵפָה מִתַּחַת יָדוֹ.

15) One who causes the public to eat sacrificial foods outside the Temple courtyard;[a] **16) One who calculates years and establishes new months outside the Land of Israel;**[b] **17) One who causes the blind to stumble,** which includes giving bad advice or causing a person to sin;[c] **18) One who inhibits the public from performing a mitzva;**[d] **19) A butcher who** allowed the meat of **an animal that had a wound that would cause it to die within twelve months [*tereifa*] to emerge from his possession** to the marketplace;[e]

כ) טַבָּח שֶׁלֹּא בָּדַק סַכִּינוֹ לִפְנֵי חָכָם. כא) הַמַּקְשֶׁה עַצְמוֹ לְדַעַת. כב) מִי שֶׁגֵּרֵשׁ אֶת אִשְׁתּוֹ וְעָשָׂה בֵּינוֹ וּבֵינָהּ שֻׁתָּפוּת אוֹ מַשָּׂא וּמַתָּן הַמְּבִיאִין לָהֶן לְהִזָּקֵק זֶה לָזֶה - כְּשֶׁיָּבֹאוּ שְׁנֵיהֶן לְבֵית דִּין מְנַדִּין אוֹתָם. כג) חָכָם שֶׁשְּׁמוּעָתוֹ רָעָה. כד) הַמְנַדֶּה מִי שֶׁאֵינוֹ חַיָּב נִדּוּי.

20) A ritual slaughterer who did not check his knife before a Torah scholar;[f] **21) One who intentionally causes himself to have an erection;**[g] **22) One who divorced his wife and** then **made a partnership** with her **or business dealings between them that lead them to interact with each other,**[h] **when they both come to the court, they ostracize them; 23) A Torah scholar who has a bad reputation;**[i] and **24) One who ostracizes someone who is not liable for ostracism,** as he has abused the power of ostracism.

GLOSSES OF THE RAAVAD

"עַל אַרְבָּעָה וְעֶשְׂרִים דְּבָרִים מְנַדִּין אֶת הָאָדָם בֵּין אִישׁ בֵּין אִשָּׁה וְאֵלּוּ וְכוּ׳ הַמַּכְשִׁיל אֶת הָעִוֵּר." אָמַר אַבְרָהָם: כְּגוֹן הַמַּכֶּה הַבֵּן הַגָּדוֹל.

"A person, whether a man or a woman, may be ostracized for twenty-four matters, and they are... one who causes the blind to stumble." Avraham says: **For example, one who strikes his adult son,** as the son may become angry and hit his father, or respond in a manner that is disrespectful to him.

"חָכָם שֶׁשְּׁמוּעָתוֹ רָעָה." אָמַר אַבְרָהָם: וְיֵשׁ אֲחֵרִים הַרְבֵּה: חָכָם שֶׁהוֹרָה לְהַתִּיר בְּמַיִם שֶׁאֵין לָהֶם סוֹף לִנָּשֵׂא לְכַתְּחִלָּה (בבלי יבמות קכא,א; וראה הלכות גירושין יג,כ), וְכֵן מִי שֶׁעוֹבֵר עַל נִדְרוֹ כָּל בֵּית דִּין שֶׁנִּזְקָק לוֹ לִשְׁאֵלָה - בַּר שַׁמְתָּא הוּא (בבלי נדרים כ,א; וראה הלכות נזירות ד,טז), וְאִיכָּא טוּבָא.

"A Torah scholar who has a bad reputation." Avraham says: **There are also many others** in this category, such as: **A scholar who permitted a woman** whose husband had disappeared **in an endless body of water** to remarry ***ab initio*** (*Yevamot* 121a; see also *Hilkhot Geirushin* 13:20), **and similarly, one who violates his vow; any court that attends to his request** to dissolve his vow **is worthy of ostracism** (*Nedarim* 20a; see *Hilkhot Nezirut* 4:16), **and there are many** other such cases.

"מִי שֶׁמְּנַדֶּה מִי שֶׁאֵין חַיָּב בְּנִדּוּי." אָמַר אַבְרָהָם: דָּבָר זֶה הוֹצִיא מִמַּעֲשֶׂה דְּרֵישׁ לָקִישׁ דַּהֲוָה מִנְטַר פַּרְדֵּסָא וְכוּ׳ אָמַר לֵיהּ הַהוּא אַדְּרַבָּה, וְאָמַר לֵיהּ שֶׁלּוֹ נִדּוּי (בבלי מועד קטן יז,א).

"One who ostracizes someone who is not liable for ostracism." Avraham says: **This matter was derived from an incident regarding Reish Lakish, who was guarding an orchard,** and a certain man came and ate figs from the orchard. Reish Lakish ordered him to stop, but he kept eating, and Reish Lakish then imposed ostracism upon him. **That person** then **said to him: "On the contrary,** you are ostracized," **and** when Reish Lakish inquired about this in the study hall, they **told him that his** adversary's **ostracism was** valid (*Moed Katan* 17a).

NOTES

a. *Hilkhot Ḥametz UMatza* 8:11.

b. *Hilkhot Kiddush HaḤodesh* 1:8.

c. *Hilkhot Rotze'aḥ UShmirat HaNefesh* 12:14; see also *Hilkhot Mamrim* 6:9.

d. *Hilkhot Teshuva* 4:1.

e. *Hilkhot Sheḥita* 10:14; *Hilkhot Maakhalot Asurot* 8:9. It is the responsibility of the butcher to ensure that forbidden meat does not unknowingly reach consumers who would believe it to be permitted.

f. *Hilkhot Sheḥita* 1:26.

g. *Hilkhot Issurei Bia* 21:18–19.

h. *Hilkhot Issurei Bia* 21:27.

i. See below, 7:1.

וּבְחַיֵּי רֹאשִׁי אֵין כָּאן פִּלְפּוּל, כִּי הַדְּבָרִים שֶׁהוּא מוֹנֶה בֵּית דִּין צְרִיכִין לְנַדּוֹתוֹ, וּבְכִי הַאי גַּוְנָא לֹא הָיוּ בֵּית דִּין נִזְקָקִין לְנַדּוֹתוֹ לְר׳ שִׁמְעוֹן בֶּן לָקִישׁ, אֲבָל אוֹתוֹ שֶׁנִּדָּה וְהִקְפִּיד עַל כְּבוֹדוֹ נִדּוּיוֹ נִדּוּי

And by my life, this derivation, from the incident regarding Reish Lakish, **is not valid, since the matters he,** the Rambam, **has been listing are matters for which the court is required to impose ostracism – but in such a case the court would not have ostracized Reish Lakish.** Therefore, this should not be included in the list of matters for which one is liable to receive ostracism. **Rather,** in that case, **the one who ostracized him** did so because he **was zealous about his own honor,** and in such a situation **his ostracism is valid.**

פֶּרֶק שְׁבִיעִי

CHAPTER 7

Ostracism and Excommunication

Halakha 1

חָכָם זָקֵן בְּחָכְמָה, וְכֵן נָשִׂיא אוֹ אַב בֵּית דִּין שֶׁסָּרַח – אֵין מְנַדִּין אוֹתוֹ בְּפַרְהֶסְיָא לְעוֹלָם, אֶלָּא אִם כֵּן עָשָׂה כְּיָרָבְעָם בֶּן נְבָט וַחֲבֵרָיו.

Concerning **a sage** who is **advanced in wisdom, the** ***Nasi*****, or the president of the court, who have gone astray,**[1] the court **should not publicly ostracize** any of these individuals, due to the desecration of God's name that would result, **unless he had acted like Yorovam son of Nevat, or others like him,** who not only sinned, but also caused the public to sin.[a]

אֲבָל כְּשֶׁחָטָא שְׁאָר חֲטָאוֹת – מַלְקִין אוֹתוֹ בִּצְנִעָה, שֶׁנֶּאֱמַר: "וְכָשַׁלְתָּ הַיּוֹם וְכָשַׁל גַּם נָבִיא עִמְּךָ לָיְלָה" (הושע ד, ה) – אַף עַל פִּי שֶׁכָּשַׁל, כַּסֵּהוּ כַּלַּיְלָה. וְאוֹמְרִין לוֹ: 'הִכָּבֵד וְשֵׁב בְּבֵיתֶךָ'.

But if he had committed other, less severe **sins, he should be flogged in private** without publicizing the matter, **as it is stated: "You stumble by day, and the prophet also stumbles with you by night"** (Hosea 4:5), meaning that **even though he stumbled,** you should **conceal his** punishment **as the night** is concealed. **They also say to him:** "Preserve **your honor and stay at home,"**[b] to avoid coming into contact with people.

NOTES

a. *Hilkhot Teshuva* 3:10; see also *Hilkhot Kelei HaMikdash* 4:21, regarding demoting a person from his position if he has gone astray.

b. See II Kings 14:10.

HALAKHIC DISCUSSION

1. A sage who is advanced in wisdom, the *Nasi*, or the president of the court, who have gone astray – חָכָם זָקֵן בְּחָכְמָה, וְכֵן נָשִׂיא אוֹ אַב בֵּית דִּין שֶׁסָּרַח: *Shulḥan Arukh, Yoreh De'a* 334:42.

וְכֵן כָּל תַּלְמִיד חֲכָמִים שֶׁנִּתְחַיֵּב נִדּוּי – אָסוּר לְבֵית דִּין לִקְפֹּץ וּלְנַדּוֹתוֹ בִּמְהֵרָה, אֶלָּא בּוֹרְחִין מִדָּבָר זֶה וְנִשְׁמָטִין מִמֶּנּוּ. וַחֲסִידֵי הַחֲכָמִים הָיוּ מִשְׁתַּבְּחִין שֶׁלֹּא נִמְנוּ מֵעוֹלָם לְנַדּוֹת תַּלְמִיד חֲכָמִים,

Similarly, regarding **any Torah scholar liable to receive ostracism, the court is prohibited from hastily ostracizing him** without first engaging in careful and lengthy deliberation. **Rather,** they should **distance themselves from this matter and avoid it** as much as possible. **The pious sages** who served on courts **would boast that they never** allowed themselves **to be counted among those who ostracized Torah scholars.**[1]

אַף עַל פִּי שֶׁנִּמְנִין לְהַלְקוֹתוֹ אִם נִתְחַיֵּב מַלְקוּת. וַאֲפִלּוּ מַכַּת מַרְדּוּת נִמְנִין עָלֶיהָ לְהַכּוֹתוֹ.

This is true **even though they would be counted** among those who sentenced such a scholar to be **flogged if he was liable for flogging,**[a] since this is a Torah obligation, **and they would be counted** among those who sentenced a Torah scholar to be **flogged even** if he was liable only to receive **lashes for rebelliousness,** which are administered to individuals who violated rabbinic ordinances. The pious sages attempted to refrain from ostracizing Torah scholars, but not from punishing them for their misdeeds according to the law.

Halakha 2

וְכֵיצַד הוּא הַנִּדּוּי? אוֹמְרִין: 'פְּלוֹנִי בְּשַׁמְתָּא'. וְאִם נִדּוּהוּ בְּפָנָיו, אוֹמְרִין: 'פְּלוֹנִי זֶה'. וְהַחֵרֶם – אוֹמְרִין: 'פְּלוֹנִי מֻחְרָם'. וְאָרוּר – בּוֹ אָלָה, בּוֹ שְׁבוּעָה, בּוֹ נִדּוּי.

How is ostracism performed? The members of the court **say: "So-and-so is ostracized." If the ostracism is performed in his presence, they say: "This so-and-so,"** indicating that they are referring specifically to him, "is ostracized." **And for an excommunication,** [*ḥerem*], which is more severe than ostracism [*niduy*],[b] **they say: "So-and-so is excommunicated."** The word **'cursed'** [*arur*] can also be used, as it has multiple meanings; it **can denote a curse, an oath, or excommunication.**[c]

Halakha 3

וְכֵיצַד מַתִּירִין הַנִּדּוּי אוֹ הַחֵרֶם? אוֹמְרִין לוֹ: 'שָׁרוּי לְךָ וּמָחוּל לְךָ'. וְאִם הִתִּירוּהוּ שֶׁלֹּא בְּפָנָיו, אוֹמְרִין: 'פְּלוֹנִי שָׁרוּי לוֹ וּמָחוּל לוֹ'.

How is ostracism or excommunication revoked?[2] The members of the court **say to him: "You are released, and you are forgiven." If they revoke** the ostracism or excommunication when they are **not in his presence, they say: "So-and-so is released and forgiven."**

Halakha 4

מַה הוּא הַמִּנְהָג שֶׁיִּנְהֹג הַמְנֻדֶּה בְּעַצְמוֹ וְשֶׁנּוֹהֲגִין עִמּוֹ? מְנֻדֶּה אָסוּר לְסַפֵּר וּלְכַבֵּס כְּאָבֵל כָּל יְמֵי נִדּוּיוֹ,

How should one who has been ostracized conduct himself,[3] i.e., what activities are prohibited to him, **and how should** others **conduct themselves toward him? One who has been ostracized is forbidden to get a haircut or wash** his clothing, **similar to** the restrictions observed by **a mourner,**[d] **for the entire period of his ostracism.**[4]

HALAKHIC DISCUSSION

1. **The pious sages would boast that they never ostracized Torah scholars** – וַחֲסִידֵי הַחֲכָמִים הָיוּ מִשְׁתַּבְּחִין שֶׁלֹּא נִמְנוּ מֵעוֹלָם לְנַדּוֹת תַּלְמִיד חֲכָמִים: However, if negative rumors spread about the scholar, such as accusations of studying heretical books or drinking at inappropriate musical celebrations, or if his colleagues were embarrassed by him because God's name had been desecrated due to his conduct, they should ostracize him (*Shulḥan Arukh*).

2. **How is ostracism or excommunication revoked** – וְכֵיצַד מַתִּירִין הַנִּדּוּי אוֹ הַחֵרֶם: *Shulḥan Arukh, Yoreh De'a* 334:23.

3. **How should one who has been ostracized conduct himself** – מַה הוּא הַמִּנְהָג שֶׁיִּנְהֹג הַמְנֻדֶּה: *Shulḥan Arukh, Yoreh De'a* 334:2–4.

4. **Forbidden to get a haircut or wash his clothing, similar to a mourner, for the entire period of his ostracism** – אָסוּר לְסַפֵּר וּלְכַבֵּס כְּאָבֵל כָּל יְמֵי נִדּוּיוֹ: The *Shulḥan Arukh* states that it is also forbidden for him to wear shoes. However, the *Shakh* indicates that the accepted practice is to permit an ostracized person to wear shoes, and that the other practices of mourning also do not apply to him. One who is only partially excommunicated (as discussed above, 6:13) is allowed to get a haircut, wash his clothing, and wear shoes (*Shulḥan Arukh, Yoreh De'a* 334:12), but people should distance themselves from him to shame him (*Arukh HaShulḥan*).

NOTES

a. See *Hilkhot Sanhedrin* Chapters 16–19.

b. See Halakha 4.

c. See *Hilkhot Shevuot* 2:2; *Hilkhot Sanhedrin* 26:3.

d. See *Hilkhot Evel* 5:1–3.

וְאֵין מְזַמְּנִין עָלָיו, וְלֹא כּוֹלְלִין אוֹתוֹ בַּעֲשָׂרָה לְכָל דָּבָר שֶׁצָּרִיךְ עֲשָׂרָה, וְלֹא יוֹשְׁבִין עִמּוֹ בְּאַרְבַּע אַמּוֹת. אֲבָל שׁוֹנֶה הוּא לַאֲחֵרִים, וְשׁוֹנִין לוֹ, וְנִשְׂכָּר, וְשׂוֹכֵר.

He also **may not be invited** by others to participate in the joint recitation of Grace after Meals [*zimmun*],[1] as he cannot be a member of the quorum of three required to recite this formula, **nor may he be counted as part of the** quorum of **ten** men **for any matter that requires ten.**[2] Also, **no one may sit within four cubits of him.**[3] **However, he may teach** Torah to **others, and others may teach** Torah to **him, and he may be hired** as a laborer **or hire others** to work for him.

וְאִם מֵת בְּנִדּוּיוֹ – בֵּית דִּין שׁוֹלְחִין וּמַנִּיחִין אֶבֶן עַל אֲרוֹנוֹ, כְּלוֹמַר שֶׁהֵן רוֹגְמִין אוֹתוֹ, לְפִי שֶׁהוּא מֻבְדָּל מִן הַצִּבּוּר. וְאֵין צָרִיךְ לוֹמַר שֶׁאֵין מַסְפִּידִין אוֹתוֹ וְאֵין מְלַוִּין אֶת מִטָּתוֹ.

If he dies in a state of ostracism, the court sends an emissary **to place a stone on his coffin, meaning that they** symbolically **stone him, since he had been separated from the community.**[4] And, **needless to say, he is not** to be **eulogized**[5] **and his bier** should **not be accompanied** to burial, as he is not to be respected in any way.

Halakha 5

יָתֵר עָלָיו הַמֻּחְרָם – שֶׁאֵינוֹ שׁוֹנֶה לַאֲחֵרִים וְאֵין שׁוֹנִין לוֹ. אֲבָל שׁוֹנֶה הוּא לְעַצְמוֹ כְּדֵי שֶׁלֹּא יִשְׁכַּח תַּלְמוּדוֹ. וְאֵינוֹ נִשְׂכָּר, וְאֵין נִשְׂכָּרִין לוֹ, וְאֵין נוֹשְׂאִין וְנוֹתְנִין עִמּוֹ, וְאֵין מִתְעַסְּקִין עִמּוֹ אֶלָּא מְעַט עֵסֶק כְּדֵי פַּרְנָסָתוֹ.

One who has been excommunicated is subject to more **extensive** restrictions[6] **compared to** one who was ostracized. **He may not teach** Torah to others, **and** others **may not teach** Torah to **him. However, he** may **study** Torah by **himself, so that he does not forget his learning. He may not be hired by others, and others may not be hired by him.** Similarly, others **may not conduct business transactions with him, except for a minimal amount of business** that suffices for his sustenance.

HALAKHIC DISCUSSION

1. **May not be invited by others to participate in the joint recitation of Grace after Meals – וְאֵין מְזַמְּנִין עָלָיו**: According to the *Shulḥan Arukh* (*Yoreh De'a* 334:2, 10–11), only one who has been ostracized as a sinner may not be included in a *zimmun* or a quorum of ten, but one who has been ostracized due to a monetary matter may be included, unless the court explicitly prohibited including him in a *zimmun* or quorum of ten as part of his ostracism (see *Shakh* and *Arukh HaShulḥan* 334:11). Even a sinner or one who violated a communal decree may be included in a quorum of ten unless this was explicitly included in his ostracism (Rema, *Taz*, and *Arukh HaShulḥan*, *Yoreh De'a* 334:8).

2. **Nor may he be counted as part of the quorum of ten men for any matter that requires ten – וְלֹא כּוֹלְלִין אוֹתוֹ בַּעֲשָׂרָה לְכָל דָּבָר שֶׁצָּרִיךְ עֲשָׂרָה**: It is technically permitted to pray with the ostracized person in the synagogue. However, it is customary to expel him to avoid crowding, as people must maintain a distance of four cubits from him (Rema).

3. **No one may sit within four cubits of him – וְלֹא יוֹשְׁבִין עִמּוֹ בְּאַרְבַּע אַמּוֹת**: This applies to all people other than his wife and children (*Shulḥan Arukh*) and other members of his household. It is forbidden to stand within four cubits of one who is ostracized, and it is similarly forbidden to enter his home, as the entire home is considered equivalent to four cubits. If one who is ostracized enters within four cubits of someone else, that person need not move (Rema).

HALAKHIC DISCUSSION

4. **Since he had been separated from the community – לְפִי שֶׁהוּא מֻבְדָּל מִן הַצִּבּוּר**: The *Shulḥan Arukh* states that if the individual was ostracized due to a monetary matter, the ostracism is revoked after his death. Hence, he should be properly eulogized, and his coffin should not be symbolically stoned. If one who had been ostracized repented, but the ostracism had not yet been revoked, even if he had been ostracized for transgressing the pronouncements of the Sages, he is to be granted an ordinary burial.

5. **Needless to say, he is not to be eulogized – וְאֵין צָרִיךְ לוֹמַר שֶׁאֵין מַסְפִּידִין אוֹתוֹ**: Similarly, his relatives should not rend their garments or bare their shoulders in mourning over him (*Shulḥan Arukh*). However, those attending the burial do stand in a row and console the mourners, and he is buried in ordinary shrouds (*Taz*).

6. **One who has been excommunicated is subject to more extensive restrictions – יָתֵר עָלָיו הַמֻּחְרָם**: *Shulḥan Arukh*, *Yoreh De'a* 334:2. It is permitted to speak with the one who is excommunicated, as long as the court did not explicitly impose this additional stringency upon him (*Shulḥan Arukh*). However, one should speak with him only as much as necessary, and should not engage in excessive speech with him, as one does with a mourner (Rema).

Halakha 6

מִי שֶׁיָּשַׁב בְּנִדּוּיוֹ שְׁלֹשִׁים יוֹם וְלֹא בִקֵּשׁ לְהַתִּירוֹ – מְנַדִּין אוֹתוֹ שְׁנִיָּה. יָשַׁב שְׁלֹשִׁים יוֹם אֲחֵרִים וְלֹא בִקֵּשׁ לְהַתִּירוֹ – מַחֲרִימִין אוֹתוֹ.

Regarding **one who remains in his** state of **ostracism for thirty days,**[1] which is the standard duration of an ostracism,[a] **and does not ask to have it revoked,**[2] the court **ostracizes him a second** time. If **he remains** in his state of ostracism for **another thirty days and** still **does not ask to have it revoked,** the members of the court **excommunicate him.**

Halakha 7

בְּכַמָּה מַתִּירִין הַנִּדּוּי אוֹ הַחֵרֶם? בִּשְׁלֹשָׁה, אֲפִלּוּ הֶדְיוֹטוֹת. וְיָחִיד מֻמְחֶה מַתִּיר הַנִּדּוּי לְבַדּוֹ. וְיֵשׁ לְתַלְמִיד לְהַתִּיר הַנִּדּוּי אוֹ הַחֵרֶם, וַאֲפִלּוּ בִּמְקוֹם הָרַב.

How many judges are necessary for the court to **revoke** an **ostracism or excommunication**[3] after the one who was ostracized has repented his actions?[b] This can be done **with three** judges, **even if** they are simple **laymen,**[c] **and a single** judge who is an **expert** on Torah law[d] may **revoke the ostracism alone. A student has** the authority **to revoke ostracism or excommunication, even in proximity to** his **teacher.** This is in contradistinction to the dissolution of a vow or an oath, which a student is permitted to perform only with the permission of his teacher.[e]

GLOSSES OF THE RAAVAD

"בְּכַמָּה מַתִּירִין הַנִּדּוּי אוֹ הַחֵרֶם בִּשְׁלֹשָׁה הֶדְיוֹטוֹת וְיָחִיד מֻמְחֶה מַתִּיר הַנִּדּוּי לְבַדּוֹ." אָמַר אַבְרָהָם: אֵינוֹ כֵּן, אֶלָּא כְּחֶשְׁבּוֹן הַמְנַדִּין כֵּן צָרִיךְ הַמַּתִּירִין וְכַחֲשִׁיבוּתָן. וְאֶפְשָׁר כָּל זֶה כְּשֶׁיִּרְצוּ לְהַתִּירוֹ תּוֹךְ זְמַן הַנֶּדֶר, אֲבָל כְּשֶׁיִּשְׁלַם הַזְּמַן כָּל שְׁלֹשָׁה אוֹ יָחִיד מֻמְחֶה מַתִּירִים לוֹ.

"**How many judges are necessary to revoke ostracism or excommunication? Three judges, even if they are simple laymen, or a single expert judge.**" **Avraham says: This is not correct. Rather, the number and stature** of the judges **revoking** the ostracism must be **equivalent to** those who originally **ostracized** the person. **It is possible,** though, **that this** applies only **when** the court **wishes to revoke** the ostracism **within the** originally **specified period, but when the period** of ostracism **is complete, any three** judges **or a single expert** judge **may revoke it for him.**

אִי נַמִּי כְּשֶׁנִּדָּהוּ יָחִיד וַאֲפִלּוּ אֵינוֹ מֻמְחֶה עַל דְּבַר עֲבֵרָה, וּכְשֶׁיִּשְׁלַם לוֹ הַזְּמַן מַתִּירִים לוֹ כָּל שְׁלֹשָׁה אוֹ יָחִיד מֻמְחֶה. אֲבָל נִדּוּהוּ רַבִּים צְרִיכִין רַבִּים כְּמוֹתָם לְהַתִּירוֹ.

Alternatively, it is possible that **where an individual, even a non-expert, ostracized him due to a sin** that he committed, **when the period** of ostracism **is complete, any three** judges **or a single expert** judge may **revoke it for him. But if a number** of judges originally **ostracized him, an equivalent number is necessary to revoke** the ostracism.

HALAKHIC DISCUSSION

1. **One who remains in his state of ostracism for thirty days** – מִי שֶׁיָּשַׁב בְּנִדּוּיוֹ שְׁלֹשִׁים יוֹם: *Shulḥan Arukh, Yoreh De'a* 334:1, 13–14. The default duration of a period of ostracism is thirty days, but if the court chooses to reduce or increase this period, they have the authority to do so (*Shulḥan Arukh* 334:6).

2. **Did not ask to have it revoked** – וְלֹא בִקֵּשׁ לְהַתִּירוֹ: The *Shulḥan Arukh* states that if one was ostracized due to a monetary matter, or because he acted in an insolent manner toward a Torah scholar, and he then repented and appeased his adversary or the scholar, the members of the court revoke his ostracism immediately. However, the Rema says that they do not revoke his ostracism until the thirty-day period has passed (see *Taz* 334:6, which disagrees). The *Shulḥan Arukh* also records an opinion that if he did not repent, the court nevertheless revokes his ostracism after thirty days if he so requests, while others hold that they do not revoke the ostracism until he repents.

3. **How many judges are necessary for the court to revoke an ostracism or excommunication** – בְּכַמָּה מַתִּירִין הַנִּדּוּי אוֹ הַחֵרֶם: *Shulḥan Arukh, Yoreh De'a* 334:24. If the ostracism or the excommunication is not explicitly revoked, it remains in effect even long after the originally-specified period (Rema).

NOTES

a. See also *Hilkhot To'en VeNitan* 1:5; *Hilkhot Sanhedrin* 25:11.

b. See below, 9, 13; and above 6:12.

c. Laymen who are not expert judges may form ad hoc courts for the purpose of ostracism or excommunication, especially if they are leaders of the community.

d. See *Hilkhot Shevuot* 6:1.

e. *Hilkhot Shevuot* 6:3.

Halakha 9

In the standard printed editions there is no Halakha 8. For consistency, we have maintained this numbering.

שְׁלֹשָׁה שֶׁנִּדּוּ וְהָלְכוּ לָהֶן, וְחָזַר זֶה מִדָּבָר שֶׁנִּדּוּהוּ בִּגְלָלוֹ – בָּאִין שְׁלֹשָׁה אֲחֵרִים וּמַתִּירִין לוֹ.

In a case **where three** judges **ostracized** someone **and then left,**[1] **and this** one who was ostracized **repented** and corrected **the matter for which they had ostracized him, three other** judges **come and revoke** the ostracism **for him;**[2] it is not necessary for the judges who originally ostracized him to personally revoke the ostracism.

Halakha 10

מִי שֶׁלֹּא יָדַע מִי נִדָּהוּ – יֵלֵךְ אֵצֶל הַנָּשִׂיא וְיַתִּיר לוֹ נִדּוּיוֹ.

One who has been ostracized and **does not know who ostracized him** and therefore is unable to go to him to have the ostracism revoked **should go to the *Nasi* so he can revoke his ostracism.**

Halakha 11

נִדּוּי עַל תְּנַאי, אֲפִלּוּ מִפִּי עַצְמוֹ – צָרִיךְ הֲפָרָה. תַּלְמִיד חֲכָמִים שֶׁנִּדָּה עַצְמוֹ, וַאֲפִלּוּ נִדָּה עַצְמוֹ עַל דַּעַת פְּלוֹנִי, וַאֲפִלּוּ עַל דָּבָר שֶׁחַיָּב עָלָיו נִדּוּי – הֲרֵי זֶה מֵפֵר לְעַצְמוֹ.

Conditional ostracism,[3] meaning ostracism that was imposed but will only take effect on the condition that a certain event will occur, **even if** the individual conditionally **ostracized himself, requires nullification,**[4] regardless of whether the condition was fulfilled. **A Torah scholar who ostracized himself,**[5] **even if he ostracized himself on the** condition that **such-and-such** a sage agreed to the ostracism, **and even** if he did so **for a matter for which he was liable** to be **ostracized,**[a] **may nullify his own** ostracism.[6]

GLOSSES OF THE RAAVAD

"תַּלְמִיד חָכָם שֶׁנִּדָּה עַצְמוֹ וַאֲפִלּוּ נִדָּה עַצְמוֹ לְדַעַת פְּלוֹנִי." אָמַר אַבְרָהָם: זֶה אֵינוֹ מְחֻוָּר. אִם כֵּן יְהוּדָה לָמָּה לֹא הֵפֵר לְעַצְמוֹ, וְעִם כָּל זֶה קָשֶׁה לִי יַעֲקֹב לָמָּה לֹא הִתִּירוֹ

"A Torah scholar who ostracized himself, even if he ostracized himself on the condition that such-and-such a sage agreed to the ostracism, may nullify his own ostracism." Avraham says: This is not clear; if this position **is correct, why did Yehuda,** who ostracized himself due to his failure to fulfill his guarantee to bring Binyamin back to his father, **not nullify his own** ostracism? **Yet** in any case **it is also difficult for me** to understand **why Yaakov did not revoke** Yehuda's ostracism.

HALAKHIC DISCUSSION

1. **Three judges ostracized someone and then left – שְׁלֹשָׁה שֶׁנִּדּוּ וְהָלְכוּ לָהֶן**: *Shulḥan Arukh, Yoreh De'a* 334:25.

2. **Three other judges come – בָּאִין שְׁלֹשָׁה אֲחֵרִים**: Some say that the judges revoking the ostracism must be as great in wisdom, fear of God, importance, and age, as those who originally ostracized him (*Shulḥan Arukh*; see also the glosses of the Raavad on Halakha 7). However, if they come to revoke the ostracism after the completion of the period originally set, any three judges or a single expert judge is sufficient (*Shakh* in the name of Raavad).

3. **Conditional ostracism – נִדּוּי עַל תְּנַאי**: *Shulḥan Arukh, Yoreh De'a* 334:30.

4. **Even if the individual ostracized himself, it requires nullification – אֲפִלּוּ מִפִּי עַצְמוֹ צָרִיךְ הֲפָרָה**: This is true even if he fulfilled the condition that would prevent the ostracism from taking effect. But if it was clear to the one who was ostracized at the time of the imposition of the condition that he would be able to fulfill his condition, no revocation of the ostracism is required (*Shulḥan Arukh*).

5. **A Torah scholar who ostracized himself – תַּלְמִיד חֲכָמִים שֶׁנִּדָּה עַצְמוֹ**: *Shulḥan Arukh, Yoreh De'a* 334:33.

6. **Even for a matter for which he was liable to be ostracized, he may nullify his own ostracism – וַאֲפִלּוּ עַל דָּבָר שֶׁחַיָּב עָלָיו נִדּוּי הֲרֵי זֶה מֵפֵר לְעַצְמוֹ**: Some say that he cannot revoke it for himself if he was liable to be ostracized, or if he ostracized himself utilizing an oath (*Shulḥan Arukh*).

NOTES

a. See above, 6:14.

Halakha 12

מִי שֶׁנִּדּוּהוּ בַּחֲלוֹם, אֲפִלּוּ יָדַע מִי נִדָּהוּ – צָרִיךְ עֲשָׂרָה בְּנֵי אָדָם שֶׁשּׁוֹנִין הֲלָכוֹת לְהַתִּירוֹ מִנִּדּוּיוֹ. וְאִם לֹא מָצָא – טוֹרֵחַ אַחֲרֵיהֶם עַד פַּרְסָה.

One who was ostracized in a dream,[1] and thus should be concerned that the dream is a divine sign that he is under rebuke, and requires atonement to lift the divinely-imposed ostracism, **even if he knows** the person **who ostracized him** in his dream, nevertheless **requires ten men who study halakhot to revoke his ostracism. If he cannot find** such men, **he** must **exert himself** and search for **them up to a parasang,** equivalent to approximately four kilometers, a standard limit for a person to travel to fulfill an obligation.[a]

לֹא מָצָא – מַתִּירִין לוֹ עֲשָׂרָה שֶׁשּׁוֹנִין מִשְׁנָה. לֹא מָצָא – מַתִּירִין לוֹ מִי שֶׁיּוֹדְעִין לִקְרוֹת בַּתּוֹרָה. לֹא מָצָא – מַתִּירִין לוֹ אֲפִלּוּ עֲשָׂרָה שֶׁאֵינָם יוֹדְעִין לִקְרוֹת. לֹא מָצָא בִּמְקוֹמוֹ עֲשָׂרָה – מַתִּירִין לוֹ אֲפִלּוּ שְׁלֹשָׁה.

If he walks this distance and still **cannot find** such men, he can **revoke his** ostracism **with** the participation of **ten** men **who study Mishna. If he cannot find** such men either, he can **revoke his** ostracism **with** the participation of men **who** merely **know how to read the Torah. If he cannot find** even men of this stature, **he** can **revoke his** ostracism **even with** the participation of **ten** men **who do not know how to read.**[2] **If he cannot find** even **ten** men **in his area, he** can **revoke his** ostracism **even with** the participation of **three** men, since this revocation is merely a request for divine mercy.

Halakha 13

מִי שֶׁנִּדּוּהוּ בְּפָנָיו – אֵין מַתִּירִין לוֹ אֶלָּא בְּפָנָיו. נִדּוּהוּ שֶׁלֹּא בְּפָנָיו – מַתִּירִין לוֹ בֵּין בְּפָנָיו בֵּין שֶׁלֹּא בְּפָנָיו. וְאֵין בֵּין נִדּוּי לַהֲפָרָה כְּלוּם, אֶלָּא מְנַדִּין וּמַתִּירִין בְּרֶגַע אֶחָד כְּשֶׁיַּחֲזֹר הַמְנֻדֶּה לְמוּטָב.

Concerning **one who was ostracized in his presence,**[3] his ostracism **may be revoked only in his presence.**[4] **If he was ostracized in absentia,** his ostracism **may be revoked either in his presence or in absentia. There is no** minimum amount of time that must pass **between ostracism and nullification**[5] of ostracism. **Rather, the** members of the court may **ostracize** him **and revoke his** ostracism **at the same moment, if the one who has been ostracized returns to good** behavior.

NOTES

a. See *Hilkhot Tefilla UVirkat Kohanim* 4:10; *Hilkhot Rotze'aḥ UShmirat HaNefesh* 13:5; and *Hilkhot Evel* 14:3.

HALAKHIC DISCUSSION

1. One who was ostracized in a dream – מִי שֶׁנִּדּוּהוּ בַּחֲלוֹם: *Shulḥan Arukh, Yoreh De'a* 334:35. Even if the ostracism was revoked in the dream, he nevertheless needs to go through a procedure to have his ostracism revoked (*Shulḥan Arukh*), since it is possible that the ostracism in the dream was truthful, but the revocation was an idle aspect of his dream (*Shakh*).

2. If he cannot find…even with the participation of ten men who do not know how to read – לֹא מָצָא מַתִּירִין לוֹ מִי שֶׁיּוֹדְעִין לִקְרוֹת בַּתּוֹרָה: Some say that his ostracism can be revoked only by ten men who study halakhot or *Mishna*, but they do not all need to revoke it at once. Rather, it is sufficient for them to do so sequentially (Rema).

3. One who was ostracized in his presence – מִי שֶׁנִּדּוּהוּ בְּפָנָיו: *Shulḥan Arukh, Yoreh De'a* 334:29.

4. May be revoked only in his presence – אֵין מַתִּירִין לוֹ אֶלָּא בְּפָנָיו: Some say that if the ostracism was revoked when he was not present, it is, in fact, revoked (Rema).

5. There is no minimum amount of time that must pass between ostracism and nullification – וְאֵין בֵּין נִדּוּי לַהֲפָרָה כְּלוּם: *Shulḥan Arukh, Yoreh De'a* 334:6–10.

וְאִם רָאוּ בֵּית דִּין לְהַנִּיחַ זֶה בְּנִדּוּיוֹ כַּמָּה שָׁנִים – מַנִּיחִין כְּפִי רִשְׁעוֹ. וְכֵן אִם רָאוּ בֵּית דִּין לְהַחֲרִים לָזֶה לְכַתְּחִלָּה, וּלְהַחֲרִים מִי שֶׁאוֹכֵל עִמּוֹ וְשׁוֹתֶה עִמּוֹ אוֹ מִי שֶׁיַּעֲמֹד עִמּוֹ בְּאַרְבַּע אַמּוֹת – מַחֲרִימִין, כְּדֵי לְיַסְּרוֹ וּכְדֵי לַעֲשׂוֹת סְיָג לַתּוֹרָה עַד שֶׁלֹּא יִפְרְצוּ הַחַטָּאִים.

If the court sees fit **to leave this** person **in his** state of **ostracism** even **for several years, they** may **leave him** as long as necessary, **according to his wickedness.**[1] **Similarly, if the court sees** fit **to excommunicate this** person **from the outset**[2] without first ostracizing him,[a] **or to** introduce stringencies that go beyond ordinary excommunication, such as to also **excommunicate anyone who eats with him, drinks with him, or stands within four cubits of him, they** may issue such decrees of **excommunication, in order to discipline** the individual **and to establish a safeguard for the Torah, so that sinners do not violate** its laws.

אַף עַל פִּי שֶׁיֵּשׁ רְשׁוּת לְחָכָם לְנַדּוֹת לִכְבוֹדוֹ, אֵינוֹ שֶׁבַח לְתַלְמִיד חֲכָמִים לְהַנְהִיג עַצְמוֹ בְּדָבָר זֶה, אֶלָּא מַעֲלִים אָזְנָיו מִדִּבְרֵי עַמֵּי הָאָרֶץ וְלֹא יָשִׁית לִבּוֹ לָהֶם, כְּעִנְיָן שֶׁאָמַר שְׁלֹמֹה בְּחָכְמָתוֹ: ״גַּם לְכָל הַדְּבָרִים אֲשֶׁר יְדַבֵּרוּ אַל תִּתֵּן לִבֶּךָ״ (קהלת ז, כא). וְכֵן הָיָה דֶּרֶךְ חֲסִידִים הָרִאשׁוֹנִים, שׁוֹמְעִין חֶרְפָּתָן וְאֵינָן מְשִׁיבִין.

Although a Torah **scholar has the authority to ostracize** people **to** protect **his** own **honor,**[3] **it is not** proper or **praiseworthy for Torah scholars to conduct themselves in this way.**[4] **Rather, they** should **ignore the words of the ignoramuses and pay no attention to them, as Solomon said in his** great **wisdom: "Also do not pay attention to all the matters that they speak"** (Ecclesiastes 7:21). **This** practice of not responding to insults and attacks **was** also **the way of the early pious ones: They would hear their disgrace and not respond,** disregarding concern for their personal honor and distancing themselves from anger.[b]

וְלֹא עוֹד, אֶלָּא שֶׁמּוֹחֲלִין לַמְחָרֵף וְסוֹלְחִין לוֹ. וַחֲכָמִים גְּדוֹלִים הָיוּ מִשְׁתַּבְּחִין בְּמַעֲשֵׂיהֶן הַנָּאִים וְאוֹמְרִין שֶׁמֵּעוֹלָם לֹא נִדּוּ אָדָם וְלֹא הֶחֱרִימוּהוּ לִכְבוֹדָן. וְזוֹ הִיא דַּרְכָּם שֶׁל תַּלְמִידֵי חֲכָמִים שֶׁרָאוּי לֵילֵךְ בָּהּ. בַּמֶּה דְּבָרִים אֲמוּרִים? בְּשֶׁבִּזּוּהוּ אוֹ חֵרְפוּהוּ בַּסֵּתֶר.

Not only that, but they would even **forgive the one who had disgraced them, and pardon him. The great sages would take pride in their proper deeds, declaring that they had never ostracized a person nor excommunicated him for** the sake of **their** own **honor, and this is the way that Torah scholars should act. In what** case **is this statement said? When they were disgraced or insulted in private.**

HALAKHIC DISCUSSION

1. **If the court sees fit to leave this person in his state of ostracism…they may leave him as long as necessary according to his wickedness – וְאִם רָאוּ בֵּית דִּין לְהַנִּיחַ זֶה בְּנִדּוּיוֹ כַּמָּה שָׁנִים מַנִּיחִין כְּפִי רִשְׁעוֹ:** The *Shulḥan Arukh* (*Yoreh De'a* 334:7) states that if the person who has been ostracized does not change his ways (according to the Taz, this means that he does not regret what he did and repent, even if he desists from continuing to offend) the court should not revoke his ostracism, so as not to diminish the effectiveness of their deterrence.

2. **If the court sees fit to excommunicate this person from the outset – וְכֵן אִם רָאוּ בֵּית דִּין לְהַחֲרִים לָזֶה לְכַתְּחִלָּה:** Similarly, the court has the authority to increase the stringency of the terms of excommunication, for example by refusing to bury a deceased relative of the one who has been excommunicated, or not to circumcise his son (*Shulḥan Arukh*, see also *Shakh*), or to expel his children from school or his wife from the synagogue, until he accepts the court's ruling (Rema; see also Taz, who expresses reservations about this ruling, and see *Arukh HaShulḥan* 334:6).

3. **Although a Torah scholar has the authority to ostracize people to protect his own honor – אַף עַל פִּי שֶׁיֵּשׁ רְשׁוּת לְחָכָם לְנַדּוֹת לִכְבוֹדוֹ:** *Tur, Yoreh De'a* 334.

NOTES

a. See above, Halakha 6.

b. See *Hilkhot Deot* 2:3, 5:13.

HALAKHIC DISCUSSION

4. **It is not praiseworthy for Torah scholars to conduct themselves in this way – אֵינוֹ שֶׁבַח לְתַלְמִיד חֲכָמִים לְהַנְהִיג עַצְמוֹ בְּדָבָר זֶה:** The later authorities mentioned additional reasons to hesitate from ostracizing people in contemporary times. For example, the *Shulḥan Arukh* (*Yoreh De'a* 334:48) rules that in a case where a person was ostracized because of a sin he had committed, but the civil ruler decreed a punishment against anyone who supported the ostracism, one is obligated to face the danger of potential punishment in order to strengthen Torah law. However, if the ostracism was decreed due to an interpersonal matter, one is not obligated to risk punishment. Furthermore, the Rema writes that although there is an obligation to protest against those who commit sins, one is not obligated to lose money for this purpose, and therefore it is common practice to be lenient, and not to protest against sinners, out of concern that they might cause bodily or monetary harm to the protesters. However, the authorities (see *Pitḥei Teshuva*) also said that in the absence of a clear and present danger, one should fulfill the mandate "You shall not fear due to any man" (Deuteronomy 1:17). The Rema (334:1) also writes that one should not refrain from ostracizing a person, even if there is concern that this will lead the one who was ostracized to go astray. Conversely, though, the *Taz* states that today, halakhic authorities generally hesitate to ostracize people due to the concern that this may lead the one who was ostracized to refrain from repenting (334:23; see also the additional considerations that he mentions). *Pitḥei Teshuva* quotes several authorities who disagree with the *Taz*. See appendix: "Ostracism and Excommunication."

אֲבָל תַּלְמִיד חֲכָמִים שֶׁבִּזָּהוּ אוֹ חֵרְפוֹ אָדָם בְּפַרְהֶסְיָא – נֶעֱנַשׁ, מִפְּנֵי שֶׁזֶּה בִּזָּיוֹן תּוֹרָה. אֶלָּא נוֹקֵם וְנוֹטֵר הַדָּבָר כְּנָחָשׁ, עַד שֶׁיְּבַקֵּשׁ מִמֶּנּוּ מְחִילָה, וְיִסְלַח לוֹ.

But if a Torah scholar was disgraced or insulted in public, it is prohibited for the Torah scholar to relinquish the honor due to him, and if he relinquishes it, **he is punished, because this is a desecration of the Torah** itself. **Rather, he** must **take vengeance and hold a grudge** against the offender **like a snake, until** the person **asks him for forgiveness, and he** should then **forgive him.**

בְּרִיךְ רַחֲמָנָא דְּסַיְּעַן

Blessed is the Merciful One, who has assisted us.

Appendices

Sefer HaMadda

Summaries

Hilkhot Yesodei HaTorah

The Scientific Description of the World in *Hilkhot Yesodei HaTorah*

The Rambam begins his *Mishne Torah* with a description of the Creation, stating that these lofty realms of knowledge are the ones which the Sages called the "Act of Creation" and the "Design of the Divine Chariot," (*Ḥagiga* 13a) and that they constitute the basis for loving and fearing God. This statement provoked a fierce debate among leading Torah scholars over the generations, concerning the relevance of these sciences to the worship of God, as well as the discrepancies between the Rambam's claims and the accepted views of the modern scientific community.

Martyrdom

The commandment to give up one's life for the sanctification of God's name has received much attention throughout Jewish history. The talmudic discussion of this subject was greatly developed during the period of the early authorities and afterward, with new questions receiving special focus. The authorities debate various issues, such as whether it is permitted to allow oneself to be killed even when there is no obligation to do so, and whether one may take his own life to avoid being handed over to gentiles.

Interring Printed Sacred Texts

The prohibition against erasing one of the names of God includes the obligation to preserve sacred writings from being desecrated and destroyed. After the invention of the printing press and the ensuing publication of large numbers of books, the authorities had to address various relevant questions in this regard: Is it possible to burn such books instead of interring them? What is the status of recycling containers with respect to interment? Finally, what should be done with newspapers that contain holy texts?

Hilkhot Deot

Medicine in the Talmud and in the Rambam

The treatments of diseases in ancient times, including the ones presented in the rabbinic sources, included many folk remedies such as incantations and the use of various substances. Over the generations, the extent to which these guidelines of the Sages should be accepted in practice was subject to debate, either because their knowledge on the subject was limited, or due to changes in the nature of the world. Likewise, the Rambam's statements in *Hilkhot Deot*, which include instructions on how to avoid illnesses, have been refined by the authorities and presented as recommendations alone, reflecting the best knowledge available at the time.

The Obligation to Wear a *Kippa*

Although the *kippa* is considered a symbol of the Torah-observant Jew, the source of the obligation to wear it is unclear. In this regard, the authorities differentiate between covering one's head when reciting holy texts and doing so on a regular basis, when going about one's daily business. They cite sources and present arguments for each of these situations, while discussing various other aspects of the obligation to cover one's head.

Hilkhot Talmud Torah

Torah Study for Women

For generations, the prevailing reality in Jewish tradition was that a woman's Torah education took place entirely within the home, and was limited to practical laws, matters of tradition, stories from the Written Torah, and ethical teachings. However, the sweeping changes of the modern world ushered in significant shifts in the scope of Torah study for women. Rabbinic opinions were divided over these developments. Authorities also had to grapple with determining which areas of study were suitable for women to pursue.

Earning a Livelihood from Torah Study

The Rambam expressed his extreme opposition to those who financed themselves through their Torah studies, viewing it as a desecration of God's name and an affront to the Torah itself. Subsequent rabbinic authorities, however, distanced themselves from this stance. They delineated boundaries and conditions under which receiving public compensation to be able to engage in Torah would be permissible. These later scholars also addressed the permissibility of accepting payment for teaching Torah, despite an apparent talmudic prohibition in doing so.

Ostracism and Excommunication

During the talmudic era, ostracism and excommunication were widely used as forms of punishment. These punishments prohibited contact with the excommunicated individual and isolated them from the community. Over time, their use transcended mere punitive measures, evolving into a mechanism for compelling adherence to newly enacted decrees. However, in recent centuries, the use of ostracism and excommunication has diminished due to changes in the social structure of the Jewish community and changes in the attitude of gentile governing authorities.

Appendices

Hilkhot Yesodei HaTorah

The Scientific Description of the World in *Hilkhot Yesodei HaTorah*

At the start of the second chapter of *Hilkhot Yesodei HaTorah*, the Rambam declares that the way to attain the love and fear of God is to reflect on His "wonderful, great deeds and creations." To this end, he devotes chapters 2–4 to a description of the structure of the universe, including some details on angels, astronomy (the "spheres"), and the basic forms of matter (the "four elements"). According to the Rambam, the topics of these chapters (along with chapter 1) are the "Design of the Divine Chariot" and the "Act of Creation," which together comprise the wisdom of the "*pardes*" (see 4:13).

However, the Rambam's scientific description in these chapters (especially chapters 3–4) is not in line with accepted modern scientific concepts. This leads to the question of how these claims should be treated, for the Rambam presented them at the very start of his *Mishne Torah*, and even treated them as important aspects of the foundational principles of the faith.

Already in the Rambam's own time many Sages rejected his opinions, and a significant proportion of these disputes, which were most acutely expressed in the "Maimonidean Controversy" in Spain, Provence, and other countries, focused on *Sefer HaMadda*. Indeed, a ban was placed in this period on studying *Sefer HaMadda* and the *Guide of the Perplexed*, and at the height of the controversy these works were even burned (see *Encyclopedia Ivrit*, vol. 24, pp. 558–560). It should be noted, however, that the controversies usually centered on the Rambam's worldview (which were considered an expression of foreign philosophy, mainly Aristotelian), not his scientific claims, which were probably viewed as established scientific assertions (except by Rabbi Hasdai Crescas in *Or Hashem*).

These proponents of these approaches, which continued throughout the generations, forcefully rejected many claims in *Sefer HaMadda*, including its scientific chapters. For example, the *Gra* objects to the Rambam's definitions of the "Act of Creation" and the "Design of the Divine Chariot" (*Beur HaGra* on *Shulḥan Arukh, Yoreh De'a* 246:18), while elsewhere he sharply criticizes statements of the Rambam in *Hilkhot Avoda Zara* (11:11), contending that "he was drawn after the accursed (Greek) philosophy" (*Beur HaGra* on *Shulḥan Arukh, Yoreh De'a* 179:13). Rabbi Tzadok HaKohen of Lublin also expressed reservations about the Rambam's worldview: "The Rambam, who explained the Act of Creation as referring to the natural sciences of created beings, found this useful in the service of God, may He be blessed, for loving and fearing Him. However, if this is true for him, it is not true for most of those who occupy themselves with these sciences, and he should not have established the knowledge of such topics as part of his *Hilkhot Yesodei HaTorah* at all. (For the) knowledge of such subjects is not required for Torah believers, especially since many of his claims are not true, according to [gentile] scholars of the current day. In sum, what is the connection between the words of the scholars of the nations of the world and the words of the Torah, which is from Heaven, that their claims should be made foundational principles of the Torah? ..." (*Sefer HaZikhronot*, Third Mitzva).

According to these opinions, the scientific content of these chapters in *Mishne* Torah is not a matter of halakha, but rather a description of the world according to the knowledge and views of the Rambam's time. These claims of the Rambam should not be treated as an integral part of the Torah and halakha, and consequently they are not undermined by new data and contemporary concepts.

A summary of this common attitude can be found in a statement of Rabbi Kapaḥ (in his commentary to the start of the third chapter of *Hilkhot Yesodei HaTorah*), which is based on a principle established by the Rambam himself in the *Guide of the Perplexed* (3:14). The Rambam wrote there that when it came to scientific topics, the opinions of the Sages were sometimes inaccurate because they did not have the complete scientific knowledge, and in those cases their knowledge was not part of the tradition of Israel (unlike the words of the prophets) but rather "they [themselves] were the [preeminent] scholars of those periods in these fields, or they learned them from the scholars of those periods," and therefore we should always prefer "the reality whose existence has been proven" (*Guide of the Perplexed* 3:14). Rabbi Kapaḥ further explains that the Rambam's claims in these chapters have no source or tradition in the words of the Sages, but are based on the scientific knowledge that existed at the time. Consequently, when scientific concepts change, one should not continue to remain loyal to the old concepts, "and this has nothing to do with the Jewish faith." In his view, there is a difference between assertions that are "truly a tradition of the Sages, [handed down] from one man to another," which must be maintained, and ideas that are not part of such a tradition, regarding which there is no problem with contesting them.

On the other end of the spectrum, the opinion of the Lubavitcher Rebbe is that all the Rambam's statements in *Mishne Torah* – even those that do not deal with practical mitzvot but instead describe the world – are halakhic rulings in every sense of the term, and are fixed, binding, and unchanging. In contrast, anything the Rambam wrote in his other works that are not halakhic, such as the *Guide of the Perplexed*, are not binding and eternal (see *Torat Menaḥem, Hitvaaduyot, Motza'i Shabbat Ḥayyei Sarah* 5739 [unedited], 34). According to this approach, the Rambam's statements in *Mishne Torah* originate from the Talmud and other words of the Sages, and therefore the source and root of all his claims on matters of science and nature, especially on issues as fundamental as the foundations of the faith, are necessarily from the words of the Sages. Accordingly, one must fully accept the views of the Rambam even when they contradict the findings of science (see *Ma Rabbu Maasekha Hashem*, pp. 29–30).

Without taking a side in this dispute, the basic guiding principle of the Rambam in his decision to include these topics at the beginning of his halakhic work is clear: For the Rambam, it is genuinely important from a religious and even a halakhic perspective to engage and delve into the science of the nature of the world. This is the best way, in his opinion, to fulfill the mitzvot of loving and fearing God.

Martyrdom

The Talmud and ruling authorities discuss in depth the case of a Jew who is forced by gentiles to violate a prohibition of the Torah. The basic rule laid out in the Talmud is that one may not transgress one of the three cardinal offenses: idolatry, forbidden sexual relations [*arayot*], and bloodshed, even if his life is in danger. He is commanded to be killed rather than commit the sin. One thereby fulfills the mitzva to sanctify God's name, which is derived from the verse: "And I shall be sanctified among the children of Israel" (Leviticus 22:32). With regard to all other prohibitions, however, a person should transgress and not be killed, in line with the halakhic rule that one should "live by them" (Leviticus 18:5) and not die by them. In other words, a mitzva should not be observed if it endangers one's life. Beyond these general rules, the Talmud and authorities provide other important distinctions, such as whether the incident occurred in private or in public, and whether the gentile is acting for his own pleasure or in order to force the Jew to violate mitzvot (see *Sanhedrin* 74a – 75a; *Hilkhot Yesodei HaTorah*, chap. 5).

According to the Rambam (5:1–4), if the situation does not require one to give his life in sanctification of God's name it is actually prohibited to do so. The reason is that if the mitzva to sanctify the name of God does not apply, the standard law takes effect, which is that one is obligated to preserve his life and he may not endanger himself even for the purpose of fulfilling the mitzvot. Those who rule in accordance with this opinion have criticized in harsh terms anyone who wishes to relinquish his life when the halakha does not demand it of him. The Rambam states that such a person "is held liable for his own life" (5:1), and some even claim that he is a murderer and that he has not sanctified God's name at all (see Ritva on *Pesaḥim* 25a; Meiri on *Sanhedrin* 74b; *Bayit Ḥadash* on *Yoreh De'a* 157). Some authorities, however, maintain that although it is generally prohibited to do so, one may give up his life if he is "a great and pious person," who sees "that the generation treats the matter [in question] lightly" (*Nimmukei Yosef* on the Rif, *Sanhedrin* 18a; *Sefer HaḤinnukh* 268).

In contrast, *Tosafot* (*Avoda Zara* 27b) and the Rosh (*Avoda Zara* 2:9) contend that even in a situation where there is no obligation to die in sanctification of God's name a person has the right to opt not to commit the sin even at the expense of his life, and he does not thereby violate a transgression. The *Shulḥan Arukh* rules likewise (*Yoreh De'a* 157:1). Some add that not only is it permitted, but it is even an attribute of piety and one should follow this approach (*Sefer Mitzvot Katan*, Positive Mitzvot 3). In support of their opinion, these authorities cite an *aggada* from the Jerusalem Talmud (*Shevi'it* 4:2), where it is related that Rabbi Abba bar Zimna gave up his life when a gentile tried to force him to eat an animal carcass. Other authorities quote another aggadic statement that appears in the midrash (*Mekhilta DeRabbi Yishmael*, *Yitro* 6; see also *Vayyikra Rabba* 32:1), dealing with those who give up their lives for the fulfillment of the mitzvot: "Why are you going out to be killed? Because I circumcised my son; why are you going out to be burned? Because I read from the Torah; why are you going out to be crucified? Because I ate matza" (Ran on the Rif, *Shabbat* 22b). The authorities also point out that Hananiah, Mishael, and Azariah risked their lives in order to avoid bowing down to an image, despite the fact that the image was not an object of idol worship, according to the Talmud (see *Nimmukei Yosef* on the Rif, *Sanhedrin* 18a). Some claim that it is permitted to do this only when the gentile's aim is for him to violate the tenets of his religion, since then he sanctifies God's name, not if the gentile is acting only for his own pleasure (Rabbeinu Yeruḥam, *Toledot Adam VeḤava* 18:3). The *Shulḥan Arukh* implies likewise; see *Shakh* on 157:1.

As the halakha, the *Shulḥan Arukh* rules in accordance with the opinion of *Tosafot* that one may allow himself to be killed even if he is not required to do so by law (but only when the gentile is not acting for his own pleasure, as maintained by Rabbeinu Yeruḥam; *Shakh*). This ruling was indeed put into practice by many over the generations, who gave up their lives for the fulfillment of regular mitzvot during times of persecution (for a discussion on the period of the Holocaust, see Responsa *Mimaamakim* 5:14).

Suicide in order to avoid being handed over to a gentile

Another case where the boundaries of sanctifying God's name have been expanded is the option of suicide, rather than giving oneself up to the gentile who wishes to force him to sin. On occasion, Jews have chosen to kill themselves before the gentiles reached them, either because they feared that those gentiles would compel them to violate the Torah or because they did not wish to die at their hands. This act of suicide apparently deviates from the laws of the sanctification of God's name as presented in the Talmud, but it was indeed carried out in different periods on account of decrees of persecution. This act of martyrdom even became a symbol and a model of sanctification and self-sacrifice. There are the familiar stories from Jewish history of the suicides at Masada and Gamla during the revolt against the Romans (these episodes are recounted in the works of Josephus Flavius, from where they were transcribed into the Hebrew book *Josippon*). The Talmud (*Gittin* 57b) relates the story of four hundred children who were taken captive by the Romans for immoral purposes, and in order to avoid that fate they all jumped into the sea and drowned. Likewise, during the Crusades (the Rhineland massacres of 1096) entire communities gave up their lives and even killed themselves in acts of heroism before they could be caught by the gentiles, as depicted in the lamentations and liturgical poems composed to commemorate those sad events.

The early authorities were asked whether such conduct was justified halakhically, and if so, under what circumstances. *Tosafot* imply that when a person fears that the gentiles are going to torture him in an unbearable manner and thereby force him to violate his faith, he is permitted to commit suicide, like the children in the story from *Gittin*, and there is even a mitzva to do so (see *Tosafot*, *Gittin* 57b, *Avoda Zara* 18a). Other authorities cite the related story of King Saul, who preferred to fall on his sword rather than fall into the hands of the Philistines (I Samuel 31:1–7). In this context, the early authorities quote the midrash (*Bereshit Rabba* 34) that deals with the prohibition against suicide: "'But I will demand your blood for your lives' (Genesis 9:5) – [this verse comes] to include one who strangles himself. Perhaps [it is prohibited even in a situation like that] of Saul? The verse states 'but.' Perhaps [even in a situation like that] of Hananiah, Mishael, and Azariah? The verse states 'but'" (*Oreḥot* Ḥayyim, The Law of Loving and Fearing God, 1, cited in *Beit Yosef*, *Yoreh De'a* 157; Responsa of Maharam of Rothenburg (Berlin edition), *Likkutim*).

The deeds of those who took their own lives during decrees of persecution were justified by authorities of the ensuing periods, and such individuals were even considered righteous and holy. However, early and later authorities who lived many years afterward were more hesitant when it came to issuing rulings in this regard, for they were reluctant to permit such actions in practice (see *Terumat HaDeshen*, 96; *Bayit Ḥadash* on *Yoreh De'a* 157; *Shakh* on *Yoreh De'a* 157:1).

Another case, which unfortunately became a practical issue during the massacres of 1096, but which is even more problematic halakhically, is killing one's children before they can be captured by gentiles, to prevent them from being raised as Christians. It seems that there is no account of this form of the sanctification of God's name in the Talmud or *midrashim*. Some authorities maintain that it is prohibited, and one who does so is a murderer (cited in *Oreḥot Ḥayyim*, The Law of Loving and Fearing God, 1; see also *Bedek HaBayit* on *Yoreh De'a* 157). In contrast, certain early authorities offered various justifications of this extreme act, by extending the stories of Saul and the other *midrashim* to include cases where they wished to prevent children from conversion (*Oreḥot Ḥayyim*, The Law of Loving and Fearing God, 1; Responsa of Maharam of Rothenburg (Berlin edition), *Likkutim*; *Sefer Mitzvot Katan* (Zurich ed.), First Day, Mitzva 6; see in detail the anthology *Kedushat HaḤayyim VeḤeruf HaNefesh*, especially in the article by A. Grossman).

In recent generations, the authorities have discussed in further depth the possibility of sanctifying God's name through suicide due to the desire not to die at the hands of the enemy. The authorities disputed whether killing oneself in order to sanctify the name of God is permitted only in situations where one's motive is to avoid violation of the faith, or even when the background is national in character, that is, the desire not to be killed by enemy forces. Since this was the case for Saul, some include the national motive in the sanctification of God's name, and thus the people at Masada and Gamla fulfilled the mitzva and were permitted to do so according to the halakha (see Rabbi Goren's article:

"Gevurat Matsada Le'or HaHalakha"). Others contend that the action they took was counter to the wishes of the Sages (see Rabbi Neria's *"Hitabdut Anshei Matsada BaHalakha"*).

The Torah states: "You shall eradicate all the places where the nations from whom you are taking possession served their gods...You shall smash their altars, and you shall shatter their monuments, and their sacred trees you shall burn in fire...You shall not do so to the Lord your God" (Deuteronomy 12:2–4). The *Sifrei* in *Parashat Re'e* (section 61) derives from the juxtaposition of these verses that it is prohibited to erase a single letter from one of the names of God. A *baraita* cited by the Gemara in Tractate *Shevuot* (35a) lists seven names of God that may not be erased, and the Rambam (*Hilkhot Yesodei HaTorah* 6:2) rules that one who erases a single letter from one of these names is liable to a flogging.

In addition to the prohibition against eradicating the names of God, it is prohibited to eradicate sacred texts, and there is a corresponding obligation to take the necessary steps to ensure that they do not perish of their own accord or reach a disgraceful state. A mishna in Tractate *Shabbat* (115a) rules that one may rescue all sacred writings from a fire on Shabbat and that they require interment if they became tattered. It is likewise stated in a *baraita* (*Megilla* 26b) that articles of sanctity, such as covers for phylacteries and *mezuzot*, must be interred. These rulings are accepted as halakha by the Rambam (*Hilkhot Tefillin UMezuza VeSefer Torah* 10:3–4; *Hilkhot Yesodei HaTorah* 6:8) and the *Shulḥan Arukh* (*Oraḥ Ḥayyim* 154:3–5). In the words of the Rambam: "With regard to all sacred writings, [including] their commentaries and their explanations, it is prohibited to burn them or eradicate them through direct action. Likewise, sacred writings that became tattered... should be interred." Most of the authorities differentiate between the prohibition against eradicating a name of God, which applies by Torah law, and the injunction against eradicating sacred writings, which is prohibited merely by rabbinic law (as implied in *Hilkhot Yesodei HaTorah* 6:8; see responsa of the Tashbetz 1:2; Responsa *Ein Yitzḥak* 1:5; *Tzitz Eliezer* 3:1; however, it can be inferred from the *Magen Avraham* on *Oraḥ Ḥayyim* 154:9 that the prohibition is from the Torah even with respect to other sacred texts).

Until the invention of printing some six hundred years ago, books were handwritten and there were relatively few of them around. The invention of the printing press and the improvement of printing methods over the years led to a significant increase in the number of holy books that were printed. This in turn resulted in a large increase of the number of sacred writings that required interment, for the consensus among most authorities is that printed works have the same sanctity as handwritten books (Responsa *Mas'at Binyamin* 99; *Taz* on *Yoreh De'a* 271:8; Responsa *Ḥavvot Ya'ir* 109; *Arukh HaShulḥan Yoreh De'a* 282:16; *Tzitz Eliezer* 3:1; some, however, such as Responsa *Ḥayyim BeYad* 80, maintain that printed books do not have the same level of sanctity as handwritten texts). These developments have caused genuine problems, for in many places holy texts have ended up in filthy places and have even been used by gentiles for unseemly purposes (see e.g., Responsa *Shevut Yaakov* 3:10).

In light of these changes, the ruling authorities have reevaluated the issue of interring printed works. Some have permitted burning sacred writings that were not printed for the purpose of sanctity, such as pages designed to be used solely for editing, to prevent them from ending up in the trash (Responsa *Meshiv Davar* 2:80; see Responsa *Ein Yitzḥak, Oraḥ Ḥayyim* 5, where this is permitted in exigent circumstances and under various restrictions; see also *Ḥazon Ish, Yoreh De'a* 164:3). Some even permit the burning of sacred writings that have become so tattered that they are no longer usable (Responsa *Shevut Yaakov* 3:10, where it is stated that these should be burned and their ashes buried near the grave of a Torah scholar). In contrast, other authorities prohibit any form of burning holy texts (Responsa *Beer Sheva* 43; Responsa *Knesset Yeḥezkel, Yoreh De'a* 37).

In our time, a related, frequently asked question concerns placing sacred writings in containers intended for paper recycling. Some authorities permit placing in such containers those sacred texts that do not contain a name of God (Responsa *Iggerot Moshe, Oraḥ Ḥayyim* 4:39; see also *Iggerot Moshe, Yoreh De'a* 1:172; a similar ruling is given in Responsa *Si'aḥ Naḥum* 74; see also Responsa *Aseh Lekha Rav* 3:28). Other authorities, however, maintain that one should not act in accordance with this leniency (see *Peninei Halakha, Likkutim* 1, 5:14; and the website of the Zomet Institute). Likewise, many questions have been raised about newspapers and similar publications that contain some holy writings, whether they are included in the category of sacred texts that require internment. It is stated in Responsa *Iggerot Moshe* (*Yoreh De'a* 1:172): "In practice, I do not check newspapers to see if they contain a name [of God], because I maintain that the only concern is the Tetragrammaton, which is virtually never printed in newspapers. If, however, I happen to see any one of the seven names in a newspaper, I am stringent and tear it from its place in the newspaper, and hide it away. But this is a mere stringency" (see the website of the Zomet Institute for responsa on destroying texts such as the *alonei Shabbat* pamphlets, which contain sacred writings).

Hilkhot Deot

Medicine in the Talmud and in the Rambam

The Mishna, and the Gemara in greater detail, lists numerous cures for various ailments (see for example Mishna, *Yoma* 8:5–6; *Shabbat* 14:2–4, and Gemara, *Gittin* 68b – 72a, *Shabbat* 66b – 67a, 109b – 110b). Many of these cures mentioned in the Talmud are folk remedies, incantations, and methods of healing using different substances.

Over the generations, the ruling authorities discussed the appropriate attitude one should adopt toward these cures of the Talmud. Reservations were expressed about their use as early as in the time of the geonim. In a response to a question about the remedies presented in Tractate *Gittin*, the geonim noted that the talmudic Sages were not doctors, and their statements in this field do not constitute a mitzva, but rather they are offering a description of the treatments they observed in their time. For this reason, the geonim concluded that one should rely upon the cures of the Talmud only after examining them and receiving the approval of expert doctors that they pose no danger (*Otzar HaGeonim*, Responsa, *Gittin* 68b; see *Yam shel Shlomo, Ḥullin* 8:12). Rabbi Avraham, son of the Rambam, similarly states (in his introduction to the work *Ma'amar al Derashot Ḥazal*, "Essay on the Expositions of the Sages") that there is no obligation to accept and believe in the statements of the Sages on medicine in the same way that we accept their opinion on the interpretation of the Torah, because the various remedies that appear in the Talmud have not been shown to be effective. The Maharil takes a firmer stance, arguing that it is prohibited to try and cure with the medicines that appear in the Talmud, because "one cannot understand their essential nature, and when people fail, the words of the Sages will be mocked and scorned" (collected comments from the end of his work, cited in the gloss of Rabbi Akiva Eiger on *Shulḥan Arukh, Yoreh De'a* 336:1; see *Sedei Ḥemed, Maarakha Reish,* 54).

The tosafists explain the topic differently, implying in several places that while the cures of the Talmud were indeed effective in their time, the natural order has changed, to the extent that methods presented in the Talmud as proper treatments are actually dangerous (*Tosafot* on *Moed Katan* 11a; for the general claim regarding a change in nature, see *Tosafot* on *Avoda Zara* 24b and *Ḥullin* 47a). This basic claim that nature has changed is invoked by many authorities on medical and other issues (see e.g., *Terumat HaDeshen* 271; Responsa of the Rashbash 913; Rema, *Shulḥan Arukh, Even HaEzer*

156:4; *Magen Avraham* on *Oraḥ Ḥayyim* 173:1; Responsa *Ha'elef Lekha Shlomo, Yoreh De'a* 257).

In addition to cures for various illnesses, the Talmud also provides health guidelines for nutrition, washing, relieving oneself, engaging in sexual relations, and other such matters. The Rambam, for his part, presents the proper conduct a person in general, and a Torah scholar in particular, should observe in order to preserve his bodily health. Most of these halakhot, which appear in *Hilkhot Deot,* chapters 4 and 5, can be classified as preventive measures, and some of his recommendations are accepted by modern medical experts (such as the importance of regular exercise). Nevertheless, it seems that his statements should not be taken as binding laws that may not be violated, but rather as medical recommendations and the Rambam's advice based on the best medical knowledge of his time (see *Magen Avraham* on *Oraḥ Ḥayyim* 240:29; Responsa *Iggerot Moshe, Ḥoshen Mishpat* 2:76). It should also be noted that the Rambam himself states that he is presenting general guidelines for a healthy individual, or for someone who does not have access to a doctor, whereas one who has taken ill should act in accordance with the medical literature (*Hilkhot Deot* 4:21–22).

The Obligation to Wear a *Kippa*

There is no clear halakhic source in the Mishna or Gemara for the obligation to cover one's head when engaged in a sacred task, or for the broader obligation to wear it throughout the day. However, it can be inferred from the Talmud that it was the standard practice to don a head covering, to the extent that one of the regular morning blessings marks its placement on the head (*Berakhot* 60b, *Hilkhot Tefilla UVirkat Kohanim* 7:4). Several talmudic sayings and stories indicate that the head covering was a badge of dignity and honor, and it served as an especially distinguishing sign for Torah scholars (see, e.g., *Kiddushin* 8a). Furthermore, it is an expression of the wearer's fear of Heaven, an acknowledgment that "the Divine Presence is above my head." Rav Huna, son of Rav Yehoshua, praised himself for never having walked four cubits with an uncovered head (*Kiddushin* 31a; *Shabbat* 118b; for more sources, see *Beur HaGra, Oraḥ Ḥayyim* 8:2).

The ruling authorities discuss the topic of covering one's head in two contexts. The first is when reciting "expressions of sanctity," sacred texts and rites, while the second is the general obligation to have one's head covered all the time, whether walking or remaining in place.

When reciting sacred texts

Several early authorities state that it is prohibited to have a bare head when engaging in various holy tasks. The Rambam (*Hilkhot Tefilla UVirkat Kohanim* 5:5) states that the appropriate attire for prayer includes a head covering. The *Beit Yosef* (*Oraḥ Ḥayyim* 91) cites other opinions of the early authorities in this regard: Rabbeinu Peretz maintains that one who enters a synagogue with his head bare should be rebuked, and Rabbeinu Yeruḥam states that one should not recite a blessing with an uncovered head. The source for these views, according to the *Beit Yosef,* is tractate *Soferim* (14:12), which presents a dispute as to whether it is prohibited to mention the name of God with a bare head. The *Beit Yosef* contends that those authorities rule in accordance with the stringent opinion in tractate *Soferim,* and they prohibited prayer and the recitation of blessings with an uncovered head because one cannot say God's name in that state. The same conclusion can be inferred from the *Terumat HaDeshen,* where it is stated (section 10) that one may not pray or recite blessings when his head is uncovered, "on account of a frivolous attitude toward Heaven, for he mentions the name of the Omnipresent not in a manner of awe and trepidation." However, the *Kol Bo* (section 11) implies that the reason why one may not stand to pray with a bare head is because one would not rise in that fashion before dignitaries. If so, the law might depend on the local custom. Some infer from a close reading of the Rambam that it is prohibited for this reason only when praying, but one may recite a blessing bareheaded (see *Yabia Omer* 6, *Oraḥ Ḥayyim* 15:3).

In contrast, the Maharshal states in a responsum (72) that it is not prohibited to mention the name of God or engage in sacred matters with an uncovered head. He maintains that the views presented in tractate *Soferim* should not be ruled as halakha, and he even cites proof from a midrash (*Vayikra Rabba* 27) that one may pray with a bare head. In practice, however, since the practice is accepted as prohibited by the masses, the Maharshal recommends for Torah scholars to be stringent in this regard, due to the appearance of prohibition (see *Or Zarua* 2:43, which cites a custom of the rabbis of France to recite blessings bareheaded; *Beur HaGra, Oraḥ Ḥayyim* 8:2; *Peri Ḥadash, Oraḥ Ḥayyim* 91:3).

With regard to the halakha, the *Shulḥan Arukh* rules in accordance with the stringent opinion, stating that some prohibit the mention of God's name with a bare head, and therefore, one who enters a synagogue in this state should be rebuked (*Oraḥ Ḥayyim* 91:3). Likewise, "one should not stand [to pray] with an uncovered head" (91:5). Most of the authorities accepted the *Shulḥan Arukh*'s ruling as halakha, although they disagreed over whether the mention of the Divine name with a bare head is prohibited as an attribute of piety or as a fundamental law (see the various opinions cited in *Yabia Omer* 6, *Oraḥ Ḥayyim* 15:6). In addition to the basic requirement of a head covering, certain authorities maintain that one must also wear a hat or some other extra head covering when praying and reciting Grace after Meals, since that it how one would stand to address important personages (*Mishna Berura, Oraḥ Ḥayyim* 91:12, 183:11, *Arukh HaShulḥan* 91:6; see also *Piskei Teshuvot* 2:10 for sources that refer to the importance of this practice according to kabbalistic teachings).

Wearing a *kippa* as a general practice

A different question is whether one is obligated to cover one's head at all times, irrespective of whether he is engaged in a sacred task. As stated above, the talmudic sources indicate that covering one's head was a sign of the fear of Heaven, and some were careful not to walk four cubits bareheaded. The context implies that this was an act of piety, rather than an obligation, and some ruling authorities state as much (*Darkhei Moshe, Oraḥ Ḥayyim* 2:2; *Magen Avraham, Oraḥ Ḥayyim* 91:3; *Birkei Yosef, Oraḥ Ḥayyim* 2:2). The Rambam likewise lists not baring one's head as one of those practices that come under the heading: "Torah scholars conduct themselves with exceptional modesty" (*Hilkhot Deot* 5:6).

However, the *Shulḥan Arukh* formulates this requirement as a halakhic ruling: "One may not walk four cubits with an uncovered head (*Oraḥ Ḥayyim* 2:6), and some understand this as absolute prohibition, not merely an attribute of piety (Responsa *Tevuot Shemesh, Oraḥ Ḥayyim* 33; the *Arukh HaShulḥan* states likewise in 2:10, citing "some of the great authorities"). Furthermore, the *Taz* (*Oraḥ Ḥayyim* 8:3) rules that since gentiles go around bareheaded, this law has become fully obligatory, due to the prohibition against following gentile practices. The Responsa *Mahari Berona* likewise states (section 34) that one who walks around with an uncovered head is considered to be following gentile customs and is in violation of "the precepts of Jewish practice" (see Responsa of the *Ḥatam Sofer* 5:191).

Although numerous authorities reject the opinion of the *Taz* with regard to the prohibition against following gentile practices, many others state on the same lines that covering one's head has developed from a pious custom into a more binding obligation, since it symbolizes one's acceptance of the mitzvot, and serves to distinguish between those who observe the commandments and those who do not, and is thus of great importance to God-fearing Jews (Responsa *Yeḥaveh Daat* 4:1; *Yalkut Yosef* 91:9; see *Arukh HaShulḥan* 2:10). Some accept the opinion of the *Taz* only with respect to praying bareheaded, because gentiles are particular to have their heads uncovered only when praying (*Iggerot Moshe, Oraḥ Ḥayyim* 4:40, where it is even suggested that one who prayed with his head bare might be required to repeat the prayer; for a dissenting view, see *Yalkut Yosef* 91:9).

In this context, the authorities discuss the issue of wearing a *kippa* in a place where this might be a problem, such as when visiting gentiles in positions of authority or when one is at work. It is stated in Responsa *Shevut Yaakov* (3:5) that one may be lenient in this regard due to the imperative to maintain peace with the government, and thus one may address ministers bareheaded. He adds that for the same reason the leniency also applies when gentiles come to visit a synagogue, despite the statement of the *Shulḥan Arukh* against people entering a synagogue with a bare head (see Rema, *Yoreh De'a* 150:3). The *Iggerot Moshe* (*Oraḥ Ḥayyim* 4:2) also rules leniently for the sake of earning a livelihood, if one's workplace requires its employees to have their heads uncovered (see *Terumat HaDeshen, Pesakim UKetavim* 203, which permits taking an oath in God's name with a bare head in a place where the gentiles require it).

With regard to the obligation to cover one's head, Rabbi Shlomo Kluger (Responsa *Ha'elef Lekha Shlomo* 3) suggests a compromise position. He contends that covering part of the head is obligatory for all, even when walking less than four cubits, while the attribute of piety refers to covering one's entire head. Others reject this novel idea, arguing that it is not based on any of the sources (*Iggerot Moshe, Oraḥ Ḥayyim* 1:1).

Beyond the discussion regarding the basic obligation to cover one's head, several halakhic debates focus on the scope and details of this law, such as how large the head covering must be, and whether one may cover his head with a hand or some other part of his body (see *Yeḥaveh Daat* 4:1; *Iggerot Moshe, Oraḥ Ḥayyim* 1:1; *Mishna Berura* 2:11–12; *Peninei Halakha, Likkutim* 1:7).

Hilkhot Talmud Torah

Torah Study for Women

The obligation to study Torah is one of the mitzvot that the Sages teach applies only to men and not to women. From the verse "You shall teach them to your sons" (Deuteronomy 11:19), the Sages derived (*Kiddushin* 29b) that a person is obligated to teach only his sons Torah, but not his daughters. From this, the Sages further inferred that the personal obligation of Torah study does not apply to women. Amidst a discussion concerning the law of the *sota*, the *tanna'im* disagree as to whether a father should teach his daughter Torah, or if doing so is considered problematic. According to ben Azzai, a father is obligated to teach his daughter, whereas according to Rabbi Eliezer, it is forbidden, for "anyone who teaches his daughter Torah, it is as if he has taught her nonsense" (*Sota* 3:4).

With regard to the accepted halakha, the Rambam rules that a woman is not obligated in the mitzva of Torah study (*Hilkhot Talmud Torah* 1:1), but she receives reward if she does so: "If a women studies Torah, she receives reward for doing so;

however, her reward is not comparable to the reward that a man receives for studying Torah, because she is not commanded in the mitzva" (1:13). Furthermore, the Rambam rules in accordance with Rabbi Eliezer's opinion that it is forbidden for a father to teach his daughter Torah, and explains that the prohibition is because most women's minds are not sufficiently focused to be able to study effectively: "The Sages instructed that a person should not teach his daughter Torah, due to the fact that, in the case of most women, their minds are not sufficiently focused to be able to study effectively, and so when they study, they misunderstand the material and thereby render the words of Torah into insubstantial matters, due to their poor understanding." The *Shulḥan Arukh* (*Yoreh De'a* 246:6) accepts the Rambam's rulings in this matter.

The halakhic authorities discuss the parameters of

the prohibition against teaching Torah to women. The Rambam limits the restriction to the Oral Torah, adding that one who teaches their daughter the Written Torah is not considered as though he had taught her nonsense. Nevertheless, the Rambam writes that ideally, a father should not teach even the Written Torah to his daughter. Later authorities limit even this later restriction, explaining that it does not include teaching the simple meaning of the Written Law, which may be taught even initially, and that this is, indeed, the prevalent custom (*Taz, Yoreh De'a* 246:4, and see *Tzitz Eliezer* 9:3:4–5).

The Rema (*Yoreh De'a* 246:6), citing several early authorities, makes an additional important point regarding this law. A woman is obligated to learn the laws that pertain to her daily life, so that she will know how to conduct herself in accordance with the halakha. "For if she does not know the laws of Shabbat, how will she observe Shabbat?" (*Sefer Hasidim, Margaliyyot* 313). However, there are some authorities who insist that even with regard to practical halakhot, women should not study directly from halakhic works, but rather they should receive the information through the oral transmission of tradition, from mother to daughter (Responsa *Maharil* 199; and see *Arukh HaShulḥan, Yoreh De'a* 246:19).

In general, for much of Jewish history, women did not study Torah in any organized fashion, and it was sufficient for them to be educated at home in matters of ethics and to receive the family tradition regarding laws pertaining to the home and family. Nevertheless, there were individual women in every generation who did engage in in-depth Torah study, beginning with Berurya, the wife of Rabbi Meir, who was renowned for her scholarship (see, for example, *Tosefta, Kelim, Bava Metzia* 1:6), and continuing with famous female scholars in later generations who taught, preached, and even wrote responsa (see, for example, Responsa *Maharshal* 29; Responsa *Tashbetz* 3:78; for a general historical survey, see the book *Nashim Lamdaniyot* by Shlomo Ashkenazi). The authorities justified these cases of Torah study by individual women, explaining that the prohibition applies only to the majority of women, with regard to whom there is the concern that they will render words of Torah as insubstantial matters. However, individual women whose minds can focus on study are permitted to study Torah. This applies in the case of gifted women who are able to study on their own (*Perisha, Yoreh De'a* 246:15), or when it is evident that a particular woman's intention is to study wholeheartedly and she has the intellectual capability to do so (Responsa *Tov Ayin* 4; and see *Birkei Yosef, Yoreh De'a* 246:6).

Changes in Women's Torah Study in Recent Centuries

The reality that women's Torah education was predominantly transmitted within the informal home setting underwent a significant transformation during the twentieth century and onward. As young people began leaving their parents' homes to pursue general studies and vocational training, and with it, gained significant exposure to outside cultures, the power of familial tradition waned considerably. This prompted a need to provide daughters with institutionalized Torah instruction in order to fortify them against being led astray by negative cultural influences. As such, with the backing of several leading rabbis, Torah seminaries exclusively for girls were established, such as Sarah Schenirer's pioneering Beit Yaakov schools, where the students were taught Torah and fear of Heaven. While the core curriculum – the study of the simple meaning of the Written Torah, and of practical halakhic observances – was already permitted by earlier authorities, as mentioned above (see Responsa *Moznayim LeMishpat* 1:42), the very creation of formal Torah institutions for female students marked a groundbreaking innovative development. The Ḥafetz Ḥayyim endorsed this systemic change, given the new realities facing the Jewish world, while also adding the directive that girls should study the ethical teachings of the sages from works such as *Pirkei Avot* and other classical Jewish ethical works (*Likkutei Halakhot, Sota* 20:1; Responsa *Iggerot Moshe, Yoreh De'a* 3:87). However, there were some rabbinic leaders who steadfastly opposed any deviation from the conventional educational practice, insisting that, at the very least, the curriculum should be limited as much as possible to what was customary in the past, and that study should only take place from classic works that had been authored specifically for women, and which contained practical halakhic rulings and anthologies of faith and ethics (Responsa *Divrei Yatziv, Yoreh De'a* 139–140; *Shevet HaLevi* 6:150).

In contemporary times, many authorities have advocated further broadening the scope of women's Torah study to additional areas, although opinions remain divided on the appropriate parameters. Some authorities rule that daughters should not be taught Mishna at all, with the exception of *Pirkei Avot* (Responsa *Iggerot Moshe, Yoreh De'a* 3:87). Others rule that it is proper to teach the Oral Torah extensively to girls and women, but without actually delving into the Talmud itself (see, for example, the article by Rabbi Lior in *Elonei Mamrei* 120). Others insist that it is even permissible to teach girls in-depth study of the Talmud. Proponents justify these expansions as an extension of the Ḥafetz Ḥayyim's original argument. They explain that in the current climate, ensuring the religious growth of girls and women requires a much broader knowledge of all areas of Torah, beyond the fact that such study is necessary for the practical observance of the laws (see the statements of Rabbi Lichtenstein cited in Rabbi Navon's article in *Teḥumin* 28). Others justify these expansions by arguing that in the current reality, where women are educated in many general fields, any woman who wishes to study the Oral Torah should be considered like the minority of women in previous generations who were permitted to study Torah (see the article by Rabbi Henkin in *HaDarom* 61, and Responsa *Aseh Lekha Rav* 2:52). Some have suggested that the change is based on the idea that during times of great need, it is possible to adopt ben Azzai's opinion that one is actually obligated to teach one's daughter Torah (Responsa *Mikveh HaMayyim* 3, *Yoreh De'a* 21; and see *Eshel Avraham, Peirot HaNoshrin* on *Sota* 20).

The Lubavitcher Rebbe approached this issue from a different angle. While conceding that the initial impetus to expand women's Torah education stemmed from spiritual decline and a fear of rebellion, he viewed the growth of advanced women's Torah study as an ultimately positive development – a step toward the redemptive future when "the earth will be filled with knowledge of the Lord, as the water covers the sea" (Isaiah 11:9; *Shulḥan HaMelekh, Hilkhot Talmud Torah*, p. 206).

Earning a Livelihood from Torah Study

The issue of the relationship between Torah study and earning a livelihood has long preoccupied Jewish scholars. The Mishna and Talmud present differing perspectives on this issue, with debates continuing until modern times. Beyond the general issue of the appropriate balance between a person's Torah study and their earning a livelihood (see, for example, the dispute between Rabbi Yishmael and Rabbi Shimon bar Yoḥai in *Berakhot* 35b), the authorities explored whether it is permissible, and if so, if it is advisable, for a Torah scholar to dedicate himself exclusively to Torah study while being supported financially by the community. This issue depends on whether it is permitted or proper to benefit financially from one's Torah study, and on the extent to which it is appropriate for the community to support its Torah scholars in order to enable them to be focused on their studies.

The Rambam was the first to devote an in-depth discussion to this question. In his commentary to *Pirkei Avot*, on the mishna: "Rabbi Zadok says: Do not make the Torah a crown to glorify yourself with, nor a spade to dig with" (*Avot* 4:5), the Rambam discusses what he describes as a prevalent phenomenon of Torah scholars who do not work for a living but instead support themselves from an allowance provided to them by the community. The Rambam goes to great lengths to prove that there is indeed a halakhic prohibition against doing this. Based on the above mishna, the Rambam understands that it is forbidden to profit financially from one's Torah study. Furthermore, he insists that doing so constitutes a desecration of God's name, as the masses will think that Torah study is just an occupation like any other, from which one can earn a living. He details the various professions in which different *tanna'im* and *amora'im* engaged, as recounted in the Talmud, and emphasizes the fact that they chose to earn their livelihoods through their own labor rather than benefit from the community's support. The Rambam also emphasizes this in *Hilkhot Talmud Torah*: "Whoever sets his heart on engaging exclusively in Torah study and not working, but rather finances himself from charity, by doing so he has desecrated the name of God, scorned the Torah, and extinguished the light of the religion. In addition, he brings harm upon himself, and has removed his life from the World to Come, for it is forbidden to derive benefit from the words of Torah in this world" (3:10).

However, many rabbinic authorities disagreed with the Rambam's stance, deeming it proper, in certain cases, for scholars to study unfettered by financial concerns.

The Kesef Mishne (in his commentary to the Rambam's *Hilkhot Talmud Torah*) argues that there is no issue with Torah scholars financially benefiting from other's financial support. He cites various talmudic sources emphasizing the importance of financially supporting Torah scholars. In his view, the prohibition in *Pirkei Avot* against making Torah into "a spade to dig with" refers only to one whose primary motivation in studying Torah is in order to make money. However, one who engages in Torah study for its own sake, accepting public funding only in order to allow him to focus fully on studies, does not violate this prohibition. Nevertheless, he agrees that one blessed with the ability to earn a livelihood through his own efforts is forbidden from accepting communal support. However, a Torah scholar who is unable to support himself may indeed receive financial assistance.

The Tashbetz (Responsa *Tashbetz* 1:142–148) elaborates extensively on this issue, siding with the Kesef Mishne, and ultimately ruling that provisions should be made to ensure that Torah scholars in the community will be free to study Torah without the distraction of having to worry about earning a livelihood. He argues that not only is it permitted for a Torah scholar to be supported by the community, but that the community has an obligation to do so. The community must provide for Torah scholars' sustenance so that they can study Torah without interruption, and so that they not be denigrated in the eyes of the masses due to their poverty. In his view, this obligation applies also to Torah scholars holding official positions, such as a dean of a yeshiva, and to students engaged in Torah study throughout their lives (see Responsa *Tashbetz* 146 concerning who is defined as a Torah scholar with regard to these matters). Beyond the community's obligation, there is also a great mitzva for wealthy individuals to support Torah scholars. Nevertheless, the Tashbetz agrees that it is a pious attribute for a Torah scholar not to rely on the community, but to earn his livelihood through his own labors. The exceptions to this are Torah scholars appointed over the community who, were they to also work, would be belittled by the masses (Responsa *Tashbetz* 148). In support of his arguments, he cites various proofs from the words of the Sages, including the midrash about Issachar and Zebulun (*Bereshit Rabba* 99:9), according to which the tribe of Zebulun engaged in commerce, and with the money they earned, they supported the tribe of Issachar, thereby enabling them to engage exclusively in Torah study, and that both tribes merited reward for this arrangement.

Most authorities follow the path of the Kesef Mishne and the Tashbetz, permitting Torah scholars to be supported by the community, however they offer various distinctions. Some write that a person is forbidden from imposing himself on the community, but if the community chooses on its own initiative to support Torah scholars so that they can learn, a Torah scholar may accept their support, and that doing so even affords honor to the Torah (*Arukh HaShulḥan, Yoreh De'a* 246:39–40). Some add that a rabbi officially appointed over a community is permitted to accept financial support from the community, and it is even preferable that he do so, for otherwise his words will not be accepted by the community (*Derisha, Yoreh De'a* 246:10, and see Rema, *Yoreh De'a* 246:21). Moreover, some authorities write that the dean of a yeshiva, and those who disseminate Torah to the masses, commit a sin if they refuse financial support, for if they are forced to dedicate their efforts to earning a living, it would impair their studies and ability to teach and instruct, as required of them (*Yam Shel Shlomo, Ḥullin* 3:9, and see *Shakh, Yoreh De'a* 246:20). The Rema (*Yoreh De'a* 246:21) adds that an elderly or sick person who is unable to work for a living is certainly permitted to benefit from his Torah knowledge and receive financial support in order to study.

The Kesef Mishne provides a second argument to justify Torah scholars receiving financial support. He says that even if the Rambam's claims are fundamentally correct in principle, in practice, scholars and their students had to accept payment from the community, for had they not done so, no one would have been able to dedicate their lives to Torah study, and the Torah would have been forgotten. As such, this constitutes a case of: "It is time to act for the Lord, they have violated Your teaching" (Psalms 119:126). The Sages derived from this verse that sometimes, in extenuating circumstances, one must "act for the Lord" to bolster the Torah even in ways which involve "violating Your teaching" by negating certain Torah precepts (see *Berakhot* 54a). Many authorities attach this argument to their allowances on this matter, and even determine, based on it, that if a Torah scholar is capable of dedicating his entire day to Torah study, then he should do so, and that refraining from doing so should not be seen as a pious attribute (*Beur Halakha* 231; Responsa *Iggerot Moshe, Yoreh De'a* 2:116; *Yabia Omer* 7, *Yoreh De'a* 17). Some later authorities rule that, in principle, the halakha is in accordance with the Rambam's opinion; however, because it is impossible today to achieve greatness in Torah while also being preoccupied with earning a livelihood, one should rely on the argument of "a time to act for the Lord" and permit it (Rabbi Yosef Kapaḥ on *Hilkhot Talmud Torah* 3:10). However, some emphasize that all of these allowances are not to be taken as general permission for anyone who desires to learn to accept financial support to do so, but are intended specifically for those who wish to dedicate their entire lives to study and teaching, and who otherwise would be unable to achieve greatness in Torah. For such people, the principle of "a time to act for the Lord" is applied. However, one who does not intend to dedicate his entire life to teaching must, after studying for a few years and acquiring a basic knowledge of Torah, work for his livelihood (*Peninei Halakha, Likkutim* 1:1:18).

Taking remuneration for teaching

Beyond the general discussion about financially benefiting from Torah study, the authorities deal with a more specific discussion on this matter. From the Talmud (*Nedarim* 36b – 37a) it emerges that there is a prohibition against teaching Torah for payment: "See, I have taught you statutes and ordinances, as the Lord my God commanded me" (Deuteronomy 4:5), from which the Sages derive: "Just as I, Moses, studied Torah from God without charge, so too, you should teach Torah free of charge." According to the Gemara, this prohibition applies specifically to the teaching of the Oral Torah and not to the Written Torah, for various reasons. The authorities further limit this prohibition in various ways that enable people to dedicate their lives to teaching Torah. *Tosafot* (*Ketubot* 105a) distinguish between occasional instruction, for which one may not charge money, and a person who dedicates all his time to teaching Torah, such that he does not have the time available to earn a livelihood from other work. In such a case, according to *Tosafot*, "the community is obligated to provide for his sustenance." Others write that such individuals may only receive reimbursement for their lost time, i.e., the money they would have earned if they had been working instead of teaching (*Haggahot Maimoniyyot, Hilkhot Talmud Torah* 1:6). The *Shulḥan Arukh* (*Yoreh De'a* 246:5) accepts these permissions as the practical halakha.

Ostracism and Excommunication

Ostracism [*niddui*] and excommunication [*herem*] are halakhic means of punishment mentioned in the Mishna (see *Eduyyot* 5:6). The Talmud (*Moed Katan* 16a) derives from the Written Torah that one can ostracize and excommunicate those who disobey the law, and further discusses the details of these punishments. The Rambam (*Hilkhot Talmud Torah*, Chapters 6–7) and the *Shulḥan Arukh* (*Yoreh De'a* 334) codify these laws, listing twenty-four instances of transgressions in which ostracism should be used. Essentially, ostracism is the isolation of a person from the community; they are not to be included in any matters requiring a quorum of ten men, and no one may sit within four cubits of them. Excommunication is similar, but more severe, prohibiting business or Torah study with the excommunicated individual.

The purpose of these punishments is twofold: punishing the transgressor, especially for contempt of Torah scholars or their decrees; and compelling the transgressor to repent and accept the court's ruling, especially in a case of one who was initially punished for refusing to obey the court's ruling. From various stories in the Talmud, it is apparent that the use of ostracism, referred to in Aramaic as "*shamta*," was common. This included even excommunicating Torah scholars for ruling against the majority (*Eduyyot* 5:6; *Bava Metzia* 59b) and excommunicating transgressors (see, for example, *Eiruvin* 63a, *Pesaḥim* 52a, *Kiddushin* 70a, *Ḥullin* 132b).

Although originally ostracism and excommunication served as means of punishment for transgressions, their application was expanded and they were used to enforce compliance with decrees issued by the early authorities. When the court or community wished to enact a new decree, they would enact it with the force of an excommunication, declaring that anyone who acted against the decree would be excommunicated. In the language of the early authorities, these were referred to as "community excommunications." Such excommunications were common in the era of the early authorities, and among the most famous are two of the excommunications of Rabbeinu Gershom Meor HaGola, one prohibiting taking a second wife in addition to one's first wife, and the other prohibiting divorcing a wife without her consent.

Some early authorities understood that underlying such excommunications is a form of oath (since the word *ḥerem* can also refer to an oath), and that national leaders have the authority to place the whole community under oath, just as Joshua did when he placed the nation under oath not to rebuild Jericho after it was destroyed (Joshua 6:28; and similarly, in other places in the Bible). Therefore, violating an excommunication is prohibited just like violating an oath (Ramban's *Laws of the Excommunication*, pages 293–297). Other early authorities disagreed, noting that, under the standard laws of oaths, it is impossible to place an oath on future generations, whereas community excommunications do apply to future generations. Instead, they explain that the force of community excommunications derives from the decree itself. When the community or court enacts a decree, the decree itself contains within it the stipulation that whoever violates the decree will be excommunicated (Responsa *Rosh* 5:4, 7:9). Regarding these excommunications, the halachic authorities discuss whether one who violates a community excommunication is automatically excommunicated, or whether the excommunication takes effect only once the transgressor has been declared a violator of the excommunication. They also discuss how such excommunications are to be annulled (see Responsa *Rashi* 70; Responsa *Rivash* 33; *Tur* and *Shulḥan Arukh*, *Yoreh De'a* 334:22).

Along with the development of the concept of a community excommunication, the use of individual ostracism and excommunication in their original sense also continued. In the responsa literature, there are many examples of individuals who were excommunicated, especially for not obeying the law, or for insulting a Torah scholar (for a few examples of the many cases, see Responsa *Rif* 146; Responsa *Rashba* 1:713; *Terumat HaDeshen* 274; *Avkat Rokhel* 179; *Shevut Yaakov* 3:99; *Noda BiYehuda*, vol. 1, *Yoreh De'a* 70; *Ḥatam*

Sofer, Yoreh De'a 222; *Torah Lishma* 257). Well-known individual ostracisms and excommunications include, for example, the excommunication that the Jewish community of Amsterdam placed on Baruch Spinoza, and the excommunication placed on those individuals who were involved in Sabbateanism.

Reduction in the use of ostracism and excommunication

In recent centuries, the use of ostracism and excommunication has diminished, for several reasons. First, the effectiveness of ostracism depends on the pressure created by being isolated from the community. This situation existed as long as a person's membership in the community was a given reality, with members of the community having no other place to go. However, when Jews in the Diaspora began to be able to live outside the communal framework, ostracism lost its power. Moreover, there was a concern that if a transgressor was excommunicated, it might actually cause him to leave the communal framework entirely and cast off all restraints. In such a case, instead of the desired effect of leading a person to repent, excommunication could actually lead them to refrain from repenting and totally reject the Jewish way of life. This concern was raised by halakhic authorities who discussed whether one should excommunicate a person if there is a concern that he will go astray or lead his children and family astray (see Rema, *Yoreh De'a* 331:1 and in the commentaries of the Taz and Shakh; Responsa *Ḥatam Sofer, Yoreh De'a* 322; for a more general discussion see *Derisha, Yoreh De'a* 334:8 and *Taz, Yoreh De'a* 334:23).

The Radbaz (Responsa *Radbaz* 1:187) adds another very important factor. Although, in his opinion, transgressors should be punished even if there is a concern that the transgressor will totally reject a Jewish way of life, nevertheless "the leader of the generation should be moderate in such matters, since not all people are equal, and not all transgressions are equal… and so the use of excommunications is dependent on the discretion of the judge who leads the community, provided that all their actions are done for the sake of Heaven" (see Halakhic Discussions to *Hilkhot Talmud Torah* 7:13).

A second reason for the reduced use of ostracism was that the gentile governments in many places prohibited Jews from using it, seeing it as undermining the government's exclusive authority. Such interference by gentile governments goes very far back in history, and the early authorities already address situations in which gentile rulers punished someone who obeyed an ostracism issued against someone for going to a gentile court for judication (*Terumat HaDeshen* 276; *Shulḥan Arukh, Yoreh De'a* 334:48). Another aspect of this interference arose in a later period as authorities aimed to integrate Jews into general society; ostracism's separatist nature was seen as an obstacle. The power of ostracism lies in belonging to an insular Jewish community, and so the authorities saw it as an obstacle to their goal, and often prohibited its use. In many places, the authorities completely banned the imposition of ostracism or excommunication, and many halakhic authorities note that all the laws of ostracism apply only when the ruling government permits it, but in countries where the government does not allow ostracism, it is prohibited due to the principle that: "The law of the kingdom is the law" (see, for example, Responsa *Noda BiYehuda, Yoreh De'a* 1:66, in the glosses there; Glosses of *Imrei Barukh* to *Shulḥan Arukh, Yoreh De'a* 334; *Arukh HaShulḥan, Yoreh De'a* 334:1; Responsa *Minḥat Yitzḥak* 3:112).

Image Credits